MEDIA
Librarianship

edited by
John W.
ELLISON

Neal-Schuman Publishers, Inc.
New York   *London*

Published by Neal-Schuman Publishers, Inc.
23 Cornelia Street
New York, NY 10014

Library of Congress Cataloging in Publication Data
Main entry under title:

Media librarianship

   Bibliography: p..
    Includes index.
    1. Audio-visual library service. I. Ellison, John
William, 1941–
Z717.M45 1984   025.1′77   84-2145
ISBN 0-918212-81-2

Contents

Preface

If you want to be accepted and even liked, then do not say anything which has not already been said, nor do anything which has not already been done. Do not disagree with anyone. Do not say anything new. Best of all do nothing at all. Then you will be a great scholar in the eyes of the world. On the other hand, if you want to be a great scholar, do things your own way and wait. People will get used to you.

—Harry Wolfson

MEDIA *Librarianship* presents an introduction to the theory and practice of media librarianship and serves as a basic handbook for potential media librarians and a valuable source for practitioners. This book introduces the concept of media librarianship and, when appropriate, presents practices and solutions that fit the library context. Librarians in academic, public, special, and school settings will all find this book valuable because it addresses topics without regard to type of library.

Some of the theory and practice of media librarianship can be applied to situations both in and out of libraries; however, this book addresses those theories and practices that relate specifically to libraries. Both the major and finer points are presented so the reader can make comparisons.

Topics addressed in this book cover the broad scope of media librarianship, from its genesis to why and how we go about the business of selecting, organizing, disseminating, and managing film, tape, record, and twenty other non-print format services in the context of libraries. The history, philosophy, theory, practice, and state-of-the-art of media librarianship are identified and presented so important aspects of American society's information and entertainment needs are recognized as essential and basic elements of a free democracy.

Media librarians know that their role in libraries is more than "bringing people to books" or "public relations" or "gadgets." They have the potential to help make the notion of "information transfer" a reality for large numbers of people, particularly those who have not been served by libraries. The media librarian's mission is to help develop the full potential of individuals, to help guarantee equal and unrestricted access to information, and to expedite access and transfer of information. This mission is *not* a platitude that is stated and forgotten. It is the basis for all decision-making and action taken by the media librarian.

In preparing this book, I have drawn upon my experience as a public, medical, school, and academic librarian and teacher of media librarianship. Thus, I attempted to select contributors who bring similarly diverse experiences to their writing. Their varied experiences and perceptions of media librarianship make their contributions particularly meaningful, although not always accepted by the traditional librarian community.

No attempt was made to have each contributor conform to a particular writing style. The individual contributors' choice of essays, chronologies, annotated bibliographies, or bibliographical essays reflects their personal approach to the subject.

The terminology used is as varied as that found in the libraries where media librarians work. Terms like "non-print" and "non-book" are generally unappealing, if not repulsive, to media librarians. They also find the use of "media" to describe materials other than paper print items equally offensive. *Media* will be used consistently throughout this book to refer to combined formats such as hologram, film, filmstrip, audiotape, map, model, record, book, slide, video, picture. *Non-print* will be used to describe formats other than books and paper print matter.

Media librarians can work with all print and non-print forms of information and entertainment in the context of a library. They are not to be confused with school media specialists, media specialists, audio-visual specialists, or educational technology specialists. The chapter "What Are Media Librarians?" provides a detailed description of what a media librarian is and is not.

Many people in the library profession confuse media librarians with other academic media fields. The media librarian's education is usually much broader and has an entirely different focus from those in other academic media fields. Here is a comparison of some differences between the media librarian and the educational communication specialist:

Media Librarian	*Educational Communication Specialist*
Library focus	Classroom focus
User focus	Teacher focus
Outreach and walk-in activities	Walk-in activities
Lifelong focus	K-12 focus
Systems design process	Instructional design process
Enrichment and educational emphasis	Educational emphasis
Strengths in selection, acquisition, and organization	Strengths in design, production, and utilization
Lifelong growth	Educational institution development

Most media librarians balance their academic preparation with print and non-print courses. They can comfortably work in reference, user services, and technical services as well as in the library's media department. Depending on the size of the library, media librarians, like other librarians, usually find themselves assigned diversified responsibilities in print services and in the library's media department.

Some chapters in this book are articles from previous publications. Little has been written specifically on media librarianship and by so few people that this book attempts to collect some of the more important writings and develop topics not treated in the literature for this audience.

Special thanks go to the many media librarians who, as students, demanded their own literature and who currently work tirelessly in libraries to create the integral media collections and programs so essential to full library service. Finally, I wish to thank Rita Maedl for her patience and assistance in the preparation of the final manuscript.

John Ellison

THE PROBLEMS

Media Librarianship:
The State-of-the-Art

Paul B. Wiener

"America is growing at a rate of ten billion words per minute."*

Few would disagree that media librarians today are a proud, dedicated, increasingly conspicuous lot. Their resourcefulness, if not yet legendary, is almost obsessive. Yet these professionals remain easier to characterize than their profession. As the 1980s shift into second gear, can we still talk as intelligently and confidently about media librarianship as book-oriented librarians can about their work? Is it an elephant best described by twenty blind men, or an animal that can be recognized and nurtured by all? The state-of-the-art is never a stable state, yet today's evidence points to a profession growing in so many directions and requiring such a diversity of complex skills and styles from its practitioners that, taken as a whole, its thousand fragments look like pieces of a blank puzzle: if they are finally put together, the only picture seen is one of accomplishment.

In 1906, long before the electronic media dominated the delivery of information and entertainment to the masses, Melvil Dewey wrote:

> The "library" has lost its etymologic meaning and means not a collection of books, but the central agency for disseminating information, innocent recreation, or, best of all, inspiration among the people. Whenever this can be done better, more quickly, or cheaply by a picture than a book, the picture is entitled to a place on the shelves and in the catalog.[1]

What seemed then to be a reasonable, workable, and admirable goal has escalated into a dazzling, expensive array of library services and technologies with so much potential that their providers now sometimes confuse actual with desirable applications.

THE IMPACT OF TECHNOLOGY

Only a few decades ago, media librarianship concerned itself primarily with collections of sound and visual images—films, slides, recordings,

---

*Ad for an NBI computer word-processing system in *The Wall Street Journal*.

filmstrips, photographs, prints, and microforms. In the 1960s, mainframe computers and television complicated the role of libraries. Media librarians began to divert some of their energies from building collections that served visible, mobile patrons to delivering images and information to invisible users who needed only to move a dial. The 1980s finds libraries of all types involved with cable television, videodisks, micro-computers, program production, online data retrieval, computerized catalogs, electronic resource-sharing, and miniaturization technology that makes a microfiche as outsized as a brontosaurus.

The impact of these developments on traditional library concerns has been great, sometimes shattering. Classifying and conserving materials, serving the idiosyncratic needs of individual users, upgrading pro-fessional standards and status, paying for acquisitions, relying on institutional integrity for efficiency and identity, meeting social and legal guidelines for access to all materials—all have been challenged. Libraries have begun the awesome task of trying to keep up with the sophisticated media needs of an impatient public, and with the predictions of educators, engineers, businesspeople, and librarians that a technological fix is all that is necessary to bring an impoverished institution back to health.

The evident accomplishments and trends point to the boundless imagination of media librarians. The educational use of microprocessors (in school media centers especially) is increasing by ten percent a month.[2] Books, films, and videotapes teaching "media literacy" are on the rise. The new *Academic American Encyclopedia* was recently the first encyclopedia to be produced for online retrieval. Media librarians are beginning to demand and write previewing policies and to review media for microcomputer programs.[3] The Museum of Broadcasting in New York City has become the prototype for a network television program research library accessible to the public—a counterpart of Vanderbilt University's well-established network evening news library that has been operating since 1968 (though whether this material is a source of entertainment, opinion, or fact has not been officially deter-mined). The Television Licensing Center has gained an important foothold in the provision of off-air-copied PBS programming to schools and libraries.

Videogames, microcomputers with entertaining self-instructional programs, and commercial databanks like The Source that permit users to scan late-breaking news, job opportunities, transportation schedules, stock prices, or store sales are now available in public libraries, and users are flocking to them. With much fanfare and controversy, Clarkson College (Potsdam, N.Y.) has begun to replace its card catalog with a computerized catalog and many of its reference books with microforms and databanks. At the University of Nebraska, an interactive, computer-assisted videodisk teaching foreign languages has been developed which combines text, graphics, and animation. The Port Washington (New York) Public Library continues, after more than ten years, to lend video recording equipment to patrons and conduct workshops on its use, to amass an impressive collection of local history on videotape, and to organize photography exihibitions of national significance. Many other public libraries using public access cable television channels (or having origination centers on their premises) are broadcasting or creating programs on books, telling stories to children, or covering local performers and civic events. Congressional hearings, however, threaten to repeal laws requiring cable franchisers to provide unregulated public access scheduling.[4]

Project Media Base of the National Commission on Libraries and Information Science studied and publicized the need for a new national audiovisual database[5] (which has existed for health professionals for years in AVLINE). The National Film Board of Canada has adopted the British PRECIS indexing system for its new film catalog. The *Educational Film Locator's Guide* has demonstrated what creative networking can do for film access, filmography, and classification. A host of new periodicals on videotext, video software, cable TV, database management, microcomputers, and satellite transmission have appeared. It is an impressive list of new services and it is only a small selection. Were it not for one small fact, it would be enough to silence all but those most skeptical of the success of media technology in extending the library's institutional longevity. The fact is, most of the kinds of information reported above come from the library media—the print media, at that. The questionable objectivity and perspective of the professional journal hardly makes it an ideal information source.

To be fair, I should mention the video programs *Goodbye Gutenberg* and *Fast Forward*, and films like *The Mind Machines*, *Now the Chips Are Down* and *The Library of Congress* (BBC version), all of which either graphically detail many current library media applications or demonstrate the video and computer technologies with the greatest potential for library application. Computers are now being used to create databanks for law firms, the newspaper industry, hospitals, the banking, insurance, and credit industries, and law enforcement agencies. These are "media libraries," in fact if not in name. Most, however, don't affect our present concerns, except insofar as they draw off potential colleagues to jobs in private industry. Computers are also being used to index and access individual frames of information on instructional videodisks. Deirdre Boyle, though, tells an alarming anecdote of how it took a year and a half to transfer fifty-four thousand slides onto a videodisk at MIT, and another fourteen months to catalog only eight percent of them for computer access[6]—proof that energy, like money, cannot be saved unless someone else spends it first.

A word should be said about past innovations. One of the most intelligent was Ottawa's IRTV project, which lived from 1968 to 1971. Funded by Bell Canada, the Ottawa Board of Education had cable television sets installed in every classroom in five public schools. Classes then received film and video programming from a central program library switching station, if program, time, and channel were reserved in advance. Though apparently well-received, it went the way of most pilot projects, although subsequent evaluation proved it to be highly economical, taken in the long view.[7] This optimal coordination of media programming, community planning, and technological creativity has no counterpart in today's educational media library setting.

Taking another tack, it would seem that the combination of new copyright restrictions, color film fading, incompatible recording, display, and retrieval systems, the business failure of many small film distributors, and the widespread transfer of 16mm to video format is now *decreasing* both the accessibility of many important collections and titles to buyers and renters, and the value of many media acquisition policies. Why the several producer industries and the public, academic, and national libraries failed to assiduously, routinely preserve audiovisual media output over the past century is one of the mysteries of media librarianship. No doubt collectors and profiteers of rare sound and image recordings are grateful for the oversight. Where were the pirates when we needed them?

MEDIA AND LIBRARY LITERATURE

Librarians' professional journals do not generally allocate much space to non-print media developments. *School Library Media Quarterly*, in fact, remains the only periodical exclusively devoted to media librarianship, though media librarians may in good conscience consider as their own such serials as *Media and Methods, Educational Media Yearbook, Instructional Innovator, Instructional Technology, Sightlines,* and *Film Library Quarterly.* The broad coverage of *Library Journal* and *American Libraries* also provides exposure to the various success stories, trends, and inventions for readers interested in the branch of librarianship called media. *Library Trends, Special Libraries,* and *Drexel Library Quarterly* have also devoted considerable space to non-print media librarianship, though very sporadically.

Despite a wide assortment of software review columns and services, including the exhaustive work of the Educational Film Library Association (though there is no *New York Times Book Review, Choice, New York Review of Books,* or *Publishers Weekly* for the audiovisual media), many media librarians continue to complain of the difficulty of previewing and evaluating non-print media, as if it should be easy, or as if selecting print media were a model of efficiency. Their complaint has a variety of explanations. Some film distributors have withdrawn their previewing policies for several financial reasons—increased mailing costs, slow turnaround time, unethical use of preview items. Complaints are also related to the time it takes to evaluate many items intelligently, to the difficulty of finding and scheduling qualified previewers, to the variety of formats (often of the same program) available, and to the constant flood of catalogs, brochures, conferences, and festivals that tempt librarians. Implementing separate selection criteria for each medium and training librarians to apply them, however, would be burdensome, if not unrealistic. Many conscientious media librarians nevertheless believe that time-consuming evaluation is demanded by expensive, sophisticated media packages and feel pressured to choose the best, most appropriate item in the face of shrinking budgets.

BUDGETING FOR MEDIA

In recent years, traditional public and educational library budgets for audiovisual media have not averaged above 6.3 percent of their total materials acquisition budgets,[8] though they have never been much higher. (For academic libraries, it was 2.6 percent, excluding microforms. In public school media centers, audiovisual acquisitions and equipment combined were nine percent of the total.[9]) The majority of educational media sales go to public schools and lower grades (sound filmstrips are still the second largest market), where government funding has been most conspicuous. According to Tom Hope, "many firms that rely entirely or predominantly on sales to the educational market are having a difficult time staying alive"[10] (partly because they are small companies, partly because services are now being sold in place of goods). The expense of, and increasing dependence on, sophisticated hardware by schools wishing to use popular video and computer programming naturally frightens many administrators and cuts deeply into small budgets. Harder to deal with is the ignorance of high-level educational bureaucrats, which causes a Kafkaesque maze of purchasing and budgeting procedures.

One result of this budgetary terrorism is that much of the available money goes to a few big producers and distributors—those who can offer the most "economical" packages, the most familiar material, or the most captivating, extensive advertising. Although our growing dependence on communications conglomerates may seem to be of little consequence, it is not paralleled in the educational print market, where the relatively low cost of media makes alternative, teacher-selected materials still easily accessible to learners and users. But the aggressiveness with which ABC; PBS; IBM; *The New York Times*; Time, Inc.; Films, Inc.; Warner Communications; and a few publishing houses have begun to dominate media sales and delivery suggests that maybe our sophisticated technology will bring to its users only an increasingly slick, standardized product that media librarians will feel pressured to buy. Local resistance to programming created chiefly on the east and west coasts is beginning to be heard[11]—a protest against the tendency of mass media to homogenize content. Interestingly, the major designer of local television "action" news programming style all over the country is located in Marion, Iowa.[12]

This is not really new. But that is just the point. If we are not to be mere ushers of conglomerate programming, the great variety of channels, programs and formats promised by cable TV, videodisk, computer technology, and optical, laser, and microwave transmission will require not only a corps of engineers and instructional technologists (and co-workers) to create original, local software and delivery systems—we will also need educators, administrators, politicians, and informed citizens who recognize the need for alternatives, who can restructure their organizations, who can train and attract quality media managers, and who will risk spending money to insure that media are used to address individual needs, abilities, and tastes. Though many media librarians are demonstrating such awareness, talent, and strength, there is little evidence that library schools have helped them reach this point, or are preparing their successors for the complex management and business skills required in their positions.

MEDIA LIBRARIANSHIP AND LIBRARY EDUCATION

It is no secret that, excepting those pursuing careers in public schools, media librarians are the most self-taught, self-selected of library personnel. Given the current scope of "media" courses offered in library schools, this continues to be necessary. Perhaps it even encourages the independence and resourcefulness required of most media librarians. A study in 1976 showed that courses in library schools dealing in any way with media (liberally defined) represented thirteen percent of total course offerings. More than half of these, however, were offered, and taken, to satisfy state certification requirements for public school media specialists.[13] Of more concern was the finding that many library schools did not list courses relating to media offered *outside* their own programs.[14]

One measure of the difficulty in arousing librarian interest in collecting, much less reading, such statistics, is that the 1980 *Library Education Statistical Report*, compiled and published by the Association of American Library Schools, failed to include any statistics relating media to library school programs, courses, laboratories, faculty, or student interests. The 1981 *ALA Yearbook* doesn't cover "media" under any obvious heading, if anywhere.

It is easy to fault library school curriculum design, but it may be that media librarianship is not a fit subject for academic preparation. Is thirteen percent of total course offerings so bad, considering the percentage of courses devoted to other specialized areas? Maybe that is all a library school is capable of giving. Most library schools now offer courses in microforms, computers, or online services, though the attention they pay to audiovisual media does not approach that found in Canada or England.

WHO ARE MEDIA LIBRARIANS?

Media librarians are still in the process of creating their own discipline. They are more responsive to environment than to tradition, and they are accepting the possibility that much of their work, unlike traditional librarianship, does not need a narrowly-focused, academic (thus necessarily conservative) preparation. Curricula change far more slowly than current media technology. But even though library schools are not sending media librarians out into the marketplace with the kind of established, immediately applicable expertise they are giving to music, medical, or children's librarians, media librarians continue to be hired. Where are they coming from, and what are they practicing?

Some, of course, come from programs in instructional and educational technology. Others combine learned library skills with personal interests; they work or talk their way into positions. Some have backgrounds in commercial film or television production, broadcasting, business management, journalism, computer sales or programming, public relations, and educational administration. Many are never called "librarians." This parallels the wide-ranging non-professional backgrounds of print librarians a few generations back.

MEDIA COLLECTION DEVELOPMENT

The functions of media librarians are almost as varied as the positions they occupy. But unlike their print counterparts, most media librarians today are not primarily concerned with the two areas that make all librarianship possible: building collections and organizing collections, physically or symbolically. They are too busy with other tasks. Collections of software now tend to defy easy classification. Indeed, today's media librarians are involved with receiving and delivering signals, with sharing resources, protecting copyrights, preserving filmstock and magnetic imagery, organizing media events, producing materials, managing computerized distribution centers, evaluating costly hardware, helping teachers, and publicizing their own services. These functions, too, are paralleled by "print librarians"—not that they are easy to define anymore. They may think in print, but they work with media. Indeed, much "print" now is "published" only on tapes, terminals, and printouts.

But the well-known inaccessibility of many media materials frustrates patrons and professionals alike. Whether due to copyright restrictions, perishable stock, nonchalance, inadequate reviewing, lack of a *Books in Print* for non-print media (*Non-Books in Non-Print*?), or simply to the difficulties of cataloging materials that have a dozen or more points of access, it remains a problem endemic to the profession and one that must be faced head-on. And while the problem is being addressed, resources are disappearing. More people will learn their video and radio history from illustrated texts than from original, vintage recordings. Film history, on the other hand, which has always counted on a great storehouse of 16mm titles, will become warped by the limits that time and convenience will place on available titles.

Not that rare, magnificent collections of audiovisual media are not constantly being unearthed and preserved. The Academy of Television Arts and Sciences-UCLA Television Archives recently acquired twenty-seven million feet of Hearst Corporation news film. The University of South Carolina is acquiring sixty million feet of sound and silent Fox Movietone News film. Brandeis University recently restored and is circulating vintage Yiddish American films. The Oral History Program of Columbia University will soon get forty thousand acetate discs of WOR (New York City) radio programs since 1937 (which are being organized by a young non-librarian). A private collector, former film librarian David Chertok, has a personal library of rare jazz films, which he edits and presents in touring programs. And of course the work of those pioneers of collection and restoration, the Museum of Modern Art, the Library of Congress, and the Eastman House Museum, never stops. Nor does the work of the many libraries and library departments, such as the Library of Congress Division of the Blind and Physically Handicapped which, in providing books to the visually impaired, are instrumental in developing audio collections and services. Individual media librarians can do little purchasing of rare materials. Their expertise, however, enables them to rout out sources of such material, encourage donations, and promise excellent curatorship, and influence their own institution's receptivity to acquiring or buying valuable, often prestigious, materials.

Still, for most of us the funds for acquiring rare collections are lacking, and the technology for restoring much original stock doesn't yet exist. The newer delivery systems are directing attention to the newer software, and the excitement they generate among users and librarians dims interest in archival management and research and keeps media librarians busy just keeping up. Moreover, like anybody else, media librarians often take current programming for granted, routinely erase much of what they record, and have no way of knowing what may be worth preserving.

Perhaps in response of the confusion of responsibilities, and to the subtle depersonalization visited upon the best of us by the techno-structure sponsoring our positions and possessing our clients, many media librarians have made professional status and role definition their chief concerns. At least that is the impression gained by surveying recent articles in professional journals. It is easier for special interest groups— school librarians, instructional technologists, database searchers—to organize around issues of their own certification, networking capabilities, publicity needs, professional standards, opposition to censorship, and relationship with peers and administrators than it is for them to agree on cataloging standards, or on how to institute professional school curricula, create new journals, or write original print or audiovisual reference materials. Like print librarianship, media librarianship is embedded in social rather than intellectual issues, despite the bedrock of advanced research and engineering that underlies our work.

Library school and educational technology programs rarely attract those with strong ambitions in science, with two interesting conse-quences for libraries: their graduates unconsciously perpetuate the gap between the possible and the practical, the efficient and the bureau-cratic; and they tend to be overly optimistic about the part they can play in applying the new technologies to library functions and client needs. Their own research often appears self-serving. Some of the most effective media librarians come from outside the established programs. Those who complete doctoral programs—few are from library schools—base many of their theses on surveys of existing studies and services,[15] and on examinations of staffing and organizational structures. First-hand examination of program content, historical studies, classification schemes, format development, or the writing of comprehensive, an-notated mediagraphies are rare. Clearly, the intellectual aspects of media librarianship have yet to be fully explored—or encouraged. The newer media themselves, meanwhile, have yet to prove a useful, expedient vehicle for conferencing, or for improving work performance. The proper exercise of media librarianship is still open for discussion.

There can be little doubt that the limited library school coverage of non-print media, the dearth of appropriate professional journals and communication channels, and the lack of agreement among media librarians as to their professional and intellectual interests all result from their having no central organization to represent them. This is reflected, too, in the absence (outside the overworked Library of Congress) of a central registry for new audiovisual media. AECT exists for the technology-oriented, AASL for those employed by schools, and EFLA for the film nuts among us, but there is no analog of the American Library Association, nor any prospects for one. Given the tendency of large organizations to explode into fragments of special interests, perhaps we are only conserving energy.

THE FUTURE OF MEDIA LIBRARIANSHIP

Is media librarianship, then, a profession to be refined in the academy, standardized and defined in the marketplace and the library, organized and unionized by skilled workers whose common interests are known to one another? Many factors would seem to work against these possibilities. The peculiar strategies of funding media programs and purchases makes unified efforts difficult to accomplish. That non-print media are essentially group productions makes it hard to identify and assign the responsibilities of managing them at their many stages of utilization. The newness and rapid change rate of media technology far outstrips our merely human efforts to establish reliable procedures to work with it. The printing press has been around for five hundred years and the book for thousands. The print media have unified and educated us for several millennia and, until recently, have defined information.

But the differences between print and non-print formats are probably less significant than we realize: their common social functions unite them. Early critics feared that books and printing would destroy memory and concentration, idle workers, and lead to tyranny by the masses. Today's critics of television and video/computer technology echo these worries and produce "evidence" to bolster their opinions. The free, widespread access to popular books in libraries is hardly more than a century old. It has not increased literacy, only reflected it. Access to non-print media in libraries is only slightly younger; it has not decreased literacy, only made it less threatening. Traditional libraries are undergoing the most serious financial crisis of their reign—the Denver Public Library has just decided to impose an annual fee of $100 on individual patrons living outside the Denver city limits—but this hardly affects the publishing industry or the explosion of print-based information. (It has been suggested, however, that the use of computers in libraries both to store research publications and to analyze circulation data will have the dual effect of clearing shelves of rarely-used items, and of convincing faculty that compulsive, promotion-oriented research is a wasted effort which librarians will no longer encourage.[16] Media libraries show every sign of growth and ingenious service, despite indications that access to media information and entertainment will become centered in the home and office (that, too, could have been said about books). Surely the state-of-the-art of media librarianship will change by the time this essay is published. Have we seen the future, then, and is it ours?

The most promising situation is often the least understood. For the first time we have the capability of preserving virtually forever any image or piece of information we want, and of sharing it with anyone, anywhere. It is a librarian's dream and we are probably in the heyday of media librarianship. Only recently have information and imagery begun to be produced faster than we can even hope to keep up with them. We should be proud to have amassed many wonderful collections of media and thus preserve something of our cultural heritage.

The library is beginning to move out of the realm of librarianship and closer to the world of communications. The same central databanks, transmission lines, manufacturers, satellites, cable systems, and broadcast centers are being used in businesses and homes that enterprising media librarians are using to create new services. But we may be the servants, for the electronic media exert a power that warps time and perception in its bid for infinite expansion.

We will continue to collect, organize, and transmit. That is our pleasure and our job. Those of us who continue in the 1980s to be associated with agencies already identified as libraries, who specialize in collecting perishable imagery, or who blithely accept the inevitability of our misnomer in a world of confused specialization may call ourselves media librarians. The rest of us will simply, if not humbly, do what we do and call it work.

References

1. Melvil Dewey, "Library Pictures," *Public Libraries*, 11 (1906), 10-11.
2. Inabeth Miller, "The Micros Are Coming," *Media and Methods*, 16:8 (April 1980), 32.
3. Sheila Evan-Tov, "Help Through the Software Maze," *Media and Methods*, 18:2 (October 1981), 25.
4. Henry Geller, "Putting the Lock on Cable," *Channels of Communication*, (December-January 1982), 61-62.
5. *Problems in Bibliographic Access to Non-Print Materials—Project Media Base: Final Report.* (National Commission on Libraries and Information Science, 1979).
6. Deirdre Boyle, "Video Fever," *Library Journal*, (April 15, 1981), 849-52.
7. G. Harry McLaughlin, *Educational Television on Demand: An Evaluation of the Ottawa IRTV Experiment*, Occasional Papers No. 11, Ontario Institute for Studies in Education (Ontario, 1972).

8. *Bowker Annual of Library and Book Trade Information*, (New York: Bowker, 1981), pp. 276, 278.
9. *Statistics of Public School Libraries/Media Centers, 1978 Fall*, (Washington: National Center for Educational Statistics and Lance Hodes Westat Inc., 1981), p. 7.
10. Thomas W. Hope, "In the Matter of Money," *Instructional Innovator*, 26:5 (May 1981), 10-13.
11. Richard Reeves, "Along Tocqueville's Path - Part I," *The New Yorker*, (April 5, 1982), 78.
12. *Media Probes: TV News* (16mm film), produced by Martin Ostrow, distributed by Laybourne/Lemle, Inc., 1980.
13. Karen S. Munday and John W. Ellison, "A Systematic Examination and Analysis of Non-Print Media Courses in Library Schools," *Expanding Media*, Deirdre Boyle, ed., (Phoenix: Oryx Press, 1977), pp. 293-97.
14. Ibid.
15. Janet G. Stroud, "Research Methodology Used in School Library Dissertations," *School Library Media Quarterly*, 10:2, (Winter 1982), 124-34.
16. Daniel Gore, "Something There Is That Doesn't Love a Professor: 'The Mismanagement of College Libraries' Revisited," *Library Journal*, (April 1, 1982), 686-91.

Bibliography

Many works covering libraries, media, communications, broadcasting, literacy, and publishing were consulted as background material in developing the themes of this essay. They are particularly valuable in that they are multidisciplinary in approach, often viewing libraries and library services from broad and unusual perspectives. Many do not discuss libraries or media librarianship per se, but offer information and insights about social, educational, and cultural trends that bear directly on our work and on the directions we may be heading. Following is a selective list of some of the more comprehensive or provocative works.

Bahr, Alice Harrison. *Video in Libraries: A Status Report, 1979-1980*. White Plains, N. Y.: Knowledge Industry Publications, Inc., 1980.

Bell, Daniel. *The Winding Passage*. Cambridge, Mass.: Abt Books, 1980.

Cherry, Susan Spaeth, ed. *Video Involvement for Libraries*. Chicago: American Library Association, 1981.

Cipolla, Carlo M. *Literacy and Development in the West*. New York: Penguin Books, 1969.

Cornish, Edward, ed. *Communications Tommorow: The Coming of the Information Society*. World Future Society, 1982.

Dranov, Paula; Moore, Louise; and Hickey, Adrienne. *Video in the 80s*. White Plains, N. Y.: Knowledge Industry Publications, 1980.

Goldstein, Seth. *Video in Libraries: A Status Report, 1977-78*. White Plains, N. Y.: Knowledge Industry Publications, 1977.

Green, Claire, ed. *The Print Publisher in an Electronic World*. White Plains, N. Y.: Knowledge Industry Publications, 1981.

Grove, Pearce S. *Nonprint Media in Academic Libraries.* Chicago: American Library Association, 1975.

Hutchinson, Joseph Allan. *A Status Study of Educational Media Services in Selected Institutions of Higher Education in the United States.* Ph. D. dissertation, Louisiana State University, 1981.

King, Donald W., et al. *Telecommunications and Libraries: A Primer for Librarians and Information Managers.* White Plains, N. Y.: Knowledge Industry Publications, 1981.

Mahoney, Sheila; Demartino, Nick; and Stengel, Robert. *Keeping PACE with the New Television.* New York: The Carnegie Corporation of New York and VNU Books International, 1980.

Mattelart, Armand. *Multinational Corporations and the Control of Culture.* Atlantic Highlands, N. J.: Humanities Press, 1979.

Robinson, Glen O., ed. *Communications for Tomorrow.* New York: Praeger, 1978.

Rochell, Carlton, C., ed. *An Information Agenda for the 1980s.* Chicago: American Library Association, 1981.

Schramm, Wilbur. *Big Media, Little Media: Tools and Technologies for Instruction.* Beverly Hills, Calif.: Sage Publications, 1977.

Sigel, Efrem et al. *Books, Libraries and Electronics: Essays on the Future of Written Communication.* White Plains, N. Y.: Knowledge Industry Publications, 1982.

Sigel, Efrem, ed. *Videotext: The Coming Revolution in Home/Office Information Retrieval.* White Plains, N. Y.: Knowledge Industry Publications, 1980.

Smith, Anthony. *The Geopolitics of Information: How Western Culture Dominates the World.* New York: Oxford University Press, 1980
_____. *Goodbye, Gutenberg: The Newspaper Revolution of the 1980s.* New York: Oxford University Press, 1980.

Telecommunications and Libraries: A Primer for Libraries and Information Managers. White Plains, N. Y.: Knowledge Industry Publications, 1981.

Williams, Raymond, ed. *Contact: Human Communication and Its History.* New York: Thames & Hudson, 1981.

Worth, Sol, and Gross, Larry. *Studying Visual Communication.* Philadelphia: University of Pennsylvania Press, 1981.

Information, Not Books

John W. Ellison and Judith S. Robinson

Seeking a justification for the existence of libraries in the library literature is like pursuing a bibliographic will-o'-the-wisp. A rationale is often implied, even assumed, but it continues to be vague. One would expect every book on librarianship to contain one chapter on "philosophy," but authors tend instead to jump into long discourses on "service" without addressing the essential "why service" question. Others openly admit "There is no articulated philosophy of library science which is available for use by researchers confronting the major questions facing the discipline."[1]

The fact that libraries prevail does not justify their existence. Their inability to rely upon a sound philosophical justification for their existence leaves them ill prepared to establish goals and directions essential to meeting the needs of the changing society. Clarifying the role of libraries in society would provide the basis for a profession to truly serve its publics and to adjust effectively to a changing society. The following three principles seem to summarize the basic philosophy of an information-serving agency in our culture:

1. The primary purpose of libraries is to help guarantee equal and unrestricted access to information in our society.
2. The second purpose of libraries is to help develop the full potential of individuals in our society.
3. The third purpose of libraries is to expedite access to and transfer of information.[2]

It is difficult to disagree with the notion that the foremost purpose of libraries is to help guarantee equal and unrestricted access to information in our society. David Dehler, a lawyer, has expressed what could be viewed as the basis for our existence when he wrote:

> Now the right to information is a fundamental human right and therefore does involve considerations of principle. And therefore, although principle cannot dictate the precise policy to adopt, principle does require (1) that the problem of the right to information should be, at the policy level, among the priorities; (2) that a fundamental objective of the policy must be to make available to all persons true and complete information, i.e., the creation of an informed and sound public opinion; and (3) that in making available such information no distinction be made between the so-called elite, the establishment, the in-group, on the one hand, and the so-called ignorant, the poor, the dis-established, on the other.[3]

Can libraries honestly claim that they do not emphasize service to the elite, the establishment, and the in-group? Surveys of public library users, for instance, indicate that they are college-educated, white, urban, and in white-collar occupations. By not recognizing the individual cognitive styles of their potential public, librarians limit library use largely to those individuals who are willing to access information through print sources. Acceptance of the notion that the role of libraries is to help guarantee equal and unrestricted access to information implies that libraries have a responsibility to make information, regardless of format or delivery system, available to all citizens of our society. Limiting access to information because of its format is nothing less than a covert form of censorship. Dorothy Broderick, in discussing the library's responsibility for organizing and providing knowledge for society, has said, "Note, the word is knowledge, not books, and the librarian who fails to use all media is narrowing the world he offers to his users."[4]

The concept of the supremacy of print must be replaced by the concept of the supremacy of information. Our society recognizes the power of information and may well reduce support for institutions that limit access to information by restricting the formats in which it is available. The public's growing awareness of alternatives to print was illustrated in a recent syndicated cartoon which showed a library user commenting to the librarian at a "service" desk:

NO   VIDEOTAPES . . . NO   CASSETTES . . . NO   RECORDS . . . NO PRINTS OR PAINTINGS TO BE LOANED OUT . . . WHAT THE HECK KIND OF A LIBRARY IS THIS ANYWAY?

If the secondary purpose of libraries is to help develop the full potential of individuals in our society, then it is obvious that all formats of information must be made available to meet the variety of individual cognitive and enrichment styles represented by our diverse publics. Robert Gagne has emphasized that "no single medium is likely to have properties that make it best for all purposes."[5] A responsible library should attempt to meet individual needs. Lester Asheim has summarized the library's charge in this way: " . . . the librarian has a role to play in identifying the most effective means for the dissemination of different kinds of messages to serve different purposes for different audiences."[6]

Finally, the third purpose of libraries is to expedite access to and transfer of information, irrespective of format. Expediting access relates to the acquisition, retention, and classification of information. Transfer of information includes such activities as referral and each aspect related to the dissemination of information from the source to the user. Size of image, sequencing of information, cognitive style are just three of hundreds of transfer factors which should concern librarians.

ACCOUNTABILITY OF LIBRARIES

Libraries in America have entered an era of public accountability. Citizens, administrators, and politicians are demanding that libraries and other publicly supported institutions provide services that justify public investment. The inflation and reduced federal spending of the 1970s have resulted in diminished public funding, forcing many libraries into heightened competition with other agencies for shrinking resources. At the same time, results of a 1975 Gallup survey indicated that one third of Americans had either never used a library or had not visited one in the past decade, and half of our population had not used any library in the previous two years. A more recent study by Yankelovich, Skelly and White for the Book Industry Group showed "Slightly more than twenty-six percent of the population use the library."

Why do so many Americans avoid libraries? Can it be because libraries are not providing what people desire and need? Library performance has always been difficult to measure, and they have tabulated quantitative statistics while desiring ways to truly estimate the real quality and impact of their services. They have compiled statistics on circulation, acquisitions, reference questions, and even the number of people entering and exiting their buildings, realizing that these numbers don't tell them what they really want to know, but needing some gauge for estimating their worth.

Perhaps more significantly, they have divided the public into two camps—"users" and "non-users"—and have tried to study how libraries relate to the lives of each. In many of these studies, they have learned that a library user tends also to be a "reader." In other words, users seek information and material for personal growth largely in print form. Both the 1975 and 1978 Gallup surveys corroborate this. Book loans and use of reference materials were the library services most frequently used by library users responding in the Gallup studies, while use of non-print resources such as films, recordings, and loan of art prints was considerably lower.

Interestingly, the Gallup polls showed library non-users to be somewhat print-oriented also. While the most frequent reason for non-use of libraries in the 1975 Gallup study was lack of interest or need (35%) almost one third of the responses related specifically to print resources in the library. About thirty percent of these non-users said they didn't use libraries because they didn't read, they had enough books at home, they preferred to purchase their own books, or felt they could satisfy their information needs outside the library through newspapers, magazines, and other media. Ironically, the 1978 Gallup study reported that seventy-two percent of library users responding said they would be extremely, very, or slightly interested in borrowing films, records, and tapes, while sixty-one percent of all respondents (library users and non-users) expressed an interest in these formats.[9]

FORMAT DISCRIMINATION

The reason that many library users and non-users associate the library with print resources is directly related to the kinds of materials and services that many libraries offer. Don Roberts summarized his findings from a 1976 study: "My study last fall and in subsequent follow-up has proven that there is a strong disregard and lack of respect for non-print media in the profession."[10] This conclusion is not a fresh revelation for those who work closely with non-print. Many of us recognize that, with few exceptions, libraries are promoters of information predominantly in print format. This philosophy has been communicated to the public when national associations have promoted "The Right to Read" or "You Are What You Read" rather than "You Are What You Know," and when libraries have published listings in local newspapers of "New Books at the Library" rather than "New Materials at the Library." However, on a more subtle level, libraries express the same negative bias when they permit certain practices in relation to non-print services.

One of these practices is the failure to provide equal bibliographic and physical access for these services. Lack of equal bibliographic access is sometimes a result of failure to catalog non-print materials adequately, or segregating the print and non-print catalogs. Certain library policies can also have the effect of limiting physical access to these resources. Some libraries may enforce a policy which requires a separate borrower's card for non-print resources. Others may require stricter loan periods, fines, or fees for materials other than print, or impose age restrictions on use and circulation of non-print materials. Physical access may also be discouraged by locating non-print service areas in low visibility sections of the library and failing to publicize these locations. These examples will not change significantly as long as job ads read: Media person wanted with MLS from an accredited library school.

RATIONALE FOR INCLUSION

Some libraries feel they are really committed to non-print services, but this commitment is often for questionable reasons. In some cases, they introduce non-print services because it results in good public relations or because it is fashionable. However, when commitment does not accompany a new service, the service falters and is not developed to its full capacity.

Another motivation for developing non-print is that local, state, and federal monies have sometimes been available to fund special projects. Again, this rationale expresses little or no commitment, and the service tends to be dropped when outside funding is eliminated. These programs may also falter when they are not accompanied by professionally prepared staff capable of creative program development. This means hiring non-print staff with more than one or two "media" courses from a library school.

Finally, many libraries, lacking the basic knowledge of the inherent communication properties of each medium and delivery system, view non-print services only as a means of increasing book circulation. This view was expressed in an article by a library educator who wrote, " . . . I think that media is used to best advantage when it serves as a catalyst to return children willingly to the world of print."[11]

FORMAT DISCRIMINATION IN LIBRARY EDUCATION

The bias toward print in libraries has been paralleled by a similar bias in library education,[12,13,14] blatant in some instances, while subtle in many others. One of the subtle ways this bias can become evident is through terminology. For instance, the term "media," which includes all formats of communication, is used by some faculty only in reference to materials other than print. Similarly, information science is frequently equated with computers, rather than as a broader discipline concerned with the properties and behavior of information and its organization, dissemination, collection, storage, retrieval, interpretation, and use.

Occasionally, omissions in library education help to instill a bias toward print. Course syllabi, bibliographies, and handouts sometimes limit or omit references to non-print resources. Some faculty may reject student projects concerned with non-print. Faculty may spend class time discussing professional print associations, while making little or no reference to AECT, NAVA, ASIS, etc. Classes may be cancelled for library conferences, but little encouragement may be provided for student attendance at information science or non-print conferences. Some reference and cataloging courses are still taught with little or no discussion of non-print information sources.

Some library school curricula demonstrate a print bias by covering all non-print in a separate course, rather than in an integrated curriculum of courses dealing with information in diverse formats.[15] In such programs, a large majority of course offerings may focus on print formats. Students may be advised to take one token non-print course but ten or eleven print-oriented courses for an MLS degree. Faculty advisors may communicate to students that non-print courses are valuable only for those planning to enter school media centers or pursue "media" librarianship as a career.

Sometimes library school offerings appear to include up-to-date course work in non-print but actually treat these topics cursorily. Pauline Wilson summarized this tendency in relation to information science curricula, which face problems somewhat similar to non-print in some library schools:

> ... in far too many schools—possibly even the majority—the information science component of the curriculum is merely cosmetic in nature, either a new name for an old course fluffed-out with updated language or a simple overview that constitutes little more than current awareness.[16]

Ideally, there should be no discrimination between print, non-print, and computerized channels of information. Library educators should be preparing students to select, acquire, organize, disseminate, manage, and analyze all forms of information to meet the public's needs. Maybe Geddes was right when he titled an article, "AV: Too Important to Leave to the Library Schools."[17]

Ultimately, society is adversely affected when librarians and library schools limit the range of formats through which information can be obtained. The question is, why have library educators and librarians allowed themselves to disregard information in many formats that the public wants and would use?

LIBRARIES AND PRINT

The neglect of non-print in both libraries and library schools reflects the reluctance of the profession to adapt to the technological, informational, and social changes of the past few decades. It is ironic that while our society has embraced these formats as vital and desirable elements of modern life, many librarians and library educators continue to view them as innovative and experimental. This perspective is understandable when we recall that libraries evolved alongside print technology. For decades, print was the sole vehicle for mass communication of ideas. As a result, print itself became an end in the eyes of many librarians, rather than a means for human communication. When additional means of communication were developed which supplemented or substituted for the printed page, these were considered by many librarians to be deviations or frills.

An automobile executive once declared that his company was not in the business of selling cars, but selling transportation. A similar distinction can be made for libraries: They do not exist to provide books, but to provide information and enrichment. If library professionals could embrace this philosophy, libraries might begin to truly keep pace with society's needs. Information is too valuable in today's society for librarians not to recognize its value to library users. They must, as a profession, agree on the role of libraries in our society. With such an agreement, they could extend service to a wider spectrum of the public and take new pride in their profession.

References

1. John M. Christ, *Toward a Philosophy of Educational Librarianship* (Littleton, Colo.: Libraries Unlimited, 1972), p. 15.
2. Lynn Lundgaard, the University of Oklahoma, Norman, Okla. Discussion, July 8, 1981.
3. David Dehler, "The Right to Information," *Revu de l'Universite d'Ottawa* 44 (October-December 1974), pp. 169-70.
4. Dorothy M. Broderick, "On Misplaced Devotion," *School Library Journal* 11 (January 15, 1965), p. 34.
5. Robert M. Gagne, "Media and the Learning Process," Presentation at the 1968 Division of Audiovisual Instruction Conference, Dallas.
6. Lester Asheim, "Introduction: Differentiating the Media," *Library Quarterly* 45 (January 1975), p. 3.
7. The Gallup Organization, *The Role of Libraries in America* (Frankfort, Ky.: Kentucky Department of Libraries and Archives, 1975), p. 8.
8. "Book Industry Study Finds U. S. Still Is a Nation of Readers," *Library Journal* 103 (December 15, 1978), p. 2466.
9. The Gallup Organization, *Book Reading and Library Usage: A Study of Habits and Perceptions* (Princeton, N.J.: The Gallup Organization, Inc., 1978.)
10. Don Roberts, "'Printism' and Non-Print Censorship," *Catholic Library World* 48 (December 1976), p. 223.
11. James L. Thomas, "Turning Kids on to Print," *Audiovisual Instruction* 22 (September 1977), p. 34.
12. John W. Ellison, "Now Hear This! . . . A Potpourri of Reader Reaction to Ten of Library College Thought," *Learning Today* 10, (Winter 1977), pp. 41-44.
13. Richard Palmer, "Interaction, Future Shock, ASIS and the Library Schools," in *Information Politics*. Proceedings of the ASIS 39th Annual Meeting, San Francisco, October 4-9, 1976.
14. Tefko Saracevic, "Information Science Education in the 1980's? A Blunt Offering for a Debate Coupled with Questions for Study and Recommendations." *Information Management in the 1980's*. Proceedings of the ASIS Annual Meeting, 1977, Vol. 14.

15. Karen Munday and John Ellison, "A Systematic Examination and Analysis of Non-Print Media Courses Taught in Library Schools," *Journal of Education for Librarianship* 16 (Winter 1974), pp. 184-94.
16. Pauline Wilson, "Impeding Change in Library Education: Implications for Planning," *Journal of Education for Librarianship* 18 (Winter 1978), p. 161.
17. George Geddes, "AV: Too Important to Leave to the Library Schools," *Library Review* 28 (Spring 1979), pp. 14-18.

Librarian Cum Information Professional

Don Roberts

Does it make any sense to become a media librarian, or to remain one once you do? Isn't all the talk about information science and management these days, and hasn't it long since been agreed that, once library schools and the profession dropped the use of "science," they would get their credibility elsewhere? Service, maybe. In the age of information and mass communications the words librarian, library, and library school have become anachronistic, to say the least.

In the late 1960s and early 1970s I found myself teaching in an unaccredited library school which had computer terminals in the school offices, a fully functioning media lab, including production capability, and many courses integrated with various information formats. To invite only authors to speak in the school would have been unheard of. And, oh yes, we did have courses to help the students learn to communicate better, both among themselves and with future employers and clients.

Now, the sixty-year-old library school at the University of Minnesota is threatened with closure. It has agreed not to take in any more students; some of the faculty have resigned and will be moving on; and in the interim there will be some soul-searching about what will become of the school. An astonishing administrative fiat early last year called for a task force "to examine the feasibility of developing a substantially re-structured program that would provide opportunities for curricular and research activities in information processing and management as well as in the more classical aspects of librarianship." This school, which got into information science very late and into media hardly at all, is now faced with some narrow options that all but insure its demise.

In my best years as a librarian, much of my work was experimental and looked upon with doubt and disfavor by many of my fellow librarians. The distrust of innovation and the continual revolutions in information handling and communication techniques have created a schism in which "traditional librarians" and those who would be "change agents" have become pawns in a game presided over by administrators who either do not understand the forces at work or choose not to acknowledge them. So you may want to take a good look at the notion of "librarian" and "library" before you get into the attitudes and institutions which characterize much of the profession. If you have strong feelings about the importance of information work as something which is interactive with the information environments around it, as opposed to serving as a purveyor of "canned" information from elsewhere, you will want to give both the training schools and possible employers a very close look. Do not be overly impressed with your own zeal on the subject of change, because it might take you ten to twenty years of "yeoman's service" to get to a place within an information network where you could effect the necessary changes.

I think it best that you erase the word librarian from your mind temporarily and concentrate on imaginary job descriptions and titles that might be employed in some radio or TV station, information company/cartel, info and referral network, hypothetical library, or whatever. Think about the transitions ahead—if you agree that radical changes *are* ahead and that the library as we know it may be on its way out.

PREPARING FOR YOUR CAREER

If you ar thinking of preparing yourself for work in a specific library or information system, try to take a close look at the planning that the library is doing for the next ten or twenty years of service. It is particularly discouraging to prepare yourself for future work and find yourself dispensing outmoded services, so you need to look at the way the libraries/information centers are wired for the future. What will be the picture for public data services in the library? Will they be available to homes, offices, and other institutions and businesses? Are the technological expectations of the staff on a par with the surrounding community, and if not, why not?

If you find out that the library has accepted the status quo and is rationalizing that as a way to avoid future responsibilities, you must ascertain whether the library can make it as a sentimental, museum-style service and then decide whether or not you want to go with that. If you go into some kind of training for work there, you may want to make sure that the education does not lead you into conflicts. It is very possible to get training which will be diametrically opposed to the work you will do, and I don't recommend that unless you expect to leave the job in a relatively short time. I have known people who received money for part of their education from an institution or business they were bound to leave at a future date. The ethics of this are debatable, though it seems to be common practice.

One sure way to examine a library or information center for integrity and future interest is the way it treats children and young adults.

Libraries generally view children by reader status (e.g., summer *reading* programs) or as recipients of light entertainment or homework assistance. It seems to make no difference whether young people are learning algebra in the fifth grade, doing complicated science projects in grammar school, cutting their teeth on microcomputers, or playing music in Suzuki groups—they are still relegated to a vision in someone's memory of the way children used to be. This is pathetic and must be changed. Will the agent for change be you? We desperately need imaginative, innovative information people to work with children.

The most neglected group in library and information service are so-called young adults. The best that has been done for them is a slightly updated version of children's reader services plus some special programming. There have been some projects which were carried out earlier under LSCA funds which held some promise of turning this around. But for the most part the services to this age have been even less imaginative and intelligent than for children. Yet they are the next generation of voters, the people who may or may not become information workers and provide the possibilities of innovative, fresh insights for the information services of the future. We must remain inventive and open enough to provide service to this most challenging group of information users.

Here are some other librarian/information people needed: *information synthesizers/abstractors*, people who can boil down information to help information consumers with their "overloads." *Information networkers*, people who are especially attuned to interfaces, especially those which are interactive and audiovisual. *Information translators*, people who can change information from format to format, language to language, transmission device to receiving device, facilitators who know how to work with electronic engineers, AV technicians, and other resource people to keep the interfaces going. *General systems thinkers* comprehensively examine the properties of information and their role in all aspects of society. *Futurists* look at trends and developments and use their observations to pro-actively plan for desired futures. *Information brokers* and *managers*, who know how to wheel, deal, and swap for information and services, people who are good cross-field runners, politicians, and hustlers. *Multimedia catalogers* and *accessors/information philosophers*, who will make sure that the limitations of our national library do not limit our clients' access to information. *Multimedia selectors* of software, people who select by subject matter and in different formats compatible with communities they serve, because the time is past when people are so specialized that they can only select print. *Information programmers*, who are trained to deal with cable television, radio, telephone messages, computers, information packages, political considerations, public relations, etc. Finally, *information scientists* (yet to be defined) need to be taken out of their roles and given the responsibility of working actively with the others mentioned. As long as their talents are relegated to "housekeeping" functions, library and other information services will be in trouble.

You may want to consider the new information service configurations starting to pop up here and there. There will be more and more opportunities of this kind as we witness the "paradigm shifts" ahead. For example, you may want to try to work for yourself as an information broker/consultant, taking the place of diminished or phased out public and private information services. These configurations constitute "libraries without walls" or invisible libraries, using telephone and computer services (sometimes on a yearly fee basis) to provide services that would otherwise be unavailable. Another version of this would be to set up an inter-company information service to keep costs down and information active.

Or how about an information co-op, modeled perhaps on food co-ops? This co-op could hire trained information workers as coordinators with the skills and organizational ability to supervise volunteers and provide information services to members. Thus volunteers and members could access wide-ranging resources via time-sharing, microcomputers, subscription services, periodicals, etc., that few would be able to afford otherwise. The service could be very sophisticated without anyone necessarily owning anything except shares in the co-op.

Look in the want ads in *The New York Times* and other papers for current job titles and descriptions for information work. Compare these to the titles and descriptions in library journals. Then you may want to compare both of them to the curriculm of schools you are considering attending or have attended. If you come up with some dichotomies, you may want to write to possible employers and ask them where they suggest you get training or additional training.

Look at the proceedings of information futurists conference, such as the one held by the World Future Society in Washington, D.C. in the summer of 1982, to see what is predicted for information professionals. Then compare the predictions with the audiotapes of the programs of a recent conference of the American Library Association to see where the matchups are, and where the "future directedness" of ALA is. Especially useful would be to focus on the overall themes within the programs and how they were reflected in the subject matter of the invited speakers.

Study the areas of work you are interested in (public service, private industry) to see how the budgets compare for information service; and, more specifically, what percentage of those services go to the salaries of professional personnel. Are the salaries commensurate with other professionals in the organization and in similar organizations? If not, why not? How does this compare to the search you made in the newspapers and library journals? You may be surprised to find that many municipalities and businesses pay their information workers far less than other "skilled" workers. So you may not want to enter into the work only later to have to be "victimized" by the "insensitivity" of the institution or company.

Write to an association which you may depend upon in the future for your professional updating, such as ALA, ASIS, AECT, or SLA, and ask them to provide you with the name of an exemplary person in your area with whom to discuss information work. These are some of the possible topics to try: What is information science and how does it relate to mass communications and popular taste? How is right brain/left brain theory being applied to information handling? How will the acceleration of "smart machines" affect the amount of creativity in information work? How is building and space design changing to accommodate the rapid changes in equipment and software? How many information formats do you personally work with and how do you see the integration of these in information systems? What would you suggest for professional preparation in light of the rapid changes predicted in information handling in the next decade, especially in terms of digital/disk/chip technology? Could you rank you professional concerns by importance? You may also want to ask for a reading list on present and future problems of information handling.

Marshall McLuhan said that we are constantly using the new media to do the work of the old. This is especially so in libraries and information centers. Examine the uses made of media by local library and information centers and see how this influences your choices of employment. For example, many libraries use TV only for surveillance. Are films used predominantly to draw people into the building? Phones are the lifeblood of reference services; how imaginatively are they used by the systems you observe? What plans do the information centers you visit have for upgrading and changing their information technology for the work ahead? How interactive are they? Do they permit branching, possible two way connections with homes, offices, "wired" businesses, and libraries to receive and send signals? What are the potentials, especially in new or remodeled buildings, for space-age communications?

Try to get the proceedings of the sessions held in your state to prepare for the White House Conference on Libraries. See how these reflect today's and tomorrow's needs in information handling and if there is something to follow up there. If you are really serious about information handling, you may have to leave your city or even your state!

Peruse the latest index volume of *Library Literature* for the hot topics of the profession. See who is writing what. This might provide you with clues to take your search further. There are always buzz words, slogans, awards, equipment, and software mentioned. Scan these index volumes and then go on from there. See which categories have the most entries and then see what conclusions you can make from that.

Many people who are interested in preserving the library as a place of "free access to knowledge" are unwittingly doing so in a way that insures its demise. The example that comes to mind is the *Library News*, published by the Urban Libraries Council. This well-intentioned publication and the group that sponsors it express the belief that the continued dominance of print services is the way the library will survive. Thus, they invite authors to speak in favor of the library as an institution. But we know that things have changed radically, especially since the Second World War, and that a library must be fully integrated to draw the public into it. If we continue to support groups, institutions, and services that insist upon the dominance of print, we are asking for obsolescence and demise.

If you get interested in any library school for advanced study, I would suggest you check into more than the faculty and their qualifications (particularly the dean) and the courses offered. Especially important to check are the courses suggested by the library school in other departments of the university. But even more important is the "between the lines" information, including what kind of equipment the school has and what is available to students, what kind of guest lectureships are sponsored by the school, the amount of input that the information community has in the way the school operates, and how it anticipates the needs of the surrounding community. Too often there is an incestuous tendency that keeps a school cycling within itself and its own accreditation committees. Be especially wary of a school that does not have much respect within its own academic community.

The first step is to put out of mind that information is material: a book, a film or videotape, microfiche, whatever. Look at information as a process that is sometimes recorded in this or that format. Any format will give the information a different life, and it will also distort it. Try to keep in mind that a lot of information is created only as part and parcel of that format itself. How will this fact influence your future chances for employment? If you devote yourself to a format and the format is on its way out as a dominant communication medium, what will that mean for your employability? What will happen to a periodicals librarian when serials become increasingly electronic, or a fiction specialist formerly dealing in novels who must now specialize in videotapes? It may be expedient to consider the content and process of the subject matter and special collections rather than specialize in a format.

For the less taken but soon-to-be-more-taken path, I suggest something even more radical. Forget degrees and the usual paths into library work. Whether or not you have some kind of degree, you may want to find a way to work within information/communications networks. Keep in mind that many businesses (and soon the institutions) will be less and less willing to give credibility to degrees. Why? Because these pieces of paper reflect training of the past, which has virtually nothing to do with the present or future. I'm not saying the potential employer may not give some importance to this or that paper qualification; but what kind and for what reason? I think we can assume that employers will soon be more interested in skills and performance first, and degrees second.

You may want to look for schools that teach communications skills of many kinds: computer schools, radio and television broadcasting schools, vocational-technical institutes, business and secretarial schools, etc. And you may also want to look at possible corporate training programs, e.g., computer, specialized telephone equipment, word processor, broadcasting, and cable companies. If you could compare the changes in vocational-technical training in the last few years, you would begin to realize that there are ways you can do the work you want to do without a master's degree.

Another possibility is to attend trade shows associated with conferences and exhibitions which have to do with information and communications. A good example are the shows labelled "consumer electronics." See what is being shown, talked about, and sold to help individuals, businesses, and institutions with their communications. Check the pitches at the booths and by the speakers. What are the companies such as Bell Telephone, ITT, Apple, Texas Instruments, Kodak, and Zenith up to and how does what they are selling relate to your future as an employee?

One thing you may discover in exhibits, conferences, schools, institutions, and companies is that almost no one knows what information and communication is. It is awesome to see the splendid displays put on by the giant corporations and cartels, just as it is impressive to see the booths fronted for the Library of Congress and other public information conglomerates and spinoffs and discover that the "in" vocabulary and attitudes incorporated are little more than lingo and graphics.

You must ultimately return to your own mind, your preference, and your natural abilities. Obviously, there are traps here, too, but my feeling is that you must be in accord with your own beliefs and especially with your own way of doing things. If you are going to be a happy, creative information worker in the late twentieth century, you must be attuned to yourself in your work. Training and personal performance are becoming more and more important. I am not saying that ideals are not important. They are—but only when they are welded to present training and performance. This will mean continuous retraining for most of us, learning from the young, and a lot of humility. And it will mean, more than ever, paying particular attention to the environments in which we live, especially the creative, changing environments.

If you have already resigned yourself to a work model of some kind, you may not need this chapter. You can obviously make your lifestyle a work of art, and get a certain amount of satisfaction from that. You may even be able to find a personal life which is compatible with that. In any case, I would suggest that you be very careful about the specialization you choose within your field. Years ago a fellow professional chose to work in periodicals because she felt that it was the most stable and interesting part of the library. She retired early when her department was the first to be computerized. The sentiment was suddenly removed.

"Change" is an overused word nowadays, and change for change's sake is one of the bugaboos of information professionals. I am constantly asked when the changes will stop, when the formats will standardize. The answer is that they will never stop, and that a lot of the changes are going to be unnecessary, full of hype and dollars, and that they will cause a lot of consternation—all the more reason why information professionals must be on top of them rather than reacting against them and thus being manipulated by them. As the bumper sticker says so aptly: "If you think education is expensive, try ignorance."

People who would work in libraries and information centers are in an increasingly difficult position, not only because the continuity that has characterized the work in the past has largely fallen away, but even more so because the assumption that print resources contain the totality of knowledge has continued to erode. This has caused a great deal of disorientation among the professionals who have been leaders, administrators, and teachers. The reactions to this disorientation have been disparate and have tended to reinforce and extend the uncertainty.

In order to prevent the continued stultification of information work we must look at the options very carefully. Otherwise, we are subject both to the dehumanization of information and to new dangers in the workplace. OSHA now receives more complaints about radiation and other side effects from CRTs than any other "tools" in the workplace. If precipitous changes in working conditions are not watched closely, we will find our results eroded by the very tools of change to which we have adapted.

To go back to an earlier point, information begins with the physical/mental aspects of life, not with its symbols. We cannot understand symbols without our sensory organs, our nervous systems, and our subconscious. Human communication took place on the planet three or four million years before we got around to the things that have been so venerated in library school courses such as "The History of Books and Printing." The insistence of the library profession on "durable records" and the resultant limited, materialistic view of information has not only blinded people to their own information physiology and psychology, but it has also impeded the possibilities of change within their work. Thus the people involved have become allied with the producers and distributors of information, often to the detriment of all concerned. What has been considered "ephemeral," entertaining, or otherwise unacceptable because it has not been materialized in print (or now in microfiche or in a database) has been relegated to a secondary place.

Your ultimate possibility in the present will be within this exciting if unsettling time of information integration. This will even be true for those who choose to work in quasi-traditional library situations, where "tradition" will have to include everything from LP, 78 rpm, and 45 rpm records to the early videodisks, because all these will have to be stored in our sentimental libraries. But for those who will be constantly changing their orientation to embrace the latest information laser systems, holographic storage, digital LPs, documentary films, and video encyclopedias there will be challenges of ever-increasing and mind-boggling kinds.

These future formats should be lighter, more compact, less expensive, and capable of more flexible economic distribution than the ones we have now. And the ultimate hope is that the professionals who handle these information packages will be equally fluid and capable of movement and change. If these professionals are able to bring both sides of their brains plus their personalities into the arenas of work, all the better. The ultimate hope is to keep information *humanized*, open to input from all kinds of media and available to our whole selves.

It will be much easier for you to prepare to be an information worker than a librarian, and it will be a lot better if you can keep yourself open to all information jobs, formats, and networks. You are an adaptable, technological human being, not limited to paper and ink or microfiche nor computerized digits for inputs, and innately capable of sophisticated information services. The exciting possibilities are subject to many potentially frustrating limitations, primarily rationalizing and traditional backpedalling, but it is my hope that you will be one of those "pathfinders" who will fight their way through to the new possibilities which await discovery and implementation. Go for it!

Even if you decide to specialize in the past and to work within the mazes of memories, I hope you go all the way with that too. Your work will be hazarded by the latest fads in information handling, just as your more contemporary counterparts will be limited by the restraints imposed by those who would have the past dominate information services. The marketplace will be against you, because companies, corporations, consultants and the like will be selling their versions of the future rather than helping you with the past. Our "information age" has never been more dependent upon information and information workers, and this will continue to be so. Good luck with the many roads ahead.

Smile, This Is the Real World

Kenneth R. Fielding

Y OUR first day on the job as P.L.'s new media librarian goes very well. The boss, who is all smiles, tells you that they want someone to really take charge of that film collection. Films are going to be big in libraries in the future, and "we want to get in on the ground floor." The boss also mentions a record collection that lies scattered hither and yon and notes that "our last cataloger quit and went to the Yukon." The job will also include responsibility for displays and exhibits. "Nothing too elaborate. Just a few store window displays. You can do that in a few hours each month." And P.L. should add videotapes, videodisks and even get into production. "No reason why we can't also make a few films or tape a few meetings every now and then?" The boss wants a complete media service and all you can say is "Wow! What an opportunity!"

So you begin to check into old P.L.'s media services to date. You could find several things. Perhaps P.L. has a clerk (who also works circulation, processing, and types adult booklists), seven Canadian travel films (and there are two legal letters in your box from the Canadian Travel Film Library), and two hundred records (one hundred Mozart, one hundred Haydn). Or, you may find a reasonably well-established media collection. Since 1955, the library has purchased, received as gifts, borrowed on indefinite loan 125 16mm film titles and also a thousand records. In that same period, twelve different people have had responsibility for media (and one of them went stark raving mad back in 1961!).

P.L. may also have some rather unusual equipment to support its media services. One library I worked for had a ceiling projector for use by paraplegics. With this device, the pages of a book on microfilm could be projected onto a ceiling. The totally paralyzed user could thus enjoy Dickens, Cooper, Chaucer, and the Federalist papers. You could find such a device at P.L. or perhaps, if you would look carefully behind the snags and that old smock on the lowest shelf in the children's circulation desk, you would discover the library's stereopticon slide viewer and twenty-four slides showing Niagara Falls in 1934.

Typical? Unfortunately, yes, for most libraries with so-called media departments acquired these devices almost in absence of mind. There was probably no comprehensive plan to guide the purchase, the cataloging, or the care of non-print items. Someone thought it might be a good idea to buy a few classical records. There was, after all, a music study group in town. Someone else donated the ceiling projector or an ancient movie projector. The former director liked travel films and contracted with the Canadian Travel Film Library to deposit so many titles every quarter. Maybe the State Library also deposited films at key points throughout the state.

There really had never been a full-time media person. The former film librarian might have been the children's assistant or a senior circulation clerk who went to the movies a lot. One of my first positions entailed responsibility not only for films but also for display and exhibit preparation, publicity, meeting room use, and several reference shifts each week.

Non-print, after all, was not a full-time job. It was something assigned to enable a staff member to have enough work to fill out a forty-hour week. Also, the newest staff member was usually assigned to film or record work. He or she could learn the ropes, could even mess things up without hurting anything very much. After all, media services were only a sideline, nowhere near as vital as print services.

And old P.L. also never took good care of those few media materials they did possess. Films received aid in extremis. The Mozart record was so warped that one could jump from the first movement to the fourth without having to listen to the second and third. Standard operating procedure in these circumstances involved throwing out the film or record without replacing it or having it repaired. Or, the mutilated item would be returned to the shelves with the fond hope that the next borrower would not notice the damage.

As one might suspect, there was also no space for media services. The records might be shelved in the 780 section right next to the music scores. In this version of the integrated library, the records would protrude into the aisle where they could easily be dislodged by unwary users. Film shelving might be found in the middle of a room or else sequestered in the work room.

Work space for P.L.'s media librarian would be at a premium. Possibly, desks, work tables, even typewriters might be shared with other staff. Displays might be unpacked on the same tables as orders. The film rewinds for inspecting film would be under another table or in the basement. Records to be cataloged would be in a corner next to the radiators. Most important of all, P.L. would not have any money to speak of for media. The media budget of a thousand dollars would be used for recordings, paintings, film, and other materials plus freight costs for traveling exhibits plus needed equipment repairs. Our media librarian could be forgiven for sudden heart failure at this point. Obviously, P.L. wasn't really interested in media for their own sake. Media were merely an appetizer designed to entice more readers into the library; an image-making device to show skeptics that the library had entered the twentieth century.

So, our media librarian learned a great truth. The most dangerous "radical" in librarianship is not one who advocates equal rights for women or gays or other minorities. Nor are those who advocate intellectual freedom really an embarassment. After all, most of these people don't want to change the structure, they merely want to be included within it. But the media librarian, through advocacy of the so-called "non-print devices" and supporting technology, could radically alter the existing structure and philosophy of the library.

The philosophical differences between print and media are reflected in several ways. Media materials are often used differently from print. Books, magazines, and other print forms are designed for use by a single individual. Though we may read aloud to a group, reading generally is a solitary activity. Indeed, therein lies much of its attraction. Media formats—records, film, TV, displays—provide a group experience and are most cost-effective when seen and/or heard simultaneously by a large group.

THE MEDIA LIBRARIAN AND THE COMMUNITY

These differences in usage are reflected in the ways that print and media librarians view the community. Print librarians in selecting materials, tend to seek out respected individuals—board members, state consultants, colleagues—for purchase suggestions, rather than the community at large. The community's input is often perceived in terms of censorship or as a threat to intellectual freedom. One must oppose attempts to remove books from the library, particularly if the censor does not represent all community views. But print librarians seem equally reluctant to add books suggested by pressure groups even if such suggestions are in no way political or religious. I know of a recent attempt by an historic housing district to have its public library purchase a few paperbound Victorian house plans. The attempt, which ultimately did result in the purchase of a few books, was very much opposed by the library as an unwarranted intrusion.

The media librarian, generally, takes a different view of the community. Often, media librarians will actively solicit community advice on selecting films and other non-print media. The high cost of film and videotape may make this a logical step. We do not want to spend two hundred dollars on something no one will ever use. More importantly, however, the media librarian will soon discover that the key to making media successful is strong communicty support.

The media librarian will be concerned about censorship and will not want to politicize the media collection. But he or she may also find that by working with potential censors—fundamentalist church schools, patriotic societies, women's and gay liberation groups—potential opposition can be neutralized. Rather than building alliances within the profession, as do print librarians, the media librarian may find it more convenient to seek allies among the community groups. The greatest threat to the department may not be the John Birch Society but, very possibly, the profession.

Print and non-print or media librarians will have other differences. The print librarian will observe that only five thousand films were circulated in a total library circulation of five hundred thousand items. Since film circulation thus accounts for only one percent of the total circulation, why spend fifteen percent of the materials budget on media materials? The media librarian will argue that volumes are not a true index of film use. Half a million books probably represent half a million people. Five thousand films represent not five thousand people but one hundred thousand to one hundred and fifty thousand. Film, after all, is a group medium, and one film generally reaches twenty to thirty people. Thus, the media librarian will conclude that the figure of fifteen percent is, if anything, far too low.

Similar observations will be made about records and displays. The twenty thousand records circulated annually reach an audience of sixty thousand to seventy-five thousand. The ten displays in the downtown Mall may be seen by as many as twenty-five hundred people weekly. And the library may produce a TV program that reaches a million people a year. Obviously, our media librarian cannot expect to get more money by using these figures at a budget hearing. But their use suggests another major difference between print and media services. To the print librarian, items such as volume, titles circulated, etc., are the key. To the media librarian, it is people as indicated in audience figures and reactions that are most important.

Technology is another area in which we find differences in philosophy. Print use doesn't usually involve technology though newspaper on fiche and microfilm do require supporting equipment (one could argue that fiche and microfilm are actually media department materials). The print librarian is thus spared from having to operate and repair machines.

The inability to operate and repair specialized media equipment on the other hand, can prove acutely embarassing to the media librarian. I remember with great pain my first attempt to play back a videotape we had just made of a library story hour. As our Board watched the snowstorm on the TV monitor, I squirmed in agony and consternation before I finally discovered that I had placed the player in the record mode. Video is not the only problem machine; 16mm film projectors can do wonderful things to film if improperly threaded. Cassette and record players and overhead, slide, and filmstrip projectors can also provide hours of "entertainment" for the unwary or the inept. Of course, knowing how to operate media equipment is not enough. One must also be able to help maintain the equipment and even, at times, make simple repairs and adjustments.

Setting up exhibits and displays can also present many technical difficulties. Flat exhibit panels can severely test the library that lacks proper facilities. At one library where I was employed, the main exhibit space was a long window trough on the mezzanine floor, a site far removed from normal traffic flow. For art objects, we require not only space but power and possibly special lights. These problems are compounded if the exhibit is some distance from the library.

Media materials generally require more care than printed materials. Books are usually returned undamaged and need only to be reshelved. But 16mm films, for example, must be carefully checked for sprocket damage, breaks, and other problems before they can be reshelved. Film inspection equipment, incidentally, is one of the more expensive items in the well-run media service department. Records should be checked after each use and cleaned frequently. Failure to do so can ruin the collection. Even paintings, sculpture, multimedia kits, and slides need regular inspection to detect scratches, dents, and abrasions. A well-run media department will spend much more time just keeping software and equipment in repair than any print department will spend caring for its materials.

It is obvious that much of the knowledge needed for successful media management is not available in any concise, organized form. For example, print librarians can find "good collection" described in the *Standard Catalog for Public Libraries* or the *Harvard Guide to American History* or the AAAS list as well as current review sources such as *Kirkus*, *LJ*, or *Choice*. Though there are reviews for film (EFLA, *Landers*) and records (*Booklist*) there are nowhere near as many comprehensive guides available for the media librarian.

The lack of sufficient reviewing sources is not the only problem for the media librarian. The print librarian finds all unabridged editions of Shakespeare to be pretty much the same. Bindings and print may vary, but the play will be the same. Not all film versions of Hamlet are necessarily the same. The librarian has to consider technical quality, cast, and background music, among other criteria, in making a choice. We must consider sound quality, publisher, and performers when buying recordings.

Because there are more variables to consider, the media librarian takes longer to select titles and finds it necessary to preview purchases. He or she also has to be more intuitive than the print librarian to determine what the community needs. And the best way to do this is to involve the community. Thus the media librarian must also know a great deal about the community: how it is organized, how its different components interact, what its real needs are. He or she must be able to interact effectively with the different groups in order to help fill their needs. The media librarian also must know many more theoretical, operational, and mechanical procedures. The display artist needs to be aware not only of freight costs and shipping schedules but also how to use many different graphic tools. The film librarian must know how to effect simple repairs to keep an unreliable projector running.

The importance of knowing sources of traveling exhibits and technical qualities of good film are not important in a profession whose organizational principles are based on the book. Small libraries have children's and adult departments based on the book. Larger libraries have subject departments—based on print services. Librarians who head these departments or who just work in them must know a great deal about books; must be able to give book talks, write book annotations, prepare booklists. But where, in this structure, is there a place for the media specialist?

Usually, media service, if it exists at all, is a minor function of a book department. Or, if it is a separately administered service, the media head is usually subordinated to a print librarian such as the adult services librarian. A media librarian ultimately proves his or her worth by displaying a keen interest and knowledge of books. This bias, of course, means nothing if the media librarian is content to remain a second-class citizen in the library. The media librarian who is not bothered that his or her department is the first one to receive cuts and the last one to receive increases will probably be a joy with whom to work. And, if our friend is also an assistant reference librarian or a cataloger or a chidren's assistant, he or she can spend more time in these areas. Those media librarians who want to see their departments prosper, however, will probably have difficulties. This will be especially true if their services suddenly become popular. And media services, after all, do tend to become very popular.

Films, for example, are an ideal way to entertain members of a lodge or a church group. They are also very useful in education and training. Videotapes, 8mm films, and records are excellent items for home loans and for group use. Once the public becomes aware that the library has such material and is willing to lend it, circulation often increases dramatically.

The potential of media is such that the media librarian can often increase circulation with minimal effort on his or her part. Simply promoting the collection through lists or occasional newspaper or radio spots can bring many new faces into the library. Minor policy changes can also produce significant results. When one public library transferred its record collection from book shelves to record browsers, circulation increased almost one hundred percent. By allowing our users to borrow the library's 16mm projector, we greatly increased film use since our collection became much more accessible.

The most dramatic improvements are achieved through increased funding. Even small, unplanned increases can produce very positive short-term results. There is nothing like a few new films or videotapes or a few dozen new records or cassettes to revitalize a somnolent department. Of course, the novelty soon wears off as users, having now seen or heard all the new purchases, demand more new titles.

To sustain the high interest in media, the collection and the service must be constantly refreshed, and this requires a fair share of the money. Fortunately, some states, such as New York, have been able to provide additional monies for media development. One library, for example, obtained $50,000 in federal grant funds in 1970 and 1971. This money allowed the library to add 150 new films, purchase new 16mm projectors, screens, and a film inspection machine. Circulation doubled and the collection increased not only in size but in depth as the media librarian added new police and fire training films, films on drugs, black history, and business management.

Unfortunately, any improvements in media—from small improvements due to intelligent policy changes, to miraculous growth attributable to a greatly increased budget—can create great problems. Media services are fine if they don't grow, but when they begin to improve and to have impact, the more traditional departments may begin to feel threatened in a number of ways.

One of the first areas of conflict will involve staff assignments. Perhaps the media librarian, who also works reference or circulation or processing (or all three!), may experience role conflicts and ask to spend more time on non-print. A no-win situation could quickly develop whereby the administration might have to slight either reference or media services. The administration could elect to transfer support staff to media services, leaving the media head to endure role conflicts. But the transferee's departure could also weaken another department without greatly enhancing the media department's effectiveness. New staff may be hired, but, other departments will argue, why give new staff to the media department when their own operations are understaffed? Intense conflicts may arise. The situation is aggravated when there are several print librarians and only one media librarian. The media librarian may have to learn to be a better administrator—more tactful yet firmer—than print librarians, lest the media librarian's staffing problems serve to discredit media services.

Space can also be a problem. Where do you put those new films? Where can additional record browsers be housed or new TV equipment be safely stored? Often, two or more departments will end up wanting the same space.

Sharing is not always the answer. For example, we might find shelves for reserve books behind the circulation desk. Here, too, are the films shelved for pickup by users. So, old P.L. on some days reverberates with the sound of films crashing to the ground as a clerk, looking for a reserve, makes a wrong turn. Even more fun can be had, of course, if we put projectors destined for loan in the same area as the films and reserve books.

When sharing is not feasible, the library may make some rather novel arrangements. Sensitive media equipment that abhors dampness is stored in the wet basement of a library; records and cassettes are found next to radiators or near electrical equipment. Yet, the media librarian who complains about such problems is likely to be told that he or she is fortunate to have any equipment or materials at all.

Damage problems also fall upon unsympathetic ears. The media librarian who has the automatic film inspection and cleaning machine in the basement is indeed lucky, for many libraries with film collections do not bother to inspect or clean films at all. Most libraries, as we have seen, simply prefer to discard broken films, warped records, or damaged equipment and are not at all pleased when told that such damage could be avoided entirely or at least greatly lessened with proper maintenance and care. After all, one doesn't need an inspection machine for books or newspapers!

The media librarian's complaints will not be well-received. Instead, as problems mount, media librarians may be asked why they failed to consider the problem of damage before purchasing additional projectors. Perhaps they should tighten circulation procedures so as to avoid such extensive damage to records, films, and equipment in the future. Perhaps the library has tried long enough to make media services a reality. Having thus offered it a fair trial, the library might now consider alternatives. Let someone else, perhaps the system headquarters or the central library, acquire films. Let the museum handle exhibits. Let the teens buy their rock and roll records at the record shops. Let adults rent TV equipment and tapes from the local dealer. After all, these are not library functions.

These criticisms may not be uttered too loudly when money is plentiful but will emerge basso profundo when budgets are tight. Why should a department that has such problems and can cause such disruptions continue to receive funding when the more traditional departments are in danger of losing staff, materials, or equipment? How can one justify non-print anyway? Underlying such criticisms will be the print librarians' strong dislike for most non-print. Television is, after all, commercials—vapid, repetitious, and untruthful. TV is bad drama, insipid comedies, and brassy newscasts. Film is often even worse. One can crowd only so much violence into a twenty-three inch screen. And recordings (excepting classical, some jazz, and show music) are for the young at heart and small of brain. Non-print materials are simply not intellectually stimulating. Intellectually mature children are said to prefer books to TV or movies; intellectually responsible adults are known for their disdain of most TV.

How does one fight such a situation? Ironically, some media librarians outdo the print librarians in their concern for rules and procedures. Some media departments impose punitive measures such as heavy fines (the death penalty for late returns of projectors) and restrictive loan policies. Some units may demand that film users procure a separate registration in addition to their library cards. Some restrict record loans to adults.

In selecting films, records, and audiotapes, some media staffs pore over every review. Films receiving any negative comments are not purchased. The reviews, after all, are infallible and quite superior to the local community as a selection tool. Recordings produced by unknown companies are seldom if ever purchased. Nor do some departments ever consider such exotica as videotapes, videodisks, or 8mm movies.

The need for dignity becomes obsessive as the sorely pressed media department attempts to justify its existence to the print people. Such librarians feel that their very survival depends on the support of their fellow staff members (rather than the community), and they seek this support even at the expense of good community service.

Good community service demands more than just close attention to rules and procedures. Obviously, we can not countenance vandalism, theft, or careless handling of non-print materials and equipment. And we should utilize every source of information available—reviews, articles, previews—whenever possible in selecting items for non-print collections. But our greatest ally in our effort to develop and sustain service is our community.

OBTAINING COMMUNITY SUPPORT

First, we have to determine what our community wants. And we do this by contacting not only the most established community groups— Rotary, Toastmasters, Kiwanis—but also less well-known groups— churches of all denominations, human service agencies, and ethnic organizations. We can discover their existence and their programs through local newspapers and radio and TV coverage. We can also follow leads provided by users and interested staff members. Some of these groups may help us pressure our own administrations to provide media service or work with us to produce media programming. Finally, we should regularly conduct systematic community analysis to determine non-print needs.

Once the community has begun to take our services seriously, we must nourish increased use through intelligent policies. The greatest virtue we can incorporate into our procedures is flexibility. Library rules often constitute an effective barrier between the library and its public. Though the rules supposedly promote the efficient use of materials, they may instead discourage use. We cannot afford to turn users away if we want our departments to survive. So, we might overlook some fines. Sometimes damage to materials is inevitable; the user was not careless, but just unlucky. Sometimes we have to trust people. The public will reward our flexibility and friendliness by using our services and materials in increasing numbers, thereby enhancing our department's chances for survival in the print-oriented library. Increased use of non-print may even help the library to shed its image as an austere, snobbish institution.

Indictments of media services can be not only incessant but also quite persuasive, especially if posed by bright people. It may be effective, as evidenced by increased use, but can we really afford it. After all, one 16mm color film can cost two to three hundred dollars and up. Three-quarter-inch color videocassettes can range from one to three hundred dollars per program. Reproductions of great paintings, sculpture reproductions, can cost from fifty to two hundred fifty dollars depending upon the supplier and quality of the product. Rather than spend three hundred dollars for one 16mm film, why not use the same sum to acquire twenty to thirty books from the jobber?

We could, of course, argue that records, cassettes, and 8mm films cost no more than books. The average record costs between eight and ten dollars and cassettes cost no more. Even 8mm film is not expensive, and many titles range from fifteen to twenty dollars. Furthermore, a three hundred dollar film is seen by at least twenty people every time it circulates. A fifteen dollar book is used by only one person. The per capita cost for both items is thus about the same—fifteen dollars.

Probably, our argument, so well-thought-out and well-phrased, will fall upon deaf ears. Even if our point is conceded, our friends in the print services departments might well add that other agencies can do the job better. Also, they may praise us as valued people who would be so much more effective as reference librarians. Why destroy ourselves over something that may very well not be worth all of our pain?

If we should fail to heed logic, we may become endlessly embroiled in those petty little in-house conflicts that supposedly have nothing to do with media service. No one objects to films, but why must we transport them on book trucks belonging to the reference department? Why are our record users always so noisy? Or, everyone likes our displays but regrets that we are always leaving paste or scissors around. Obviously, we are not very popular.

No one will come to our rescue either. Our fellow media librarians are not going to be of much help, because their own situations are probably as precarious as ours. There are film and video roundtables and committees in many state associations and in the ALA, but these have little influence locally and little real prestige and power even within their parent associations. State media consultants, where they do exist, have their own survival problems. New York State disbursed its film collection a few years back, undoubtedly in the interests of economy. And of course, most state consultants are graduates of the print departments of big city libraries. Obviously, they will not be our first line of defense. And thus we may find ourselves quite alone except for some non-print faculty in library schools.

But we need not give up, for non-print does indeed have a place in the library. Information, after all, comes in many legitimate formats—books, magazines, recordings, films, pictures, videotapes, even exhibits. The library has the obligation to preserve and collect information in all formats relating to our history, our culture, and our times. Failure to provide information simply because it is not in print constitutes a violation of intellectual freedom. One day, those print librarians may be held accountable to their public, if they are not already, and their budgets may suffer.

Can people learn from non-print? Before there was the word, there were the five senses, which included sight and sound. Early man learned from these senses, and modern man, when he reads, translates words back into their original components—sights and sounds. Who then is more intellectual: Fellini and Bergman or Shakespeare and Freud? Can we not hear poetry as well as read it? Which inspires us more: a book on modern Israel or a display featuring artifacts and maps? Need we apologize for non-print? Never.

Of course, librarians may accept our positive answers to these questions. But how will they react to our desire to produce our own non-print material? Good media librarians shudder to think of their response, and yet the production of films, slides, videotapes, and audiotapes, is a natural outgrowth of an interest in non-print. Production, furthermore, is an excellent way of involving the community. It is also a superb way of providing an exciting record of community history and culture.

The simplest form of non-print production would probably involve audiotapes. The media librarian needs an inexpensive recorder and microphones. A passable record of community events such as council meetings or community concerts could be developed without further editing. The resulting tapes could be circulated to individuals or agencies. With a better quality tape recorder and microphones and possibly by adding editing equipment, the library could improve tape quality. With a two-channel recorder, the library could produce bilingual materials or add music to dramatic performances or speeches. The library could even produce its own radio broadcasts.

Slides and photographs could also be prepared by library staff in response to community needs. Parades, high-school athletic contests, graduations, and theater presentations could be preserved through slides and photographs. With proper equipment, synchronized slide/tape presentations could be produced.

Film and video production could be the fulcrum of a sophisticated media service. The community could be heavily involved in many phases of production—writing, camerawork, performance, editing, post production, even distribution. The finished products could be easily loaned through the usual library outlets and could also be broadcast on local TV. Similar experiences could be achieved through a community-oriented program of displays and exhibits. Residents and groups would not only view the displays but could also contribute objects, do graphics, help in design, and set up.

But old P.L., which after so much difficulty has finally accepted a general media service, now faces a new threat. How indeed can a library accommodate a production service within the library structure? As with any general media service, staffing a reproduction service would be the first major hurdle. But staffing production would entail an additional problem of finding the right staff, particularly staff who will work with the people from the community.

If the library was interested only in exhibit work or slide and audio production, a satisfactory person might already be on board. But our librarian could not simply begin arranging exhibits or taping or photographing community events without considerable training and experimentation. Proper exhibits work would require knowledge of sources, insurance, and freight regulations. Our librarian would also have to know or learn how to survey potential sites inside and outside the library. To tape meetings and other community events properly, the librarian would have to master several pieces of audio equipment (mike, recorders, possibly editors) and become adept at anticipating and solving on-site problems. Our library photographer would also have to master intricate equipment—camera, lenses, filters, etc.—and might find it convenient to develop his or her own prints and slides. It is very possible that the time needed to master even one of these duties and then to properly maintain the service would leave our librarian with little time for anything else.

Film and video production would require an organizer (who would make contacts, write scripts, arrange taping and rehearsal dates), a camera person (who might also do editing), and a technician to maintain and repair equipment. This would moreover constitute merely a skeleton crew, one quite inadequate for a heavy production schedule. It is doubtful that many libraries would have any professional communications specialists on board. Nor would most libraries be in a position to train staff to do camera work and editing. Thus, the library would have to hire specialized staff.

Librarians wishing to hire such staff would soon find the usual library hiring procedures inadequate. Most camera persons, artists, and technicians cannot meet civil service requirements. They lack the MLS and in fact might not even be able to pass the clerk-typist examination due to "insufficient" typing abilities. Most librarians who can type and who have an MLS cannot also run cameras. New methods of staffing a film or video production facility will be needed.

One library, for example, hired camera people and technicians via contracts. The principal cameraperson, who also did editing work, was an independent who contracted with the library to provide certain video services on a per-project basis. The library also had an auxiliary cameraperson and a technician under contract. State and federal monies were used for the contractual expenses.

Other libraries might prefer to use volunteers from the community. Someone in the community, perhaps the library itself or a cable station or a nearby school or college, could provide volunteers with the requisite training and coordination. With luck, the library might end up paying very little money for a viable TV or film production service.

Unfortunately, even if the costs were low, old P.L. could end up with another kind of problem. Independent contractors would not legally be library employees and thus would not be subject to library rules and procedures. The contractor or volunteer could work when he or she wanted. The result could be a major service with great potential impact which the library could not direct.

Additionally, our profession has no standards whatsoever for judging video or film. The conventional standards applied to broadcast TV and commercial film are invalid. Our equipment is not as good. Nor do we engage professional performers, Broadway set designers, or union technicians. No one locally, no one at the state library, no one in authority in the library world can determine if the library gets its money's worth. Consequently, media librarians who are engaged in production look outside librarianship for performance standards, for technical know-how, for advice. We make the acquaintance of local corporate and cable TV people or visit local or area film and video schools. Because these agencies can answer our questions and because many also show some interest in our efforts, we will tend to pay very little attention to the library profession.

What role will the community play? We have already observed their signal importance in helping us develop non-print collections. Community agencies can play an even larger role in non-print production.

Not only will local churches and cultural clubs be the subject of our programs, but they will become so familiar with our services that many will feel competent to suggest when, what, and even how we should tape or film a subject. Not every suggestion will be inscribed in stone, but we media producers will soon learn how to incorporate our goals and community interests into a common product.

But if our role models are in non-broadcast film or TV rather than librarianship, if our media staff are virtually independent of library controls, what will happen to the library? The trend toward two distinct philosophies within the library, which began when old P.L. acquired its first records many years ago, now reaches its culmination when we decide to do non-print production. Can our structure accommodate this? How can the library administration, the library profession, integrate these two divergent forces? Indeed, what is our justification for doing so?

First, libraries cannot afford to be divided. Society, by and large, is indifferent to our mission. Non-users, after all, outnumber users by at least three to one and possibly by as much as nine to one. Second, media services, particularly videotape and film, are an ideal way to reach large groups. A library-produced TV program, for example, has the potential of reaching nearly everyone in a community. Non-print offers us the potential of transforming community indifference into positive acceptance and support not only for non-print but for all library services.

Third, libraries are charged with collecting information on the community and the world in any format that proves useful to the public. Often, community information can only be preserved on audiotape or videotape or some other non-print material. How else can we record the visit of a famous person or capture the spirit of a parade or pageant?

Fourth, books and non-print are not really competitors but simply different avenues to understanding. The ideal study of the New Deal era, for example, should include textbooks, newspaper articles, magazine stories, recordings of 1930s music, speeches, radio broadcasts, posters and other display items of the period, and films and/or videotape copies of news events, etc. Remove any one of these formats—the books, the films, the displays—and we thereby reduce our understanding and diminish the quality of our potential learning experience.

Finally, good media services require extensive planning and thought. An administrator who seeks to develop a media service will soon find that the need to plan for its implementation can have a positive effect on print services as well. Non-print can thus contribute to the efficiency of all library services and bring positive results to all phases of librarianship.

Censorship of Media Materials

John S. Robotham

LIBRARIES are institutions that provide — or at least should provide—materials for recreation, information, and inspiration in as many media of communications as are appropriate to their purposes. And not only will they supply a range of media, but they will have available, in those media, a variety of formats. Thus, the media librarian faces a multiplicity of choices, making the work more difficult, certainly, and also more challenging.

One problem is simply in knowing something about what is available in each medium, and in being able to judge it. The great number of items produced and the lack of adequate reviews for many of them make this a formidable task. Another problem lies in the librarian's budget—usually too small. Some media items are far more expensive than the librarian is used to, and they may also require special equipment. And, if a great variety of media is purchased, will that make the collections in all media too sparse to be of value? Then there is the matter of a collection's organization. Should films and records be shelved with printed material on the same subject, or are they housed separately? How is the catalog handled, so that all material on a subject is apparent to the user? Is special shelving necessary? These are all questions the media librarian must consider.

None of these difficulties should deter the media librarian from thinking about the need for any medium, however, because any or all may be important in providing the best library service. Poetry, plays, and, of course, music, come fully to life only when they are seen or heard. Hearing a poet read or seeing a play performed is an entirely different experience from reading the work. So it might be important for the library to provide recordings (in a variety of formats) or films (also in several formats). Or the library might present a live poetry reading or a live performance of a play. And libraries frequently do so.

Certain kinds of informational needs might also be best served by providing several media. Some people learn better with one medium than another. Some prefer print, others might want pictures, and still others need someone actually showing them how something is done. Other situations may call for the acquisition of various media. Seeing a wildlife film is certainly different from reading about wildlife, for instance. Some examples of each medium have their own justification for existing, and need no other; film art, or video art, for example, cannot be duplicated in any other medium. None of this means that one medium is better than any other. It just means they are different, and the media librarian has to think about each one.

Unfortunately, many librarians are slow to accept the need for new media, or new formats, if, indeed, they accept them at all. This has been true every time something different has arrived on the library scene. Paperbacks were a long time gaining acceptance in libraries and even today are not in evidence in some libraries. Other print forms, such as pamphlets and periodicals, might well be more widely and variously used in libraries, if librarians opened their thinking to possibilities for providing good service, regardless of the source or form of the material.

And, without a doubt, recordings in their various formats, and films and other pictorial media are still not fully accepted by the profession. This attitude, whether or not it is unwitting, results in censorship—and it is censorship of the worst kind. Censorship by librarians is worse than outside censorship, because it is mostly undetectable. It is easy for librarians to justify, even to themselves, the decision not to purchase any item, because of budget, space, or other considerations. When the special problems connected with films or recordings are added, any number of arguments can be adduced in support of not starting such a collection.

If a film collection, for example, is started, the same arguments can be, and usually are, marshaled in favor of not giving full service. Thus, the films are not thought of simply as part of the collection, but rather as a sort of fringe service, as popular as they may be. These limitations take a number of forms. One of the commonest is an age restriction, usually justified on the grounds that films are expensive, and ignoring the fact that very expensive art books or technical books are given out freely. The hours of public service in a media department or record room are often fewer than the rest of the library. The location of these departments in the library may also make access difficult, often involving stairs, and sometimes so hidden away that many library users don't know they exist. Fees may even be charged for some services, in what used to be known as the free public library. Libraries are, of course, simply following the public's lead in this respect. Films have long been regarded as having a greater impact than print, and as more likely to lead to antisocial behavior.

A difficult problem for media librarians, and one that applies to film more than any other medium, should be mentioned here. Films, because of their form, do not reveal their contents as easily as other media. A book can be flipped through and the potential borrower can decide on the spot. Recordings usually have their contents, as described by the producer, in plain view. But for films, media librarians must write annotations, especially since most films will not even have been reviewed anywhere. The media librarian can suggest a preview, of course, and usually will. But a preview is time-consuming, and many borrowers will not bother. Thus, the annotation is very important. But, the media librarian must be very careful to avoid labeling the film in some way, so that the potential borrower is not prejudiced. It may be quite tempting for the media librarian to try to avoid controversy through the use of a warning in the annotation, either for fear of the borrower's reactions to the film, or because the media librarian personally disapproves of it. Thus, in trying to avoid an attempt at censorship from outside, the media librarian may censor the film beforehand. Describing the film briefly, without falling into any of these traps, and at the same time saying what is necessary, may be difficult, and annotations are worth a good deal of thought.

In addition to not acquiring items, limiting access in various ways, and labeling films in their annotations, media librarians have been known to cut footage out of films that they or others might disapprove of, or to cover up parts of book illustrations with ink or paint. These methods, although obviously more easily detectable as censorship, are worse in that they alter the intention of the filmmaker or illustrator. It would have been better had the media librarian not acquired the item in the first place.

Librarians and library clerks have taken other forms of direct action in the case of materials of which they disapproved or items they thought might prove controversial. They have, for example, simply hidden books, or placed materials in an office, or never processed them. Sometimes items are put in the collection but not in the catalog, or they are cataloged but with no indication that they are in a special location or collection. Even if an enterprising or lucky user happens to find one of these items—and if the user is young—the clerk at the desk may try to discourage its use. None of this is meant to imply that these practices take place in all libraries or even most, but these practices are common enough, and the profession must do all it can to discourage them.

Librarians are not the only censors, of course. They are, after all, part of the society in which they work, and they have their own fears, prejudices, and doubts. They are also usually very vulnerable in their jobs, and unless they have a great deal of courage they are not likely to risk those jobs in defense of some book or film that they personally may find distasteful.

Nevertheless, many librarians have fought to defend their selections against the censor. And they have had to with some frequency. As each new medium is added to libraries, it is followed faily closely by complaints. Complaints about offensive material depend, of course, to some extent on the kind of material collected and on the public's awareness of that material. Pamphlets hidden away in a vertical file are not conspicuous, and their use usually depends on the librarian's pointing out their existence. Even then, the librarian may extract one pamphlet for one person's use. Pamphlets also look innocuous. If the library circulates works of art, on the other hand, they are often displayed for public viewing, and they may be large and brightly colored, bringing any possibly offensive item quickly into public awareness. Films, although their contents are not readily apparent, are shown, usually, to groups, and are large images which may be brightly colored. They also usually use sound, thus enforcing their message. All these elements make their use more powerful than many other media. And, when one adds the public's perception of the power of film to influence behavior, there is a good likelihood that a censor will appear.

There are, undoubtedly, still many more attacks on books than on films, but this may reflect the relatively small number of films in libraries, the relatively small number of film collections, and the kinds of films collected. There also appear to be few complaints about recordings, works of art, and other media, but this also, in all likelihood, is an indication of the number of such collections, and the contents of the collection.

Two complaints about recordings will serve to show that, as in other media, the range of possible complaints is as wide as the range of available recordings. One was a Vincent Price recording of stories by Carl Carmer, Oliver Wendell Holmes, and similar authors about witches, ghosts, and goblins. It is not a recording one would expect to be controversial, but in one of the stories the hands of a witch were cut off, and that was the basis of the complaint. In the other incident, the library was playing some recordings as part of a program. Among these recordings were some by Pete Seeger, and that was enough for the outraged complainant, who managed to bring the wrath of the city's mayor down of the library. In this case, as in many others, the library stood firm and the complaint evaporated.

Attacks on films in libraries go back at least to 1950. Since in 1949 there had only been fifty libraries circulating films in the whole country, complaints go back almost to the beginning of this service.[1] Add to this the fact that libraries at that time were collecting only the most sober of films, and it is easy to see why this was the first recorded attack on films in libraries. There may, of course, have been unrecorded attacks, and, in fact, this is far more common than those that are described in the literature or reported in any way. I know this from my own library experience of more than 30 years and from what others have told me in my research into the subject. As one long-time film librarian told me, "When complaints came in those days, we didn't put them in writing." For good reasons, most complaints are probably still not put in writing. Governing bodies of libraries, and administrators too, often consider a complaint to be an inadequacy on the part of the librarian, and they may start to look for things they can remove from the library, including the librarian. Or the librarian may remove the offending item, and, naturally enough, not wish to report this initiative.

Any complaint should be recorded, however. This doesn't necessarily mean to make it public, which could be foolish, but to make it known to the library administration or governing body, so that they will be ready to back you up if the complaint goes any further, or so they can prepare for other complaints.

Controversial library materials vary so widely in content and style that it is impossible to predict what will be attacked. One of the best examples of this fact comes from one of the best documented film censorship cases. It happened in California in 1970 where the librarian said she " . . . made a conscious effort to avoid films which might be patently controversial."[2] *Little White Crimes* was one of the films that seemed to draw the most wrath, with suggestions that it promoted socialism and was subversive, although any librarian might assume that it is all right to be against white-collar crime. The other eighteen films were also standard library fare and included *The Hand* and *The Rock in the Road*. But all were condemned by the would-be censors, a good indication that it is probably not possible to avoid complaints even if one tries.

In the 1950 incident, the films were such that most librarians would not expect an attack. This case happened in Peoria, and the films that couldn't play there were *Brotherhood of Man*, based on *Races of Mankind*, a pamphlet by Ruth Benedict and Gene Weltfish; *Boundary Lines*, another harmless, animated film about the elimination of boundary lines between people; and *Peoples of the USSR*, a Julien Bryan film about the various racial and cultural groups in the Soviet Union. This last film, ironically, had been banned in the Soviet Union but had been used as a U.S. armed forces training film. The librarian justified his removal of the films on the grounds that the Library Bill of Rights didn't include films, a striking example of the way some librarians have treated films differently from books.[3]

The New York Public Library was itself the censor in 1957, when it withdrew from a television program it had helped prepare. This program, "The Faces of War," took the position of being against war as a solution to mankind's problems. Norman Cousins and Margaret Mead participated in the program, and it seemed beyond reproach, but the trustees said the library must not take sides.[4]

Kenneth Anger's 1963 film, *Scorpio Rising*, about California's motorcycle gangs, was involved in at least two unrecorded incidents. In one case, at a western university, a trustee objected to the film being shown. When he was asked why he said, "Have you looked at it in slow motion under a magnifying glass?" The film was also shown at an eastern public library at about the same time. Locally, this showing caused such a sensation that the chief of police took to opening the librarian's mail.

By the 1970s, film collections, or at least film showings, were becoming fairly common in libraries, and complaints reflected this fact. As with books, some films are consistently attacked, although they may seem more innocuous than others. *The Lottery*, based on the short story by Shirley Jackson, in which villagers perform a meaningless though violent ritual simply because it is traditional, has been attacked with some regularity. One can, perhaps, understand the actions of the banners, even if one doesn't approve. The film and the story are designed to make the viewer or reader think. And depth of thought has not usually been a characteristic of would-be censors—although they can sometimes be made to see the point of the library's having an item, if it is explained to them. It is harder to understand attacks on *Death of a Legend*, an Audubon Society film about wolves, or the films of Alfred Hitchcock, such as *The Birds, Psycho, Suspicion,* and *The Thirty-Nine Steps.* But, as I said—and can't repeat enough—anything is likely to be attacked by somebody.

About Sex, although it has won awards and been very well-received by many individuals and organizations, is a veteran of numerous censorship attempts. It also provides a lesson in the tactics of censors. One thing attackers have done is to tell untruths about the film and its producer. Whether or not these errors of fact are told knowingly, they have had an effect on sales, and, consequently, they have prevented people from seeing the film who might have benefited from the information in it.

It was said, for example, that the film was made with federal funds, and that it was sponsored by Planned Parenthood of America. Neither of these statements is true. The script was wrongly attributed to a controversial writer on sex. It was claimed that the producer of the film also produced pornographic films, and that one of the shots in the film had come from a pornographic movie. Neither claim is true. A potential buyer was told that the film had been banned in several states, although it had not. Some groups were told that if they showed the film they would lose funds because they were giving illegal information. Not true, of course. Other tactics included quoting out of context, threatening a library with loss of funds if it didn't withdraw the film, and juxtaposing scenes or words to give a different impression from that conveyed by viewing the film itself.

Another complaint came in the form of a letter from the local chapter of a national organization, on that organization's stationery, demanding that a library remove the film from its collection. There was an implied threat in the body of the letter itself, and appended was a list of the organization's local advisory board, which was made up of a number of locally prominent people. The answer to this letter also provides some useful responses to such complaints. The librarian pointed out that previously the film had circulated a hundred times without a complaint. He then mentioned the many awards and endorsements the film had received, including respected local organizations. He said he realized their objections were sincere, but he remained politely firm about continuing to use and circulate the film. Finally, he sent copies of the correspondence to the listed members of the group's advisory board, some of whom may not have been aware of this move on the part of an organization with which they were connected, and who, perhaps, would not have approved of censorship if they had known. This response seems to have worked, since the incident went no further. There are, of course, times when no logic, endorsement, statement of fact, or anything else has an effect. The librarian's time of trial may then begin, and other methods will have to be sought.

Just as materials that are attacked vary widely, so do those doing the attacking. Censors are not limited to the lunatic fringe of the right-wing, as some have suggested. They come from all parts of the political and social spectrum. They can be of any age, race, ethnic group, occupation, or educational or economic level. Lawyers, teachers, high and low government officials, the clergy, scientists, a variety of ethnic groups, business people, and the police are a few of the groups that come to mind who have wanted to prevent somebody from seeing, hearing, or reading something.

A Clockwork Orange was banned by a college president, who had not seen it. Say Goodbye was objected to by hunters. The NAACP objected to a library showing of Birth of Nation. "Women Library Workers" found How to Say No to a Rapist and Survive offensive. Parents didn't want a high school to show A Child Is Born. The Anti-Defamation League objected to showing of two Leni Riefenstahl films, Olympia and Triumph of the Will. The director of a drug abuse clinic wanted to suppress a film critical of methadone. Homosexuals didn't want Boys in the Band to be shown. There are more examples, but the point should be clear. We all find something offensive. The question is, how do we respond? If we can't allow others to make up their minds about a book or a film we find offensive, we certainly should not be librarians.

In spite of the great variety of would-be censors, there are certain characteristics they seem to have in common. Almost invariably they will deny being censors. What they want to do is to ban this particular item, which they regard as harmful. And since they know best, they know the rest of us shouldn't be allowed access to it. Censors also tend to be quite literal-minded. Satire and irony elude them, as does anything that isn't straightforward in its technique. They often appear to be humorless. And they are frequently very emotional when they make their complaints.

This last characteristic leads us naturally to consider ways to deal with attempts at censorship, because the first thing everybody will tell you to do is stay calm. And everybody is right. But staying calm is not very easy when somebody is yelling at you or is even visibly upset. You must try, however. And you must try to avoid fruitless argument, particularly about the merits of the item in question. The point is that it is the right of others to see the film, hear the recording, read the magazine, or view the picture. There are many reasons for selecting an item for a library collection, and presumably there were good ones for selecting this item. These reasons may be mentioned to the complainant, but no library should cave in and withdraw anything simply because there is an objection to it. It is amazing how many times that seems to happen, however, when with a little firmness the incident would probably go away.

In any case, it is the librarian's job to defend the collection, and so a calm, polite, but firm manner is definitely called for. But what does one do when the calm politeness fails—when the attackers continue to attack, insisting that the offending item be removed from the library? Although most complaints vanish after the first burst of emotion, some refuse to go away. Some complainants are, in fact, organized into groups, even having statewide or national affiliation. And that kind of group tends to be persistent.

At this point, we have to go back to what the library should have done before the censor appeared. One exercise that might have helped is the writing of a materials policy. (I use "materials policy," rather than the more common "selection policy," because the statement should include the withdrawal of items as well as their acquisition.) Materials policies serve more purposes than fighting the censor, and indeed they may not be of much apparent use for that purpose. It seems to me they do serve the cause of intellectual freedom, however, if only indirectly.

Materials policies cannot be very specific about what a library should acquire or discard, but they do give a librarian general guidelines for building a collection in that library's community. Thus, if the policy is well-thought-out and attention is paid to it, it can help the librarian avoid being the one to censor materials. We all find some things offensive, and we sometimes have difficulty selecting such items for our libraries. But if we keep the library's purpose in mind, we can overcome this antipathy.

A sound materials policy that has been thoughtfully approved by the library's governing body will also give the librarian a feeling of some security as he or she wanders through the thickets of the selection or withdrawal of library materials. One must not feel that this policy provides an impregnable fort, however. Governing bodies have been known to ignore it completely, at the first whiff of a complaint. And the complainant often will not care what the policy is.

Even the would-be censor, though, may be impressed by a thoughtfully written policy. And even if the actual words don't convince him or her, the fact of its existence shows that the selectors are working within a framework that serves the community, and that they are responsible professionals. This purpose is also served by some of the library profession's documents that are discussed later in this chapter, and these documents are often appended to a library's materials policy, thus tying that policy to the policies of a nationwide professional organization.

A procedure should be established so that any complaint can be dealt with in a calm, orderly fashion. The use of a complaint form, at this point, is recommended. These forms vary greatly, however, and some librarians don't believe in their use at all. Some kind of written record does seem useful, though—if the complaint reaches that stage. What the librarian should not do is to whip out a form at the first approach of a complainant. In any case, if a form is used, great care should be taken in its wording so that the complainant is not further exasperated by the form itself or given the wrong impression.

Some sort of review mechanism is now necessary to decide if the acquisition of the item was indeed valid, or if an item acquired many years earlier should now be discarded. Occasionally the complainant has a point, as when information is misleading or incorrect. The review procedure might be anything from the only librarian looking again at the reasons for acquisition to a review committee at a high level of the administration in a large library. The important point is that there be a procedure.

The basic defense of any medium in a library is the same as for any other medium. There are, however, differences in perception, by librarians as well as by the public, that may make the defense of some media more difficult. One of these differences lies in what the librarian does with the medium. Films, filmstrips, and possibly slides are often shown by the librarian to a group in the library. This use of film is much more common than a similar use of other media, as, for instance, a booktalk. Indeed, it may be the only use to which the library puts film. But, when a library has a film showing, it is seen as approving of the films. It is, therefore, necessary to explain that this is not so. (The same problem arises with books and other media, but to a much lesser extent.) The library is showing the films because of a felt or expressed need, just as it might acquire *Mein Kampf* because people wanted to read it, and not because they approved of the contents.

Films are regarded as having a greater power than print, so a film may be attacked but the book on which it is based is not. I personally believe the reaction depends on the individual or on the presentation of the material, and not merely that one medium is more powerful than another. Others, including librarians, seem to disagree, however. The point is that the selector makes no distinction among media, but selects what seems to be best for a particular purpose. And since no one can know with any certainty what the differences in effect are, all media must be treated alike.

Another difference between film and the other library media is not a perception but a matter of use. Film, by its nature, is almost always seen by a group. As for other media, books may be read aloud, but most often are not. Other print media hardly ever are. Videotapes are often seen by an individual. Recordings are usually listened to by one person. Even exhibits are often looked at by one person at a time. So film is, in this respect, different. Although a film is borrowed by an individual, it is probably seen by a large group, even including many people who will never use anything else the library has to offer. Thus, its potential for reaching a much larger audience than any other medium is great—as is its potential for reaching the would-be censor. This is particularly true because the viewers probably have not chosen the film themselves but are only seeing it because someone else planned the program.

Because films are seen in a group, the viewing experience is different in another way from experiencing other media. Members of an audience influence one another. This would be particularly true of library films, which are commonly borrowed to show to members of some organization. After the showing, the audience, knowing one another, would probably comment on the film, and a would-be censor might quite easily stir up others to do something. One way to partially avoid potential censorship problems is to strongly recommend that the borrower preview the film. Even if the borrower won't take the time to preview it, the librarian can discuss the film's likely audience with the user and can point out some features of the film. As with annotations, the librarian must be careful not to prejudice the user.

If, after the review procedure, the complainants continue pressing the library to conform to their wishes, the librarian may want to turn to outside help. Local help may be available. The librarian should have formed a good working relationship with the local press, local politicians, and local organizations. The governing body of the library should have been prepared for such a possibility, as should any friends of the library group. And if the librarian has built a good collection and provided good service to the public, there will be a reservoir of library users from whom to draw support. The support of the groups like these has helped win a lot of censorship battles. The support of the library's governing body is, of course, crucial—although librarians have continued battling without it—

but the good will of a variety of groups thoughout the community is of great importance. It is, in fact, the librarian's job to win this good will, regardless of censorship attempts.

Help from outside the community may or may not be wanted, depending on the circumstances. But even if the librarian has done a good job of surrounding the library with local friends, interested organizations can provide useful information. Contact a variety of organizations and see what they have to offer. State library associations have intellectual freedom committees which may be helpful. They may provide copies of the appropriate library documents, such as the Library Bill of Rights and its various interpretive documents, or the librarian's Code of Ethics. These documents are helpful to the librarian in several ways. They help keep the goals of the library and the conduct of the librarian firmly in mind. They can be shown to would-be censors, and although they probably won't make a difference, they will at least show that the librarian is acting under a nationally recognized professional code, not just out of idiosyncrasy. And they can be shown to friends of the library, particularly the governing body of the library, to help them understand what the library and the librarian are all about. Many of these people should have seen these documents already, and even discussed them, if the librarian had been doing a really good job. But this, sadly, is the kind of work most of us neglect. If the state association can't supply these materials, the Office for Intellectual Freedom of the American Library Association certainly can.

State library associations can also supply other written material, such as items on similar cases, and suggestions for dealing with the situation. They might even send a representative to discuss the case with the librarian, if that seemed desirable. Librarians sometimes feel, justifiably, that someone from outside the community would be wrongly perceived and would hurt more than help. So, each situation must be assessed individually.

An organization of particular interest to film librarians is the Educational Film Library Association (EFLA) at 43 West 61st Street, New York, NY 10023. They will send the librarian printed material on censorship cases, possibly even on a particular film. They can put the librarian in touch with others who have been through the censor's mill; discussing the problem with someone who has been there provides solace. It can also help with specific suggestions from a colleague who knows some of the problems. Nobody but the person on the scene will know all the problems.

This organization also adopted, in 1979, a "Freedom to View" statement, which was subsequently endorsed by the American Library Association. This document applies to all audiovisual materials, but, of course, the emphasis is on film. Ideally, such a statement should not be necessary if library materials are regarded in the proper way. Given the perception of films as different, however, it probably was important to promulgate such a statement. Documents of this kind can be used in a number of ways, before any confrontation develops, and in the hope that, if enough groundwork is done, the number of attacks will at least be lessened. Ronald F. Sigler, a film librarian and teacher who has seen the censors up close, suggests the following uses:

1. Have your governing authority adopt the *Freedom to View* statement as policy, along with other intellectual freedom statements such as the Library Bill of Rights or the School Library Bill of Rights.
2. Print the statement in your film/video catalogs.
3. Post it prominently in your circulation area.
4. Include the statement in your materials selection policy.

If these steps are taken, obviously the document begins to serve as an educational tool. Most importantly, this and similar statements help the governing body understand the librarian's role. And the governing body should, ideally, give some thought and discussion to the points covered. Then they may be ready to support the librarian in time of trouble. The other methods of distributing the document will, one hopes, help educate the general public, or at least the borrowers of film, so perhaps they won't attack you, and may even help, when the censor appears. It seems useful to reprint this document here:

Freedom to View

The FREEDOM TO VIEW, along with the freedom to speak, to hear, and to read, is protected by the First Amendment to the Constitution of the United States. In a free society, there is no place for censorship of any medium of expression. Therefore, we affirm these principles:

1) It is in the public interest to provide the broadest possible access to films and other audiovisual materials because they have proven to be among the most effective means for the communication of ideas. Liberty of circulation is essential to insure the constitutional guarantee of freedom of expression.
2) It is in the public interest to provide for our audiences films and other audiovisual materials which represent a diversity of views and expression. Selection of a work does not constitute or imply agreement with or approval of the content.
3) It is our professional responsibility to resist the constraint of labeling or pre-judging a film on the basis of the moral, religious, or political beliefs of the producer or filmmaker or on the basis of controversial content.
4) It is our professional repsonsibility to contest vigorously, by all lawful means, every encroachment upon the public's freedom to view.

It is a strong statement, and perhaps every librarian should read it with the morning cup of coffee. It needs to be kept in mind.

An organization that all librarians should know is the National Coalition Against Censorship, 132 West 43rd Street, New York, New York 10036. Its members are a large group of organizations in the arts, communications, education, religion, and other fields. The Coalition holds programs, publishes a newsletter, sends out literature, and deals in various ways with censorship problems. If a librarian, or anybody else, contacts them with a censorship problem, they will send out appropriate literature, refer the librarian to appropriate individuals or organizations in the area of the library, and, in some cases, give specific advice. This last service is important. Most organizations won't give advice that isn't of the most general kind. But the Coalition, dealing daily with these situations, has probably heard it all, and one can learn from their knowledge.

The American Civil Liberties Union, and its state affiliates, is also a good organization to know. They have earned their reputation of defending the most unpopular of causes. They are primarily known for providing legal advice but may give other pertinent advice as well.

A Friends of the Library group may be of help, if they have been well-organized, and particularly if intellectual freedom and the library's role has been discussed with them. They have the advantage of being local people who can talk to their friends and neighbors, and they won't be seen as outsiders.

It may be of some use if the librarian reads both current news and background material on the subject of censorship. It helps to be aware of items that are being attacked, or that have been, to know what others do before and after the censor comes.

Of first importance for anyone concerned with intellectual freedom is:

Newsletter on Intellectual Freedom. Chicago: American Library Association. Bimonthly.
This periodical reports on attempts to censor items in all media, both in libraries and elsewhere. There are also reports of judicial decisions, reviews of pertinent books, and other news dealing with censorship.

A periodical that film librarians, particularly, but also anyone else who needs, or wants, to know about censorship problems, should read regularly is:

Sightlines. New York: Educational Film Library Association, Inc. Quarterly.
A regular feature is the "Freedom to View" column. It sometimes reports on cases at some length and also provides comment and other film censorship news. This

periodical has also run other articles dealing with various aspects of intellectual freedom.

A book that discusses in detail some of the points raised in this chapter is:

Robotham, John, and Gerald Shields. *Freedom of Access to Library Materials.*
 New York: Neal-Schuman Publishers, Inc., 1982.
Subjects discussed include age, racism, and sexism, who the censor is and what is censored, and how to greet the censor.

A different kind of book that might give the librarian an idea of what it is like to face a censor is:

Anderson, A. J. *Problems in Intellectual Freedom and Censorship.* New York:
 Bowker, 1974.
Thirty fictional case studies (some based on actual incidents) present very real situations in which librarians might find themselves. There are examples from college, public, school, and special libraries concerning problems with films, books, recordings, exhibits, and programs. Questions after each study make the reader think.

Another book that libraries might find of value is:

Busha, Charles H. *An Intellectual Freedom Primer.* Littleton, Colo.: Libraries
 Unlimited, 1977.
This collection of essays deals with censorship in—among other areas—the visual arts, the performing arts, and film. Although they are concerned with society as a whole, not specifically libraries, these essays are useful to the librarian because they discuss a variety of media and because they discuss societal attitudes and responses to them.

Reading about intellectual freedom, talking to friends and colleagues, and making preparations in the form of policies and procedures can give information, inspire noble thoughts and deeds, provide solace in time of trouble, and sometimes even obtain material help. But in the end, the librarian is on his or her own, and if there is a full-blown censorship case, it may get very lonely. One's job and future are sometimes on the line, and little help from one's colleagues or the profession may be forthcoming. Of course, one might go through an entire career without this happening, just as a police officer may never be shot at. But a librarian, like a police officer, must know that anything can happen. Furthermore, it is the librarian's professional responsibility to fight the censor. It is an occupational hazard, and if one isn't prepared to accept the consequences of this responsibility, one had better find some other line of work.

But there can be a happy ending to this seeming tragedy. If one is firm and has made sufficient preparations, the chances are that even the worst of situations will be happily resolved. There is ample precedent to prove that this is not daydreaming. Furthermore, probably the best defense is to provide a good collection and good service to the community, two objectives that should be the goal of every librarian anyway and should in addition, give the librarian great personal satisfaction. What more could anyone want?

References

1. Gloria Waldron, *The Information Film* (New York: Columbia University Press, 1949), p. 149.
2. Ronald F. Sigler, "A Study in Censorship: The Los Angeles 19," *Film Library Quarterly*, Vol. 4, No. 2 (Spring 1971), 36.
3. Ronald F. Sigler, "Freedom to View," *Sightlines*, Vol. 11, No. 1 (Fall 1977), 3-5.
4. *The New York Times*, November 11, 1957, p. 1.

MEDIA
LIBRARIANS

What Are Media Librarians?

John W. Ellison

A great deal of confusion surrounds the term "media librarian." No two people in or outside the library profession seem to agree on what such a person is, does, or how they should be educated. Some librarians consider persons educated in educational technology, instructional communications, instructional design or audiovisual education, who work in a library situation, as media librarians. Others consider school media librarians synonymous with media librarians. Still a smaller group of librarians consider specialists with a degree in the areas of video, music, photography, film or graphics, and working in libraries, as being media librarians. Literally speaking, none are correct.

Without long dictionary or textbook definitions, it can be generally agreed that "media" is the plural for "medium." Medium as used in the context of libraries includes newspapers, magazines, films, videotapes, books, phonorecords and nineteen other single format items. The individual formats we handle in library information transfer usually are considered a medium. Therefore, attaching the plural "media" to the word "librarian" would mean *a person who is educated, knowledgeable, and can work with all formats of information transfer in the context of a library*. This simplistic definition of a media librarian will not be universally accepted (much like the term library), but this definition is supported by traditional usage and logic.

Assuming this definition was universally accepted, we could proceed to make other assumptions. For example, persons educated (through course work or real world experience) in exclusively one medium such as film, video, print, or photography should be called film, video, print, or photography specialists. Those persons educated in educational technology, instructional communication, instructional design, or audiovisual education may well be knowledgeable in several non-print formats, but lacking the print education or knowledge gained from experience, would prevent them from being considered media librarians. They should be called non-print generalists since they lack the print knowledge needed for them to be media librarians. Print librarians who are not adequately prepared to manage non-print services should be

Parts of this essay originally appeared in *Catholic Library World* 52 (December 1980) pp. 233–34.

called print reference, print public service, or print catalog librarians, according to their position.

School media librarians, or "specialists" as they are often called, come close to being media librarians by their title and responsibilities. However, many states have such restrictive academic requirements, and many library schools are so steeped in print tradition that few school media librarians receive more than a smattering of formal non-print education. This situation in many cases is contrary to course titles and descriptions which so often indicate a strong preparation in all media. It is common to see a school media librarian almost totally lacking in knowledge of any medium other than print, with a transcript suggesting extensive preparation in all formats of information transfer (media). Finally, as students, school media librarians are generally confined to a structured curriculum limited to schools, while students prepared to be media librarians are usually not restricted to a type of library curriculum unless by personal choice.

At present, the formal education of media librarians usually takes one of two forms. Either they have two degrees; one in traditional librarianship and the second in the broad concept of non-print, or they have attended one of the few library schools with a strong media curriculum that combines studies of print and non-print in one degree program. One method of acquiring a media librarianship education over the other is not necessarily better. Some advantages and limitations exist in both approaches. The obvious major advantage in having two degrees in two areas of study (print and non-print) is the time and depth dedicated to the subjects. The major drawback is the duplication that must take place in two degrees with many similarities. Study of media (print/non-print) in a single degree program has its merits, but the major drawback is the limited exposure to complicated course content a person will receive when two curricula are combined into a one degree program. Duplication can nearly be eliminated, but it is still not possible to overcome an academically restricted curriculum because of the short length of some one degree programs. To compound this problem, think a few moments about the information/computer science needs of today's media librarian and then mentally develop an academic program that would properly prepare this person to work in any one of a variety of media positions.

There are three major concerns I have regarding the preparation of media librarians. The first is the almost total lack of interest library schools show in media librarianship. They have made some changes in course titles to include non-print without much regard for course content. In addition, they have added few faculty with the education, knowledge, and experience to properly teach in a media librarianship program. Second, some persons are graduating from degree-granting programs with one or two courses in "non-print" with the notion they are adequately prepared to function in non-print services in an academic, public, or special library. Even worse, some employers have the idea that a librarian with one or two non-print courses or workshops is adequately prepared to manage non-print services in a library. Still other employers believe paraprofessionals with no special non-print training or practical experience can manage non-print services. A frightening situation, to say the least. However, for some librarians it seems natural, since they feel a library degree is all that is required to make a person qualified to accept any available professional library position. The old axiom, you can't manage what you don't know, has little or no meaning to them.

Finally, I am deeply concerned that libraries in general are not seeking to employ more multidisciplinary candidates and putting pressure on academic programs to prepare more such candidates for the job market. Libraries generally cannot afford the luxury of hiring an information specialist or educational technology person exclusive of a library science education. Persons going into programs (and employers) should give more thought to strong multidisciplinary programs which prepare persons for what is now a multichannel information society. Under the current circumstances we all have to live within limitations. However, it is unnecessary to restrict ourselves with limited or inadequately prepared personnel who cannot meet the information needs of the library community.

The advantages of having a media librarian over a film specialist, for example, or a non-print generalist are numerous. Media librarians will usually have a good background in traditional librarianship combined with non-print library services. Therefore, they require little more than the normal orientation usually provided for a new librarian. By the nature of their education, they are knowledgeable about twenty-three non-print formats and the selection, organization, management and programming necessary to develop non-print library services. Finally, most media librarians will see the broader aspects of services rather than the limited "educational" view often possessed by non-print generalists or the extremely narrow perspective of some film specialists. This is not to say non-print generalists and film specialists have no place in libraries. However, the community's needs, size of the library, and goals of the library play a more significant role when selecting individuals with such limited academic or practical backgrounds.

The image of non-print in libraries has often been negative because unqualified personnel were employed to develop, select, organize, and manage the services. The horror stories that some of these people tell about how they select, supervise, and develop programs and manage these services leave one in shock. Most of these stories can be directly related to inadequate academic preparation in media librarianship. But the most frightening thing about the horror stories is that many of the people telling them are unaware that the potential problem may rest with *them* rather than the *media* or the *people* they often blame. They have accepted positions for which they are not academically prepared and/or lack the acquired practical knowledge; and, what is worse, they make judgments by the same inadequate yardstick. High level criteria should be used to employ a media librarian as any other librarian. And certainly when examining academic preparation, few print reference librarians would be employed without courses in basic reference, government documents, collection development, plus one or two advanced reference courses as the very minimum preparation. Why should we accept less rigor when examining the academic preparation or practical knowledge of a media librarian? Maybe that old axiom is raising its ugly head again.

The media librarian engages in a variety of activities, depending on the type of library and identified needs of the library community. Since the degree and extent of each activity is relative to a given situation, no absolute list of activities performed by media librarians has been compiled. The following is an attempt to represent the basic competencies a media librarian should have when accepting a professional entry-level position. The extent of knowledge depends to a large degree on the depth of education and amount of experience a person may bring to the position.

Each competency was checked against the bibliography and informally verified by several working media librarians. A formal verification is currently being conducted by surveying every identified media librarian in the United States.

Media librarians and library directors may find these competencies valuable for self-assessment, evaluation of a media department and criteria for selecting media librarians. Special caution should be exercised when determining the degree of accomplishment or knowledge one should have in each category. Generally, persons independent of a given library with knowledge and work experience in media librarianship can provide a more objective assessment of the activities of a library's media department and the reasonable degree of accomplishment which should be expected for each competency.

Some media department services and activities follow the personal and sometimes narrow dictates of the media librarian without much regard for the library community being served or the full potential of a given media department. Use of specified competencies can be both a point of reference and outline for discussion of where a media department should go. Both library administrators unfamiliar with media department services and entry-level media librarians should find this list of competencies a reference point for growth and development of a comprehensive media department program.

MANAGEMENT FUNCTIONS

- Determine overall policies
- Confer with director regarding operations, programs, and budgets
- Schedule use of facilities
- Identify the criteria for selection of personnel
- Develop a staff/administrative manual
- Develop job descriptions
- Supervise personnel
- Compile, tabulate, and analyze data for reports
- Schedule inventory of equipment
- Conduct evaluation of adequacy and suitability of facilities, equipment, materials, and services
- Establish policies for maintenance of materials and equipment
- Prepare the media services' bulletin or newsletter
- Maintain professional status (keep up in the field)
- Inform users and non-users of available services
- Prepare promotional materials
- Determine goals and objectives of media services
- Identify legislation which affects media services
- Develop written criteria for evaluating materials and equipment
- Protect the right of unrestricted access of materials by users
- Have outside evaluation every three years
- Determine appropriate computer functions related to media
- Develop one media service-initiated program per month for the library staff or community
- Develop a plan for advancement of staff
- Plan operation and maintenance services
- Plan arrangements of space and furniture

- Plan and develop other service units within the department
- Conduct training for personnel
- Prepare work schedules
- Assign duties
- Evaluate work of personnel
- Schedule inventory of materials
- Plan and implement community relations activities
- Develop grant proposals for federal, state, and private funded projects and programs
- Terminate personnel
- Evaluate holdings
- Prepare annual report
- Participate in facilities planning
- Prepare a formal selection and review policy
- Invite and accept suggestions from users and non-users about services
- Make everyone aware of the laws (e.g., copyright) regarding media services
- Maintain a current collection of bibliographical materials used in the selection and acquisition of materials and equipment
- Develop staff self-evaluation program
- Administer tours and orientation programs
- Work with an advisory committee who assists in reviewing needs, policies, quality of services, etc.
- Prepare a multiple-year project plan with goals and objectives

RESEARCH FUNCTIONS

- Administer an annual library community needs assessment study
- Determine the need for conducting research to support the goals and activities of media services
- Develop a plan of assessment and evaluation of the media program based upon the established goals and objectives

- Administer for economic analysis of the department (cost-effectiveness)
- Engage in research activities relative to media
- Disseminate research information and findings
- Apply research findings to the operation of the department

DESIGN FUNCTIONS

- Design new materials (non-print)
- Instruct others in the design of materials
- Design publicity materials (print)
- Follow a systematic design procedure when producing materials

PRODUCTION FUNCTIONS

- Assist in production of programs and materials
- Duplicate materials
- Record (video or audio) meetings, speeches, programs, and performances
- Process and print photographs
- Operate lettering and drawing devices
- Microfilm materials
- Photograph activities
- Administer film or video productions

INSTRUCTIONAL FUNCTIONS

- Conduct in-service workshop on use of equipment
- Plan a program of media library instruction
- Guide reference and research work for small or large groups
- Conduct in-service workshops on use of materials

- Orient users to materials and equipment
- Instruct others in the production of materials

MAINTENANCE FUNCTIONS

- Inspect materials for damage
- Maintain equipment
- Purge collection to eliminate unused and out-of-date material
- Repair materials
- Supervise a storage and care program for materials

PREVIEW, EVALUATION, SELECTION, AND ACQUISITION FUNCTIONS

- Search catalogs and shelflist for ordering and duplication of materials
- Preview materials
- Select materials
- Evaluate materials
- Acquire materials
- Read evaluative reviews on materials
- Assign accession or inventory numbers
- Evaluate equipment
- Acquire equipment
- Select equipment
- Read evaluative reviews on equipment

UTILIZATION FUNCTIONS

- Set up equipment
- Give instruction on the use of equipment
- Demonstrate effective utilization of equipment

- Operate equipment
- Locate requested materials for rent
- Demonstrate effective utilization of materials

DISSEMINATION FUNCTIONS

- Establish policy for distribution of materials
- Schedule use of materials
- Deliver and collect materials
- Maintain distribution files and records
- Establish policy for distribution of equipment

- Schedule use of equipment
- Deliver and collect equipment

ORGANIZATION FUNCTIONS

- Establish cataloging procedures
- File orders and notices
- Abstract materials
- Write annotations for in-house publications
- Establish classification procedures
- Compile materials list
- Write reviews for professional publications

Bibliography

American Association of School Librarians. *Certification Model for Professional School Media Personnel.* Chicago: American Library Association, 1976.

Case, Robert N., and Lowrey, Anna Mary. *Behavioral Requirements Analysis Checklist.* Chicago: American Library Association, 1973.

Chisholm, Margaret E., and Ely, Donald P. *Media Personnel in Education: A Competency Approach.* Englewood Cliffs, N.J.: Prentice-Hall, 1976.

"A Competency and Task List for Specialists and Technicians in Media Management, Media Product Development, and Instructional Program Development" *Audiovisual Instruction,* November 1974. pp. 22-69.

Gerber, Gloria S. "Occupational Task Inventory for Media Specialists." Unpublished paper, State University of New York at Buffalo, 1980.

Post, Richard. "College and University Functional Learning Resource Program Evaluation." Unpublished paper, Ohio University 1980.

The History of Media Librarianship: A Chronology

Amy R. Loucks-DiMatteo

Before media centers could be established, non-print technological instructional aids had to be developed. Before libraries could be established, "books" had to be written. But before books could be written man had to learn how to write. Thus the beginnings of today's library media centers must be traced back to the earliest beginnings of writing more than 5,000 years ago.[1]

THE following is a chronology of the history of media librarianship. Although the term "media" includes both print and non-print materials, this history primarily explores the development of non-print materials.

The information is arranged chronologically. The symbol (c.) preceding a date indicates that the date has been approximated. The symbol (___) indicates that a date has not been determined, but an effort has been made to fit the information in the proper place in the chronology. The dates and information listed have been taken directly from the sources cited; therefore, it is likely that the reader will find some conflicting dates and information.

Non-print media probably originated in the Orient, where shadow shows entertained the people for over two thousand years.[2] A reliance upon visuals has been demonstrated since early history through cave wall drawings, Egyptian pictographs, Babylonian maps, clay tablets, medieval art works, Renaissance woodcuts, and early illustrated books.[3]

Mesopotamia, the country between the Tigris and Euphrates rivers, introduced writing to the world. The Sumerian people who inhabited Mesopotamia used the cylinder seal to mark and identify their property.[4] Other cultures developed early forms of writing which were of two basic types: cuneiform and hieroglyphics. Cuneiform writing resembled wedge-shaped characters and was used by the Sumerians, Akhadians, Babylonians, Assyrians, and the Persians. Egyptian hieroglyphics used figures or objects to represent sounds or words.[5]

Over a thousand years passed from the development of syllabic writing until alphabetic writing was developed. Although a contribution of the Near East alphabetic writing was adapted as an instrument of communication by the Greeks. The twenty-six character alphabet used today in Western cultures was developed by the Romans.[6]

1700 B.C.	The Babylonians were the first to establish libraries. (Cushing)
1100 B.C.	The first libraries of historic times were found in the temples of Ancient Egypt. (Thompson)
1100 B.C.	Royal libraries were in existence in Phoenicia. The most famous royal library was Assurbanipal at Ninevah. (Thompson; Parsons)
____	The first of the great private libraries were supposed to have been as early as Pisistratus of Athens, and Polycrates, tyrant of Samas. (Parsons)
900–700 B.C.	The kings of Assyria maintained a collection of thousands of clay tablets written in cuneiform. (Hostrop)
400 B.C.	The private libraries of Euripides, Aristotle, and Plato were in existence. (Hessel)
300 B.C.	Schools with libraries were in existence in Athens. (Hostrop)
300 B.C.	The first known books were the clay tablets of Mesopotamia and the papyrus rolls of Egypt. (Hostrop)
____	The first integration of print and non-print was found in the first picture book: *Orbis Pictus* (Comenius)
384–322 B.C.	Aristotle was the first known systematic collector and classifier of books. He developed the concept of a classification hierarchy and was given the title of first librarian. (Hostrop; Grove)
80 B.C.	Tyrannion, a grammarian, reclassified and recataloged Aristotle's library. (Strabo)
300 A.D.	One library in Rome contained 62,000 volumes. (Hostrop)

400	Twenty-eight public libraries were in existence in Rome. (Hostrop)
400	The codex, constructed from folded leaves which were bound together on one side, took the place of papyrus rolls. (Hostrop)
600	The Rule of St. Benedict gave monasteries the responsibility for making books and creating libraries. (Hostrop)
____	The first public library was established in Athens five hundred years before the Christian Era by the tyrant Pisistratus. (Parsons)
____	The first public library was established in Rome during the close of the Pre-Christian Era by Asinius Apollo. (Parsons)
____	The Library of Alexandria in Egypt was known as the first research library with its "...incomparable resources of the first real and greatest collection of intellectual materials or data ever assembled in antiquity..." (Parsons)
mid 1400s	Johann Gutenberg of Mainz, Germany, invented the printing press. (Hostrop)
1583	The first use of a decimal classification system was by Lacroix du Maine, who classified Henry III's library. (Dewey)
1600	Libraries began to resemble present day libraries with books on open shelves and tables for readers. (World Book Encyclopedia)
1683	The first academic library in the United States was the Harvard College Library. It was begun by a small collection of books donated by Reverend John Harvard, and it was the largest library in the country for 200 years. (Bowker, 1964; Fay; Hostrop)
1700s	Six college libraries were founded: Yale University in 1700; Princeton University in 1746; University of Pennsylvania in 1755: Columbia University in 1757; Brown University in 1767; Dartmouth College in 1770. (Fay)
1731	Benjamin Franklin founded the first subscription library in the American colonies, "The Library Company of Philadelphia." (Bowker; Hostrop)

1796	New Jersey established the first state library. In the 1800s other state libraries were established: South Carolina in 1814; Pennsylvania in 1816; New Hampshire and New York in 1818. (Fay)
1800	The United States Library of Congress was established, the largest library in the U.S. (Hostrop)
1817	The large map collection of Christoph Daniel Ebling, a German scholar, was purchased after his death by Israel Thorndike and donated to the Harvard College Library. (Mullins)
1822	The first free public library was the Juvenile Library of Dublin, New Hampshire. (Kane)
1854	The first large public library to be established was the Boston Public Library. (Chamber's Encyclopedia)
c. 1866	The United States Library of Congress map collection was established. (Grove)
1871	Jacob Schwartz created the Cutter number system which preserved the alphabetical order of authors in classification systems. (Grove)
1876	Melvil Dewey's classification system was first issued. (Grove)
1880s	The first academic slide libraries were established at Bryn Mawr College, Cornell University, Dartmouth College, the University of Illinois, Princeton University, and the University of Michigan. Prior to 1884, these collections consisted of lanterns slides (3¼" x 4" slides with the image printed on glass). (Grove)
1882	The first music library was established: Brooklyn (New York) Public Library. (Bowker, 1964)
1884	Henry C. Badger was appointed as the first map curator at the Harvard College Library, which contained about 14,000 sheets. (Grove)
1887	The first library school was established at Columbia University, New York City, by Melvil Dewey. (Bowker; Encyclopedia Americana, 1980)

1891	The first circulating picture collection was established at the Denver (Colorado) Public Library, by John Cotton Dana. (Bowker; Smith)
1894	Paper or contact prints of motion pictures were deposited at the Library of Congress for copyright purposes. (Grove)
1894	A motion picture deposit was begun at the Library of Congress. (Information)
c.1897	The Library of Congress Division of Music was organized. (Thompson)
1902	The first graduate library school was the New York State Library School. (Bowker, 1964)
1903	A phonorecord collection was established at the Library of Congress. (Grove)
1903	The Lowe Theatrical Library, the first theatrical library in the United States, opened at Harvard University. (Encyclopedia Americana, 1957)
1904	The photo-offset press was developed. (Hostrop)
1904	The first circulating print and framed paintings collection was established at the Newark (New Jersey) Public Library by John Cotton Dana. (Bowker, 1964)
1906	The New York State Library had 60,000 prints. (Grove)
1906	Lantern slides became widely used as teaching aids in universities. (Grove)
1906	Melvil Dewey recognized the importance of non-print materials to libraries when he wrote: "Libraries are rapidly accepting the doctrine for which we have contended for many years, that what we call books have no exclusive rights in a library. The 'library' has lost its etymologic meaning and means not a collection of books, but the central agency for disseminating information, innocent recreation, or, best of all, inspiration among the people. Whenever this can be done better, more quickly, or cheaply by a picture than a book, the picture is entitled to a place on the shelves and in the catalog." (Grove)
1910	Henry Evelyn Bliss constructed his subject classification system which eventually included non-print media. (Bliss)

c.1910   The Bell & Howell Film Company had a film library of over
            a thousand silent and two hundred sound 16mm motion
            pictures. (Saettler)

1911   The Edison Film Library was established. (Saettler)

1913   A gift from a local citizen established the first phonorecord
            collection outside the Library of Congress, at the St. Paul
            (Minnesota) Public Library. (Bowker, 1971)

1914   Librarians began to review and evaluate the mass media.
            Public demand, plus the evaluation involvement stimu-
            lated the collection of non-print formats in libraries. Public
            libraries in large cities developed large collections of
            photographs, pictures, postcards, clippings, and other
            formats in an effort to provide the public with non-print.
            (Grove)

1914   The first phonorecord collection was established at the St.
            Paul Public Library in Minnesota. (Bowker 1964)

1914   The Kansas City (Missouri) Public Library circulated
            music rolls for the player piano. (Clement)

1914   *The Public Librarian*, a library journal, advocated the
            acceptance of phonorecords in libraries. (Edison)

1914–15   The *American Library Annual* reported that a public
            library in St. Joseph, Missouri, used the Edison Home and
            School Kinetoscope to illustrate stories narrated for chil-
            dren (Pringle)

1915   A statewide film exchange was proposed by James Gillis, a
            California state librarian. (Grove)

1915   The St. Paul (Minnesota) Public Library record collection
            had ninty-three recordings for limited use only.
            (Johnston)

1915   The August issue of *Library Journal* was devoted entirely
            to the music collections of the public libraries in the United
            States. (Bowker)

1915   Many public libraries maintained picture collections.
            (Parker)

1916   The first photographic department in a university library
            was established at Harvard University. (Bowker, 1957)

1917   The Chicago Bureau of Visual Instruction established the first instructional film library in a city school system. (Saettler)

1919   The Kern County Library, California, had a lantern slide and stereographic (three-dimensional slide) collection and established a phonorecord collection. (Clement)

1920   Audiovisual materials began to be handled as a normal part of library service. (Quinly)

1920   More than twenty-four state universities had film services. (Nolan)

1923   The first collection of circulating phonorecords was established in the Springfield (Massachusetts) Public Library. (Grove; Bowker, 1964)

1924   Audiovisual librarianship was introduced into the organizational framework of the American Library Association. The proposal that marked the beginning of ALA's formal audiovisual activity came from outside the Association. Ben Howe, a representative of the motion picture industry, suggested to the Council of the ALA that libraries should be the principal institutions for the distribution of educational films and should serve as information centers concerning entertainment and industrial films. Ben Howe's suggestion sparked ALA to create a Visual Methods Committee. (Clement)

1924   The American Library Association formally recognized the importance of films to library service and appointed a committee on Relations Between Libraries and Moving Pictures. (Cocks)

1926   The Graduate Library School was established at the University of Chicago to provide education beyond the first professional degree and offered a PhD. in library science. (Encyclopaedia Britannica)

1927   The Carnegie Corporation of New York authorized the distribution of "College Music Sets" for music study in college libraries. (Grove)

1928   The first PhD. in library education was granted at the University of Chicago Library School. (Encyclopedia Americana, 1962)

1928   The Carnegie Corporation assisted college libraries in the
            purchase of phonorecords, which were later identified by
            audiovisualists as "disks." (Shores)

1928   Fifty-three academic institutions had libraries with music
            collections, but only twelve of the collections held sound
            recordings. (Pierre)

1929   The first library to circulate educational films was the
            Kalamazoo (Michigan) Public Library. (Bowker, 1964)

1930s   Public libraries began to develop extensive film services.
            (Pringle)

1930s   Libraries began to put journals and newspapers on micro-
            film. (Encyclopedia Americana)

1931   The   Music   Library   Association   was   organized.
            (Bowker, 1958)

1933   Louis Shores determined that the library must have a range
            of subjects, levels, and formats in its collection to match
            the interests of individuals. (Shores)

1934   The Department of Geography at the University of Chicago
            planned to develop a map library of 400,000 sheets.
            (Development . . .) In 1968, the size of the collection was
            approximately 210,000 sheets. (Special Libraries Associa-
            tion)

1934   A resolution was sent to the American Library Association
            Committee on National Planning by the Visual Methods
            Committee, which recommended the establishment of
            regional demonstration centers for audiovisual aids. The
            proposal was not implemented. (Clement)

1934   The talking book was added to library service for the blind.
            (Encyclopedia Americana, 1957)

1935   Louis Shores introduced the first audiovisual course at the
            library school of Peabody College in the South. The course
            was taught by Milton Lanning Shane from 1936 to 1940.
            (Shores)

1935   The United States National Archives set up a division of
            motion pictures and sound recordings. (Grove)

1935   The Museum of Modern Art Film Library was established in New York City by a Rockefeller Foundation Grant for the preservation, distribution, study, and development of films. (Grove)

1936   The American Library Association set a standard for 35mm film as best suited for research and library work. This decision was made at the Richmond Conference. (Doss)

1936   Visual aids were distributed through the city libraries of Kalamazoo, Michigan, and Pasadena and Long Beach, California. (Dunn)

1938   The first Cooperative Microfilm Project was established at Harvard University. (Bowker, 1964)

1939   A $5,500 grant from the Rockefeller Foundation funded a Joint Committee on Educational Films representing the American Library Association, the American Film Center, the Association of School Librarians, and the Motion Picture Project of the American Council on Education. The purpose was to "encourage library experimentation in the handling of educational films ... to cooperate with such libraries and to facilitate the exchange of information between them, to devise uniform methods for recording experiences and to encourage their use, and to report from time to time on the experiments." (Williams)

1940s   Maps began to be accepted as legitimate materials for libraries. (Wood)

1940s–1964 Major phonorecord collections established. Late 1940s– Sibley Music Library, Eastman School of Music; 1958– Stanford University Archives of Recorded Sound; 1958– Archives of New Orleans Jazz at Tulane University; 1961– Historical Sound Recordings Program of Yale University; 1964–The Syracuse University Audio Archives. (Grove)

1940   Hundreds of universities and school systems had established audiovisual libraries. (Grove)

1940   At the suggestion of Carl Milam, the former Visual Methods Committee was merged with the former Radio Broadcasting Committee to form the Audiovisual Committee of the American Library Association. (Clement)

1941	Gerald D. McDonald surveyed literature and visited libraries and submitted a report to the American Library Association concluding, "Thus far librarians have done virtually nothing in the handling of films and very little even in providing information which would further their use." (McDonald)
c.1942	The first major public library film collection began in Cleveland, Ohio. (Palmer)
1942	Film lending became a routine part of library service. (Quinly)
1943	The term "media" appeared in the *Post War Standards for Public Libraries*, published by the American Library Association, defined as: " . . . books, periodicals, newspapers, pamphlets, maps, film, pictures, recordings, music scores, and similar material." (Post War . . .)
1944	Fremont Rider, Librarian at Wesleyan University, proposed that microcards be used in libraries, "both to reduce the space required for the catalogs of their growing collections and to produce more responsive catalogs." (Encyclopedia Americana, 1980)
1945	A Motion Picture Project was formed at the Library of Congress (Grove)
1947	The Carnegie Corporation awarded a grant to the American Library Association for building lending collections of films. (Encyclopedia Americana, 1957)
1947	The Carnegie Corporation awarded a grant to support a Film Advisory Service at the American Library Association. The purpose was to demonstrate that public libraries could serve as distribution centers for audiovisual materials, in addition to books. (Saettler)
1947	The American Library Association obtained a grant of $27,000 from the Carnegie Corporation for a "two year program to provide for film advisory service to help libraries establish film lending service." (Clement)
1947	Librarians and audiovisualists were two separate entities. Many schools had a separation of library and audiovisual facilities. At this time, the separation of the two was strongly backed by school administrators, teachers, librarians, and audiovisualists. (Shores)

1947   The Worcester Free Public Library had one thousand circulating phonorecords. (Grove)

1947   The Florida State University Graduate School of Library Service and Training was established. The school was committed to the audiovisual education of librarians and teachers. The school also advocated the unification of audiovisual departments with the library instead of keeping them as separate entities. (Shores)

1947   "Listening posts" were introduced into the reading room at the Florida State University Materials Center. The listening post consisted of a jack and eight headsets. (Shores)

1947   Dr. Charles Hoban was the first full-time professor appointed to a library school faculty at the Florida State University Graduate School of Library Training and Service. He was a strong force in the audiovisual movement and co-wrote, with his father and Zisman, the first textbook in the audiovisual field. (Shores)

1948   Phonorecords became a routine part of library service. (Quinly)

1948   The Audiovisual Committee of the American Library Association was made a board which allowed for a sub-committee structure. The various committees were not wholly successful in their efforts to establish cooperation and communication with other national associations. (Clement)

1948   A mimeographed manual entitled *Processing Audio Visual Materials* was put into use at Indiana University for library science courses. (Processing . . .)

1948   The first manual on integrated cataloging was published by the Materials Center at Florida State University. (Shores)

1949   The American Association of School Librarians sponsored the publication *Audiovisual School Library Service*, by Margaret Rufsvold. The book gave detailed information to guide the traditional book-oriented librarian in establishing an instructional materials center. (Rufsvold)

1950   The "Statement of Guiding Principles" in the *Evaluative Criteria 1950 Edition*, suggests that " . . . schools should have available, organized in the library or as a separate department, audiovisual materials for use in the educational program." (Evaluative Criteria . . .)

1950s   Major film collections in academic libraries were not established until this period. (Grove)

1950s   The "Rapid Selector," developed under the guidance of Ralph R. Shaw, the librarian of the United States Department of Agriculture, was the first machine specifically designed for searching the literature of a subject. It combined document images with binary coded identification, both stored photographically on roll film. (Encyclopedia Americana, 1980)

1950s   Louis Shores developed the concept of the generic book which is " . . . the sum total of man's communication possibilities . . . the evidence of life." The generic book recognizes that subject, level, and format may affect communication. "In the concept of the generic book there is no such thing as non-book material." The generic book has six format classes: print, graphics, projections, transmissions, community resources, and programmed media. (Shores)

1950s   The 35mm color slide was established as a necessary and integral part of a slide library. (Grove)

1950–60   Phonorecord archives were established in the Music Division of the Library of Congress, Indiana and Stanford University Libraries, and the New York Public Library. (Nolan)

1952   A survey was undertaken by the Association of College and Research Libraries to examine the extent to which audiovisual services had developed in the United States universities and colleges and to examine the patterns of service. The findings of the research implied that the development of audiovisual collections was still at an early stage. (Bennett)

1953   Edgar Dale, a theorist, viewed libraries as experiencing a transitional phase, " . . . shifting from being a repository of ideas in print to a repository of ideas on film, on tape." His "cone of experience," and other ideas have contributed to the development of a learning resource concept. (Dale)

1954   C. Walter Stone, a strong proponent of the unification of print and non-print, insisted that libraries utilize a "cross-media" approach for the benefit of students, teachers, and administration. (Stone)

1954   The Library of Congress printed catalog issued two new sections: one for music and phonorecords and another for filmstrips and motion pictures. (Schmeckebier)

1954-55   The San Jose (California) State College began the first program for curriculum materials specialists. (Saettler)

1955   Over 250 libraries were lending film, 192 through membership in a cooperative film service, with the remainder owning individual film collections. (Bowker, 1957)

1955   Irving Lieberman conducted a study of audiovisual instruction in library education. He reported a need for a graduate program for audiovisual specialists. (Lieberman)

1955-57   The American Library Association Special Committee on the Bibliographic Control of Audiovisual Materials surveyed libraries in an attempt to assess their non-book holdings and found the following holdings of non-book media. 115 libraries had motion picture collections (31 academic, 46 public, and 50 school) and 176 libraries had phonorecord collections (56 academic, 72 public, and 48 school). (Hamman)

1956   The Southern Illinois University unified their audiovisual department and library, as did Purdue, San Jose State, St. Cloud (Minnesota), and the University of Colorado. (Shores)

1960   *Instructional Materials*, by Louis Shore, was the first book devoted to the concept of unifying library science and audiovisual education. (Shores)

mid 1960s   The crusade for the unification of audiovisual departments and libraries was moving toward acceptance. (Shores)

1965   MEDLARS (Medical Literature Analysis Retrieval System) files were made available by the National Library of Medicine for use by other libraries. (Lancaster, p. 78)

1967   The New York Public Library was the largest public library in the United States. (Hostrop)

1968   Trevor N. Duprey conducted a study of college libraries and identified unnecessary competition between audiovisualists and librarians. (Duprey; Modern . . .)

1968   Trevor N. Duprey conducted a study of problem areas in adopting a learning resource center approach. (Duprey; Ferment . . .)

1968   Sidney Forman conducted a survey of 1,193 college libraries which indicated that 10 percent of the libraries were involved in implementing some aspect of the learning resource concept, and 37 percent were planning to introduce part of the concept in the future. (Forman)

1969   The crusade for the unification of audiovisual departments and libraries was successful. *Standards for School Media Programs* was jointly published by the American Library Association's American Association of School Librarians and the National Education Association's (NEA) Department of Audiovisual Instruction. (Shores)

1970   The number of libraries in the United States was broken down as follows (statistics from the U.S. Office of Education): 7,000 public libraries, 1,500 academic libraries, 1,200 two-year college libraries, 3,500 special libraries, 450 law libraries, 800 medical libraries, 475 military libraries, 125 institutional libraries, and 50,000 elementary and secondary school libraries. (Hostrop)

1970   The Bureau of Libraries and Educational Technology was established by the U.S. Office of Education. (Hostrop)

1970   The American Library Association published the *Guidelines for Audiovisual Materials and Services for Public Libraries*. Included were definitions, standards for service, materials, space, equipment, and personnel. It stressed the importance of non-print media in all formats. (Audiovisual Committee . . .)

1970   Robert Brundin surveyed the development of learning resource centers on junior college campuses. He concluded that the development of learning resource centers in junior colleges was an attempt to make the library the "heart of the campus." (Brundin)

1970   Richard Vorwerk studied the organizational status and
            environmental demands of academic libraries. He found
            that newer forms of media were being excluded in academic
            libraries because administrators weren't quite sure what to
            do with them. (Vorwerk, 1970)

1972   John W. Ellison conducted the first study of learning
            resource centers on university and college campuses. He
            identified principles that validated the concept of an
            integrated learning resource center which would include
            both print and non-print materials. (Ellison)

1973   Melvil Dewey is said to be the "Father of American
            Libraries." F. Dean McCluskey is said to be the "Father of
            American Audiovisual Education."

1973   Andrew Carnegie is said to be the "Father of Library
            Philanthropists." (Hostrop)

Footnotes

1. Richard W. Hostrop, *Education Inside the Library Media Center*. Hamden,
   Conn.: Shoe String Press, 1973, p. 3.
2. Pearce S. Grove, *Nonprint Media in Academic Libraries*. Chicago: American
   Library Association, 1975, p. x.
3. John L. Nolan, "Audio-Visual Materials." *Library Trends* 10, (October 1961),
   p. 262.
4. Hostrop, p. 3.
5. Ibid., pp. 2-4.
6. Ibid., pp. 4-5.

References

American Library Annual. New York: R.R. Bowker, 1957.
Audiovisual Committee, Public Library Association. *Guidelines for Audiovisual
   Materials and Services for Public Libraries*. Chicago: American Library
   Association, 1970.
Bliss, Henry Evelyn. "Economics in Libraries." *Library Journal* 28 (1910).
The Bowker Annual of Library and Book Trade Information. New York: R.R.
   Bowker, 1957.
The Bowker Annual of Library and Book Trade Information. New York: R.R.
   Bowker, 1958.
The Bowker Annual of Library and Book Trade Information. New York: R.R.
   Bowker, 1960.
The Bowker Annual of Library and Book Trade Information. New York: R.R.
   Bowker, 1964.

The Bowker Annual of Library and Book Trade Information. New York: R.R. Bowker, 1971.

Brundin, Robert. "Changing Patterns of Library Service in Five California Junior Colleges." PhD. Dissertation, Stanford University, 1970.

Chamber's Encyclopedia. vol. 8. London: Pergamon Press, Ltd., 1967.

Clement, Evelyn G. "Audiovisual in Libraries; the Past." Paper presented at the 95th ALA Conference, ISAD Audiovisual Section Program, July 1976. ERIC document #ED 129 328.

Cocks, Orrin. "Motion Pictures and Reading Habits." *Library Journal* 43 (February 1918): 67-70.

Comenius, John Amos. *The Orbis Pictus.* Syracuse, N.Y.: C.W. Bardeen, 1887.

Dale, Edgar. *Challenges to Librarianship.* Tallahassee, Fl.: Florida State University, 1953.

_____. "Development of the Collection of Maps at the University of Chicago." *Science* 79 (February 23, 1934).

Dewey, Melvil. *Dewey Decimal Classification and Relative Index.* 16th ed. Lake Placid Club, N.Y.: Forest, 1959.

Doss, Milburn Price, ed. *Information Processing Equipment.* New York: Reinhold, 1955.

Dunn, Fannie W., and Schneider, Etta. "Practices in City Administration of Visual Education." *Educational Screen* 15 (November 1936).

Duprey, Trevor N. *Ferment in College Libraries: The Impact of Information Technology.* Washington, D.C.: Communication Service Corporation, 1968.

Eason, Tracy. "A Selected Bibliography of AV Media in Library Literature, 1958-69." *Wilson Library Bulletin* 44 (November 1969): 312-319.

Edison, Thomas. "Mechanical Arts and the Library." *Public Library,* 19 (1914).

Ellison, John W. "The Identification and Examination of Principles Which Validate or Refute the Concept of College or University Learning Resource Centers." PhD. Dissertation, Ohio State University, 1972.

Encyclopaedia Britannica 1, vol.#10. Chicago: Encyclopaedia Britannica, Inc., 1978.

Encyclopedia Americana, vol.#17. New York: Americana Corporation, 1957.

Encyclopedia Americana, vol.#17. New York: Americana Corporation, 1962.

Encyclopedia Americana, vol.#17. New York: Americana Corporation, 1980.

Evaluative Criteria. Washington, D.C.: Cooperative Study of Secondary School Standards, 1950.

Fay, Lucy E., and Eaton, Anne T. *Instruction in the Use of Books and Libraries.* Boston: The F.W. Faxon Co., 1924.

Fleming, Bennett. "Audio-Visual Services in Colleges and Universities in the United States." *College and Research Libraries* 16 (1955): 11-19.

Forman, Sidney. "Innovative Practices in the College Library." *College and Research Libraries* 29 (November 1968): 486.

Grove, Pearce S. *Nonprint Media in Academic Libraries.* Chicago: American Library Association, 1975.

Hamman, Frances. "Bibliographic Control of Audiovisual Materials: Report of a Special Committee." *Library Resources and Technical Services Bulletin* 1 (Fall 1957): 180-89.

Hessel, Alfred. *A History of Libraries.* Metuchen, N.J.: Scarecrow Press, 1950.

Hostrop, Richard W. *Education Inside the Library Media Center.* Hamden, Conn.: Shoe String Press, 1973.

_____. *Information Bulletin.* 23. Washington D.C.: The Library of Congress.

Johnston, W. Dawson. "Symposium of Music in Libraries: St. Paul Public Library." *Library Journal* 40 (August 1915): 574.

Kane, Joseph Nathan. *Famous First Facts*, 4th ed. New York: H.W. Wilson, 1981.

Kujoth, Jean Spealman. *Readings in Nonbook Librarianship.* Metuchen, N.J.: Scarecrow Press, Inc., 1968.

Lancaster, F. Wilfred. *Information Retrieval Systems*, 2nd ed. New York: John Wiley and Sons, 1979.

Lieberman, Irving. *Audiovisual Instruction in Library Education.* New York: Columbia University School of Library Service, 1955.

McDonald, Gerald D. *Educational Motion Pictures and Libraries.* Chicago: American Library Association, 1942.

Mullins, Lynn S. "The Rise of Map Libraries in America During the 19th Century." *Bulletin* 63 (March 1966).

Nolan, John L. "Audio-Visual Materials." *Library Trends* 10 (October 1961): 261-67.

Palmer, Joseph W. "Surveying the Future of Public Library Film Service." *New York Library Association Bulletin*, 30 (April 1982): 1-8.

Parker, John Austin. "A Brief History of the Picture Collection." *Wilson Library Bulletin* 30 (November 1955): 257-58.

Parsons, Edward Alexander. *The Alexandrian Library.* New York: Elsevier Press, 1952.

Pierre Key's International Music Yearbook, 1928. New York: Pierre Key, Inc., 1928.

Post War Standards for Public Libraries. Chicago: American Library Association, 1943.

Pringle, Eugene A. "Films in Public Libraries." *Drexel Library Quarterly* 2 (October 1961): 261-67.

Processing Audio Visual Materials. Bloomington, Ind.: Indiana University, 1948.

Quinly, William J. "Audio-Visual Materials in the Library." *Library Trends* 5 (October 1956) 294-300.

Richardson, Ernest Cushing. *Classification: Theoretical and Practical.* 3rd ed. New York: H.W. Wilson, 1930.

Rufsvold, Margaret. *Audio-Visual School Library Service.* Chicago: American Association of School Librarians, 1949.

Saettler, Paul. *A History of Instructional Technology.* New York: McGraw-Hill Book Company, 1968.

Schmeckebier, Laurence F., and Eastin, Roy B. *Government Publications and Their Use.* Rev. ed. Washington, D.C.: Brookings Institution, 1961.

Shane, M. Lanning. "Audiovisual Aids & the Library." *College and Research Libraries* 1 (March 1940): 143-46.

Shores, Louis. *Audiovisual Librarianship*. Littleton, Colo.: Libraries Unlimited, 1973.

Smith, Josephine Metcalfe. *A Chronology of Librarianship*. Metuchen, N.J.: Scarecrow Press, 1968.

Special Library Association, Geography and Map Division, Directory Revision Committee. *Map Collections in the United States & Canada: A Directory*. 2nd ed. New York: Special Library Association, 1970.

Stone, C. Walter. "The Place of the New Media in the Undergraduate Program." *Library Quarterly* 24 (October 1954).

Strabo. *The Geography of Strabo*. New York: Putnam, 1917.

Thompson, James Westfall. *Ancient Libraries*. Berkeley, Calif.: University of California Press, 1940.

Thompson, Oscar, ed. *The International Cyclopedia of Music and Musicians*. Rev. ed. New York: Dodd, Mead, 1958.

Vorwerk, Richard J. "The Environmental Demands and Organizational Status of Two Academic Libraries." PhD. Dissertation, Indiana University, 1970.

Williams, Edwin E. "ALA Notes." *Wilson Library Bullentin* 14 (June 1940): 778-79.

Woods, Bill M. "Of Map Librarianship - A Very Personal Report." *Bulletin* 76 (June 1969): 4-6.

World Book Encyclopedia, vol. 12. Chicago: Worldbook-Childcraft International, Inc., 1982.

Media Organizations and Associations

Joseph W. Palmer

T HE associations concerned with the development of media resources and services are numerous and varied. They range from large multi-faceted organizations such as the American Library Association to specialist groups such as the Feminist Radio Network and the Association for Media Based Continuing Education for Engineers. These and dozens of other groups operating at the national level are described in the directory pages of the *Educational Media Yearbook*.

Why are these groups needed? What functions do they perform? Primarily, they enable persons with similar media interests to exchange ideas and information and to keep their knowledge current and growing. Media associations stimulate thought, research, and innovation. They allow media people to work together to achieve desired ends. They help professionals to obtain support and recognition from their institutions and society.

Important activities of media associations include the publication of journals, newsletters, manuals, monographs, research reports, and non-print publications. Some produce reviews and mediagraphies. Of great importance are conferences and workshops where members can meet, learn, and plan together. Many organizations lobby for legislation favorable to media services, form liaisons with other library/media groups, and develop standards and guidelines.

The media librarian should not overlook local and statewide media organizations. They offer the individual more opportunities to partic-ipate actively by attending meetings and being on committees. Further-more, they often address themselves more directly to topics of local concern. Almost every state library association has a media-interest subgroup. An example is the Film/Video Roundtable of the New York Library Association. There are also groups that address the needs of school media specialists. Often, these are independent of the state library association. The *Bowker Annual of Library and Book Trade Information* contains listings for "State, Provincial and Regional Library Associa-tions" and for "State School Library Media Associations." The three national associations with which every media librarian should be familiar are the American Library Association (ALA), the Association for Educational Communications and Technology (AECT), and the Educa-tional Film Library Association (EFLA).

AMERICAN LIBRARY ASSOCIATION

As early as 1924, ALA established a Committee on Relations between Libraries and Moving Pictures, but it was not until the 1940s that the association played a significant leadership role in fostering access to audiovisuals through libraries. It started in the early forties with demonstration film forums in public libraries. Developed under the auspices of ALA, these forums used motion pictures and follow-up discussions to reach the population with messages designed to generate a sense of national identity in a time of domestic and international crisis. This led to the deposit of public information films in some libraries during the war, which in turn led to the first public library film collections of real consequence.

After the war, ALA was eager to stimulate a greater commitment to audiovisual education through libraries. In a memorable convention address at the 1946 ALA Conference in Buffalo, John Grierson, father of the documentary film movement, urged ALA members to "get out from behind our desks and institutions and make our various powers of enlightenment a dynamic force in our communities everywhere" and to do this by using "all the bright new media and techniques which now lie in our hand in an ingenious and amazing world of new illuminations and new skills."

With grants from the Carnegie Corporation, ALA employed Patricia Blair to serve as ALA Film Advisor from 1947 to 1951. She engaged in a prodigious program which educated librarians about film as a library resource and stimulated the establishment of dozens of public library film collections and of the first two public library film circuits in the United States. Film was the foot in the door for audiovisual media in libraries.

During the 1950s and 1960s there arose a great national concern with improving the quality of education, maximizing instructional effectiveness, and equalizing educational opportunity. This led to the massive distribution of federal monies to schools, colleges, and libraries, and to the proliferation of media theory and resources. Non-print media became available in unprecedented quantity and variety in schools and libraries. Librarians with audiovisual responsibilities were often enthusiastic and optimistic but they also felt frustrated and without leadership.

In 1967, ALA formed an Audiovisual Task Force to investigate their needs. The 1969 AV Task Force Survey Report concluded that problem areas included inadequate training in library schools, insufficient reviews and bibliographic control of non-print, and a lack of respect and recognition for media within the profession. It cited audiovisual librarians' "continuing need for identity, recognition, and appreciation, as well as for information and help" and suggested that ALA "study [the] needs for a membership organization within librarianship and a national office staff which could provide advisory and coordinating services relating to audiovisual services provided by libraries."

ALA did not implement these suggestions but instead chose to strengthen support for audiovisual services within existing divisions and to promote an all-media (print/non-print) approach to library services. Finances were at least partially responsible for this decision. ALA had wanted to retain the position of Film Advisor after the expiration of the Carnegie grants, but it had decided this was not possible without subsidy. In 1969, ALA put its all-media philosophy into action by making its review journal, *Booklist*, resolutely multimedia. Another ALA serial publication of special importance to media librarians is *Library Technology Reports*, with its frequent in-depth evaluations of audiovisual hardware.

Today, nearly every division of ALA has audiovisual sections, committees, and/or activities. Most active are the Audiovisual Committee of the Public Library Association (PLA-AVC) and the Video and Cable Communications and Audiovisual Sections of the Library and Information Technology Association (LITA-VCCS and LITA-AVS). In 1975, PLA-AVC published *Guidelines for Audiovisual Materials and Services for Large Public Libraries* and *Recommendations for Audiovisual Materials and Services for Small and Medium Sized Public Libraries*. In 1980, LITA-VCCS published a second edition of its excellent *Video and Cable Guidelines*. The Association of College and Research Libraries published *Guidelines for Audio-Visual Services in Academic Libraries* in 1968. In 1979, it began to include reviews of non-print media in its review journal, *Choice*.

The Association for Library Service to Children engages in a variety of media activities including the publication of annual lists of "Notable Films of Interest to Children," "Notable Filmstrips of Interest to Children," "Notable Recordings of Interest to Children," and "Prints and Posters of Interest to Children." The Young Adult Services Division publishes an annual list of "Selected Films for Young Adults."

Totally dedicated to the integration of print and non-print in school media centers is the American Association of School Librarians (AASL). Their interaction with the Association for Educational Communications and Technology is close and ongoing. It resulted, in 1969, in the publication of joint AASL-AECT Standards for school library media centers. This landmark publication formally advocated that print and non-print services and resources merge in a consolidated school media center. The standards were revised in 1975 and published as *Media Programs: District and School*.

Today, although great progress has been made, the problems noted in 1969 by the Audiovisual Task Force still exist. ALA's decision to foster an all-media approach to library service and not to ghetto-ize non-print librarians in a separate division may have been a good one. However, its inability to establish an ALA office with staff to provide advisory and coordinating services is regrettable. At present, non-print activities and interest groups are scattered throughout the various ALA divisions. Joining ALA does not allow one to be active in any of these unless one also joins the specific division. Consequently, there are numerous groups—all with different memberships—working in overlapping areas, with no effective coordination or centralized leadership. This greatly weakens the ability of ALA to provide leadership and support to media librarians.

ASSOCIATION FOR EDUCATIONAL COMMUNICATIONS AND TECHNOLOGY

AECT traces its beginnings to the National Education Association's Department of Visual Instruction (DVI). Established in 1923, DVI evolved into the Department of Audiovisual Instruction (DAVI) which flourished in the decades following World War II. The effective use of films for the training of large numbers of armed forces inductees had generated great enthusiasm for the idea of audiovisual aids to instruction.

In the 1950s and 1960s, there was an intensification of this interest accompanied by increasingly sophisticated technology and large infusions of federal money for educational innovation. There was also a gradual change in DAVI because of the development of learning theory. DAVI's emphasis shifted from a concern with audiovisual materials per se to the learning process in general and to the scientific investigation of how technology could be effectively applied to the instructional process. Concern was directed increasingly towards the systems approach to instruction, the recognition of individual differences, and the provision of media-assisted individualized instruction. As a result, DAVI changed its name, in the early seventies, to the Association for Educational Communications and Technology (AECT). (Technology can be defined as the application of scientific methods and the products of science to the solution of practical problems.)

Today, AECT is an organization of both practitioners and researchers. It has nine divisions and is affiliated with a large number of national organizations (including AASL) and more than fifty state organizations. Its divisions reflect its diverse concerns: Information Systems, Telecommunications, Research and Theory, Instructional Development, International, Industrial Training and Education, Educational Media Management, Media Design and Production, and School Media Specialists.

AECT produces materials in print and non-print formats including monographs, filmstrips, and 16mm films. Journals include *Instructional Innovator*, which is geared to the practitioner, and two research quarterlies, *Educational Communications and Technology* and *Journal of Instructional Development*. A recent monograph was *Professional Negotiations for Media/Library Professionals: District and School*, a "how to" guide to collective bargaining. This concern with professional status and development is also reflected in a major undertaking of AECT at this time: the establishment of a certification process for educational technology professionals.

Certification is offered in three areas: Instructional Development, Materials Design and Production, and Media Management. Candidates may apply for more than one certificate. Each requires adequate professional preparation, including several years of full-time experience in a position with major educational communications and technology responsibilities, and the passing of an examination. Certification is renewable every five years. It is noteworthy that applicants must sign a copy of the AECT Code of Ethics prior to receiving certification.

EDUCATIONAL FILM LIBRARY ASSOCIATION

World War II, which had such a significant impact on the development of AECT and on ALA's audiovisual activities, also led to the establishment of the Educational Film Library Association (EFLA). In 1942, the Educational Film Lending Library Committee was formed to help the government distribute war information films to agencies that could reach the general public. Rather than disbanding when this mission was accomplished, the Committee reorganized as the Educational Film Library Association.

Since 1943, EFLA has been fostering quality educational film production, distribution, and utilization through its publications and activities. It is currently expanding its scope to include video as well. Originally, membership was divided between state departments of education, school systems, public libraries, and museums. Today, membership also encompasses producers, distributors, government, labor, health agencies, and individuals.

Since 1946, EFLA has published *EFLA Evaluations*—influential evaluations of 16mm films prepared by volunteer committees of specialists. Other publications include the quarterly journal *Sightlines*, a monthly newsletter, *EFLA Bulletin*, and a number of specialized filmographies, handbooks, reports, and directories.

EFLA sponsors the annual American Film Festival, which is held in New York City each spring. Non-theatrical films in nearly fifty categories compete for prestigious awards which have considerable influence on film sales. Winners are sent on tour the following year and are screened in schools, universities, and libraries across the nation. The Festival also provides an opportunity for persons interested in educational and non-theatrical films to meet and confer. The Festival now also includes a video competition. In 1982, ribbons were awarded to videotapes in a dozen categories ranging from Video Art to Social Issues, Training and Management, and 30/60 Second Public Service Announcements.

OTHER ORGANIZATIONS OF INTEREST

In addition to ALA, AECT, and EFLA, other organizations make valuable contributions to the media professional. Economic problems have hindered the ability of some to be as active as they would desire. Indeed, the long established and esteemed National Association of Educational Broadcasters declared bankruptcy and dissolved in 1981. Professional associations need and deserve the media professional's participation and support if they are to survive and be effective.

Associations with which the media librarian should be familiar include:

Association of Media Producers A trade association with approximately one hundred members, AMP monitors developments in the field and publishes surveys and analyses of educational media trends and sales. It is an active lobbyist for legislation favorable to media.

Consortium of University Film Centers Approximately fifty university film rental libraries belong to this organization, many of which rent 16mm films at fees far below those charged by distributors. The *Educational Film Locator* is a union list of films in CUFC collections.

Film Library Information Council Established in 1967 to provide national leadership to public library audiovisual specialists, this organization's activities have dwindled in recent years. Its main activity at present is the publication of *Film Library Quarterly*, a journal featuring articles on the film art and on significant developments, genres, and artists in the area of documentary and non-theatrical film and video. It also features authoritative reviews of film and video from a public library point of view.

Health Sciences Communication Association HESCA is the larger of two associations devoted to the use of media in the health sciences. The other organization is the Health Education Media Association.

International Association for Visual Literacy This association encourages the cross-disciplinary study of visual communication. Among its concerns are research on still pictures, motion pictures, and video, and the application of research findings to classroom techniques. IAVL holds an annual conference and publishes the *Journal of Visual/Verbal Learning*. In addition, it offers programs at AECT conferences.

National Audiovisual Association Since 1939, when eight dealers united to form the National Association for Visual Education Dealers, NAVA has grown to be the single most important organization in the audiovisual industry. Manufacturers, producers, distributors, and other industry workers form the bulk of its eighteen hundred members, but there are also some associate members drawn from the users of audiovisual media. NAVA serves as an information clearinghouse, sponsors training institutes and an annual conference, and is an active lobbyist. Among its important publications are the invaluable *Audiovisual Equipment Directory* and *The A-V Connection,* a "guide to federal funds for audiovisual users."

Bibliography

Covert, Nadine. "Educational Film Library Association (EFLA): Influential Force in Media," in *Educational Media Yearbook 1977*. Ed. James W. Brown. New York: Bowker, 1977.

Frame, Ruth. "The ALA and Nonprint Media," in *Educational Media Yearbook 1977*. Ed. James W. Brown. New York: Bowker, 1977.

Galey, Mina Ruth. "Professional Certification by AECT," in *Educational Media Yearbook 1981*. Ed. James W. Brown and Shirley N. Brown. Littleton, Colo.: Libraries Unlimited, 1981.

Grierson, John. *Grierson on Documentary*. Ed. Forsyth Hardy. New York: Praeger, 1966.

Hitchens, Howard. "AECT as a Professional Organization," in *Education Media Yearbook 1981*. Ed. James W. Brown and Shirley N. Brown. Littleton, Colo.: Libraries Unlimited, 1981.

Palmer, Joseph W. "Contributions of the Carnegie Corporation to the Development of Public Library Film Service." *Journal of Library History* Vol. 12, no. 4 (Fall 1977), 325-41.

_____. " '17-'74: Decades of Service." *Film Library Quarterly* Vol. 8, No. 1 (1975), pp. 18-22.

Stone, C. Walter. "AV Task Force Survey Report." *American Libraries* Vol. 1, No. 1 (1980), pp. 40-42.

MANAGEMENT OF MEDIA SERVICES

Media Center Organization

William T. Schmid

Today, media centers are found in many areas: education, business and industry, libraries, medicine, government, the military, and museums. Some media centers are small, with limited production capability, while others provide a full range of support. This chapter gives you an understanding of basic forces influencing media centers, advantages and disadvantages of various organizational arrangements, and a better idea of what positive structural changes are possible within your own environment. Many principles presented can be applied in specific areas such as television, audio production, graphics, photography, audiovisual equipment circulation, library services, printing, and learning resource centers. These concepts have application in large centers with many departments or small centers having only one full-time position. Today you may be working in a specific service area but tomorrow you may be asked to manage a large center. People in charge of large media centers often do not have a background in all production and service areas but come from a particular discipline.

TYPICAL MEDIA CENTERS

Many people are overly concerned with titles and labels. A look at two very different media centers, one in education and another in industry, can determine if there are any similarities. Figure 1 (page 100) shows a university media center with the following major operating units: coordinator of distribution, in charge of circulating audiovisual equipment and materials; coordinator of television, in charge of producing instructional videotapes and 16mm films; coordinator of learning resources, in charge of cataloging and providing playback facilities for packaged presentations such as tape/slide programs; coordinator of audio, in charge of producing all instructional audiotapes which become a part of tape/slide programs; and coordinator of graphics, in charge of producing all original art work and photography.

Figure 2 (page 101) shows the organizational chart for a corporate media center. Major responsibilities are divided between production and

Reprinted by permission of Hastings House, Publishers, Inc. from *Media Center Management: A Practical Guide* © 1980 by William T. Schmid.

FIGURE 1 University Media Center

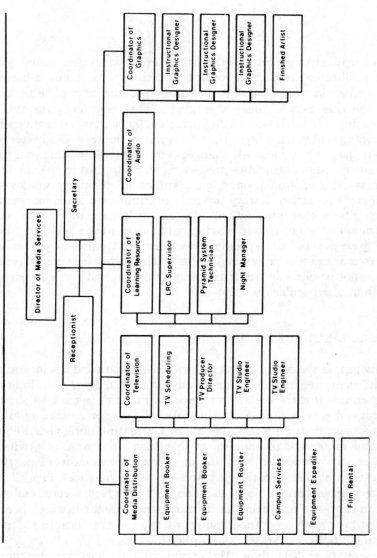

FIGURE 2   Corporate Media Center

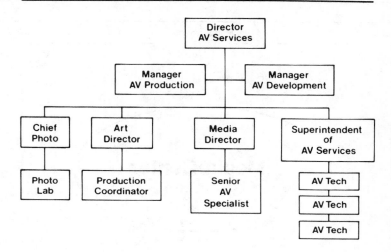

development with the following operating units: chief photographer, in charge of all still photography and cinematography; art director, in charge of producing all original art work; media director, in charge of all videotape and multimedia productions; and superintendent of AV services, in charge of the circulation of all audiovisual equipment along with playback facilities for packaged programs.

Although the titles are different, the functions are similar. In the university media center, photographic functions are handled in two areas. The coordinator of television does all cinematography while the coordinator of graphics does all still photography. In the corporate media center, all photography is done through the chief photographer's department. Other examples could be shown, but the point is to identify functions and functional relationships rather than terminology.

One additional word on terminology. This chapter has broad application for media centers in education, business and industry, libraries, medicine, government, the military, and museums. Each area has its own set of "buzz words" and labels. To use labels from each area would be confusing and awkward. Therefore the word client is used for anyone seeking service from a media center. A client can be a teacher, instructor, content specialist, student, trainer, instructional developer, librarian, trainee, or customer. Certainly the list could be longer.

ENVIRONMENTAL INFLUENCES

Any media center is the product of its environment. For this reason, no two media centers are organized exactly the same way. Most factors

FIGURE 3   Environmental Influences

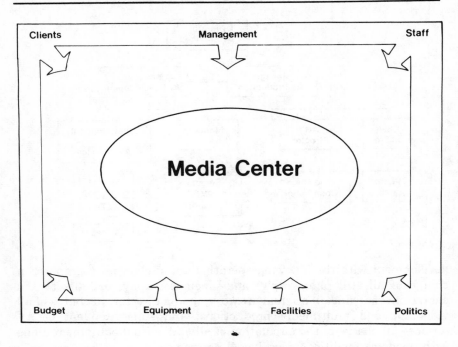

making up this environment are subtle. Figure 3 shows an operational environment consisting of clients, management, staff, politics, facilities, equipment, and budget. Arrows indicate all these have a direct influence on how media centers are organized. No matter what type of organization the media center serves, these influences quickly establish boundaries of growth.

Clients

People who use a media center, whether they be students, instructors, administrators, or employees, basically are concerned about convenient, reliable service. Human nature indicates we all patronize services which are easiest to use. Client needs represent a real and appropriate influence on the very organizational foundation of a media center. Any media director who does not recognize and work effectively with client needs will not have a successful operation.

Management

The media manager's own concerns have a direct influence on media center structure. Any manager should strive for convenient, reliable service, but this starts with a well conceived organizational chart showing direct lines of accountability. The growth of informal procedures between clients and media staff might be a first indication of deficiencies in the formal organizational structure and necessitate cause for change in that formal structure.

A basic requirement of any media center organizational structure must be to facilitate the efficient utilization of personnel, equipment, materials, and space. Without staff and facilities, a media center cannot function. Since there never seems to be enough staff and facilities, it is imperative they be used wisely.

The ideal media center organizational structure should also provide for lateral and vertical staff advancement. If there are chances for professional development, any new employee coming into a media center is likely to be more enthusiastic and encouraged to perform effectively. Large media centers with many positions have a built-in advantage for advancement. However, the small center should be organized to allow at least for staff development on a variety of projects.

Support from upper administrative levels is extremely helpful while a lack of support can greatly restrict the potential growth of a media center. With the very survival of a media center hanging in the balance, upper-level administrators have a direct influence on the organizational structure of a media center. These administrators usually have no background in instructional technology. Media center managers must continually tutor upper-level administrators regarding advantages and disadvantages of non-print materials. Without such continuing education techniques, these administrators often have simplistic answers to complex problems regarding media center operations. Many administrators view media centers as pure overhead, a cost center that could easily be eliminated during tight budgets. Media center managers in any organization must document the positive cost-effective contribution of their operation.

Staff

No single factor has more direct influence on a media center than staff. Personnel considerations are two-dimensional: number of staff members and, more important, staff talent. Most people fall into the easy trap of defining media capability in terms of equipment, facilities, and budget. Without talented staff, none of these can be fully developed. A talented staff can take mediocre equipment, facilities, and budget and provide valuable services, but the reverse is not necessarily true. A mediocre staff will not be saved automatically by superior equipment, facilities, and budget. A talented staff is equally important for both the well-endowed and the struggling media center.

Politics

Many people do not think of politics as a major influential force in media center management. Political factors pertain to the power of individuals and groups that make decisions. Some of this decision-making is formal, following the organizational structure of the school, company, library, or organization.

Political factors can be defined in the library setting where state and national politicians can make or break the cause of media. Local politics can also be defined in terms of the bureaucratic power structure in every school system, library, or business. Who reports to whom and with how much clout can have an effect on media center operations. The media center director is always better off reporting high up in the admin-istrative structure. In education the media center should be directly linked with the instructional process and the success of students, while in business the center should contribute directly to profitable perfor-mance.

Realistically, much of the decision-making process can also take place on an informal, subtle level, not nearly as visible but equally effective. Decisions should be made on the basis of an objective review yielding key facts. However, other less objective factors also enter, because decision-making is a human enterprise, subject to all the human drives of pressure, greed, advancement, power, prestige, patronage, and influence.

The media director should be aware of informal lines of influence which, although not easy to detect, can have much influence on a media center's fate. The behind-the-scenes realities of who likes whom, who gets invited to the right cocktail parties, who can influence, and who has the real power to make decisions must be recognized and dealt with effectively. A media center director may report to a vice president in charge of corporate communications who is just a figurehead with little real power. However, a junior executive in finance who is a strong proponent of media and also a close personal friend of the president's could have much influence. In the game of politics, media managers must learn to recognize the teams and play the game accordingly. The subtle nuances of political power can be a tremendous force shaping the media center organizational structure.

Facilities

Staff and equipment must be housed in adequate facilities. There is a direct relationship between good facilities and the media center's ability to meet service demands. A major challenge for media managers is to make upper level administrators aware of the unique architectural requirements in a media center which influence service capability. Electrical, air conditioning, acoustical, and work-flow relationships represent just a few of the many design considerations which must be properly addressed to ensure a smooth, efficient media center operation.

Equipment

Equipment capability has a direct influence on service effectiveness. Few people in media can resist the temptation of new equipment with the promise of increased capability. However, increased capability is often available only for a price. Equipment technology has advanced much faster than our ability to develop effective programs. The major challenge is to make the perfect match of the right equipment for the right purpose.

Budget

Another obvious factor with a direct influence on operations is budget. There is probably no single area of greater concern for a media director than budget. Many managers feel budget, not personnel or facilities, makes all things possible. Without a good budget little is possible. A realistic budget makes it possible to attract talented staff and equip them with the tools to turn out superior products and services.

THREE ORGANIZATIONAL APPROACHES

All organizational models include a wide variety of services. There seems to be a growing management philosophy that diverse media services have much in common. Hopefully this is a healthy departure from the days when, for example, librarians and audiovisual people stayed in their own camps. People were either "print" or "non-print." Some even felt print was better than non-print, and others supported the reverse. This gave media technology its very own version of the Crusades! Now there seems to be some healthy cross-fertilization of interests. Media professionals from different support services are realizing the client is the most important common denominator. Clients do not care about format nearly as much as content and results. There is no best medium, only the best medium for a particular application. Certainly such a philosophy is not yet universally practiced, but there has been much progress.

FIGURE 4   Independent Decentralized Organization

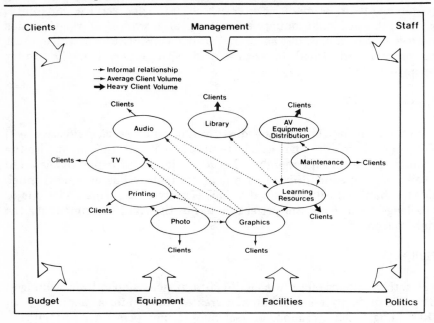

Independent Decentralized Organization

One classic organizational approach is to have autonomous services, each with its own clientele. Figure 4 shows a variety of independent services. Although titles for these services vary, the overall concept is representative. A word of explanation is appropriate for resources which could also be called a resource center or resource laboratory. Regardless of title, this area usually houses materials along with media equipment for playback, preview, and production. Each department in Figure 4 has its own facilities, staff, and budget. Arrows represent the typical direction of service. A photographic unit might serve television, printing, and graphic departments along with regular clients such as teachers or instructional developers. Broken arrows indicate typical informal relationships between service areas. Informal relationships mean there is no direct responsibility to provide service to other media support areas. In many cases, there might be a charge for services. For example, in Figure 4, if television production does not have sufficient budget it could not retain photographic services. Solid arrows indicate clients must go to each area for service. Bold arrows indicate those service areas typically having the highest client volume.

There are several good reasons why independent media departments have developed over the years. Independent media departments usually

FIGURE 5   Centralized Organization

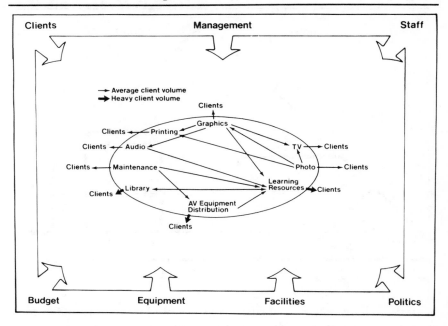

represent spin-offs from related operations. For example, service centers in education often evolved from academic programs such as a television service from the communications department, or an audiovisual service from the education department, or a learning resource center from a library studies program. Industrial television services many times developed out of public relations, training, or advertising departments. As these media areas grew they often broke away from the fostering department and became separate entities.

Personalized service and convenient location probably sum up the advantages of independent service departments. Since these service areas are usually small, the client feels there is more personalized service. Most independent areas grow out of a concentrated need and thus remain conveniently close to this need. Being logistically close to the client's work location is probably the single most important advantage of the independent media service area.

There are some inherent disadvantages with independent media departments. Users must go from one department to the next to coordinate a multifaceted media project such as a slide/tape program. The broken arrows in Figure 4 illustrate a lack of formal interdependence between services. Instead of cooperation, there may be competition. The television service may produce a videotape which more appropriately should have been a slide presentation. Because budgets are closely

FIGURE 6   Floor Plan A

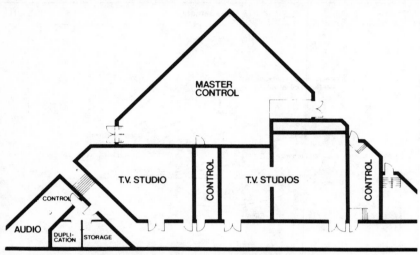

Reprinted with permission from *Video Systems* (May 1978 issue) and Instructional Center for Training and Management Development at Xerox Corporation.

related to client volume, television has a vested interest in not turning away any business, regardless of appropriate application. Independent media departments foster duplication of personnel and equipment. Television may have a graphic artist and photographer along with supporting drawing and darkroom equipment. The same expertise and facilities may also exist in the photographic and graphic service areas. A multiplicity of graphic and darkroom facilities might be justified in certain instances but in most cases is impractical. The small organizational structure in an independent media service area can restrict personnel advancement. Professional staff growth can also be limited by a lack of interaction with a variety of media professionals.

Centralized Organization

The opposite extreme from decentralized media departments is found in the total centralization of all related media areas. Decentralization was discussed first since many media services started as independent functions. Eventually, in certain cases, management saw advantages for merging separate departments into a centralized media center. In Figure 5 (page 107), broken arrows between media areas have been replaced with solid arrows indicating a strong formal interdependence through centralization. In this model, autonomous management of separate areas has been replaced with one manager over all media operations. For example, in this arrangement, photo is charged with the responsibility and budgeted to provide direct support to printing, graphics, audio, and

FIGURE 7   Floor Plan B

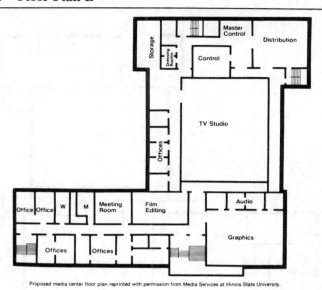

Proposed media center floor plan reprinted with permission from Media Services at Illinois State University.

television. Outside clients may have to pay for services, or an internal budget based on projected volume may be available. Although clients can still work directly with individual services, at least now they are all in one location.

In many cases the maximum centralization shown in Figure 5 will not be possible because of local environmental influences. A good compromise in a move toward centralization would be consolidation of all production areas where there is a large similar commitment to specialized staff, equipment, materials, and space. Such areas could include graphics, television, photography, maintenance, printing, and audio. The construction or remodeling cost for production areas is usually much higher than for other facilities in a media center.

Efficient design and use of floor space are additional advantages of the physically centralized media center. A good floor plan can recognize important relationships between service departments and provide for proper work flow. Several media center floor plans are shown in Figures 6 through 9, to illustrate these relationships. In Figure 6, Floor Plan A, television and audio production are located next to each other. This is done to foster the relationship that exists between television and audio in terms of projects, production talent, engineering personnel, and some equipment. A current trend is also evident in Figure 6. Master control, used primarily for engineering functions, was a relatively small area in comparison with the television studio. Now, master control tends to be much larger, accommodating editing and tape duplication. This trend

FIGURE 8   Floor Plan C

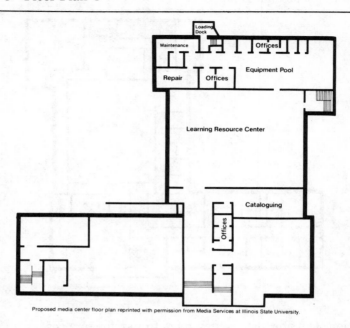

Proposed media center floor plan reprinted with permission from Media Services at Illinois State University.

has been caused by rapid development of small electronic field production equipment for productions outside the studio and simultaneous acceptance of the ¾-inch and ½-inch videocassette formats for editing and duplication. Technological developments can cause sudden changes in space requirements, so be flexible when planning facilities.

Figure 7, Floor Plan B, goes even further, with television, audio, graphics, and film all located close together. This takes advantage of the support role graphics has with audio for tape/slide programs, with television for slides and camera cards, and with film for animation flats. Audio also has support roles with film and television for specialized sound tracks. The floor plan also allows for maximum utilization of facilities. The television studio can double as a large recording studio for audio and interior shooting studio for film.

Figure 8, Floor Plan C, also shows how a good floor plan can maintain important relationships between different service areas. The learning resource center is the hub, housing program preview, audiovisual equipment practice stations, and individualized lesson playback areas. The equipment pool, along with circulating audiovisual equipment, provides immediate backup during equipment breakdowns in the learning resource center. This is especially important in programs where users are on a tight schedule to complete a certain number of mediated modules. Special short-term equipment setups can be easily handled

FIGURE 9   Floor Plan D

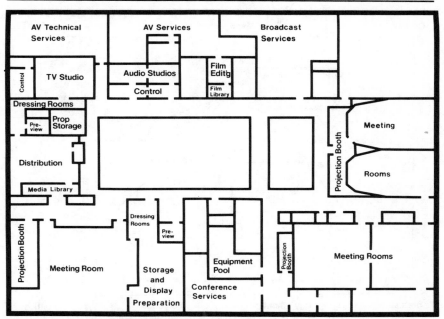

with the equipment pool next door. Repair and first-line maintenance support the equipment pool and playback equipment located in the learning resource center.

Figure 9, Floor Plan D, provides for maximum cooperation between production and service areas. Television, audio, and film are all located close together in one corner of the floor. The equipment pool for circulation of equipment is across the hall. However, this floor plan goes even further by placing three major meeting rooms with projection booth facilities on the same floor. Attractive and functional meeting rooms are strategically located close to the equipment pool. Therefore, this floor design fosters desirable cooperation among media support areas while providing meetings with a full complement of those same services. The close proximity of support services to meeting rooms is also a very realistic design for those last-minute emergencies during meetings.

Physical consolidation also promotes maximum utilization of resources. One center brings together personnel with a wide variety of media competence. This can stimulate interdependence and a teamwork approach in which the most appropriate medium is selected and used to accomplish a particular task. Individual personalities can either make or break teamwork potential, but at least the centralized media center

FIGURE 10   Hybrid Organization: Centralization with Decentralization

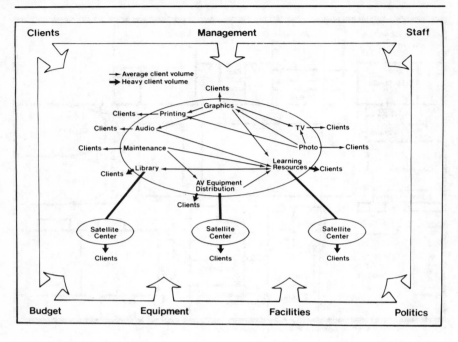

provides opportunities for such positive dynamics. This teamwork philosophy also provides media staff with professional growth opportunities through wide exposure to a variety of media approaches. By sheer size, the centralized media center allows for lateral and vertical promotional opportunities. Look back at Figures 1 and 2 and see the numerous promotional opportunities inherent in the organizational structure of a large media center. In Figure 1, someone could start as an artist with several promotional options: (1) coordinator of graphics, (2) coordinator of some related area such as television or audio, and (3) director of the center. Media people often branch out from their original interest, and large, centralized centers facilitate this growth. Clients also benefit, since the centralized approach provides one-stop, convenient service, no matter how complex the program.

The major advantages of a centralized media center seem to correct most of the disadvantages of decentralization. A stronger feeling of interdependence among media service departments is nurtured by consolidating these areas administratively and physically. Administrative consolidation provides overall budget control, eliminates some of the budget competition which can hinder objective media utilization, and fosters coordinated development. This last point is crucial since no organization can afford to have independent media departments going off in separate directions with little coordination towards common goals. The fractionized, uncoordinated growth of separate media areas results in unnecessary duplication of personnel, equipment, materials, and space, along with ineffective use of limited budgets. The centralized media center allows for the efficient use of these resources.

Despite all the advantages, the centralized structure is not without some disadvantages. The consolidated center may be labeled impersonal and because of a centralized location may eliminate easy "next-door" type service. Client convenience is directly proportional to how much a service will be used and cannot be ignored in the media center organizational structure.

Hybrid Organization: Centralization with Decentralization

Since there are inherent advantages and disadvantages in both decentralized and centralized media organizations, it is possible to apply the positive aspects of each to achieve the best of both worlds. All media departments can be centralized for overall control and efficient use of resources, while establishing decentralized satellite centers close to specific client needs. Figure 10 is exactly like Figure 5 except for the addition of satellite centers. Decentralization through satellite centers is used for library materials, audiovisual equipment distribution, and learning resources. All these services have bold arrows, indicating heavy client volume; therefore, they should be located conveniently close to client needs. Each satellite is custom designed to meet local requirements. A typical satellite center for equipment distribution might be located in a building with equipment specifically selected to serve the needs of that building. One satellite center might have a heavy concentration of 16mm projectors while another may have more slide projectors, depending on local need. Satellite centers offer another advantage in usually being relatively small so clients receive personalized service which was one of the only major advantages of the decentralized organizational structure. No media center organizational structure is ideal, but this hybrid approach allows for incorporating the advantages of centralization and decentralization.

MANAGEMENT TIPS

Once an organizational structure has been selected that fits local needs, certain operational guidelines should be employed to ensure maximum service. The following tips are proven, management techniques that can be used in any media center.

Develop Accountability

In order for any media center to operate smoothly, the entire workload must be logically subdivided into operating units. A manager who cannot successfully delegate authority will not survive. There must be an exact definition of responsibilities for two reasons: (1) to ensure each job is done quickly and efficiently and (2) to ensure staff members know the range of their responsibilities. Such a division of authority will only be successful if employees are held accountable for their performance. The organizational chart of a media center should show who reports to whom and, more important, how the work actually gets done. If informal operational arrangements evolve, several possibilities might exist: (1) someone is taking on additional duties; (2) someone is not doing their required work, forcing others to take up the load; and/or (3) the formal organizational structure no longer satisfies client needs, resulting in the use of makeshift solutions. Under any circumstances, well-planned lines of accountability must exist for management to quickly isolate problems or acknowledge accomplishments. Correction or praise should be done with dispatch. All too often the media manager is quick to criticize and slow to praise. Judicious use of accountability keeps everyone on the right track so confusion and inefficient use of time can be avoided.

Guarantee Consistency

Consistent service is crucial yet difficult to achieve. People using a media center must be able to depend on a high level of service. Most clients, when faced with the options of sporadic service ranging from very good to mediocre, or consistent average service, would choose the latter. At least with consistent average service they can plan accordingly and know the job will be completed on the date promised within quality standards. Achieving consistent service is difficult when considering the number of variables at work. These variables include fluctuations in budget, productivity of personnel, objectives of the organization, operating costs, and service volume. A continual balancing act is required between all factors influencing productivity to maintain a dependable level of service. The manager must plan ahead and project the correct mix of the above variables to ensure consistent service. Some techniques for maintaining consistent service will be covered in this chapter, since with consistency comes increased patronage.

Analyze Staff Volume

The quantity and quality of staff directly affects media center services. Variety of staff talent can heavily influence productivity, especially in production areas such as television, audio, and graphics. One artist may

FIGURE 11   Staff Productivity Formula

Formula	$\dfrac{\text{Annual Service Volume}}{\text{Total Staff}}$ = Average Volume per Staff Member
Example Graphic Production	$\dfrac{9000 \text{ Units of Finished Artwork}}{3 \text{ Artists}}$ = 3000 Units per Artist
Example Media Equipment Distribution	$\dfrac{12000 \text{ Requests for Media Equipment}}{2 \text{ Staff Members}}$ = 6000 Requests per Staff Member

work slowly yet turn out high quality work while another produces rapidly but quality may suffer. The pace and quality of each artist may also be heavily influenced by the type of assignment. Artists, just like other production people, usually have certain things they can do very well. Some managers will assign jobs based on what a person can do best, while other managers believe in giving production people a variety of assignments to broaden their experience. With either approach, an average production volume per position must emerge, in order to project future personnel requirements.

The easiest way to determine staff productivity is to take the total service volume in a given time frame and divide by the number of staff. Figure 11 shows this basic formula and how it can be applied in two very different operations. In each case, annual output for the area is divided by total number of staff to derive the average volume per staff member. If a graphics area turned out nine thousand units of finished art work in a year with a staff of three artists, the average staff load is three thousand units of art work per year. (A unit is defined as a single piece of art work such as a slide or overhead transparency.) True, this average does not take into account individual staff differences or the complexity of each task, but at least it provides a starting point for estimating average staff productivity. The same approach can work for other areas such as distribution of media equipment. In media equipment distribution, twelve thousand requests divided by two staff members yields an average staff load of six thousand requests per year. Once the average yearly production load per staff member has been established, a media manager can start to make intelligent decisions about staff requirements for special assignments or projected future volume.

Establish Growth Projections

Being able to determine how much production or service volume a staff member generates per year is a key to other valuable management

FIGURE 12   Personnel Projections

			1 yr	2 yr	3 yr	4 yr	5 yr
Graphic Production	Output	Units per Year Projected 20% Increase	9,000	10,800	12,960	15,552	18,662
		Turnaround Time[a] [days]	5	8	5	5	5
	Staff	Existing	3	3	3	4	5
		New	0	|.6|	1.3	1.1	1.2
		Total	3	3	4	5	6
Media Equipment Distribution	Output	Orders Processed Projected 25% Increase	12,000	15,000	18,750	23,437	29,296
		Turnaround Time [days]	1	2	1	2.5	1.5
	Staff	Existing	2	2	2	3	3
		New	0	|.5|	1.1	|.9|	1.8
		Total	2	2	3	3	4

[a] Total time required between submission and completion of a service request.

information. However, service quality should not be totally sacrificed for increased productivity. An appropriate balance must be maintained between output and quality.

A manager must know the average service volume each staff member can generate to make accurate growth projections. This involves a two-step process: (1) determining the factors which will influence future volume, and (2) dividing projected volume by average staff output to determine personnel requirements. There are several sources of information that can help when estimating future service volume: (1) the average increase in media center productivity experienced over several representative years and (2) expected growth of the institution the media center serves. In education, a projected increased enrollment could have a major impact on a media center. Introduction of a new product in business may require media center support for the development of sales training packages. A new state law requiring additional training for nurses may necessitate increased program acquisitions and playback facilities for the media center in a hospital. Of course, the reverse is also true with a decline in service needs which might result in media center cutbacks. The media manager must be kept informed of all pertinent developments that rely on media support.

Once volume levels are projected, staff needs can be estimated. In Figure 12, graphic production has estimated an annual growth of 20 percent so the units of finished art work will jump from 9,000 to 10,800 in the second year. Dividing 3,000 units of finished art work per artist into 10,800 results in 3.6 positions. Since the 0.6 is not a full position, graphics decides to wait a year before adding a position. By not adding the position, the turnaround time—total time required between submission and completion of a service request—jumps from five to eight days. Service requests for graphics that once took an average of five days to complete now take eight. To guarantee consistent service, it is better to increase staff when the need first becomes apparent rather than when the maximum staff load is reached. But then, who in a media center works under ideal circumstances? So, during the third year, the projected volume has jumped to 12,960 and is divided by 3,000 units per artist, to substantiate the need for at least one additional artist. Notice with the additional artist the turnaround time drops back to five days.

This approach to matching required staff with projected demand can be used for most operating units in a media center. The same approach is used in Figure 12 for media equipment distribution, charged with the responsibility to supply equipment. The only differences are type of work, average volume per staff member, and turnaround time. In Figure 12, media equipment distribution can tolerate only a one-day turnaround time. People usually desire very quick service because they do not plan ahead when ordering media equipment. Ideally it would be nice to have a turnaround time of several hours for any service; however, this chapter is not about the ideal but rather what is cost-effective and realistic. Having a large staff of artists available to complete all requests on an immediate basis is convenient but not cost-effective. Therefore, each media center operating unit must establish an acceptable balance between work volume and turnaround time. Figure 12 also shows the strong relationship between available staff, service volume, and turnaround time, given an adequate operating budget and staff working at maximum efficiency. As volume goes up and staff size remains the same, turnaround time increases. When staff is increased to keep pace with volume, turnaround time drops. This relationship must be kept in mind when projecting future volume and staff.

Do Not Overcommit

Most people in a media field enjoy providing service. They should be able to empathize with people's needs. Add to this a clientele that desires more services than are possible, and overcommitment can become the short-term cure for a long-term illness. Overcommitment starts out as a one-time exception to usual policies to help a client in dire need. No harm done? Wrong. A basic axiom of media management: the exception quickly becomes the rule. All of a sudden the media manager who made an exception for one particular case is now bombarded by other requests for the "new service." When the manager explains it was a one-time exception, there are quick retorts of special treatment for certain favorites. If the manager does not yield to the pressure, clients always go to that reliable standby, nasty phone calls followed by even stronger letters to everyone in a position of authority. If the manager succumbs to the pressure, the center quickly starts trying to provide an added service without proper provisions. The result is poor, inconsistent service with the very same clients complaining. Another media management axiom: you can't please all the people all the time, and some people you can't please at all. The moral of the story is not to overcommit in the zeal to help a client. Such action usually means the manager will win the battle but lose the war. Overcommitment, in the long run, becomes more of a disservice to clients because of an inability to deliver services on a dependable basis.

Certainly, there will be times when exceptions represent the only logical method for solving a problem. Just remember to weigh carefully the consequences of initiating exceptions to well-developed policies before making a decision. The art of knowing when exceptions are appropriate is a management skill that usually only comes with experience.

A postscript is also required on the overcommitment problem. There must be a good understandable reason why a request cannot be filled. Just saying, "It has always been our policy, " or "We have never done it," is not fair to the client. Chances of adverse client reaction drop considerably when reasons are given for not being able to complete the request. Sincerity and courtesy can also help, along with giving options for filling the request which do fall within the capability of the center.

Determine Accurate Turnaround Time

As noted earlier, turnaround time is the total time required between submission and completion of a service request. The relationship of turnaround time to other factors that affect productivity was discussed in connection with Figure 12. Turnaround time can fluctuate radically, depending on available staff and service volume. The only point to be made here is to establish a realistic turnaround time that satisfies the needs of most clients and the operational capability of the center. A realistic turnaround time for clients will vary with the service unit. For graphics, three to five days might be required, while equipment distribution might be able to fill a request within several hours. If the turnaround time does not meet the schedules and deadlines of most clients, a more realistic time frame for completing service requests must be established. Conversely, a turnaround time which is great for clients but causes chaos within the center is also unsatisfactory. A balance must be established between client needs and what is realistically possible. These two factors should establish an accurate turnaround time which then must be maintained. Once validity has been established for a turnaround time, clients will develop their planning around this time frame. A manager must do everything possible to guarantee a stated turnaround time to build credibility for the center.

Standardize Operational Procedures

A media manager maintains a constant balancing act with such variables as adequate staff, sufficient budget, desirable turnaround time, and fluctuations in service volume. When service volume and turnaround time increase, the usual answer is more staff and budget. A better solution is increased efficiency. The only way to achieve optimum efficiency is to standardize all possible operational procedures. Standardizing operational procedures means establishing the simplest set of procedures to accomplish a specific task with the least expenditure of personnel time, equipment, and materials. Each aspect of this definition is important. The simpler the procedure, the easier it is for personnel to learn and execute it, resulting in fewer errors. Mistakes and confusion quickly convert to increased personnel time. Standardization means establishing set procedures for certain types of routine jobs to save time. Assembly-line concepts should be employed whenever possible. Developing service forms that get the job done is a very important part of standardization. Keeping personnel, equipment, and materials expenditures to a minimum can release these same valuable resources for increased volume

Every effort should be made to standardize all routine requests. There are probably days when a manager feels there is no such thing as a routine request! But, objectively, routine requests probably make up 80 to 90 percent of the total service volume. Figure 13 (page 120) shows the impact of standardization using a hypothetical example. Moving from center to right, using standardized procedures, 80 percent of the routine requests can be efficiently processed in 40 percent of the available staff time, a conversion factor of one-half. This allows for special requests that are different from the norm, requiring additional staff time. An arbitrary conversion factor of three is used for special requests, resulting in 60 percent of the staff time. The ability to make time for special requests is very important since usually positive client feedback is not for satisfactory delivery of expected services, but for completion of special, out-of-the-ordinary requests. This is human nature. People who request an

FIGURE 13   Standardized Versus Non-Standardized Operating Procedures

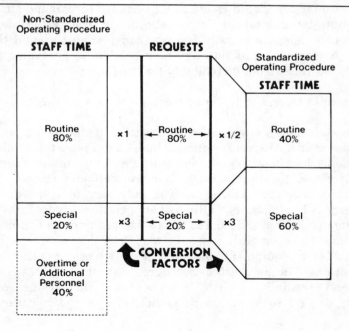

advertised service cannot be expected to be overly laudatory when they receive these services. If an airline flies a passenger from Chicago to New York on time, without incident, there is no cause for celebration, because this is what the airline is paid to do. Indeed, management might be alarmed if a passenger writes a complimentary letter about going from Chicago to New York safely on their airline! But, if the airline exerts extra effort to ensure that a passenger makes a connecting flight, there might be cause for enthusiastic praise.

Please note special requests are different from exceptions leading to overcommitment mentioned earlier. *Special requests* are within the capability of the media center, whereas *exceptions* require inordinate measures beyond normal procedures for completion. A special request might require a wide-angle lens on a slide projector instead of the standard lens. An exception might involve changing the standard lenses for wide-angle lenses on fifty projectors in fifteen locations with one day of notice! The latter request might only be accomplished through extensive personnel overtime and renting forty-five wide-angle lenses and, therefore, is not a service within the capability of the center.

Moving from center to left in Figure 13, the repercussions of not standardizing the routine can be seen. Here, 80 percent of the regular requests take 80 percent of the available staff time, using one as a conversion factor. Sufficient time for special requests is not created through standardizing routine jobs. The only way to create additional time for special requests is to consider overtime for personnel or hiring additional staff. Each approach can unnecessarily increase the budget. Efficient standardized operating procedures can create the additional time required for special projects without a commensurate budget increase.

Although many examples of standardization exist, here are some tips for improved efficiency:

- Group similar requests for processing.
- Use assembly-line techniques.
- Keep all processing steps close together.
- Design service forms that are easy to use.
- Keep alternatives to a minimum.
- Use compatible equipment.

When considering the organizational structure for a single media service department or a large media center, one must be aware of the influential impact of the local environment. Clients, management, staff, politics, facilities, equipment, and budget all have a direct influence on the organization of the media center. A realistic view of the environment will help determine what organizational options are possible. Decentralized media departments make possible personalized services, conveniently close to client needs, but lack management control and wise use of space, equipment, materials, and staff. Centralized organization establishes proper management control and cost-effective use of facilities but may lack personalized service, close to client needs. A hybrid approach can combine the advantages of centralized control with satellite centers to provide services close to clients. A well-conceived media center reflects as much as possible the surrounding environmental needs. Desirable qualities for any media center organization should include accountability, consistent service, reliable turnaround time, and standardized procedures for efficient use of staff.

Managing the Library's Media Services Department

Marie Bruce

MANAGEMENT responsibilities of the library's media services are of prime importance in establishing and maintaining a reliable, efficient service center for staff and users. There are many styles of management available to the media librarian, ranging from the autocratic, whereby all authority is vested in the manager to free-rein management, whereby all authority rests with the group and the manager is a colleague. Perhaps the most effective form of management in media services is participatory management.

Participatory management is the process of actively involving all subordinates in the decision-making process. The media librarian shares his or her authority with employees and uses their expertise and creativity to obtain the greatest gains in morale and work production. Participatory management is practiced at all levels of media services and includes both professional and non-professional staff. When subordinates are actually a part of the decision-making process, they become ego-involved and attempt to make the best contribution possible for a decision that is as good as it can be.[1]

Staff size of media services is unimportant when it comes to using participatory management because of the importance of the individual in the process of decision-making. The emphasis is on involving staff members in setting goals and objectives, contributing to decision-making, and establishing their accountability for their work. Participatory management provides an opportunity to bring out the best in everyone.

For example, allowing the audio department to control the decisions for productions results in a greater diversity of productions, a sense of commitment to the project being done, and a sense of responsibility for and accountability to the completed project.

Participatory management also frees the media librarian from the daily task of close supervision to allow him or her to concentrate on other matters. The same advantages can be applied to television, photography, printing, distribution, engineering, and graphic units. Equipment distribution can be effectively handled by an employee instead of consuming a manager's time and by so doing, personnel are concerned about correct scheduling, delivery, and maintenance of the equipment. In participatory management it becomes important for the staff to see that all aspects of equipment are taken care of efficiently since they are accountable for it. This strategy can be applied to the maintenance unit as well.

Media librarians, paraprofessionals, and clerical and student workers are involved in participatory management at their various operating levels and in effect make the director's job easier. Using participatory management as a technique of managing the media department does not result in diminished authority for the media librarian. One of the biggest unfounded fears of a media manager is the loss of authority when using participatory management. The media manager still makes decisions and exercises his or her authority, but the employees also share in decision-making and are accountable for those decisions.

FORMS OF PARTICIPATORY MANAGEMENT

Participatory management takes four basic forms:[3]

Work groups—individuals working together to achieve a set of goals, led by a manager who shares his or her authority.

Matrix or project management—restructuring of total organization to have employees work on specific projects that have a definite beginning and end. Particularly useful when there are changing project requirements over a period of time.

Collective bargaining—represents the employees in their desire for input into wages, hours, terms, and conditions of employment. Acts as a link between employer and the employee.

Industrial democracy—organization is characteristic of a democracy where emphasis is on representing employees' desires when making decisions over owner desires. Employees are heavily involved in running the organization.

The library's media department is most suited to project management and work groups since much of the work is done on an individual project basis for other departments in the library. A great deal of flexibility is possible in these two types of management allowing for different units of media services to combine for specific projects as the need arises. They in turn can be disbanded and/or regrouped for each new production request to achieve maximum production output of the staff. No other forms of management allow for such diversity in managing while at the same time making the utmost use of the staff's capabilities and creativity.

MEANS OF IMPLEMENTING PARTICIPATORY MANAGEMENT

The change to a system of participatory management in a media department cannot be accomplished overnight. It is a slow and steady process that requires adequate training of media librarians and supervisors as well as substantial preparation of the employees who may not have experienced participatory management and are reluctant, for many reasons, to see the change. It should also be noted that the more autocratic the media department director is, the more difficult it will be to implement participatory management.

The first step in implementing participatory management is to know yourself, the media department, and media. Media department directors must know their own abilities as well as their weaknesses and have a commitment for self-improvement in participatory management. Knowing employees of the department is important so that there is an understanding of their strengths and weaknesses. In order to increase productivity you must be aware of how to improve your relationship with employees to promote teamwork. The attitudes of staff members towards implementing participatory management can make or break its success. Just as importantly, the media librarian must have a strong working knowledge of media. A demonstrated ability to produce and to supervise production of media in its various formats to meet users' needs is vital to the efficient operations of media services.

Do you really know your supervisor? It is absolutely essential to know your supervisor's expectations, strengths, weaknesses, role and status in the organization, and attitudes toward participation.

Knowledge of the media services and its role in the library is also essential. What does the department do well? How are people treated and what is the morale and climate within this area? You must know how the users view the department and whether or not your service and reputation hold any rank. In what areas is there need for improvement?

Analysis of yourself as a manager, your employees, and your supervisor requires a great deal of time, thought, and effort—a thorough investigation of operations is essential for the media librarian who is considering participatory management for the department.

After completing the department/employee analysis you can begin to identify the barriers that may affect the successful implementation of participatory management. The media director must identify specific barriers in each area (i.e., manager, subordinate, supervisor, organizational), and then determine why the barrier exists and how important it is in blocking participatory management. Next you must consider if it is possible to remove the barriers and the financial and psychological costs for doing so.[4] The following list shows the possible barriers to participatory management.[5]

Organizational Barriers

Tradition
Organizational philosophies and values
Quality of policy and procedures
Quality of personnel
Organization structure
Lack of a supportive climate
Lack of a reward system for participatory management

Subordinate Barriers

Lack of competence in participatory management
Lack of desire
Lack of content knowledge
Lack of awareness that participatory management is expected
Fear
  a. of failure
  b. of rocking the boat
  c. of group ostracism
  d. of making work harder
  e. of eliminating jobs

Managerial Barriers

Manager's habits
Not understanding participatory management
Theory X assumptions
Lack of security
Fear
  a. of giving up power
  b. of being overshadowed
  c. of lack of discipline
  d. of loss of personal visibility
  e. that job won't get done

Situational Barriers

Time constraints
Task constraints
Environmental influences

Barriers to participatory management are usually of three types: controllable, uncontrollable, and capable of being influenced. Controllable factors may include inadequate time with employees as well as lack of training and interest on the part of employees. Uncontrollable factors may be the reputation of the department, structure of media services, and the area of service within the entire library. Barriers you can influence may be lack of knowledge in participatory management by a supervisor, organizational climate that is not conducive to participatory management, and a supervisor who is unwilling to spend the time to practice participatory management.[6]

The next step in moving towards participatory management in media services is to choose a course of action that will remove the barriers you can most easily control. With each small success the next barrier will become easier to remove and as your credibility improves, successive barriers will be even easier to overcome.

Once the barriers are removed it is time to begin implementing participatory management in the media department. The traditional ways of accomplishing this are discussed below.

Supportive Climate—the employees of the media department are supported, respected, and trusted by the media department management. Likewise, employees show a high level of trust of the media librarian. This is achieved through fair and equitable dealings by both parties with regard to employee rights, discipline, salary, raises, and promotions.

Suggestion Systems—media managers should encourage submission of oral and written suggestions and should acknowledge all of them. These suggestions should be considered carefully by the media librarian and when adopted the credit should be given to the person responsible for the idea.

Open Door Communications—set aside specific, uninterrupted times to talk to your employees. Try to make staff feel at ease by: removing barriers of counters and desks (body language may speak louder than your words), visiting them in their offices or the lounge instead of yours, and talking *with* them—not *to* them. Take notes on their suggestions, follow them up, and then report back to the employee on the action taken.

Brainstorming Sessions—use staff groups from different media units to generate ideas and problem-solving solutions. This should occur in an informal, non-threatening situation so that employees do not fear criticism during or after the session by either managers or other staff members.

Task Forces and Committees—these can be established to study specific issues to make recommendations to the decision-makers for their resolution. The group should: know exactly what is expected of them, have sufficient authority and resources to carry out their responsibility, be chosen for their expertise and interest, and have a specific time limit to propose actions. Meetings should be carefully planned and follow a detailed agenda. Unit supervisors should consider recommendations of the committee.

In preparing a media unit for a change to participatory management, especially in a previously autocratic structure, some non-traditional means of preparation may be necessary. Methods which are individual-centered and adopted for use by organizations are sensitivity (T-group) training, transactional analysis, and transcendental meditation. Each of these methods has as its focus improvement of individual attitudes and behavior rather than improvement of the media unit. Great care is necessary in use of these techniques, and adequate training of the manager to carry out these functions is imperative. Group-oriented methods of preparation for participatory management include Delphi Method; Nominal Group Training; Family Grouping; and Multivariate Analysis, Participation, and Structure. A full discussion of these methods may be found in William Anthony's book *Participative Management*.[7]

Proper training of the director interested in implementing participatory management in media services cannot be overly stressed. Management training in participatory management is possible, and some of the more traditional methods include management training and education; human relations training; leadership and motivation training; communications training; and management by objectives.

For example, the management by objectives technique (MBO) is a process by which the media services director and the staff jointly participate in setting goals, objectives, activities, and target dates for completion as well as the performance evaluations as they relate to the established objectives. By so doing, it is possible to evaluate the service's performance objectively according to the preestablished criteria of the entire staff. The advantages of MBO are: 1) subordinates help in planning and controlling their own performance, which results in high motivation to do a top job and 2) the integration of the service's goals, productivity, accomplishments, human resources, social interactions, and accountability.[8]

SOME CAUTIONS IN USING PARTICIPATORY MANAGEMENT

The traditional means of practicing participatory management have been available to media directors for quite some time, yet few departments practice this form of management. Reasons for this are many: lack of a systematic, coordinated means of implementation; lack of desire or training on the part of the director; it is costly and time-consuming compared to individual decision-making; there is sometimes group pressure to conformity; the quality of decisions is sometimes lower than if made by one or two experts; some compromise in decisions because of the group situation; and reluctance by the staff to become involved in the decision-making process.[9]

ADVANTAGES OF USING PARTICIPATORY MANAGEMENT IN MEDIA SERVICES

In addition to satisfying hierarchical needs of individuals, participatory management has other benefits to the individual as well as to the media department. These advantages include:

- Increased productivity.
- Better problem definition, greater range of alternatives, and better understanding of adverse consequences.
- Greater commitment to the task, the team, and the organization.
- Increased cooperation with members of management and staff.
- Reduced turnover and absenteeism.
- Individual growth opportunities increased from sharing of insight and knowledge.
- Higher trust level.
- Reduced complaints and grievances.
- Greater acceptance of changes.
- Decreased organization politics.[10]

It is hard to argue the value of these assets in the operations of a media department, and any system which provides a means for so doing should be seriously investigated.

CHARACTERISTICS OF PARTICIPATORY MANAGERS

How can a media person be identified as a participatory manager? A study conducted by Larry Greiner in the early 1970s rated thirty-nine leadership characteristics based on what 157 managers thought of participatory management. Managers chose ten characteristics they felt were representative of a participatory manager. Ranked in order, from the most to the least participative, the characteristics are:

1. Gives subordinates a share in decision-making.
2. Keeps subordinates informed of the true situation, good or bad, under all circumstances.
3. Stays aware of the state of the organization's morale and does everything possible to make it high.
4. Is easily approachable.
5. Counsels, trains, and develops subordinates.
6. Communicates effectively with subordinates.
7. Shows thoughtfulness and consideration of others.
8. Is willing to make changes in ways of doing things.
9. Is willing to support subordinates even when they make mistakes.
10. Expresses appreciation when a subordinate does a good job.[11]

Additionally, Maurice Marchant has stated that a participatory administrator should be goal-oriented, have the ability to listen and be patient, demonstrate a proficiency in keeping staff and committees focused on their assigned missions to prevent sidetracking, and an ability to tell when talk has lost its value and the time for decision and action has arrived.[12] None of these skills is easily learned; this is perhaps one of the biggest reasons participatory management is not widely practiced in libraries.

HISTORICAL DEVELOPMENT OF PARTICIPATORY MANAGEMENT

Participatory management was originally termed "democratic management," and talk of it as a management technique first surfaced in the 1920s. In 1934, J.P. Danton urged the increased use of staff resources for personnel decisions and policy formation since the management trends in library settings were towards democratic styles. Herbert Goldhor in 1940 maintained that staff should be consulted regularly in managing. Two years later, R. E. Krug stated that democratic management fostered high morale, and open communication, and that employee contributions were not yet at their peak for contributing to administration. R.A. Uleveling believed that staff should participate in decisions as long as the chief administrator was responsible for the final decision that was made. The Library of Congress adopted employee participation in 1950 and developed a handbook for its widespread use. Then, in 1952, Amy Winslow encouraged, "bottom-up management" for suggestions, staff committees, opinion polls, communications, and staff organizations. The next year she discussed staff participation in terms of the why, how, how soon, and how far.[13]

THE HAWTHORNE EXPERIMENTS

Participatory management in the general field of management was brought to the forefront with the Hawthorne experiments. Workers who performed routine tasks were involved in varying environmental conditions of light, heat, room color, rest time, and different pay scales. Almost every change the workers experienced resulted in an increase in productivity, and physical conditions did not appear to have any effect on that productivity. Mayo, an industrial psychologist who conducted the experiments, discovered that workers' attitudes are directly related to productivity. When given attention, the workers developed a feeling of importance. Mayo demonstrated that humane and respectful treatment of employees pays for itself in the long run. To summarize the Hawthorne experiments:

1. People's social and psychological needs are every bit as effective as motivators as money.
2. The social interaction of the work group is as influential as the organization of the actual work task.
3. The human factor cannot be ignored in any accurate management planning.[14]

DOUGLAS MCGREGOR'S THEORY X AND THEORY Y

Further development of participatory management occurred when Douglas McGregor established two theories which considered the behavior of people in an organization. He called these Theory X and Theory Y. A manager of Theory X is an autocratic leader and allows minimal participation in decision-making. The manager of Theory X makes the following assumptions:

1. The average person dislikes work and will avoid it to the extent possible.
2. Most people have to be threatened or forced to make the effort necessary to accomplish organizational goals.
3. The average individual is basically passive and prefers to be directed rather than to assume any risk or responsibility. Above all else he or she prefers security.[14]

TABLE 1 Likert's System 4 Approach

Organizational Elements	Characterized as
1. Leadership processes	1. High task involvement along with a high degree of personal relationships with subordinates.
2. Motivational forces	2. Economic rewards based on a compensation system developed through participation.
3. Communication processes	3. Uninhibited flow of information along all levels—upward, downward, and horizontally.
4. Interaction-influence processes	4. High degree of mutual confidence and trust between superiors and subordinates. As a result, employees are more willing to accept responsibility. The informal organization is accepted as part of the formal organization and recognized as being supportive in achieving organizational goals.
5. Decision-making	5. Widely dispersed and well-integrated throughout the organization. Employees participate in setting goals, work methods, and decisions relating to their work.
6. Control processes	6. Wide responsibility for review and control at all organizational levels. Responsibility for implementation of the control function is dispersed to all employees throughout the entire organization. Control data, such as productivity, costs, etc., are used for self-guidance and coordinated problem-solving, rather than entirely for punitive purposes.

(From Robert L. Trewatha and M. Gene Newport, *Management: Functions and Behavior.* Dallas: Business Pub., Inc., 1976, p. 431.)

On the other hand, a Theory Y manager believes in a democratic style of leadership and participation in decision-making. This representative of participatory management makes these assumptions about workers:

1. Work is as natural to people as play or rest and, therefore, is not avoided.
2. Self-motivation and inherent satisfaction in work will be forthcoming in situations where the individual is committed to organizational goals. Hence, coercion is not the only form of influence that can be used to motivate.
3. Commitment is a crucial factor in motivation and is a function of the rewards coming from it.

4. The average individual learns to accept and even seek responsibility, given the proper environment.
5. Contrary to popular stereotypes, the ability to be creative and innovative in the solution of organization problems is widely, not narrowly, distributed in the population.
6. In modern organizations human intellectual potentialities are just partially realized.[15]

LIKERT'S SYSTEM 4 APPROACH

Another approach to participatory management was developed by Rensis Likert, who believes that human assets are more important than physical assets. Managers show an interest in the employees' ideas, personal problems, and problems at work. He calls his approach System 4 and the manager helps workers to develop their capabilities, and acts as a linking pin between the group and others in the organization. Employees participate in decision-making, setting of goals, and creating new ideas.[17] (See Table 1.)

FIGURE 1   Maslow's Hierarchy of Needs

Level V	Self-actualization (achievement)
Level IV	Self-esteem (ego satisfaction, status)
Level III	Love and Belongingness (acceptance and security)
Level II	Safety Needs (protection from physical harm)
Level I	Physiological Needs (food, water, rest, shelter, etc.)

(From William P. Anthony, *Participative Management*. Reading, Mass.: Addison-Wesley, 1978, p. 20.)

MASLOW'S HIERARCHY OF NEEDS

Why do workers wish to become involved in decision-making? Maslow postulated that people have a hierarchy of human needs and after reaching a reasonable level of satisfaction of their basic physiological and security needs, they become aware of the need to have some control over their own lives. Maslow's hierarchy of needs (Figure 1 above) shows the development of workers from Level I to V, and as each need is satisfied, they progressively move up the scale.

The major points of Maslow's theory are:

1. Individuals have the same hierarchy of needs but are at different levels of need satisfaction.
2. A person will not move up the hierarchy until the level below is substantially satisfied.
3. Needs are satisfied in different quantities among individuals. What is satisfactory for one at 85 percent may only reach satisfaction for another at the 95 percent level.
4. The higher level needs are infinite in levels of satisfaction while lower order needs tend to be finite in their degree of satisfaction.[18]

FIGURE 2   Work Environment Needs

Level V	Challenging and Rewarding Work
Level IV	Promotions
Level III	Work Group Relations
Level II	Seniority Systems
Level I	Pay and Benefits Plans

(From Richard Tellier, *Operations Management: Fundamental Concepts and Methods.* New York: Harper and Row, 1978, p. 216.)

In industrialized countries, most lower order needs are easily satisfied, and people are concerned with meeting higher level needs. One of the greatest need-satisfying devices a director can use is to provide employees with the chance to participate in the decision-making process. This opportunity provides the employee with the chance to achieve ego satisfaction and self-actualization, the two highest levels of need in Maslow's hierarchy.

It is important for the director of the media department to understand the values of Maslow's hierarchy of needs. Figure 2 illustrates how Maslow's theory of needs can be translated into terms of the work environment.

HERZBERG'S TWO-FACTOR THEORY

Related to Maslow's hierarchy of needs is Herzberg's two-factor theory of work motivation. Extensive research by Herzberg in the 1950s ascertained which aspects of work affect employees' job satisfaction and how this occurs. He found two independent factors, motivator and hygiene, that determine attitudes and motivation towards work. The motivator factor comprises various aspects of the job that tend to satisfy employees by their presence but do not create dissatisfaction by their absence, for example, achievement, responsibility, recognition, challenge, and accomplishment. Hygiene, the second factor, will dissatisfy the employee if it is below standards expected by the employee but will not increase satisfaction if present in sufficient amounts. These dissatisfiers include pay, type of supervision, working conditions, and other external aspects of the job.[19]

Herzberg concluded that in order to ensure job satisfaction and productivity, managers need to maximize motivator and hygiene factors. This can be accomplished through adequate pay, comfortable working conditions, and supervision suited to the levels of the employees. At the same time, a means of providing the worker with responsibility, recognition, challenge, and a sense of achievement should also be implemented. Participatory management can be used to provide all these factors. The use of participatory management changed the work by giving employees more responsibility and the chance for individual growth. Increased motivation and creativity occur when using participatory management and the opportunity for promotion is enhanced.

THE MANAGERIAL GRID

Blake and Mouton[20] developed a model of leadership styles during the 1960s which they call the Managerial Grid. Managers are rated on their concerns for people and concerns for production on a scale of 1 (minimum) to 9 (maximum). The ideal for any manager is to achieve a 9.9 score. This indicates a maximum concern for production as well as a maximum concern for people. In this state of management the individuals' personal goals and the organization's objectives are obtained through a cooperative effort.

RESEARCH IN PARTICIPATORY MANAGEMENT IN LIBRARIES

In libraries, the idea of participatory management is a popular topic, but there is more discussion about it than there is research. The following is a summary of research conducted since 1970. Little research was done before that point.

In 1970, Louise Galloway[21] outlined how the Louisville University Library Faculty participated in the search for and selection of a new director of libraries. M.P. Marchant[22] demonstrated how staff job satisfaction was greatly affected by managerial style and the opportunity to participate in the decision-making process in 1971. He used a simplified version of the Likert model. Booz, Allen and Hamilton, Inc.[23] did a case study of the organization and staffing of the libraries of Columbia University in 1972 and gave an account of a method for involving librarians in the operation of a university library. Henry Rotan Stewart's[24] doctoral dissertation of 1972 studied staff participation in the management of twelve college libraries to determine the relationship to library performance characteristics. He found no direct relationship but concluded that staff morale was affected by managerial style; participatory management produced the happiest staff.

In 1973 Louis Kaplan[25] did some studies which reported how faculty status for librarians affected the process of participation, whether the academic department was the best model for librarians, and how unskilled introduction of participation could lead to disillusionment. Jane Flener[26] studied the staff participation in the decision-making process at ten large university libraries. Less than half the staff were interested in becoming involved in participatory management as recently as 1973.

Two years later, Louis Kaplan[27] reported study results which showed the absence of a positive relationship between job satisfaction and improvement performance. Then in 1976 Leeds Polytechnic Library School[28] completed a two-year study to determine preferences of management style. Women constituted 76 percent of the study. No choices for an autocratic manager were made; 16 percent chose participatory management; and 70 percent wanted their opinions on decisions sought. However, they made it clear that they wanted leaders to lead and managers to manage. Louis Kaplan[29] in 1977 concluded from empirical studies that the typical high level manager does not use just one decision-making style, but lets the situation dictate the mode, and a considerable amount of subordinate decision-sharing is permitted.

In 1977 Victoria Mussman[30] conducted a study of managerial style (Likert's 4 system) as perceived by the library director and by three full-time professional and clerical staff at five public libraries in the Los Angeles area. The same year, M.B. Wood[31] outlined a successful participation venture in a health services library. During 1979, M. Tunley[32] began researching the development of a participative style of management in public library service which is to be a ten-year study.

RECOMMENDATIONS

M.J. O'Connor has outlined some recommendations for libraries considering participatory management in the near future:

> There is a need to measure effectiveness of various new management techniques recently developed in library systems and . . . to research into the changing role of management in terms of participation.

There is a need to develop research on the human factor in library management across a wide range of individual topics, e.g., the role of communication, approaches to motivation, styles of leadership, impact of personality, alienation and job satisfaction, effect of group dynamics on productivity, etc.

There is a need to examine the role of leadership in library management with particular reference to the leaders' relationship with staff, users, and the larger organization within which the library functions.

A particularly neglected area in library research is the field of team management and team coordination, and this could be a subject for applied research.[33]

Media departments, no matter how large or small, should be encouraged to implement participatory management. Whatever their subject expertise, media librarians responsible for managing employees should be adequately trained to implement and effectively administer participatory management.

Adequate preparation of the media department and the staff before undertaking participatory management is vital to its success. Removal of barriers to participatory management is the first step in building a successful management program and is the media librarian's responsibility.

Changes in media services operations and methods may be suggested by staff members to obtain more efficient service. This directly benefits the user and also results in improved staff morale, production, and satisfaction.

Participatory management, when properly used, allows for innovation and creativity, resulting in a healthy work atmosphere in which the employee identifies with the media department and the library.

At its highest and most functional level, participatory management should be used by the staff for the selection and retention of the administrators who govern them. Using participatory management at that level strengthens the commitment of the library and/or administration to participatory management, and at the same time demonstrates to the employees the importance of their input into the total operations of the media department.[34]

Participatory management as a style of leadership for today's media librarian can be one of the most productive forms of management in terms of employee satisfaction, morale, productivity, and commitment to the organization. The advantages for the administrator, employee, and media department in using participatory management far outweigh the few drawbacks. Every person at every level in the system benefits from participatory management and through this leadership can grow to his or her fullest potential. There is no greater satisfaction possible in management than to view the results of a successfully implemented venture into participatory management.

References

1. William P. Anthony, *Participative Management*. (Reading, Mass.: Addison-Wesley, 1978), p. 3.
2. William T. Schmid, *Media Center Management*. (New York: Hastings House Publishers, 1980), p. 18.
3. Anthony, pp. 53-59.
4. Ibid., pp. 51-52.
5. Ibid., p. 48.
6. Ibid., p. 52.
7. Ibid., pp. 74-75.
8. Robert L. Trewatha and M. Gene Newport, *Management: Functions and Behavior*. (Dallas: Business Pub. Inc., 1976), pp. 422-24.
9. Rollin Glaser and Christine Glaser, *Managing by Design*. (Reading, Mass.: Addison-Wesley, 1981), p. 113. and James M. Banovetz, "Decision Making," in *Local Public Library Administration*, 2nd ed. by Ellen Altman, ed. (Chicago: American Library Association, 1980), pp. 93-94.
10. Edwin Flippo, *Management: A Behavioral Approach*, 2nd ed. (Boston: Allyn and Bacon, 1970), p. 352. and Glaser, *Managing by Design*, p. 112.
11. Robert Albanese, *Management: Towards Accountability for Performance*. (Homewood, Ill.: Richard D. Irwin, Inc., 1975), pp. 495-96.
12. Maurice P. Marchant, "Participative Management, Job Satisfaction and Service," *Library Journal* 107(8) (April 15, 1982), p. 784.
13. Amy Winslow, "Supervision and Morale," *Library Trends* 3 (July 1954), pp. 42-43.
14. Robert M. Fulmer, *The New Management*, 2nd ed. (New York: Macmillan, 1978), pp. 36-37.
15. Theo Haimann, *Management in the Modern Organization*, 2nd ed. (Boston: Houghton Mifflin, 1974), p. 346.
16. Ibid., pp. 346-47.
17. Robert B. Buchele, *The Management of Business and Public Organizations*. (New York: McGraw-Hill, 1977), p. 178.
18. Anthony, pp. 20-21.
19. Richard Tellier, *Operations Management: Fundamental Concepts and Methods*. (New York: Harper and Row, 1978), pp. 216-17.
20. Robert L. Blake and Jane Mouton, *The New Managerial Grid*. (Houston: Gulf Publishing Co., 1978).
21. Louise Galloway, "Academic Librarians Participate in the Selection of a Director of Libraries," *College and Research Libraries* 33 (3) (May 1972),. 220-21.
22. Maurice P. Marchant, *Participative Management in Academic Libraries*. (Westport, Conn.: Greenwood Press, 1976).

23. Booz, Allen and Hamilton, Inc., "Organization and Staffing of the Libraries of Columbia University," *Association of Research Libraries*, (1972), 27.
24. Henry Stewart, *Staff Participation in the Management of College Libraries*. (Ann Arbor, Mich.: University Microfilms, 1972).
25. Louis Kaplan, "Participation: Some Basic Considerations on the Theme of Academe," *College and Research Libraries* 34(5), (September 1973), 235-41.
26. Jane G. Flener, "Staff Participation in Management in Large University Libraries," *College and Research Libraries* 34(4), (July 1973), 275-79.
27. Louis Kaplan, "The Literature of Participation: From Optimism to Realism," *College and Research Libraries* 36(6) (November 1975), 473-79.
28. J. Hall, "Student Preference for Leadership Styles," *Assistant Librarian* 72 (June 1979), 86-88.
29. Louis Kaplan, "On Decision Sharing in Libraries: How Much Do We Know?" *College and Research Libraries* 38(1) (January 1977), 25-31.
30. Victoria Mussman, "Managerial Style in the Small Public Library," *California Librarian* 13(3) (July 1978), 7-20.
31. Muriel B. Wood, "The Organization of Successful Participative Management in a Health Science Library," *Bulletin of the Medical Library Association* 65(2) (April 1977), 216-23.
32. Malcolm Tunley, *Public Library Management: The Development of a Participative Style of Management*. (Wales: Current Research at College of Librarianship Wales, 1979).
33. M.J. O'Connor, *Research in Library Management* (Wetherby, West Yorkshire: British Library Research and Development Reports, 1980).
34. John Ellison, "Selecting Library Administrators—the Key to Participatory Management," *The Library College Experimenter* 3(2) (May 1977), 19-24.

Systematic Analysis (Marketing) and Media Librarians

John W. Ellison and Kathy J. Lucisano

By their very nature, non-print materials are the most dynamic of library services. Effective media use elicits participation, and continued media use hangs on the degree of participation. Media people who work outside of libraries almost universally accept as fact that information about and input from their users are essential ingredients for their success: witness Nielsen, Arbitron, and other market rating services. They would never think of establishing a collection, developing a program, or creating a presentation without first knowing the needs and wants of their audience. Unfortunately, this is not always the case in the library profession.

A great deal of confusion seems to exist in library circles when terms like "community analysis," "needs assessment," and "marketing" are used. The anti-marketing editorials in several issues of *Library Journal* best illustrate this clash. Each term has received its share of character assassination without much attempt at understanding the term or the potential value of the technique in helping media librarians better understand the information needs of their library community, be it academic, school, special, or public.

Each of these terms represents a technique that media librarians can use to systematically assess the information needs of a community. None of these techniques is unique to library planning; in fact, each has been adapted from successful business or sociological perspectives to provide libraries with powerful planning tools. *Community analysis* has been defined as "an organized, thoughtfully planned attempt to determine the factors, such as population characteristics, cultural and educational facilities, occupational patterns, community goals and attitudes, and administrative structure that relate to the library."[1] This process usually includes collecting the demographic information from secondary sources prior to analysis. *Needs assessment* is a systematic process of collecting, organizing, and analyzing primary data about the information needs and interests of the potential library community. This process is usually characterized by a systematic survey of primary sources——the people.

Needs assessment can be defined as the determination of the quantitative and qualitative extent of the discrepancies between what is and what is required. *Marketing,* according to Philip Kotler, the author of *Marketing for Nonprofit Organizations,* and the leading authority on the subject, " . . .is the analysis, planning, implementation, evaluation, evolution, and control of carefully formulated programs designed to bring about voluntary exchanges of values with target markets for the purpose of achieving organizational objectives. It relies heavily on designing the organization's offering in terms of the market's needs and desires, and on using effective pricing, communication, and distribution to inform, motivate, and service markets."[2]

Marketing systematically examines the product (benefits being sought), price (all costs including time, effort, and hassle), place (locations and hours), promotion (advertising and non-personal communication), and people (all personal forms of comunication like word of mouth) variables as a unified package. For libraries, marketing attempts to systematically determine the needs and wants of the potential community and adapt the library for the purpose of making better decisions. The key here is "exchange of values" rather than money. Market segments or homogeneous groups are identified, rather than the total library community. This variable or element approach to a library community provides an opportunity for specific identification of needs and the direct impact these needs may have on the library. It differs from both community analysis and needs assessment in that it systematically examines all aspects of the library service process rather than just data collection. That is why the word "mix" is so often found in the marketing literature.

The essence of professional media librarianship is being able to listen and allow the library community to directly define their own needs and so allow individual users unrestricted access to information. It is important to keep this definition as broad as possible.

The tools of community analysis, needs assessment, and marketing in no way remove any part of the media librarian's primary obligation to meet the community's information needs. They simply provide three somewhat different systematic approaches to information collection, organization, and analysis prior to formal planning, decision-making, and implementation. The systems selected to accomplish the goal of formally learning about the library community should not detract a library board and library staff from broadly defining the type of services needed in a library community. These three approaches represent only one aspect of an overall management input process and are not an end in themselves.

The remainder of this chapter will discuss the rationale for systematic library community analysis using a combination of the three techniques discussed thus far. The term *systematic analysis* will be used since aspects of all three tools combined will be examined.

RATIONALE

Systematic analysis still seems to be a strange and difficult animal to libraries almost forty years after the American Library Association established minimum standards for public library service and charged that:

> Continuous and periodic study of its community should be made by the library in order to know people, groups, and institutions thoroughly, and to keep up with development and changes.[3]

There is much agreement, though, that such analysis is essential to library planning. Geddes defined library planning as involving the following steps:

- research to develop characteristics on the history of the community and the library,
- analysis of the community with a projection of trends,
- analysis of present services and the budget,
- study of the . . .collection,
- evaluation measured by acceptable standards,
- a series of conclusions and remarks

but stresses that "before any determination of need can be made, there must be a clear-cut knowledge of what the community has been, what it is, and most particularly, what it will be,"[4] This integrated approach to planning thorough library service has been reflected by several landmark library-community studies, including those by Martin (*Library Response to Urban Change. A Study of the Chicago Public Library*, ALA, 1969, and *Deiches Fund Studies of Public Library Service*, Enoch Pratt Free Library, 1963-74) and Monat (*The Public Library and its Community: A Study of the Impact of Library Services in Five Pennsylvania Cities*, Pennsylvania State University, 1967). Palmour has stressed this need for consolidated library projection in *A Planning Process for Public Libraries* (ALA, 1980).

But in reality, the media librarian need look no further than the vast array of technologies available to find the rationale for systematic analysis. The key word is change. Technology, media, and in turn library service all change regularly. To add another dimension, the library community itself changes continually: new users, regular users with new information needs, users newly literate in a new technology all attest to the situation. Systematic analysis is essential to keep the media library relevant.

WHY SYSTEMATIC ANALYSIS?

"Why do we need the information garnered from systematic analysis?" asked the Library-Community Project, working to establish adult education as a foremost library service in the late 1950s. Their answer is most succinct:

> to be able to know what books and other materials we need to buy.
> to enable us to set goals for planning and services.
> to help us to plan special activities.
> to enable us to develop an effective public relations program.
> to establish working relationships with other agencies and organizations.
> to give the staff insight and understanding about the community based on concrete knowledge.
> to determine the library's educational role in the community.[5]

Essentially, their conclusion was that such information is essential to effective library service.

To add to this pragmatic list, we can turn to Martin's observations of 16 years earlier:

> to provide information for locating and planning a new library building . . .
> to guide staff-selection policies . . .
> to introduce a new assistant to the area . . .
> to provide information to persons interested in the locality.[6]

Croneberger and Luck pointed out that systematic analysis can prove an ongoing evaluation of the library's services:

> The purpose of community analysis should not be only to facilitate the achievement of goals and objectives, but also to provide updated information to challenge these goals and objectives as current responses by the library to changing public.[7]

Allie Beth Martin has suggested systematic analysis on the basis of the accountability principle.[8] For public libraries, at least, users and potential users hold the purse strings, and therefore the library is accountable to their information needs. Such an argument could hold true as well for corporate, school, and academic libraries to some extent.

Systematic analysis would provide not only an ongoing integration of the community and its needs in the media library's planning process, but also a continual expression of interest by the library in the community itself.

Systematic analysis is also a way to democratize the library, to make sure that it remains "public." Martin aptly put it:

> A community survey is a means for overcoming the narrow social base on which much public library service rests. Libraries justify many books and services in terms of "demand." For a public institution in a democracy this is one possible basis for determining policy. It is a questionable basis, however, when demand is taken as the request of the minority who happens to be attracted by present library offerings. . . .Community analysis identifies the total community picture as against that part of the picture which can be seen from the library's information desk.[9]

Of course, the other extreme has been advocated by librarians from Berelson to Childers: that a thorough community study is necessary to determine which groups will be served and which will not since, as Berelson believes, the library "cannot be all things to all men, (and) must decide what things it will be to whom."[10]

A study done for the Detroit Public Library from 1970 to 1976 disclosed some important lessons in community analysis which reinforce the case for formal systematic analysis:

> First, assumptions about a community based solely on superficial appearances can be painfully inaccurate.
> The second lesson is that in the task of community analysis it is essential to recognize groups, organizations, and other agencies as part of the community.
> The third instructive point to be drawn from this experience is that different approaches are needed for different communities and subgroups within them.[11]

Systematic analysis is necessary, then, for a variety of practical reasons: materials selection, library planning, public relations, staff-enhancement, evaluation, finance, and a true understanding of the community's real and potential information needs. And to move beyond minimum standards, it should be remembered that knowing the information needs and wants of the community and fulfilling them is only the beginning. Both in planning and actual service, the media librarian's ability to anticipate trends, demands, and interests by all segments of the community is an important factor in achieving dynamic library service. Only by continuously assessing services, users, and non-users—

—and by keeping up with change in the library and community—can the media librarian's role as coordinator of needs and resources be realized.

Systematic analysis is part of the larger management system: yours. It narrows the gap between "ideal" and "real"; between "means" and "end"; and, as such, is an indicator for the future. Finally, it helps provide a sense of appropriate timing, priorities, and evaluation.

RESISTANCE, OR WHY WE SELDOM DO IT

In the face of some very convincing arguments for systematic analysis, it is still a great puzzle why librarians—media or otherwise—do not undertake such projects. Over the years several authors have brought this problem to the profession's attention, but to no avail. In library school everyone learns the axiom about "knowing thy community," yet few courses teach "how."

The literature provides several conjectures as to why systematic analysis is largely ignored; perhaps the one most often cited is money. In the inflationary years since 1960, costs alone would seem prohibitive to many public officials and librarians. Lack of budget appropriations for library planning is one major reason that systematic analysis does not occur. Costs involved in study of the community can run up quickly in terms of staff time. McClarren cites "preoccupation with the day-to-day requirements of operating a library when community analysis requires a long-term commitment of time and attitudes"[12] as a hurdle to overcome.

Another barrier to execution of systematic analysis is a common belief that there is no real need for such activity.

> Knowledge of the community to be served is essential as a foundation for library management, yet libraries have not always practiced community analysis, and some still do not. The reason for this is that librarians may be unaware of deficiencies in their community knowledge.[13]

Palmour cites a reason this may be so: a reliance on fulfillment of national standards "in lieu of setting specific goals and objectives for their own library."[14] He goes on to point out the belief that measurement of library services is not a built-in part of regular library management, and that such a process could lean heavily toward endorsement of systematic analysis in many cases.

Other observations indicate a belief that librarians are simply unprepared to conduct systematic analysis. Bewley points out that ALA minimum standards calling for continuous community study suggest that libraries consult outside agencies in carrying out the task, thus reflecting the "growing awareness that libraries are generally ill-equipped to undertake complex data-gathering for a thorough community survey."[15]

One reason for this "growing awareness" is the lack of any sort of systematic analysis handbooks for the profession, as numerous authors have pointed out. (*A Planning Process for Public Libraries* is a recent exception.) Still, most guides to community study and needs assessment, as well as marketing techniques, are part of other professions' literatures, not our own. Librarians seem reluctant to cross these barriers.

It is also plausible that the lack of the nation's library schools' emphasis on systematic analysis in coursework is a contributor to this ignorance. As late as 1976, Vainstein indicated that no accredited schools of librarianship had courses devoted to systematic analysis, and only a small percentage carried units of courses on the topic, concluding that "the teaching of community analysis appears to be an implicit rather than explicit component of the curriculum,"[16] and she recommended a reconsideration of this issue in curriculum planning.

These feelings of inability to carry out systematic analysis have contributed to a larger, more serious problem: apathy towards the community on the part of many librarians, according to the 1972 Public Library Association *Strategy for Public Library Change*.[17] Such a widespread attitude obviously is a great impediment to change, as well as to the accomplishment of systematic analysis.

Media librarians also may not know how to analyze the data based on the results of a systematic survey. The volume of numbers and comments can overwhelm the novice, or results may be reported which are not actually based on the survey findings.

The lack of systematic studies may also reflect the quality of the job some media librarians are doing. Fear of finding that a community does not support a library may prevent investigation in the realm of needs.

Owens has suggested that libraries have paid dearly for rejecting community participation: "Such resistance to citizen participation has proved costly. Community support and political influence which might have been gained have not been available during crucial budget decision-making processes."[18] The reason for rejecting community participation, according to Bundy, is that libraries have a role to play in raising the social consciousness of people and helping reform the institutions that are supposed to serve them.[19] However, she feels that this notion is not within the realm of most librarians' thinking.

A reform in all of these attitudes is long overdue.

SOME POSITIVE SIGNS

Some progress has been seen in recent years to offset these observations. To foster the need for more research in systematic analysis and to coordinate continuing education programs on community study, the Community Analysis Research Institute opened its doors under Roger Greer in 1979. The Institute, now located at the University of Southern California's Graduate School of Librarianship, was conceived to establish

> . . .new methods for tailoring library and related human services to specific needs of communities . . .and to . . .provide a national focal point for research, instruction, publication, and information dissemination on community analysis and information needs relating to the planning of library and allied services.[20]

"Non-traditional" library service such as information referral and all phases of media resources, as emphasized in the last decade, have created a new awareness for systematic analysis. Obviously, such services cannot be carried out without the effective study of the community's information needs and resources, and surely implies constant library/community interaction. As more libraries integrate such services into their facilities, systematic analysis will become more of a reality.

State librarians in several states have acknowledged the need for further training in this area of service. In the last few years, Mississippi and Illinois have sponsored leading workshops on the need for and the techniques of systematic analysis.

An emphasis in the last decade on systematic analysis in non-public libraries and information centers (notably, a study done at the National Library of Medicine, among others)[21] has helped to bring the problem to the forefront. Both the Philadelphia Project[22] and the Deiches Fund Studies in Baltimore examined community segments in relation to both school and public libraries. This continued effort on the part of other libraries to examine their services in relation to the entire population of their potential users will put more pressure on libraries to join in.

A SAMPLE CHECKLIST

The argument has been made for the paramount significance of systematic analysis for the media library, and pointed to the serious absence of real studies in the face of poor guidance and training. Formal analysis demands statistical data-gathering as well as a methodical formula for opinions and comments. The following checklist of questions will help the media librarian with the practical aspect of a study.

Community Analysis

Demographic Data: Who are the library's users? Who are the non-users? Factors involved here for public, school, and academic libraries could include age, sex, occupation, income, education, and ethnic background, among many others. In a special library, what departments are users or non-users? Are they employees or "outsiders"? Some of the above-mentioned factors might also have impact.

Geographic data: Where is the library located? How does it (can it) interact with other social agencies, institutions, departments, or other libraries? Where does it fit in its own peculiar administrative structure? How does it relate to other governing bodies?

Needs Assessment

Information wants: What do library users ask for? Current or old material? In what medium? At what level? A wide range of subjects or narrow? What do non-users want? Where do they go to fill their information wants? Do they buy records, tapes, films, books? Do they rent them? If these materials were available in the library, would they become users? Is there a technology barrier? A sophistication barrier? What can be done to eliminate these barriers?

Information needs: What do library users tend to need most? What subjects are they interested in? What media do they tend to use? How open are they to other media or other subjects? How sophisticated are they? What kinds of subjects and media might they expect to turn to in a year? In two years? How restricted do they feel in accessing subjects and media? Do they know what their information needs are? Do non-users recognize their needs? Can the library make them aware of their needs? — or determine their needs?

Information resources: What subject areas are available in the library? In what media? At what level? What subjects and media are available in other libraries? What is the gap in these combined resources? What equipment is available to accommodate the media? What can be done to close the gap between users and non-users? Between needs that are satisfied and unsatisfied?

Marketing

Product: What is the mission of the library? Does it correspond to the information needs and wants of the community? Can the library actually provide the product? If not, what can be done to change the situation? Does the community realize what product is available?

Price: Is the community given the lowest possible price in terms of time and effort? Is their time and effort in the library cost-effective? What about the price to the library? Can processes or planning be streamlined to make the product more available?

Place: Are hours of operation and location(s) satisfactory to the community? Do non-users need a change here in order to become users? Is a change feasible? Would a change benefit the product?

Promotion: How is the library reaching the community? Is there appeal to both users and non-users? What is the library's image? How can non-users be drawn into the library? Are the product, price, place, and people emphasized? What about the total range of library resources? Is there any chance of misleading promotion?

People: How does the library staff interact with users and non-users? Is there interaction? Is the product always emphasized? Is each of these techniques assimilated into the library's goals and objectives as well as planning procedures? Is the process ongoing? Can the library see results? Can the results be measured? Are the results used in library decision-making?

CONCLUSIONS AND RECOMMENDATIONS

Despite what has been demonstrated to be a relatively easy, inexpensive, interesting, and vital aspect of librarianship, media libraries and librarians by and large do not study their communities because of problems they interpret in terms of money, time, irrelevancy, poor training, low motivation, or fear of results. This is a real problem for the profession revolving around the user's need to know.

Several general conclusions can be drawn:

- Systematic analysis is an essential part of library service.
- To be effective, systematic analysis must be a continuous, cyclical effort.
- In the 1980s more than ever before, because of decreasing budgets and increasing competition in the information market, libraries must be accountable to their publics.
- Many studies have shown systematic analysis to be inexpensive and extremely productive; the time and money expended were felt to be more than cost-effective.

- By following the leads in other professions (the social sciences and business administration), media librarians can supplement the small amount of literature in their field to produce a solid base of instruction in systematic analysis.

Some recommendations must be made for profession. Some professional organization or even a library school must initiate a campaign emphasizing the importance of systematic analysis and offering more workshops on the task. Librarians and their boards must recognize the need for effective and continuous systematic analysis and commit their staff and budgets to the effort. Library schools must place a stronger emphasis not only on the philosophical importance of systematic analysis but also on the practical techniques for carrying it out. Above all, media librarians must take to heart their role in the information marketplace, initiate ongoing systematic analysis in their libraries, use its results in day-to-day library planning, and realize more dynamic library service than ever before.

References

1. Phyllis Van Orden and Edith B. Phillips, eds., *Background Readings in Building Library Collections*, 2d ed. (Metuchen, N.J.: Scarecrow Press, 1979), p. 109.
2. Philip Kotler, *Marketing for Nonprofit Organizations*. (Englewood Cliffs, N.J.: Prentice-Hall, 1975),
3. American Library Association, Public Library Division, Coordinating Committee on Revision of Public Library Standards. *Public Library Service: A Guide to Evaluation, With Minimum Standards*. (Chicago: American Library Association, 1956), p. 25.
4. Andrew Geddes, "Public Libraries." In Maurice F. Tauber and Irlene Roemer Stephens, eds. *Library Surveys*. (New York: Columbia University Press, 1967), p. 181.
5. American Library Association, Library-Community Project Headquarters Staff, *Studying the Community*. (Chicago: American Library Association, 1960), p. 12.
6. Lowell A. Martin, "Community Analysis for the Library." In Leon Carnovsky and Lowell A. Martin, eds. *The Library in the Community*. (Chicago: University of Chicago Press, 1944), p. 204.
7. Robert Croneberger and Carolyn Luck, "Analyzing Community Human Information Needs: A Case Study." *Library Trends* 24, January 1976, p. 515.
8. Allie Beth Martin, "Studying the Community: An Overview." *Library Trends* 24, January 1976, p. 434.
9. Martin, p. 203.
10. Bernard Berelson, *The Library's Public*. (New York: Columbia University, Press), 1949 (University Microfilm facsimile, 1974), p. 134.
11. Croneberger and Luck, p. 522.

12. Robert R. McClarren, "The Community Analysis Survey." In *Library Buildings: Innovation for Changing Needs*. (Chicago: American Library Association, 1972), p. 135.
13. Charles Evans, "A History of Community Analysis in American Librarianship." *Library Trends* 24, January 1976, p. 442.
14. Vernon E. Palmour, "Planning in Public Libraries." *Drexel Library Quarterly* 13, July 1977, p. 34.
15. Lois M. Bewley, "The Public Library and the Planning Agency." *ALA Bulletin* 61, September 1967, p. 969.
16. Rose Vainstein, "Teaching the Elements of Community Analysis: Problems and Opportunities." *Library Trends* 24, January 1976, p. 597.
17. American Library Association, Public Library Association. *A Strategy for Public Library Change: Proposed Public Library Goals-Feasibility Study*. (Chicago: American Library Association, 1956).
18. Major Owens, "Local Leadership, Politics and Public Support." In Clara S. Jones, ed. *Public Library Information and Referral Service*, p. 138.
19. Mary Lee Bundy, *Helping People Take Control: The Public Library's Mission in a Democracy*. Washington, D.C.: Urban Information Interpreters, Inc., 1980, p. 2.
20. "Community Information Institute Set Up at Denver U." *Library Journal* 103, January 1, 1978, p. 12.
21. Paula M. Strain, "Engineering Libraries: A User Survey." *Library Journal* 98, May 1, 1973, p. 1446.
22. J.Q. Benford, "The Philadelphia Project: 10,000 Students Tell What's Wrong and What's Right About Their School and Public Libraries." *Library Journal* 96, June 15, 1971, p. 2041.

Cost Analysis of
Media Services

Patricia Ann Coty

B ELT-TIGHTENING budgets and increased competition for shrinking funds make it imperative that the media librarian justify expenditures in a meaningful way. Private industry has been successfully using cost-benefit methods for evaluation for many years; educational and social institutions have been seriously exploring these methods for the last two or three decades, with mixed success.

Currently, many educational and social institutions seek to define their goals in quantitative or measurable terms, hoping to create a standard method to evaluate their accomplishments. This can be difficult, because the output of educational and social agencies is difficult to define, much less measure. In industry, success is measured in terms of profit. Non-profit educational and social institutions, however, do not have such a yardstick and must measure their success in terms of their apparent worth to society. Additional non-monetary factors such as public image, prestige, and employee morale must also be considered.

For the media librarian, it is important to find ways to measure the effectiveness of the media center in terms related to the concerns that the parent organization considers to be important. If you are working in private industry, you must show quantitatively and persuasively that the media center in contributing positively to profit earnings. For instance, you may be producing or purchasing audiovisual programs for sales training, safety consciousness, or management effectiveness. It is your responsibility to gather evidence that these programs have had positive results and have been worth their cost.

The media librarian in a social or government institution must also identify a standard by which media services can be measured. Is your organization dealing with the dissemination of information to the public? Are they engaged in research on a medical matter? Basically, you must show how valuable media services are in reaching this goal, and that the dollars spent on media services are well-spent.

Media librarians in educational institutions must measure their effectiveness in educational terms. How is the media center improving education? The media librarian should effectively argue the merits of the media center in ways that are understood by educational administrators, showing that media services are essential for optimal learning to occur at your institution.

Although the fundamental necessity of media services may not seem to be an issue to the media librarian, it often is to the administrator and should not be overlooked. Never assume that your administration is aware of how valuable you are; rather, make a consistent effort to communicate your successes to those in charge of the purse strings. This is especially urgent in organizations with shrinking funds. Administrators make funding decisions based on their perceptions of the cost-benefits of each department, and it is the responsibility of the media librarian to do everything possible to influence that perception in a positive way. The benefits of media services must be presented in a clear, concise, and cost-related fashion. Cost data, once compiled and analyzed, should reflect the impact of media services on the goals of the library and the organization as a whole.

Because media services are commonly budgeted as separate line items in the library budget, administrators may find it easy to single them out if budget cuts are necessary. In addition, the initial capital outlay for equipment may not readily appear to be cost-effective. Because the media budget is an easy target for cuts, it is imperative that the media librarian gather and analyze all pertinent data, and be prepared at all times to justify budget allocations. In addition to keeping administrators aware of the benefits of the media center, such as data will be invaluable to the media librarian for use in program evaluation and future planning.

Whereas simple utilization data such as "requests filled" and "clients served" are useful for the media librarian as aids in scheduling work flow, they alone do not address the question of cost-benefit, which is usually most important to the administrator making budgetary decisions. Utilization figures alone may not show the relationship between the media center and the overall mission of the library. Media utilization data must be integrated with cost data and related to the library's goals.

MEASURING COSTS

How do we measure costs? The costs of media service fall into three basic categories: capital expenditures, direct costs, and indirect costs. Capital expenditures are the funds necessary for the establishment of the media center, such as construction costs and the initial outlay for equipment and furniture. Direct costs include on-going labor, material, and service costs and any other expenses that can be specifically attributed to the purchase or production of programs offered through the media center. Indirect costs, or overhead, are the costs that are required for the general operation of the media center but cannot be assigned to any one program, for example, salaries for administrative and secretarial support, office supplies, utilities, etc.

First, we will look at the calculation of direct costs. Following is an example of the direct cost summary for a set of three overhead transparencies produced in the media center.

MATERIALS

	Cost per item	×	Number of items	=	Total
Presstype lettering	$1.50		3		$4.50
Paper	.20		3		.60
Diazo film	.30		3		.90
Art supplies	1.00		3		3.00
Total					$9.00

LABOR

	Cost per hour	×	Number of hours	=	Total
Graphic artist	$8.00		1		$ 8.00
Graphic arts aide	$ 4.25		1		$ 4.25
Total					$12.25

COST SUMMARY

Materials	$ 9.00
Labor (direct)	12.25
Total direct cost	$21.25

Direct costs are usually fairly straightforward and not difficult to calculate. They are most useful when calculated on a per-item basis.

Indirect costs, which are not shown on the above summary, could easily double the total cost of producing the overhead transparencies. Whereas direct costs can and should be tabulated as each individual program is produced or purchased, indirect costs are much more difficult to assign. These are some of the expenses that would be included in calculating indirect costs for media services:

• Labor costs of administrative, clerical, and secretarial staff and non-productive labor costs of other staff (e.g., vacation, sick leave, breaks, etc.)
• Office supplies

- Replacement spare parts and equipment maintenance
- Facility upkeep (utilities, cleaning, security, etc.)
- Telephone, computer, and other communication costs
- Staff training, research, testing

All of these costs can be totaled to arrive at an annual overhead expense. From this annual expense, there are several different approaches that can be used for incorporating these indirect costs into the budget summary. One method is to divide the total annual indirect cost by the number of hours that media services were available throughout the year, to arrive at an average indirect cost per hour. This is then added to the direct cost of an item depending on how much time was involved in producing or obtaining the item. Another method is to divide the annual indirect cost by the annual direct cost budget, to arrive at a ratio which could be multiplied into each direct dollar spent on purchasing or producing an item. A third method is to divide the number of projects completed in the year into the annual indirect cost total, to arrive at a per-unit indirect surcharge.

The media librarian must decide whether indirect costs will be included in cost analyses, and if so, how they will be calculated.[1] It is at least as important that the media librarian be aware of indirect costs, since they are often substantial and are very much a part of the administrator's perception of the cost of operating the media center.

Capital expenditures, the third type of cost mentioned earlier, include the costs of establishing the media center, such as the planning and construction of the facility, the purchase of equipment and initial software, and initial staff recruitment and training. If capital costs are to be included in a cost analysis, it is necessary to depreciate them over a period of years. The number of years may differ among the various items included, based on the anticipated useful life of the building or equipment. This yearly depreciation amount could then be added to the cost analysis in a method similar to that chosen for the distribution of the indirect costs.

For the media librarian who is trying to establish a new media center, capital expenditures are a major concern and must be closely examined. For the media librarian working in an established media center, capital cost consideration will probably be limited to current and projected equipment purchases, facility construction, and staffing changes. Capital expenditures require careful justification, since they often imply change or expansion. Direct and indirect costs, on the other hand, connote maintenance of the status quo.

For precise cost analysis, cost records must be kept throughout the year, as individual programs and services are purchased or produced. If individual cost records are not kept, costs may be estimated by dividing the total number of programs acquired throughout the year into the total media services budget, to arrive at a per-unit cost. However, since the cost of individual media varies widely (for instance, compare the cost of producing three overhead transparencies with the cost of purchasing an audiocassette or a one-hour color videotape), this information will not be as useful.

CALCULATING COST-BENEFIT

Useful information can be obtained by dividing yearly media services costs with the number of users who have benefited from the department's program. If records are tabulated throughout the year reflecting the number of program users, an average cost-per-user can be calculated. This can be extremely useful to the administrator, as well as to the media librarian, in evaluating the cost-benefit of the media center. Because audiovisual programs are often used with large audiences, or used repeatedly with individuals or small groups, it can often be shown that the overall cost of media services is actually small when reduced to per-capita outlays.

Keeping data on program users can yield other interesting information. If the backgrounds of the users are known, users can be grouped by age, department, or grade level. This information can be helpful to the media librarian not only in planning future acquisitions or productions but also in justifying budget requests to administrators. Usage of media center services can also be tabulated according to media types, which may provide information on the preferences of the library community. This can be very helpful when it is time to plan for additional equipment purchases, especially if you can show that the demand for certain items is difficult to fill because of equipment constraints. Another benefit of tabulating use of the media center broken down by media types is that it provides justification for maintenance and repair expenditures.

Thus far we have discussed ways to collect and manipulate data on program costs, but one must keep in mind that cost alone does not in any way reflect the quality of the programming, or the effect of media center services on users' performances, attitudes, or abilities. It is the examination of these effects, in relation to cost, that determines the cost-benefit of the media center, and its programs. For instance, one program may be more costly per user than another, yet it might also be more effective as a learning tool. On the other hand, cost is not an automatic indicator of quality; the more expensive program might be less suited to the task at hand. Cost-effective studies can determine the least expensive method for meeting a stated minimal objective, but they cannot judge the merits of different methods so far as they exceed minimal objectives or create additional benefits. We have to be aware of the minimum degree of effectiveness that is acceptable in a given situation and the various options available to meet that particular need. Programs that exceed the minimum degree of effectiveness should be considered in terms of their additional cost, and a decision should be made as to whether the institution can afford to pay for benefits in excess of the minimum requirement.

In proposing the use of media as a cost-effective solution to a stated need, one must first identify the need, then list all possible options and methods available to meet the need and estimate costs of the various options, and, finally, make a decision based on such factors as cost, time constraints, user characteristics, and intellectual strategy (e.g., is motion necessary? Color? Is it for group or individual use?). In many cases, the need for specific intellectual strategy will be the deciding factor, even though it may presume a higher cost than other options. In some cases, time constraints will necessitate more costly programming than might otherwise have been possible, especially if staff must be paid overtime and items have to be handled "rush."

Even when constraints preclude choosing the most cost-effective method of media services, the media librarian can still find ways to assure common-sense spending. For instance, suppose that videotape has been identified as the required format for a specific project. The media librarian can at this point work to address these questions: Is there a suitable program already on the market, and if so, should this program be borrowed, rented, or purchased? If nothing suitable exists, is this something that can be produced in-house, or should a commercial production company be hired? Should we plan for repeated individual or small group showings, or will it be broadcast?

Because some audiovisual materials have a higher average unit cost than books and other print media, a greater amount of attention is often given to the selection of these materials, and the media center collection may thus be used much more than the print collection. Seldom do most of us sit down and read a book before we order it for the library; we usually rely on the recommendation of a reviewer or potential user or, worse yet, a publisher's advertisement. With audiovisual materials, however, we often view and/or hear programs in full, and even test them on sample audiences before committing ourselves to purchase. Additionally, media are usually produced or purchased only if they are perceived to meet a specific, identified need, whereas books are sometimes bought to "fill in" or "round out" a collection without identifying a specific need for a title.

The result of these common differences in selection policies can mean that the media collection is more tailored to the needs of the institution, and may indeed be more cost-effective than the print collection. This is especially likely when a small collection of audiovisual materials gets heavy use. The media librarian can and should collect all data that will support a comparison of media use with the use of other library services, not to reflect poorly on the rest of the library but simply to show the library administrator that if budget cuts must be made, perhaps the media center is not the place to begin.

Employing an analysis of the cost-benefits of media centers not only helps the media librarian in determining what to purchase or produce but also assists in the continual evaluation of media services and creates a systematic process for reporting effectiveness to those who provide media funding. It is imperative that the media librarian design methods for gathering and analyzing data on the cost-effectiveness of media services in a manner that is meaningful in terms of each individual organization, and that the resulting information is consistently conveyed to administrative decision-makers. There is danger in resting on one's laurels, because whether or not the media librarian is aware of it, the budget-making process is unending, and there is competition for funds in every organization. The media center's effectiveness, if not its very existence, may be threatened if the administration fails to perceive the benefits of media services.

References

1. For further discussion, see William Schmid, *Media Center Management: A Practical Guide* (New York: Hastings House, 1980).

Grantwriting

Nina Martin

GRANTSMANSHIP—the art of identifying needs, conceiving a plan for meeting those needs, locating funding sources, and writing and preparing proposals that appeal to the grantor—is a valuable commodity in today's marketplace. As costs continue to escalate and as agencies become more competitive in the race for available funds, it is essential that the media librarian become proficient in this area.

During the 1960s and 1970s billions of dollars were made available by both the public and the private sectors. Numerous federal programs such as the Higher Education Act, the Elementary and Secondary Education Act, the Library Services and Construction Act, and the National Institute of Education included monies for the purpose of supporting and strengthening library media programs. Private foundations such as Carnegie, Mellon, and Rockefeller generously supported libraries. As the economy waned, however, and as government programs were cut back, fewer dollars were allocated for such purposes, making the competition for funds much keener. Today only those proposals which clearly meet the criteria established by the grantor and which indicate potential for successfully meeting the objectives of the grantor are considered.

Quite different processes are used in obtaining funding from private foundations and government agencies. Generally, the format of a proposal to a private foundation is unique to that foundation. Often, too, a formal proposal is submitted only after ascertaining the foundation's interest in such a proposal. On the other hand, proposals made to state and federal agencies usually follow a fairly standard format and are the result of a request for proposal (RFP). Each will, however, require certain basic information. The purpose of this chapter is to present a systematic plan by which the reader can become proficient in identifying potential funding sources, in ascertaining the requirements for proposal submission, and in preparing proposals.

STEP 1: IDENTIFY THE NEED

The most common mistake of media librarians who submit proposals for funding is to locate funding sources and only then to attempt to identify a need which may fit the RFP or the criteria established by the grantor. This is putting the cart before the horse. More successful are the librarians who have clearly established goals and objectives for their media centers and who can identify the means by which each objective can be accomplished. This includes a systematic plan which delineates personnel needs, spatial requirements, programming activities, supporting materials and equipment, and budgetary or fiscal implications. Working from such a statement of objectives, the media librarian is able to identify those objectives for which funding is not yet available from the parent institution. These, then, become the needs for which external funding is sought.

STEP 2: LOCATE POTENTIAL FUNDING SOURCES

The most commonly used source of information is the *Annual Register of Grant Support*, a publication of Marquis which describes approximately 2,400 programs, foundations, government agencies, and corporations, many of which are potential supporters of media programs. Each entry describes the type, purpose, and duration of the grant, requirements for eligibility, application procedures, deadlines, contacts within the agency, address, and telephone number.

The Catalog of Federal Domestic Assistance, a publication of the U.S. Office of Management, is a comprehensive listing of programs administered by more than fifty federal agencies. For each of the approximately one thousand programs listed, information is given regarding funding agency, program authorization, program objectives, types of assistance provided, uses and restrictions, applicant eligibility, and deadlines. Indexed in several ways, the publication is designed to offer maximum assistance to the user.

Information in a variety of formats is available from the Foundation Center. One publication, *The Foundation Directory*, lists grants of $100,000 or more available from approximately three thousand foundations. COMSEARCH, computer printouts of foundations making grants to libraries, is also available from the Center, which has large research libraries in New York (79 Fifth Avenue) and in Washington (1001 Connecticut Avenue, N.W.).

Other sources are publications of professional groups such as the American Library Association, the Association for Education Communications and Technology, and the National Audio Visual Association, as well as more general publications such as the *Chronicle of Higher Education.*

Once a potential source of funding is identified, it is often wise to ascertain whether the agency would be interested in receiving a proposal. One method is to submit a letter of intent, containing a brief description of the need for the project and a statement of goals and objectives.

Although it might indicate some financial requirements, these should not be detailed. The usual response to the letter of intent is an indication of interest or lack of interest. Occasionally, one may be given some clarification of the grantor's guidelines, which will help in further development.

Another, perhaps more desirable one, is to contact an agency representative. This allows one to explore quickly such matters as interest, potential funding, and eligibility.

STEP 3: PREPARE TO WRITE THE PROPOSAL

Time, energy, and even dollars are wasted by media librarians who begin work on a proposal prior to obtaining needed information. Before a word is written for the formal proposal, complete instructions should be obtained from the potential grantor. These should include guidelines, precise information on developing the proposal, and the method by which it should be presented. Every word in the guidelines should be read before starting the proposal. Special attention should be given to the instructions regarding deadline for receipt of the proposal, to whom the proposal should be sent, format for submission, and number of copies needed.

A review of the literature of the field, both to learn what has already been done in the area and to profit from the strengths and weaknesses of comparable projects, should be thoroughly carried out.

STEP 4: DEVELOP THE PROPOSAL

The typical proposal requires ten components. These are:

1. Abstract
2. Introduction
3. Statement of Need/Problem
4. Objectives
5. Methodology
6. Evaluation
7. Continuation Plans
8. Dissemination
9. Budget
10. Appendixes

Abstract

The abstract of the proposal may be the most important part, since it precedes the body of the proposal and is the first part read. It is a thumbnail sketch of the entire proposal. From the abstract the reader or evaluator should be able to ascertain quickly the credibility of the agency or person seeking funding; whether the proposal meets the grantor's needs; if the project is feasible within the financial limitations; and if the applicant is eligible under the guidelines for funding.

The abstract must be brief and should clearly specify needs and goals. The length of the abstract for federal or state agencies is usually specified by number of words or pages. The abstract requested by a foundation may be in the form of a cover letter. Whatever the format, it is extremely important that it is neatly typed, easy to read, and free of typographical and grammatical errors. Although it appears first in the proposal, the abstract is ordinarily written last by the applicant.

Introduction

The introduction is the portion of the proposal in which a case is built and the applicant demonstrates the qualifications and the capability of the agency or the individual to carry out the proposed project. A brief overview of the educational background, work experience, and significant accomplishments of each individual to be involved in the project should be included, although complete résumés for each staff member to be involved are usually placed in an appendix to the proposal.

The reputation of the applicant should be substantiated. This may be accomplished by mentioning and verifying satisfactory performance on other similar projects. Documentation, in the form of letters of support, clippings, and articles, is also usually placed in an appendix. (In some cases the funding agency may specify that no such material be included.)

The important point to remember is that the introduction firmly entrenches in the mind of the reader the credibility of the applicant. The statement should include data that will reinforce that image. The imagination of the reader should be piqued by interesting, provocative writing. The introduction should flow from the general to the specific so that the reader is easily led from successful past performances to convincing future expectations.

Statement of Need/Problem

While some agencies, particularly foundations, have definite limitations regarding the area for which they are willing to provide support, others are usually interested in finding creative ways by which a population as a whole can be helped. For example, an agency will usually prefer to find a model by which library media personnel can serve, let us say, elderly people in general rather than just a few in a specified area.

Fundable needs or problems, then, should offer solutions that can be adapted or applied to a similar problem in other instances. *The greater the probability that the solution or strategy can be used by wider audiences, the greater likelihood of funding.*

The strategy, then, by which one sells a proposal is to provide evidence that the need or problem is a common one. A thorough review of the literature is a first step in finding such evidence. Once this has been accomplished, the applicant may then move to the specific situation for which a solution is sought.

The development of a problem statement is critical, usually requiring that the applicant have some expertise in the area. A good problem statement will include a specific audience having a documented need which can be addressed by the applicant. The statement must carefully identify the actual problem, not the symptoms of the problem. A well-defined problem will lead logically to a statement of goals which are broad general issues to be addressed or changes to be made leading to the point that the applicant expects to achieve. From the goals specific objectives and activities will be derived.

The proposal evaluator will look carefully for documentation that a need exists which is addressed by the problem statement and that the problem and its proposed solution were developed with input from the appropriate persons or groups and is within the purview of the applicant. It is extremely important that the proposed solution be manageable for the applicant.

Objectives

A well-written objective is composed of four parts. These are: target audience; terminal behavior; conditions under which the behavior will be performed, including timelines; and level of proficiency. It should state explicity for *whom* something is to be done, *what* is to be done, *how*, and *how well*. A competently developed objective often makes the difference between proposals that are funded and those that are not. Funding agencies are eager to see what the applicant has accomplished. Measurable objectives allow them this opportunity.

Writing an objective is relatively simple if first one thinks of the audience (whom) and defines that audience very specifically. For example, one might state only "freshmen." A much better statement would be "students entering the freshman class who need an orientation to the Learning Center."

The second step is to specifically describe the behavior or performance (what) one expects from that group. For example, one might state that they "will locate and use media." (When) and (how) might be addressed by stating "after receiving one hour of instruction on their first visit to the center." (How well) may well be stated "appropriate to their assignments."

Reading the entire objective one sees, "Students entering the freshman class who need an orientation to the Learning Center will locate and use media appropriate to their assignments after receiving one hour of instruction on their first visit to the Center." The reader can immediately see what is to be accomplished. While the method for evaluating the objective is not specified at this point, one may reasonably expect this to be explained later in the proposal's methodology. Neither, it will be noted, is there a description of the methodology to be employed in the instructional process.

The objective described above is a "performance" objective or a "behavioral" objective. Two other types of objectives are "process" and "management" objectives. Process objectives are often described as interim objectives. These are simply the small steps along the way that one must take to reach the terminal objective. They may be activities that assist and should be thoroughly explained in the methodology.

"Management" objectives, on the other hand, need to be delineated in the objectives section of the proposal because they clarify for the reader *who* is to do *what when* in order to make the problem solvable. If for example, the applicant plans to choose an advisory committee before beginning the actual project, then the reader must see that this is to be accomplished. For example, "The director of the Learning Center will nominate by June 30, 19____, thirty persons widely representative of the community from whom ten will be selected by the president of the university to form an advisory group." It clearly delineates what is to be done by whom and by what date.

Methodology

The methodology is a detailed description of how the proposed project is to be accomplished. Usually the applicant will key processes or activities to each objective listed earlier. The methodology is the justification for the budget request. It is here that the applicant provides information about staff, space, materials, and equipment which will be needed to accomplish the project's goals.

It is very helpful if the applicant employs simple graphic techniques that will help the reader understand what is being proposed. These may be simple timelines, PERT charts, or flow charts.

For example, a timeline may be as simple as the one which follows:

Activity I	May 1	July 30
Activity II	June 10	August 1
Activity III	June 15	August 1

A helpful addition to the timeline may be another column naming the person or persons responsible for the activity.

A flow chart that shows an orderly progression of activities might also be helpful. One need not necessarily employ sophisticated symbols indicating decision points, keying, or types of activities; the reader is usually most interested in seeing how the outcome is to be achieved.

Evaluation

One of the most stringently examined sections of the proposal is the evaluation design, for it is here that the applicant details how the success or failure of the project will be measured. While the applicant certainly hopes to achieve the project's goals, failure is not a disgrace. However, it *is* important that the reasons for failure be clearly identified in order to avoid the same mistake in the future.

The usual method of designing evaluation is to key an evaluation plan to each objective. Returning to the example used earlier as a performance objective, how can one measure whether the students can, in fact, "locate materials appropriate to their assignments"? It might be as simple as having someone (the media librarian or the professor) observe a sample of the students to see if they have found the correct materials. Another method might have the student record the materials used on notecards which the professor could then check. For the management objective, the evaluation would be a dated list of thirty names turned in to the president.

Most important in proposal preparation is to show evidence that evaluation will be continuous and will be used to improve the project or to redesign techniques that are not producing desired results. Whenever possible show who is to conduct the evaluation, what evidence will be gathered, how the evidence will be analyzed, reported, and used. Be aware of government regulations that protect the human subject. Definite limitations now prohibit wide distribution of questionnaires or surveys without approval of the funding agency. Use sophisticated statistical techniques only when they are appropriate.

Charting the objective may assist in clarifying this process. For example:

Objective	Evidence to be Collected	Method of Analysis	Date to be Collected	Staff Responsible
1.				
2.				
3.				

Continuation Plans

Many agencies require that the applicant show evidence that the project will not be abandoned but will be continued by the applying agency and/or will be reported through various means of dissemination so that others may benefit from what is learned. Continuation plans should include estimates of further funding needed and potential sources of such funding whether internal or external. If the project is not to be continued, plans should be shown for disposal or further utilization of materials, equipment, etc.

Dissemination

Almost all agencies specify that information, which demonstrates the efficacy of the project, the use of the funds, and the pitfalls to be avoided, be shared with other agencies and groups. Appropriate techniques for dissemination will vary according to the project. Research should be reported through the appropriate professional journals. In some cases, information regarding the project should be made available through the media, brochures, newsletters and the like during the project, as well as at its completion.

The proposal evaluator will look for specific rather than general statements. The applicant should mention names of journals or sources to which information will be submitted. Whenever possible, include evidence of interest or commitment from publishers. Samples of in-house publications may be attached in an appendix.

Budget

A carefully detailed budget is essential. Budgets should not be padded and should be based only on those items which have been specified as eligible in the grantor's instructions. For federal and state grants, the budget is not usually seen by the reader or evaluator but is closely scrutinized by the financial officers of the agency.

The budget normally is divided into two parts, personnel costs and non-personnel costs. Additionally, the submitting agency may have the option to request indirect costs. These costs, which include overhead expenses, are usually based upon a percentage of the total budget request and are negotiated with the grantor. The parent institution will, in most cases, be involved in the establishment of these costs. Personnel costs should be based on normal salaries paid within the locale and should include fringe benefits. Personnel costs may be made on the basis of a percentage of an employee's time but may not be permissible if the request is for the same work regularly being done by that person. Consulting fees are usually permissible, as are travel and other expenses incurred by the consultant.

Non-personnel costs may include funds for facilities, purchase of equipment and materials, and other items. In addition, requests may be paid for payment of utilities, postage, and printing. Travel expenses for staff are also permissible. These usually may not exceed normal state and federal allowances. The rate of inflation should also be factored into all budget planning.

Applicants are usually encouraged to provide in-kind support indicating that the individual or agency is prepared to share in the cost of the proposed program. In-kind support is usually in the form of space, utilities, and personnel support.

Appendixes

Documentation and a variety of supporting materials may be appended to the formal proposal. All such materials should be judiciously selected, neatly assembled, and pertinent to the proposal. Masses of material will be skimmed by the reader and may be dismissed as mere window dressing.

STEP 5: REVIEW THE PROPOSAL

Attempt to see the proposal through the reader's eyes. Ask the following questions:

1. Is the proposal clear?
2. Does it convey the problem to the reader?
3. Does the proposed solution fit the problem or need?
4. Does the proposal indicate familiarity with the current literature?
5. Are staff qualifications, experience, and expertise well-presented?
6. Are objectives well-stated and measureable?
7. Is the methodology complete, well-designed, easily understood?
8. Are timelines and staff responsibilities clearly delineated?
9. Is a sound evaluation design included? Does it measure the objectives?
10. Is the proposed project feasible within the constraints of staff, timelines, facilities, budget?
11. Is the budget clean, requesting funds only for eligible expenditures?
12. Do the budget and the proposal indicate some degree of institutional support?
13. Have weaknesses or holes been spotted?

If the answer to any of the first twelve questions was negative or if number thirteen was answered positively, the applicant should attempt to rewrite or strengthen the appropriate portions of the proposal. It is often possible to obtain assistance from consultants, state agency personnel, contracts and grants officers, and others for this step.

STEP 6: SUBMIT PROPOSAL

Wrap carefully for mailing. Mail in ample time to be received by the deadline. It is a good idea to obtain a receipt when the item is mailed or enclose a postcard which can be returned upon arrival.

STEP 7: WAIT

Months may elapse between the date of submission and the date of acceptance or rejection. The grantor generally will not wish to be contacted by the applicant once the grant review process has started. Try not to give up hope. While waiting keep abreast of new developments in the area of the proposal. Be prepared to negotiate. Rarely does the applicant receive all that has been requested.

Remember that a good idea is not always funded on the first try. If the proposal is rejected, try again.

Bibliography

Annual Register of Grant Support. Chicago: Marquis Academic Media, Marquis Who's Who. Latest edition.

Bass, Richard W. *Grant Money and How to Get It for Librarians*. New York: R.R. Bowker, 1980.

Breivik, Patricia Senn and E. Benn Gibson. *Funding Alternatives for Libraries*. Chicago: American Library Association, 1979.

Dyer, Esther R., Pam Berger and Jean Lowrie. *Public, School and Academic Media Centers, A Guide to Information Sources*. Detroit: Gale Research Co., 1981. Section 8.

Federal Register. Office of the Federal Register. Washington, D.C.: National Archives and Records Services. General Services Administration. Latest edition.

Hall, Mary. *Developing Skills in Proposal Writing*. 2nd ed. Portland, Ore.: Continuing Ed. Publications, 1977.

Kiritz, Norton J. *Program Planning and Proposal Writing*. Expanded Version. Los Angeles: The Grantsmanship Center, 1979.

Perry, Suzanne. "Getting a Foundation Grant Takes More Than a Good Idea, Program Officers Say." *The Chronicle of Higher Education* 25 (October 21, 1982), p. 8.

Proposal Development Handbook. Washington, D.C.: American Association of State Colleges and Universities, 1975.

U. S. Office of Management and Budget. *Catalog of Federal Domestic Assistance.* Washington, D.C.: Government Printing Office. Latest edition.

Vermont Department of Libraries, Montpelier. "Some Things You Should Know About Foundations and Foundation Grants." *The Unabashed Librarian.* No. 29, 1978, pp. 20-22.

SELECTION

Non-Print Selection: A Combination of Methods

John W. Ellison

LIBRARY material selection procedures generally fall into one of three major categories. The primary method used is the librarian selection procedure, sometimes known as the "halo" system. It is characterized by the librarian unilaterally determining the content of the collection by selecting materials based on reviews, publisher's brochures, and bibliographies. The general development direction or strengths of a collection are determined by the librarian's knowledge and feeling about the clientele's wants.

Another procedure, but usually in far less use by librarians, is the social responsibility selection procedure. This process is characterized by activist librarians who select materials based on social problems of a given library community (community is used to reflect clientele of any type of library). They tend not to wait until library users make requests to activate orders based on their feelings on local, state, and national social issues. Social responsibility librarians áre usually aware of major social, psychological, and economical needs of the library community and select materials and develop programs on what they feel is good for the community.

The systematic analysis procedure of selecting materials combines formal needs assessment, community analysis, and non-profit marketing methods to determine the information needs of a library community. This procedure puts the librarian in a process role. It is characterized by formal community systematic analysis to determine needs rather than the use of personal feelings or social issues as a criterion to select materials

Media librarians, to some extent, will use a combination of all three methods described to develop non-print collections. They usually place a major emphasis on the systematic analysis method, with limited social responsibility activity and a minimal "halo" approach. The rationale is simple. Media librarians are usually responsible for several or all disciplines covered by a library. They usually develop a procedure for

Originally published in *Catholic Library World* 53 (October 19, 1982) pp. 119-121.

selecting materials which involves a broad opportunity for participation by knowledgeable specialists, both in and outside the library, and the general population of the library community. The following are steps generally taken by the media librarian when selecting materials.

A strong philosophy of librarianship is essential if a person is to develop selection procedures that are free of bias and open to meeting the information needs of the library community. Several ingredients should be part of this philosophy. They may include notions such as unrestricted access to information, individuals, development to their full potential and the efficiency of information delivery. Media librarians in different types of libraries will have unique thrusts in their philosophies, but the three major notions presented above are usually included with different wording and emphasis. The word "service" is not used in a library philosophy because it implies supplemental to rather than an integral part of a community.

Knowing the library community served, both individuals and groups, is important in the selection process. Demographic data gathered in the process of community analysis are available from census data, college reports, telephone company records, theater attendance figures, and the library's circulation figures. This information gives the media librarian some general information and a broad scope of the potential library community clientele. It is sad to say but for many libraries this is all the information they gather to learn about their clientele.

Published and public demographic information about a library community is helpful, but it does not provide the details needed by media librarians to know both the users and non-users. To determine the individual needs and wants, a systematic needs assessment must be conducted. This formal assessment will include some type of formal survey that provides what information is needed, and equally important, what formats are preferred. Since library communities are usually large, some type of sampling method will be used which is intended to produce responses that represent the entire community. Non-library users should not be overlooked, but must be represented in this study.

Using the information extracted from a formal needs assessment, the media librarian can then specify the goals and objectives of the non-print services in the library. This same information can be used to help determine a formal selection policy. The policy will be unique because it outlines selection procedures and provides specific needs and wants as determined by the library community based on systematic analysis.

A careful examination of the media collection based on the results of a formal systematic analysis study should be conducted at this point in the procedures. Specific weaknesses in collection content and needed formats can be identified. Then a written policy should be established that outlines how to correct the deficiencies between what exists and what is needed. Short and long-range collection development plans should be developed and formally reported to the library administration, governing body, and library community.

Once needs have been identified and plans developed to rectify deficiencies, materials should be previewed. There is no better way to acquire knowledge about the overall quality of available non-print materials than seeing them firsthand. This can be accomplished by visiting non-print exhibits at conferences, commercial stores, professional meetings, media screenings, and examining materials in other libraries. Seeing material helps to develop a feeling for the quality of production different companies offer and seeing how like subjects are treated. In addition, the media librarian will have an opportunity to become well rounded in the media "literature." This opportunity is expanded and enriched when subject specialists and library users and non-users attend screenings with media librarians.

Involving library non-users in the screening and selection process is difficult, but not impossible. Non-user identification is not impossible either since they represent anywhere from ninety-three to fifty percent of the population depending on the type of library and which study is cited. The most important factors which increase non-user library involvement are: 1) the library being known and 2) the library truly caring that non-user information needs are met. Some ways of being known are accomplished by contacting special interest groups who are known not to use the library, making personal calls on non-users, attending community meetings and providing regular programming or articles in the local mass media. No library should have a defeatist attitude toward non-users. They can be reached and will be a valuable asset for the library that is successful in attracting them to the library user column.

Examination of evaluative indexes, reviews, and selective lists published by knowledgeable subject specialists can help increase the depth and breadth of the media librarian. Reviews should never be the last step in the selection process. A well-written review does nothing more than inform the media librarian that here is something worth examining with potential users and subject specialists.

Good reviews usually contain standard criteria acceptable for both print or non-print material. However, non-print reviews *must* contain elements that may not be found in print reviews. First, some qualifications of the reviewer must be provided with the review. This information gives the media librarian some idea of the potential value of the review. Second, it is also important to have reviews which provide comparisons with other material on the same subject. Third, statements of obsolescence are also extremely important since the financial investment may be large and the potential cost benefit is sometimes part of the selection criteria. Finally, media reviews must be critical rather than kind and non-evaluative. An honest critical review is beneficial while a kind review which does not make a recommendation is of little or no value to the media librarian.

Potential users should always be personally involved in the evaluation of non-print materials. Once materials arrive at the library, they should be previewed by subject specialists. It should be noted that subject specialists need not be limited to members of the library staff. Knowledgeable automotive mechanics, business people, and medical professionals with unique expertise are excellent specialists who can provide critical evaluations of non-print materials. They are also usually willing to assist the library when properly approached. All persons involved in the evaluation process should be given a preview evaluation instrument with a criteria checklist. Several forms have been published over the years. One of the better instruments is an obscure form published by Clara DiFelice, Elizabeth Miller, and Naomi Rhodes in *The U*N*A*B*A*S*H*E*D* Librarian* and reprinted in this book. It is comprehensive, easy to use, and provides the media librarian with an average score for several criteria within five broad categories and a total score for all categories under consideration. This easy-to-tabulate instrument is extremely valuable when several people are evaluating the same non-print item. It is important to identify specific strengths and weaknesses of a format or program and determine the overall rating in a matter of seconds. This instrument provides both in an easy-to-use format.

The media librarian must make the ultimate decision to purchase material. The procedures described encourage library community participation in the decision-making process, but the final decision rests with the media librarian. Budget, equipment, facilities, and potential use are but a few of the factors the media librarian will consider before making the final decision. Non-print material can be requested from the producer or distributor on "Preview for Purchase Consideration" or a "Purchase on Approval Plan." This will permit the return of unwanted material. Always state on each non-print order, "The library retains the right to return material in twenty work days if it is unsatisfactory."

It is important to consider the potential number of uses of an item. Purchase, rent, lease, rent-to-own contracts, and inhouse production are determined, in part, by the number of uses. Rental charges are approximately ten percent of the purchase cost. Add the total cost for rental (labor, postage, insurance, and forms) and the cost may reach nearly twenty-five percent of the purchase price. Of course, the item's purchase price (i.e., a $10 filmstrip compared to a $450 film) makes the ultimate figure fluctuate significantly. Consideration should also be given to cooperative acquisition plans and the cost of material maintenance, storage, and care.

Using the procedure described helps assure the media librarian that extensive and systematic participation on the part of the library community has taken place. It also attempts to develop a collection that will be used. This process is not without its shortcomings, but it should not be rejected because of anticipated problems. And it should not be rejected because of the energy required for implementation. The rewards of increased users, clientele who feel a part of the library, and the potential for increased financial support should make the effort worthwhile.

Selection of non-print material generally does not follow the same procedures as those traditionally used for print. The difference is most evident when a library is placed in a non-print service position. Library procedures are employed and the results are usually less than anticipated. Sometimes the results are so devastating that non-print materials are unjustly criticized, and services are reduced and sometimes eliminated because an unqualified person was put into a position with limited skills to successfully develop and serve a non-print collection for which a qualified media librarian should have been assigned.

Media Evaluation Form:
A Proposal

Clara DiFelice, Elizabeth Miller,
and Naomi Rhodes

AFTER persuing the many journals and catalogs for reviews on media software and finally narrowing it down a few items, how do you select the most appropriate materials? Some people order from a distributor's brochure or select an item based on reviews in professional publications, with or without personally screening each item. This process of screening and evaluation can become a crucial step in the entire selection procedure. It may be a necessary backup for justifying budget allocations, and often can be strengthened by involving subject specialists and potential users (hereafter referred to as "outside" evaluators). These are people not on the media center staff, but whose input during the selection process will assist the media specialist in developing a collection that has the potential to be utilized to its fullest.

The process of screening and evaluation can also become a barrier to building an actively used collection, mainly due to the limitations of forms available to assist in this process. Many are too complex, designed for one specific format and therefore limited in their usefulness. Others are designed for multimedia purposes and tend to be too general or superficial. Some evaluation forms are difficult to understand and require an excessive amount of time to interpret. Furthermore, the results obtained are often meaningless and may not justify the process involved.

PURPOSE

These factors were taken into consideration in devising the Media Evaluation Form presented here. The major objectives of this form are: 1. to encompass all media; 2. to be easily used by media specialists,

Originally published in *The U*N*A*B*A*S*H*E*D Librarian* 30 (1979) pp. 29-30.

subject specialists, and potential users; 3. to provide some means to compare different media formats on the same subject; 4. to provide the means to recommend selection in terms of priorities; 5. to provide an overall rating for an item by an individual or group of evaluators.

Many evaluation instruments were consulted when designing this form (see bibliography). Even though a variety of forms are available, basically they can be divided into two categories—those directed specifically at one format or those general forms used in evaluating any formats. One limitation found on the latter was that there were no questions asked which could express how the material satisfied specific criteria or considerations unique to a certain medium. For example, in evaluating multi-media kits an important consideration would be whether or not the items related to one another in a meaningful way. Such criteria are, understandably, very important in evaluating materials. However, in deciding to have this media evaluation form encompass all media, this problem of specific criteria remained a problem. It is a limitation of the form, but it is hoped that specific criteria or considerations will be dealt with by the media librarian.

With the possible exception of the informational data at the top of the form (which should be provided by the media librarian before a screening), the form is aimed at outside evaluators.

DESCRIPTION OF FORM

Probably the most important aspect of evaluating material is whether or not it will satisfy objectives set by those who may later use the material. This appears first on the form, focusing attention on the achievement of objectives. Content considerations follow next to provide more details about the material's impact.

In developing the statements on the form, various accompanying subheadings were provided to act as guidelines for a response by the evaluator. For example, in the Content section, considering the phrases "overall effect (objective) clear" and "presentation of main idea well-organized" will assist the evaluator in responding to the statement "Content achieves its purpose."

The subhedings intend to generate some concern the evaluator may have regarding the material. The "Comments" section is included to provide an optional avenue for feedback. As well, priorities of recommendation may further assist in determining how the material answers the evaluator's needs. The "Recommendation" section is probably most useful if dealt with as a recommendation for purchase, though it has been left open for interpretation.

Least in importance to the outside evaluator may be technical and physical aspects of the material. It was felt these should, however, be necessary considerations. Therefore, a section labeled "For Media Personnel Use" was included which added some technical questions particularly aimed at being useful for the media librarian's consideration.

OVERALL RATING

The rationale behind providing an overall rating of one item would be its usefulness when comparing two or more items on the same subject. The rating given by one evaluator (2.9) could easily be compared with that of an item by a group (3.4). Obviously there are other factors to be given careful consideration, but the media librarian at least can easily determine the general consensus of a group of evaluators. Hopefully, media librarians will adapt the rating system to their own purposes.

This form also allows for the comparison of different sets of criteria by determining the rating for each section. For example, if an item rates high (e.g., 4.6), under content but is weak (2.3) technically, and another item on the same subject rates strong technically but not so strong on content, it can serve as a basis for a decision between the two factors.

In providing this simplified form for the evaluation process, it is hoped that some of the headaches, insecurities, and indecisions that accompany the selection of the most appropriate materials for the media center can be reduced or eliminated. With involvement of subject specialists and potential users as evaluators, along with the media librarian, the media collection will be more reflective of the community information needs.

Bibliography

Alvir, Howard P. *The Evolution of an Evaluation Form*. Albany, N.Y.: Howard P. Alvir, 1976.

Armstrong, Jenny R. *A Sourcebook for the Evaluation of Instructional Materials and Media*. Madison, Wisc.: Special Education Instructional Materials Center, 1973.

Baird, James R. "Criteria Used to Select 16mm Films," *Audiovisual Instruction*, (April 22, 1974) pp. 22-24.

Barksdale, Mildred W. "Student Evaluation of Films Used in a Teacher Evaluation Program," *Exceptional Children* 37, 1970, pp. 39-40.

Day, Joseph A. "The Pitfalls of Evaluating Instructional Materials," *Audiovisual Instruction* (May 26, 1976) pp. 26-27.

Ellison, John and Elizabeth Smith. *Handbook of Nonbook Materials*. Unpublished Manuscript.

Johnson, Jenny. "Appraisal of Educational Materials for AVLINE," *Audiovisual Instruction*, (January 22, 1976) pp. 22-27.

Jones, Emily S. *Manual on Film Evaluation*. New York: Educational Film Library Association, 1971.

Lasher, Edward B. "Evaluative Criteria of Non-print Materials: A Compromise," *Audiovisual Communication*, (September 1975) pp. 16-17.

Oderinde, Namu O. "Instructional Material Assessment Tool," *Audiovisual Instruction*, (April 18, 1975) pp. 22-24.

_____."Pictorial Assessment and Selection," *Audiovisual Instruction*, (January 20, 1975) pp.20-26.

Report on the NCEMMH Media Selection Conference. Columbus, Ohio: National Center on Educational Media and Materials for the Handicapped, 1973.

MEDIA EVALUATION FORM

The following information will be provided:

TITLE:
Producer: Copyright Date:
Distributor: Cost:
Medium: B/W or Color:
Running Time: Recording Speed:
Guide(s) Available:

CIRCLE AUDIENCE LEVEL(S):

	Elementary	Jr. High	Sr. High	College	Adult
Pre 1 2 3 4 5 6	7 8 9	10 11 12	13 14 15		

	Strongly Disagree	Disagree	Neutral	Agree	Strongly Agree	Not Applicable
I. Material satisfies your objectives.	1	2	3	4	5	0
II. Content:						
Content achieves its purpose.	1	2	3	4	5	0
—overall effect (objective) clear						
—presentation of main idea well-organized						
Content is authentic.	1	2	3	4	5	0
—accurate, up to date, unbiased, relevant						
Content is presented appropriately.	1	2	3	4	5	0
—vocabulary and concept level(s) equal to that of intended audience level(s)						
—guide(s) adequate						
Acting, narration, and/or performance in character with content.	1	2	3	4	5	0
—not distractive						
Titles and captions are used effectively.	1	2	3	4	5	0
—title accurately reflects the content						
—key elements are highlighted when necessary						
—symbols adequately defined						

Narration, dialog, sound are used effectively.   1 2 3 4 5 0
—key elements are highlighted when necessary
—technical terms adequately defined
Examples and comparisons given to clarify and/or support content.   1 2 3 4 5 0
Scope of the subject is realized.   1 2 3 4 5 0
—full coverage
—showing insight into the subject

III. Utilization/Educational Value:
Content proves interesting for intended audience.   1 2 3 4 5 0
—holds audience attention
—stimulates interest, thinking, communication
—offers satisfactory answers or incites meaningful questions
—has human/sensory appeal
—original, inventive, creative, imaginative
Content is flexible for many uses.   1 2 3 4 5 0
—can be used with specific programs
—contains basic concepts for use as an introductory tool
Format is suitable for subject and intended use.   1 2 3 4 5 0

IV. Technical/Physical Aspects:
Material appears to be in good physical condition.   1 2 3 4 5 0
—free from scratches, breaks, faulty splices, or torn sprocket holes
Sound/image is clear (focused, free from distortion).   1 2 3 4 5 0
Editing and production are smooth, logical, effective.   1 2 3 4 5 0
—free of omissions or unnecessary redundancy
—of a suitable length and unified composition
—with effective use of color/b&w; fidelity

COMMENTS:

RECOMMENDATION: Recommended: _____   Not Recommended: _____

_____ 1st priority
_____ 2nd priority
_____ 3rd priority

Title/Position of Reviewer   Date:

Do Not Write Below This Line

For Media Personnel Use:

	Strongly Disagree	Disagree	Neutral	Agree	Strongly Agree	Not Applicable
V. Technical and Maintenance Considerations:						
Material appears durable for prolonged use. —adequate leader provided	1	2	3	4	5	0
Format is compatible with equipment/facilities for presentation.	1	2	3	4	5	0
Initial and maintenance costs are within means. —more suitable than self-produced substitute	1	2	3	4	5	0
Material satisfies specific criteria or considerations unique to format.	1	2	3	4	5	0
Material presents the subject in a way superior to comparable media.	1	2	3	4	5	0

Were reviews consulted about this material?

_____ evaluative   _____ non-evaluative   _____ none

RATING:

Media Selection Sources

Cheryll A. Bixby and June B. Cawthon

THE selection of non-print media must be based upon an awareness of the interests, abilities, and needs of the user community as well as an understanding of the philosophy, purpose, and selection policy of the library. As Katz has stated, "No one medium will meet all the needs of all the people all of the time. Individuals prefer different media for different purposes. The library has an obligation to provide many types of materials to meet the needs of users . . . This requires understanding by the librarian and competence in evaluating nonprint materials . . . ."[1]

Media selection sources vary in their usefulness to media librarians. The selector should be knowledgeable about the idiosyncracies of basic selection tools. These sources vary in their policies regarding inclusion of all available media or only recommended materials; the formats of media covered; the amount of information given for each entry; the number of reviews in each issue, if any; and the type of library for which they are intended.

The selection tools presented in this chapter represent a *basic* collection for locating and selecting non-print media. It is by no means a comprehensive listing. Sources were chosen based upon their suitability for use in school media centers and/or public and academic libraries as well as their favorable recommendation in *American Reference Books Annual* and/or the standard reviewing periodicals.

The chapter is divided into two parts. Part I covers general selection tools that provide access to multiple non-print formats. Part II lists specialized sources for individual formats. In each section, titles have been grouped according to the type of information they provide—either non-evaluative or evaluative. Sources of non-critical, descriptive information include directories, catalogs, checklists, and yearbooks. Though these tools are helpful in identifying non-print resources, the information they provide should not be used as justification for acquisition. Sources of qualitative information on non-print media include professional journals and the indexes in which they are accessed as well as selective bibliographies and mediagraphies. Evalutive sources should always be consulted before purchasing non-print materials.

Also listed in this chapter are guides and mediagraphies that will assist in the development of a basic non-print collection.

Part I
General Sources for Multiple Nonprint Formats

GUIDES

Nadler, Myra, ed. *How to Start an Audiovisual Collection*. Metuchen, N.J.: Scarecrow Press, 1978.

Written by seven experts in the field, the book provides suggestions concerning the establishment of basic collections and which indexes and review media to use. Information about needed equipment, how to staff departments, plan services and organize programs is included in this practical book.

Rufsvold, Margaret I. *Guides to Educational Media*. 4th ed. Chicago: American Library Association, 1977.

The purpose of this edition is to identify and describe 245 catalogs, indexes, and reviewing services that systematically provide information about educational media. Comprehensive rather than selective, information is provided for all grade levels and for audiences from preschool through university and adult levels.

Simmons, Beatrice T., and Yvonne B. Carter. *Aids to Media Selection for Students and Teachers*. Indianola, Iowa: National Association of State Educational Media Professionals, Division of Publications, 1982.

A selected list of bibliographies and journals which review books, periodicals, audiovisual materials, and computer software of relevance for elementary and secondary school instructional programs. Its four sections are Book Selection Sources, Periodicals and Serials, Sources of Audiovisual Materials, and Sources of Computer Technology. A directory of publishers and an author-title index are appended. This publication was formerly distributed through the Office of Libraries and Learning Technology.

Sive, Mary R. *Media Selection Handbook*. Littleton, Colo.: Libraries Unlimited, 1983.

This handbook identifies essential selection tools for building nonprint collections (exclusive of films) for users from kindergarten through community college. Entries are critically annotated and include such non-print formats as kits, filmloops and filmstrips, simulation games, transparencies, and videorecordings. A discussion of media use and selection of instructional development is also presented.

Sive, Mary R. *Selecting Instructional Media: A Guide to Audiovisual and Other Instructional Media Lists*. 3rd ed. Littleton, Colo.: Libraries Unlimited, 1983.

This selective guide describes over 700 lists of audiovisual/instructional materials at the elementary and secondary school level. All non-print formats are included in this guide as well as government and free or inexpensive publications. Entries are arranged into three sections covering comprehensive listings as well as listings by subject and non-print format. Information for each list includes complete bibliographic data, price, grade level, subject areas, time period covered, frequency of updates, and whether the list is evaluative or descriptive. Several indexes provide access by author, title, subject, non-print format, and instructional level.

Winkel, Lois., ed. *Elementary School Library Collection*. 14th ed. Williamsport, Pa.: Bro-Dart Publishing Co., 1965- . Biennial.

This edition continues the tradition of a reliable source for a basic, up-to-date collection of print and non-print materials for preschool through the sixth grade. Entries are in a classified arrangement and give annotations that include suggested priorities for acquisitions. Separate author, title, and subject indexes are included.

Wynar, Bohdan S., ed. *Recommended Reference Books for Small and Medium Sized Libraries and Media Centers 1983*. Littleton, Colo.: Libraries Unlimited, 1983.

The third edition of this source is a selective listing of over 500 titles that were reviewed in *American Reference Books Annual* in the 1983 edition. Entries are organized into 42 subject-related chapters, including types of non-print formats. Complete bibliographic and ordering information is provided for each title as well as citations to reviewing sources and codes indicating the appropriate type of library for its use. An author, title, and subject index is included.

Wynar, Christine G. *Guide to Reference Books for School Media Centers*. 2nd ed. Littleton, Colo.: Libraries Unlimited, 1981.

Basic reference tools for locating and selecting print and non-print media at the elementary and secondary school level are listed in this selective guide. Entries are arranged under subject areas corresponding to the K-12 curriculum. Information for each item includes full bibliographic data, price, and an evaluative annotation. The index provides author, title, and subject access.

NON-EVALUATIVE SOURCES

American Library Association. Task Force on Alternatives in Print, Social Responsibilities Round Table. *Alternatives in Print: An International Catalog of Books, Pamphlets, Periodicals, and Audiovisual Materials*. 6th ed. New York: Neal-Schuman, 1980.

This standard reference tool serves as an "in print" source to the media of the small, foreign, and dissident presses. The sixth edition includes over 2,600 alternative presses. Arrangement is alphabetical by publisher. Entries include publisher's name and address, ordering information, and lists of publications available arranged first by media format and then by subject. A series of indexes accesses the publisher listing by author, subject, geographic region, and titles (divided by format). Non-print formats covered include pamphlets, recordings, films, slides, and videotapes.

Audio Video Market Place: A Multimedia Guide. New York: Bowker, 1969- . Annual.

This standard reference work, formerly known as *Audio Visual Market Place*, identifies more than 4,800 organizations active in the AV field. The main portion of the directory (14th ed.) lists producers, distributors, and services alphabetically by name under state, U.S. territory, or Canadian province. Each entry gives a brief description of the AV goods and services provided. A classified index lists the names of the producers, distributors, and services under seventeen broad subject areas with some 625 subdivisions. Other useful listings include a calendar of AV conventions/meetings, a listing of associations, a listing of trade and consumer periodicals, and a bibliography of reference sources.

Educational Media Yearbook. Littleton, Colo.: Libraries Unlimited, 1973- . Annual.

This ready reference source, the media counterpart of the *The Bowker Annual*, reflects significant developments in the field of educational media/instructional technology. A mediagraphy of print/non-print resources, a guide to national and international media-related organizations, a directory of over 700 producers, distributors, and publishers of media-oriented products and a directory of public and private funding sources for media-related projects are particularly helpful to the professional involved in the selection of non-print media.

Educators Guide Series. Randolph, Wisc.: Educators Progress Service. Annual.

Free nonprint materials in various formats are indexed in this much-used series. Entries are arranged alphabetically by title under broad subject areas and give complete bibliographic and ordering information. Current titles include:
Educators . . .
 . . . *Grade Guide to Free Teaching Aids*
 . . . *Guide to Free Audio and Video Materials*
 . . . *Guide to Free Films*

. . . *Guide to Free Filmstrips*
. . . *Guide to Free Guidance Materials*
. . . *Guide to Free Health, Physical Education and Recreation Materials*
. . . *Guide to Free Science Materials*
. . . *Guide to Free Social Studies Materials*
. . . *Index of Free Materials*

Emmens, Carol A. *Children's Media Market Place.* 2nd ed. New York: Neal-Schuman, 1982.

The second edition of this work provides in-depth information in every area of children's media. The major portion of the directory is organized in twenty-one areas of interest, such as audiovisual producers, review journals, reviewers of children's media, radio and television program sources, and a bibliography of selection tools. A name index provides access to all of the individuals, businesses, periodicals, and organizations listed.

Index to Instructional Media Catalogs. New York: Bowker, 1974.

A buyer's guide to more than 630 producers and publishers for some forty types of media in nearly 150 subject areas. The subject index classifies instructional materials by media, grade level, methodology, and identifies their producers and publishers. A product and services index alphabetically lists some eighty types of equipment and services with the names of the companies is also included.

Information America: Sources of Print and Nonprint Materials Available from Organizations, Industry, Government Agencies and Specialized Publishers. New York: Neal-Schuman, 1977- . 3 issues/year.

Formerly published as *Sources,* this reference guide lists over 2,000 U.S. and Canadian organizations and their publications and services. Entries are arranged under broad subject areas and include the organization's name, address, and telephone number, purpose, and summary of information services. The listing of publications under each entry is divided by books, periodicals, pamphlets, and non-print. Prices are included if available. The listing of organizations is accessed by a subject index as well as an index of periodical titles and an index of free and inexpensive materials.

Library of Congress Catalog: Audiovisual Materials. Washington, D.C.: Library of Congress, 1952- . Quarterly.

Motion pictures, filmstrips, sets of transparencies, slide sets, video-recordings, and kits are included in this catalog formerly known as *Films and Other Materials for Projection.*

National Information Center for Educational Media (NICEM). *NICEM Indexes*. Los Angeles: University of Southern California, 1971- . Most volumes are biennial.

The NICEM series is the most comprehensive listing of commercially produced non-print educational media. Compiled according to subject area or format, each index lists entries alphabetically by title. Entries provide descriptive annotations with complete bibliographic data, ordering information and an indication of audience level. .
Current titles include:
NICEM Index to . . .
. . . *Educational Audio Tapes*
. . . *Educational Overhead Transparencies*
. . . *Educational Records*
. . . *Educational Slides*
. . . *Educational Video Tapes*
. . . *Environmental Studies—Multimedia*
. . . *Health and Safety Education—Multimedia*
. . . *Non-Print Special Education Materials—Multimedia*
. . . *Producers and Distributors*
. . . *Psychology—Multimedia*
. . . *Vocational and Technical Education—Multimedia*
. . . *8mm Motion Cartridges*
. . . *16mm Educational Films*
. . . *35mm Educational Filmstrips*

Each NICEM Index is updated in the annual supplement entitled *Update of Nonbook Media*. Online access to the more timely *A-V Online*, the NICEM database, is provided by DIALOG Information Retrieval Service.

National Information Center for Special Education Materials (NIC-SEM). *NICSEM Master Index to Special Education Materials*. 3 vols. Los Angeles: University of Southern California National Information Center for Educational Media.

Special education materials for handicapped learners are described in this comprehensive index. Print and non-print titles are arranged alphabetically with entries giving such information as author, publisher, distributor, price, physical description, academic, reading, and interest levels, a descriptive annotation, a listing of titles in series, and cross-references. A thesaurus, a user reference section and a publisher/producer/distributor directory complete the work.

U.S. National Audiovisual Center. *Quarterly Update*. Washington, D.C.: Superintendent of Documents, 1980–. Quarterly.

Formerly known as *A Reference List of Audiovisual Materials*

Produced by the United States Government, this source describes government-produced films, videotapes, slides, multimedia kits, and other non-print materials. Complete bibliographic information, as well as sales/rental data and indication of age level is provided for each entry.

Wasserman, Paul, and Esther Herman. *Catalog of Museum Publications and Audiovisuals Available From U.S. and Canadian Institutions.* Detroit: Gale Research Co., 1972- . Irregular.

Arranged alphabetically by institution, this directory indicates the media (books, booklets, periodicals, monographs, catalogs, pamphlets and leaflets, films and filmstrips, videotape programs, and others) that are prepared and distributed by museums, art galleries, and related institutions in the United States and Canada. Title and keyword, subject, periodical, and geographic indexes are included.

EVALUATIVE SOURCES

Indexes to Reviews

Consumer's Index to Product Evaluations and Information Sources. Ann Arbor, Mich: Pierian Press, 1973-. Quarterly with annual cumulation.

This access tool for consumer information contained primarily in popular as well as specialized periodicals indexes several sources for equipment evaluations. Arranged under broad subject areas, entries indicate whether the equipment has been tested, evaluated, or just described by the reviewing source.

Orlin, Leslie, ed. *Media Review Digest: The Only Complete Guide to Reviews of Non-Book Media.* Ann Arbor, Mich.: Pierian Press, 1970-Annual.

As a successor to *Multi-Media Reviews Index,* this source provides the most comprehensive listing of reviews on all media formats in over 200 periodicals, with more than 50,000 review citations per year. Part I covers educational 16mm films, feature films, videotapes, filmstrips, and miscellaneous formats; Part II indexes reviews of popular, classical, and spoken word records and tapes. In both parts, primary emphasis is on educational, instructional, and informational media.

Sources of Current Reviews

Booklist. Chicago: American Library Association, 1905- . Semi-monthly.

Films, filmstrips, slides, recordings, and video are the audiovisual formats reviewed in *Booklist*. The citation includes full bibliographic data with prices for purchase or rental, a lengthy annotation, grade levels, and cataloging information.

EPIEgram: Materials. (Educational Products Information Exchange). Stony Brook, N.Y.: Educational Products Information Exchange Institute, 1972- . Monthly (Oct - June).

The EPIE Institute is an educational consumer's union which is involved in the testing and evaluation of instructional materials and equipment. Test results and media reviews are published in two separate publications: *EPIEgram Equipment* and *EPIEgram: Materials*. This service was formerly published as *Educational Product Report* and as *EPIEgram*.

The Horn Book Magazine. Boston: Horn Book, Inc. 1924- . Bimonthly.

"Audio-Visual Review" is a section in *Horn Book* which reviews a different format such as films, records, cassettes, etc., in each issue; however, only media relating to some phase of children's literature are considered. Full bibliographic data and an annotation is given for each title reviewed.

Information Technology and Libraries. Chicago: Library and Information Technology Association, 1968- . Quarterly.

Feature articles cover communications technology and audiovisual applications as well as cable and video technology. Reviews are included.

Library Journal. New York: Bowker, 1876- . Semi-monthly (Sept. - June), monthly (July & August).

"Audiovisual Reviews & Distributors" is a regular feature in each issue of *Library Journal*. Among the formats included are 16mm films and videocassettes, filmstrips, and slides. Information, in addition to the signed review, includes full bibliographic data with both the purchase and rental prices indicated for films. Those items available for preview are identified. A list of distributors with addresses follows the reviews.

Media and Methods. Philadelphia: American Society of Educators. 1964- . 9 issues/year.

A regular feature of this magazine is a section "Have You Discovered?", coordinated by William H. Bell, which includes reviews of filmstrips, films, and books. Two other sections, "Hardware" and "Software" offer valuable information to the librarian.

Media Monitor. Ardsley-on-Hudson, N.Y.: Informedia, 1977- .Quarterly.

This newsletter lists and often annotates instructional media for use at the elementary and secondary school level. Included are filmstrips, slides, maps, audiocassettes, and other non-print formats.

School Library Journal. New York: Bowker, 1954- . Monthly (except June & July).

Since the demise of *Previews*, "Audiovisual Review" has been a regular feature in *School Library Journal*. Formats such as 16mm films and videocassettes, filmstrips, slides, multimedia kits, and recordings are reviewed. Full bibliographic data is given for each item including both purchase and rental prices for films. Each review is signed, and the item's availability for preview is indicated. At the end of the reviewing section, both a "Directory of Distributors" and an "Index to Review" is given. "AV Product showcase" appears in an occasional issue.

School Library Media Quarterly. Chicago: American Library Association, 1952- . Quarterly.

Formerly known as *School Media Quarterly*, this journal reviews various non-print materials for the elementary and secondary curriculum. Also included are reviews of selection tools.

VOYA (Voice of Youth Advocates). University, Ala.: Voice of Youth Advocates, Inc., 1978- . Bimonthly.

Films and recordings appropriate for young adults are among the formats included in VOYA. There are good reviews for films, giving bibliographic data as well as their purchase and/or rental price. In the issue examined, recordings were listed by performer or performing group with title and producer being the only information given with the exception of a code indicating the type of music such as HR: Hard Rock.

Wilson Library Bulletin. Bronx, N.Y.: H.W. Wilson, 1914- . Monthly (Sept.-June).

New films are regularly reviewed in the column "Cine-Opsis." Also, other nonprint formats are occasionally featured as well as new reference tools to access nonprint materials. Provides overview of current developments in educational media.

SELECTIVE BIBLIOGRAPHIES AND MEDIAGRAPHIES

Brown, Lucy Gregor. *Core Media Collection for Secondary Schools*. 2nd ed. New York: Bowker, 1979.

Provides details on 3,000 recommended non-print materials available for use in grades 7-12. Entries are arranged alphabetically by title under subject headings based on *Sears*. A title index and a producer/distributor directory complete the book.

Brown, Lucy Gregor, and Betty McDavid. *Core Media Collection for Elementary Schools*. 2nd ed. New York: Bowker, 1978.

The focus of this second edition is on titles produced since the first edition, *Resources for Learning*, was published in 1971. More than 5,000 annotated non-print titles for grades K-8 are listed by subject.

Free and Inexpensive Learning Materials. Peabody College of Vanderbilt University. Nashville: Incentive Publications, 1941- . Biennial.

Recommended educational aids are listed in this source under subject headings corresponding to curriculum areas taught in elementary and secondary schools. Posters, charts, maps, pictures, kits, and pamphlets are among the aids included. The annotation for each aid includes basic information such as the nature of the item, its size, price (unless free), full name and address of the distributor, and grade level. A cross-reference index guides the user to related materials within other classifications.

Hunt, Mary Alice, ed. *Multimedia Approach to Children's Literature*. 3rd ed. Chicago: American Library Association, 1983.

This selective guide lists and annotates 16mm films, filmstrips, and audiorecordings based on children's books. Entries are arranged alphabetically by book title. Author, subject, and media format indexes are included.

Melville, Annette. *Special Collections in the Library of Congress: A Selective Guide*. Washington, D.C.: Library of Congress, 1981.

Various holdings in the special collections of the Library of Congress are described in this guide. Included are collections of drawings, films, pamphlets, maps, music photographs, sound recordings, videotapes, and other non-print materials. Arrangement is alphabetical by the name of the collection and includes a personal/corporate name and subject index.

Newsome, Walter L. *New Guide to Popular Government Publications: For Libraries and Home Reference*. Littleton, Colo.: Libraries Unlimited, 1978.

This revised edition of *A Guide to Popular Government Publications* (1972) describes over 2,500 government documents considered of popular interest, many of them free or inexpensive. Entries contain full bibliographic description, descriptive annotation, price, and ordering information. New to this edition is an appendix listing guides to AV resources.

Shaffer, Dale E. *Sourcebook of Teaching Aids . . . Mostly Free: Posters and Pamphlets for Educators.* 4th ed. Salem, Ohio: DE Shaffer, 1983.

Free and inexpensive pamphlets and pictorial materials, such as posters, maps, charts, and pictures are listed in this selective guide. Entries are grouped under broad subject headings.

Equipment

The Audio-Visual Equipment Directory 1983-84. Fairfax, Va.: The International Communications Industries Association, 1953- . Annual.

This listing of all types of audiovisual equipment is arranged according to type of equipment. Within each section models are listed alphabetically by company name. Along with descriptive data, there is usually an illustration of the piece of equipment.

Consumer Reports. Mount Vernon, N.Y.: Consumer's Union of U.S., Inc., 1936- . Monthly.

A general source for objective evaluations of many types of equipment that may be used in a library, such as recording, television, and photographic equipment. Includes an annual buying guide issue.

EPIEgram: Equipment (Educational Products Information Exchange). Stony Brook, N.Y.: Educational Products Information Exchange Institute, 1972- . Monthly (Oct - June).

Reports on the results of testing of instructional equipment by the educational consumer's union, EPIE Institute.

Library Technology Reports. Chicago: American Library Association, 1965- . Bimonthly.

This comprehensive service provides detailed descriptions and in-depth evaluations of equipment and supplies related to the library profession.

Rosenberg, Kenyon C., and John S. Doskey. *Media Equipment: A Guide and Dictionary.* Littleton, Colo.: Libraries Unlimited, 1976.

A comprehensive encyclopedic dictionary of media equipment terminology for instructional media specialists, teachers, and librarians, organized in two main sections: a dictionary, defining 400 media terms, and a guide giving criteria for the evaluation and selection of AV equipment.

PART II

Specialized Sources for
Individual Non-print Formats

The specialized sources described in Part II should be used in conjunction with the more general works listed in Part I for the development of a well-rounded non-print collection.

ART OBJECTS AND REPRODUCTIONS

Guides

Ehresmann, Donald L. *Fine Arts: A Bibliographic Guide to Basic Reference Works, Histories and Handbooks.* 2nd ed. Littleton, Colo.: Libraries Unlimited, 1979.

Reference tools that access information on art works in sculpture and painting, as well as architecture, are listed in this comprehensive, annotated bibliography. Annotations are generally descriptive, though some contain critical comments. An index provides access by author, title, series, and subject.

Karpel, Bernard, ed. *Arts in America: A Bibliography.* 4 vols. Washington, D.C.: Smithsonian Institution Press, 1979-80.

This pioneering effort to gain bibliographic control over American art contains twenty-one bibliographies on various aspects of the visual arts, theater, dance, and music. Especially useful for selection purposes are three special sections dealing with visual resources on American art, a recommended listing of serials/publications for art libraries, and a survey of pictorial materials on Americana available for purchase.

Pacey, Philip. *Art Library Manual.* New York: Bowker, 1977.

A standard reference tool in art librarianship, this manual includes detailed information on the following: reference material; museum and gallery publications; exhibition/sales catalogs; microforms; sound recordings; video and film; slides and filmstrips; reproduction of art works; and loan collections of original art works.

Non-Evaluative Sources

American Federation of Arts. *American Art Directory.* 50th ed. New York: Jacques Cattell Press/R.R. Bowker, 1984.

Provides a listing of art journals and newspapers carrying art notes and criticism as well as a listing of booking agencies for traveling exhibitions. Also includes a listing of art schools and organizations arranged alphabetically by geographic location.

Brunet, M., and J. Pope, ed. *The Frick Collection: An Illustrated Catalog.* 9 vols. New York: The Frick Collection; dist. Princeton, N.J.: Princeton University Press, 1968- .

The complete holdings of this famous art museum are illustrated and fully described in this continuing series of catalogs. Each volume presents different types of works in the visual arts from various countries with entries arranged chronologically.

Cummings, Paul. *Fine Arts Market Place.* 3rd ed. New York: Bowker, 1977.

Similar in format to *Literary Market Place*, this guide lists the thousands of firms, organizations, and individuals involved in the trade. The information of exhibitions is particularly helpful, as is the extensive index.

Fundaburk, Emma L., and Thomas G. Davenport. *Art at Educational Institutions in the United States: A Handbook of Permanent, Semi-Permanent, and Temporary Works of Art at Elementary and Secondary Schools, Colleges and Universities.* Metuchen, N.J.: Scarecrow, 1974.

Art works located at selected educational institutions in the U.S. are listed alphabetically by state in this guide. Also provided is a listing of sources for information and materials which is organized by state.

Havlice, Patricia P. *World Painting Index, First Supplement 1973-1980.* 2 vols. Metuchen, N.J.: Scarecrow, 1982.

An update of the original *World Painting Index* published in 1977, this important reference work accesses reproductions of paintings appearing in 617 art books or catalogs published between 1973 and 1980 in the U.S. and abroad. Volume 1 contains an alphabetical listing by painter. Each entry gives an alphabetical listing of the painter's works along with references to books containing the reproductions and an indication of reproductions in black and white, color, or both. Volume 2 is an alphabetical listing of paintings by title with each entry giving references to the listing of painters. Also included in this source is a listing of paintings by unknown artists.

Korwin, Yala H. *Index to Two-Dimensional Art Works.* 2 vols. Metuchen, N.J.: Scarecrow, 1981.

This reference tool accesses reproductions of art works in 253 books and covers paintings, collages, mosaics, embroideries, colored drawings, murals, tapestries, and stained glass. Volume 1 is an artist index with entries providing such information as title, date, and current location of the original work; citations to reproductions of the work with indication of size and of color or black-and-white reproduction. Volume 2 contains a listing of the current location symbols used in Volume 1 and a title/subject index.

Library of Congress. *American Prints in the Library of Congress: A Catalog of the Collection.* Ann Arbor, Mich.: Books on Demand.
   A listing of original art works and reproductions owned by the Library of Congress.

Worldwide Art Catalogue Bulletin. Boston: Worldwide Books, Inc., 1963- . Quarterly with annual cumulation.
   Considerable information about art and art reproductions is found in exhibition catalogs issued by museums and art galleries in conjunction with special exhibits. The *Worldwide Art Catalogue Bulletin* provides reviews of exhibition catalogs available for purchase. The listing is arranged by place within country and is indexed by several access points.

   The selection tools listed in the section of photographs and pictures should also be consulted.

Evaluative Sources

Index to Reviews

Art Index. Bronx, N.Y.: H.W. Wilson, 1929- . Quarterly with annual cumulation.
   This Wilson index to art journals accesses reviews of an artist's work as well as reproductions/illustrations of art works. Also featured to a lesser extent are art films and photography. Arrangement is by author and subject.

Sources of Current Reviews

   Critical reviews of art exhibitions as well as feature articles on new artists and their work may be found in such art journals as *Art in America, Art News, Arts Magazine, Artforum, Art Bulletin,* and *Arts Review.*

Selective Listings

   Without access to the original art work, the evaluation of a reproduction presents a problem for the media librarian. Guidance and information on reputable art dealers may be sought from art educators and critics, art museum curators, and local art groups as well as artists themselves.

The following titles are some of the best known resources for quality reproductions. Each one gives information on sources from which reproductions may be purchased.

New York Graphic Society. *Fine Art Reproductions of Old and Modern Masters*. various editions. Greenwich, Conn.: New York Graphic Society.

Lists reproductions available from the New York Graphic Society.

UNESCO. *Catalogue of Colour Reproductions of Paintings Prior to 1860*. 9th ed. Paris: UNESCO, 1972.

UNESCO. *Catalogue of Colour Reproductions of Paintings 1860 - 1969*. Paris: UNESCO, 1972.

Films and slides provide an alternative method of presenting and experiencing art. The sections dealing with these formats should also be consulted.

Selective Filmographies

Canadian Centre for Films on Art for the American Federation of Arts. *Films on Art: A Source Book*. Lakewood, N.J.: Watson-Guptill Publications, 1977.

This highly selective filmography lists over 450 films on the visual arts. Included are projects by independent filmmakers and small distributors. Entries are arranged alphabetically by film title and contain complete bibliographic data, a summary of the film's contents, a detailed physical description and sales/rental information. Separate indexes provide access by subject and artist.

Rohrlick, Paula. *Exploring the Arts: Films and Video Programs for Young Viewers*. New York: Bowker, 1982.

Compiled by the resource director of Action for Children's Television (ACT), this guide gives descriptions and ordering information for more than 550 productions. Entries included were judged not to be sexist, racist, or unnecessarily violent. Arranged by broad subject area and then alphabetically by film title, entries give information on time, available formats, color or black-and-white, live or animated, distributors, producers and directors, date, country of origin, age levels, awards won, and an evaluative annotation. Separate indexes provide access by subject and title.

COMPUTER-READABLE DATABASES

Guide

Houghton, Bernard, and John Convey. *Online Information Retrieval Systems: An Introductory Manual to Principles and Practices.* 2nd ed. Hamden, Conn.: Shoe String Press, 1984.

A useful overview of computer-readable databases, and the major vendors through which they are accessed, is presented in this manual.

Non-Evaluative Sources

Directory of Online Databases. Santa Monica, Calif.: Caudra, 1979- . Annual.

This directory provides the most comprehensive and timely listing of bibliographic, numeric, and full-text databases produced worldwide. Each database description includes type of file, subjects covered, producer, vendor(s), access requirements, geographic and time span coverage, language(s) used in the database, frequency of updates, and a note on contents. A directory of database producers and online services is also included. A master index to databases, database producers, and online services as well as several other indexes providing various access points completes the work. Semi-annual issues of the directories as well as two issues on new and revised information update this reference tool.

Hall, James L., and Marjorie J. Brown. *Online Bibliographic Databases: A Directory and Sourcebook.* 3rd ed. London: Aslib; dist. Detroit: Gale Research, 1983.

This reference work lists 179 English-language bibliographic databases currently available for searching. Numeric databases are excluded. Detailed entries provide such information as vendor's name and address, subject areas covered, printed versions, access charge, references to relevant documentation and, in most cases, a sample record. The introduction includes a useful overview of online retrieval. Also included are a general index and two subject guides to the databases covered.

Information Industry Market Place: An International Directory of Information Products and Services. 1984-85. New York: Bowker, 1984.

Full and current contact, personnel and product information world-wide is given for more than 1,000 database publishers, online vendors, information brokers, telecommunication networks, library networks and consortia, terminal manufacturers, consultants, government agencies, and many other related firms and services.

Williams, Martha E. *Computer-Readable Databases: A Directory and Data Sourcebook.* 2 vols. Chicago: American Library Association, 1984.

The inclusion of databases in this directory is based upon their computer readability, availability to the public, usefulness for information retrieval purposes, and their availability through the major online vendors. Entries are listed alphabetically by database name or acronym and give such information as producer, subject matter and scope, year of origin, number of records in the database, frequency of updates, and price. Access is provided through indexes by producer, processor, database name, and subject.

Newsletters published by the various database vendors and producers include descriptions of new databases.

Evaluative Sources

Indexes to Reviews

There are no specialized indexes to reviews for databases. Recent issues of *Media Review Digest* do not list such reviews; however, *Library Literature* does provide access to database reviews.

Sources of Current Reviews

Evaluations of databases and feature articles on developments in online searching are included in such professional journals as *Online, Database: The Magazine of Database Reference and Review*, and *Online Review: The International Journal of Online Information Systems*.

FILMS AND FILMSTRIPS

Guides

Allen, Nancy. *Film Study Collections: A Guide to Their Development and Use.* New York: Frederick Ungar Publishing, 1979.

This practical guide aids in collection development by providing lists of monographs and periodicals in the area of film study, print and online reference sources, annotated lists of bibliographies to aid in selection and a listing of major film archives in the U.S. An index gives access by subject, title, and film study collection.

Miller, Hannah Elsas. *Films in the Classroom: A Practical Guide.* Metuchen, N.J.: Scarecrow Press. 1979.

This guide gives a basic approach to the evaluation, selection, and use of films and filmstrips in the curriculum. Included are listings of sources for films and reviews and organizations involved in promoting films in the classroom as well as a selective filmography for developing student awareness of particular topics.

Non-Evaluative Sources

The American Film Institute Catalog of Motion Pictures: Feature Films 1961-1970. 2 vols. New York: Bowker, 1976.

An enormous project begun by the R.R. Bowker Company, the goal is to provide objective and definitive information for all feature films, short films and newsreels produced in the U.S. as well as any significant foreign releases shown in the U.S. In the first volume the films are listed alphabetically with complete bibliographic data and such information as date and location of release, cast (with names of characters), shooting location, foreign titles, and a synopsis. The second volume provides several indexes by credit, literary and dramatic source, subject, and national production. Future volumes will complete this work.

Educational Film Locator of the Consortium of University Film Centers and R.R. Bowker. 2nd ed. New York: Bowker, 1980.

This catalog lists and describes all the films held by the 50 member institutions of the Consortium of University Film Centers. The 40,000 films are arranged alphabetically by the title. Each entry is fully annotated and contains mediagraphic information.

Feature Films on 8mm, 16mm and Videotape: A Directory of Feature Films Available for Rental, Sale and Lease in the United States and Canada. 8th ed. New York: Bowker, 1967- . Irregular.

This work is an alphabetical listing of 8mm, 16mm, and videotape titles available in the United States and Canada. Each entry includes information on running time, color, major stars, and director. A number of indexes make finding and ordering even easier. Supplements to each edition of *Feature Films* appear in *Sightlines*.

Library of Congress Catalog: Audiovisual Materials. Washington, D.C.: Government Printing Office, 1953- . Quarterly with annual/quinquennial cumulation.

Previously entitled *Library of Congress Catalog: Motion Pictures and Filmstrips*, this catalog lists all films, videorecordings, filmstrips, transparencies, and slides released in the U.S. or Canada that have been cataloged by LC. Entries give full LC card information.

Sprecher, Daniel, ed. *Guide to Government-Loan Films, 16mm.* 5th ed. Alexandria, Va.: Serina Press, 1980.

Films available for loan from the U.S. Government are listed in this guide. Entries are arranged alphabetically by title under the sponsoring government agency.

Weaver, Kathleen, ed. *Film Programmer's Guide to 16mm Rentals.* 3rd ed. Albany, Calif.: Reel Research, 1980.

The third edition of this work lists 14,000 16mm films available for rent. Film entries are arranged alphabetically and include distributor and rental cost. There is an index by film director. Unlike *Feature Films on 8mm, 16mm, and Videotape, Film Programmer's Guide* lists short films. In addition, the guide lists distributors not covered in *Feature Films.*

Evaluative Sources

Indexes to Reviews

Film Literature Index. Albany, N.Y.: Filmdex, Part II, Inc., Film and Television Documentation Center, State University of New York, 1973- . Quarterly with annual cumulation.

This reference tool indexes commercial and some educational film reviews found in more than 200 popular and professional periodicals. Entries are arranged under subject headings and may be accessed under title, screenwriter, director, and performer.

New York Times Film Reviews. New York: Times Books, 1913- . Biennial.

This compilation of film reviews that have appeared in *The New York Times* lists entries chronologically with date, page, and column citations to the original review. A separate, detailed index provides various access points.

Ozer, Jerome S., ed. *Film Review Annual 1983.* Englewood, N.J.: Jerome S. Ozer Publishing, 1984.

Reviews of feature films, selected from the major reviewing media, which were released over the past year in the major U.S. markets are listed in their entirety in this annual. Entries include citations to reviews found elsewhere. Several indexes provide access by film critic, cast, producer, director, editor, screenwriter, and reviewing publication, among other access points. Also included is a listing of award winners/ nominees.

Variety Film Reviews. 16 vols. New York: Garland Publishing, 1907-1980.

Film reviews that have appeared in *Variety* are listed in their entirety in this compilation. Entries are arranged chronologically and cite the date on which the original review appeared. An index by film title completes the work.

Sources of Current Reviews

AV Guide Newsletter. Des Plaines, Ill.: Educational Screen, 1922- . Monthly.

In addition to informative articles on the theory and application of AV, there are approximately 350 film, filmstrip, and television programs evaluated each year in this publication, which is directed at elementary and secondary schools. In addition, the latest materials and equipment are featured. Formerly published as *Educational Screen and AV Guide*.

EFLA Evaluations. New York: Educational Film Library Association, 1946- . 5 issues/year.

Each issue contains one hundred reviews of current films/videotapes arranged alphabetically by title. In addition to bibliographic data, there is a synopsis, comments, age level, uses, and subject areas covered for each item. Each issue includes a subject index to the films/videotapes included in the current issue and a cumulative title index, incorporating films evaluated in the current issue with those included in previous issues for the volume year. A distributors' address list follows the indexes.

Film Library Quarterly. New York: Film Library Information Council, 1967- . Quarterly.

Feature articles on topics such as filmmakers, use of films in libraries, etc., provide the primary emphasis in this quarterly; however the critical reviews are excellent evaluations from the library point of view. Bill Katz in *Magazines for Libraries* (Bowker, 1978) states: "The basic film magazine for the film librarian at the academic, public or school level."

Film News: The International Review of AV Materials and Equipment. New York: Film News Col. 1939- . Bimonthly.

A basic evaluation source for all types of libraries (elementary through college) needing reviews of films and filmstrips. Each issue includes between twenty-five and thirty signed reviews listed under appropriate subject headings. Notes on books, magazine articles, and equipment follow the reviews.

Landers Film Reviews. Escondido, Calif.: Landers Associates, 1956- . 5 issues/year.

What *Kirkus Reviews* is to books, *Landers* is to films. The 140 critical reviews in each issue are arranged by film title. Bibliographic data is followed by intended audience level (elementary-secondary), subject areas, purpose, and the review. Each issue includes a section on new multimedia instructional materials organized by producers and distributors. A subject index in each issue and a cumulative title/subject index in the June issue adds to the usefulness of the tool.

Media Review. Ridgefield, Conn.: Key Production, 1979- . Monthly.

Directed to the elementary, secondary, and college curriculum, this journal provides critical evaluations of filmstrips and filmstrip kits. Annotations include suggested grade level, cost, detailed descriptions of components, and publisher's address. Special reports on current news affecting the media specialist as well as announcements of new releases are included.

Sightlines. New York: Educational Film Library Association, 1967- . Quarterly.

Devoted to 16mm films, this publication includes "New Film/Video Releases" in each issue. Arranged alphabetically by title, each citation includes mediagraphic information, an annotation, and the audience level for the film. A subject index follows the title listing. A special feature of *Sightlines* is the inclusion of filmographies on special subjects such as science and ethics, sexuality, etc. Supplements for *Feature Films on 8mm, 16mm, and Videotape* are included in issues of *Sightlines*.

Variety. New York: Variety, Inc., 1905- . Weekly.

Includes reviews of films, recordings, and television and radio programs.

Selective Filmographies

Artel, Linda, and Susan Wengraf. *Positive Images: A Guide to 400 Non-Sexist Films for Young People.* San Francisco: Booklegger Press, 1976.

A selective list of non-sexist films are annotated in this guide for educators. Arrangement of entries is under specified subject areas.

Emmens, Carol A. *Short Stories on Film.* Littleton, Colo.: Libraries Unlimited, 1978.

Over 1,300 films released between 1920 and 1976 that were based on short stories by American authors or well known foreign authors are listed in this filmography. Entries are alphabetically arranged by author, subdivided by a listing of short story titles. Each entry gives a film title, a source note, technical information, cast and credits. Descriptive annotations are provided. A directory lists current distributors of prints of the films. There are indexes by short story or film title.

Gaffney, Maureen, ed. *More Films Kids Like: A Catalog of Short Films for Children*. Chicago: American Library Association, 1977.

This companion to *Films Kids Like* (ALA, 1973) includes 200 entirely different short 16mm films. During a two-year testing period, these were the films preferred by a group of children from three to twelve years of age. Films of general interest as well as those designed for educational use are included. Arranged alphabetically by title, the information for each film includes running time, distributor, date and place of production, annotation, reaction of the children taking part in the testing process, uses, and age level. Special features include "Film Activities Kids Like," with suggestions for related films; key to distributors; and subject index grouping films from both *Films Kids Like* (FKL) and *More Films Kids Like (MFKL) under headings.*

Goldstein, Ruth M., and Edith Zornow. *Movies for Kids: A Guide for Parents and Teachers on the Entertainment Film for Children*. rev. ed. New York: Frederick Ungar Publishing, 1980.

This selective guide lists and annotates more than 400 entertainment films suitable for children aged eight to thirteen. A directory of film companies and distributors is included as well as listing of film books and periodicals and of film organizations.

Goldstein, Ruth M., and Edith Zornow. *Screen Image of Youth: Movies About Children and Adolescents*. Metuchen, N.J.: Scarecrow, 1980.

More than 350 feature films of the past fifty years that portray young people are annotated in this filmography. Entries are grouped under fifteen subject areas such as "crime and delinquency" and "growing pains." Also included is a directory of film companies and distributors as well as a title index.

Jones, Emily S., ed. *The College Film Library Collection*. 2 vols. Williamsport, Pa.: Bro-Dart Publishing, 1971.

This selective filmography lists and describes 8mm and 35mm films suitable for use in college-level courses. Entries are arranged under broad subject categories such as the arts, philosophy, social sciences, applied science, literature, and sports. Complete bibliographic and technical data are given for each entry as well as price, year of release, LC card number, and a descriptive annotation.

Notable Children's Films. Chicago: American Library Association, Association for Library Service to Children. Annual.

This filmography identifies 16mm films for children through age fourteen judged the most notable of those released for library distribution during the past year. The annotated list, arranged alphabetically by title, is published each spring in pamphlet form. A list also appears in a March or April issue of *School Library Journal*; however, this list is not annotated.

Selected Films for Young Adults. Chicago: American Library Association, Young Adult Services Division (YASD). Annual.

The annotated list of "notable" 16mm films is arranged alphabetically by title in pamphlet form and appears as a list in a March or April issue of *School Library Journal*.

Wynar, Lubomyr R., and Lois Buttlar. *Ethnic Film and Filmstrip Guide for Libraries and Media Centers*. Littleton, Colo.: Libraries Unlimited, 1980.

Approximately 1,400 films and filmstrips are included in this guide, which contains forty-six sections on ethnic groups. Each ethnic section lists films followed by filmstrips. Annotations for each item were taken from various reviewing sources. This is a successor to the author's *Building Ethnic Collections: An Annotated Guide for School Media Centers* (1977).

GAMES, SIMULATIONS, TOYS, KITS, MODELS, AND REALIA

Guides

Hektoen, Faith H., and Jeanne B. Rinehart, eds. *Toys to Go: A Guide to the Use of Realia in Public Libraries*. Chicago: American Library Association, 1976.

This source provides useful guidelines on the establishment, maintenance, and circulation of a collection of realia. A helpful bibliography is included.

Horn, Robert E., and Anne Cleaves. *The Guide to Simulations/Games for Education and Training*. 4th ed. Beverly Hills, Calif.: Sage Publications, 1980.

This edition includes "Evaluative Essays," which consist of twenty-four essays evaluating available simulations and games; "Academic Listings," which not only identify the games and simulations by subject but also include detailed information about both computerized and manually operated games and simulations; and "Resources," which identify simulation/game periodicals and centers. Separate author, game, and producer indexes are provided.

Non-Evaluative Sources

Belch, Jean. *Contemporary Games*. 2 vols. Detroit: Gale Research, 1973-74.
  Nine hundred games and simulations, both manually and computer operated, are listed in volume 1 by subject area and then alphabetically by title. Entries include detailed information from age level to the names of designers. A brief annotation is provided. Volume 2 is a bibliography.

  Coverage of games, simulations, toys, kits, models, and realia is also provided by the *Index to Instructional Media Catalogs*, *Audio Visual Market Place*, *Educational Media Yearbook* and/or the *Educators Guide Series*.

Evaluative Sources

Index to Reviews

  The *Media Review Digest* lists citations to reviews of the nonprint formats covered in this section under the Miscellaneous Media section.

Sources of Current Reviews

  Current reviews of games and simulations, toys, models, and multimedia kits (which often include realia) may be found in many of the standard nonprint media reviewing journals listed in Part I. In addition, these materials are reviewed in several educational journals such as *Mathematics Teacher, Social Education, Instructional Innovator, Instructor,* and *Science and Children.*
  Specialized reviewing journals in the area of games and simulations include *Creative Computing, Simages, Simgames,* and *Simulation and Games.*

Selective Mediagraphies

Wieckert, Jeanne E., and Irene W. Bell. *Media-Classroom Skills: Games for the Middle School*. 2 vols. Littleton, Colo.: Libraries Unlimited, 1981.
  The focus of this guide is on games and multimedia kits that teach library and classroom skills to seventh and eighth grade students. Classroom games are listed under curriculum categories. The forty-two media games listed deal with such basic library skills as alphabetization, use of the card catalog, the Dewey decimal system, parts of a book, and the use of reference material. A section on the construction of games provides suggestions for additional activities.

HOLOGRAMS

Holography is a new and expanding field in the area of non-print media which, as yet, has few selection aids. Recent editions of *Media Review Digest* do list reviews for holograms. Graham Saxby's book *Holograms: How to Make and Use Them* (Woburn, Mass.: Focal Press, 1980) provides an overview of developments in holography as well as instructions on how to make your own holograms.

MAPS AND ATLASES

Guides

Field, Lance. *Map User's Sourcebook*. Dobbs Ferry, N.Y.: Oceana Publications, 1982.

This reference source provides a basic introduction to maps and map sources. Included are a glossary of cartographic terms and several chapters on national and international sources of maps.

Larsgaard, Mary. *Map Librarianship: An Introduction*. Littleton, Colo.: Libraries Unlimited, 1978.

Information included deals with the selection and acquisition of individual maps on through to the administration of an entire map library. Appendixes and a lengthy bibliography add to the book's usefulness.

Non-Evaluative Sources

Alexander, Gerald, L. *Guide to Atlases: World, Regional, National, Thematic; An International Listing of Atlases Published Since 1950*. Metuchen, N.J.: Scarecrow Press, 1971.

Over 5,500 atlases published worldwide are listed in this source. Entries are grouped under their respective categories and are arranged alphabetically by publisher with the exception of thematic atlases, which are listed first by subject and then by publisher within a subject area. Several indexes provide access by publisher, author, cartographer, editor and language. The *Guide to Atlases Supplement* (1977) updates this source through 1975.

Carrington, David K., and Richard W. Stephenson, eds. *Map Collections in the United States and Canada: A Directory*. 3rd ed. Chicago: Special Libraries Association, 1978.

Over 745 map collections are covered in the third edition of this valuable reference work. Arrangement of entries is alphabetical by state and by city within states. Such information as subject and chronological specializations, special map collections, number of maps, depositories, reproduction facilities, interlibrary loan, and name of map librarian is given in each entry. A detailed index is included.

Winch, Kenneth L., ed. *International Maps and Atlases in Print*. 2nd ed. New York: Bowker, 1976.
   Listed are over 8,000 detailed cartographic entries on maps and atlases available from 700 publishing firms throughout the world. Arrangement is by continent and country.

Maps published by the United States government, the single largest map publisher, can be found in the *Monthly Catalog of United States Government Publications*.

Evaluative Sources

Index to Reviews

Though there are no specialized indexing sources for reviews of maps and atlases, the *Media Review Digest* does provide access to reviews.

Sources of Current Reviews

The American Cartographer. Falls Church, Va.: American Congress on Surveying and Mapping, 1974- . Semi-annual.
   Recommended for public and academic libraries, this publication contains useful reviews of regional and local atlases in some issues.

Bulletin. Special Libraries Association. Geography and Map Division, 1947- . Quarterly.
   All aspects of geography and maps are reported in this quarterly publication. Mary Larsgaard in her book, *Map Librarianship*, refers to it as the "premier journal for U.S. map librarians, and of interest to map librarians everywhere." Articles of professional interest, bibliographies, lists of recent maps and atlases, book reviews, accession lists, and publishers' catalogs are occasionally listed.

The Canadian Cartographer. Downsview, Ontario: Department of Geography, York University, 1964- . Semi-annual.
   The scope of coverage is worldwide. Scholarly articles of a technical and historical nature are presented. Extensive reviews of maps are included.

Cartography. Canberra City, Australia: Australian Institute of Cartographers, 1954- . Annual.

Recommended for comprehensive collections, this technical journal does include articles and reviews about maps and atlases.

Geographical Journal. London: Royal Geographic Society, 1893- Quarterly.

Bill Katz in *Magazines for Libraries* (Bowker, 1978) calls this the "world's leading scholarly geographical journal." Reviews of atlases and notes on maps are included in a section "Cartographical Survey."

MICROCOMPUTING AND PROGRAMMED INSTRUCTION

Guides

Costa, Betty, and Marie Costa. *A Micro Handbook for Small Libraries and Media Centers.* Littleton, Colo.: Libraries Unlimited, 1983.

A discussion of the selection and implementation of microcomputer systems for various types of libraries is presented in this useful guide. An overview of computer hardware/software and applications for microcomputers in libraries is given. The appendixes list books, periodicals, software dealers and packages, and organizations and individuals in the microcomputing field. A glossary is included.

Miller, Inabeth. *Microcomputers in School Library Media Centers.* New York: Neal-Schuman, 1984.

As well as providing an overview of educational applications of microcomputers at the elementary/secondary level, this guide offers useful tips on the selection and evaluation of software and video technology.

Webster, Tony. *Microcomputer Buyer's Guide.* 3rd ed. New York: McGraw-Hill, 1984.

This annual guide aids the selector in comparing and choosing currently available microcomputing equipment. An overview of microcomputers, microcomputer systems, peripherals, software, pricing, and suppliers is provided. The guide is updated in March and July of each year.

Non-Evaluative Sources

Chartrand, Marilyn J., and Constance D. Williams, eds. *Educational Software Directory: A Subject Guide to Microcomputer Software.* Littleton, Colo.: Libraries Unlimited, 1982.

This directory provides in-depth subject access to over 900 educational software packages. Entries are grouped under twelve broad subject areas and are arranged alphabetically by title. Each entry includes publisher, format, hardware requirements, programming language, price, grade level, and a descriptive annotation. Also provided is a publisher and distributor listing, with notes on their previewing policies, and an annotated source bibliography.

Classroom Computer Learning Directory of Educational Computing Resources. Belmont, Calif.: Pitman Learning, 1983. Annual.

Formerly published as the *Classroom Computer News Directory of Educational Computing Resources*, this directory lists educational computing-related resources, including associations, user groups, and funding sources located in the U.S. and Canada. Entries give complete address information and are annotated. A helpful section on software contains information on directories, reviewing sources, and clearing-houses. Also included are a listing of relevant periodicals, a calendar of conferences and workshops, and a general index.

Hendershot, Carl H. *Programmed Learning and Individually Paced Instruction: Bibliography* (includes supplements 1-6). 5th ed. Bay City, Mich.: Hendershot Bibliography, 1984.

Included in this looseleaf format are sources of individualized instruction in over 200 subjects as well as descriptions of program devices designed for self-study or for students in all levels of education. The information is presented in five sections. The last section is a list of resources and references about programmed instruction.

International Software Database Corporation. *MENU: The International Software Database*. Palo Alto, Calif.: DIALOG Information Retrieval Service, 1973- . Monthly reload.

This database gives a comprehensive international listing of software vendors and their available programs. Entries are accessible by application, computer system, and publisher. Each entry gives a full description as well of such information as minimum memory requirements, related programs, compatible systems, and pricing. Complete vendor/distributor information is also provided.

Microcomputer Marketplace 1985. 2nd ed. New York: Bowker, 1984. Semi-annual.

This directory provides a comprehensive listing of organizations and services in the microcomputer industry. Complete profiles are given on manufacturers, distributors, and suppliers of microcomputer software, hardware, and peripherals. Also given are listings of associations, meetings and exhibits, and periodicals in the microcomputing field. A newly published companion volume entitled *Educational Microcomputing Market Place (1984-85)* provides the same type of information in the area of educational computing.

The Software Finder: A Guide to Educational Microcomputer Software for APPLE II, ATARI 400/800, COMMODORE PET, CBM, VIC-20, 64, RADIO SHACK TRS-80 MODELS I-III, Color Computer, and CP/M. Dresden, Me.: Dresden Associates, 1983- . Semi-annual.

A comprehensive listing of school- and college-oriented software, compatible with the computers listed, is provided in this directory. Entries are listed by topic and give information on subject, grade level, producer suppliers, price, and references to reviews, with an indication of a positive or negative review, among other details. Also included are administrative software packages. A glossary and indexes are provided.

Wang, Anastasia, ed. *Index to Computer-Based Learning: 1981 Edition.* 3 vols. Portsmouth, N.H.: Entelek, Inc., 1981.

Over 4,800 computer-based instructional programs for primary-through college-level users are listed and annotated in this source. Entries are classified and are arranged alphabetically by program title. An index provides several access points.

Evaluative Sources

Index to Reviews

Microcomputer Index. Santa Clara, Calif.: Microcomputer Information Services, 1980- . Bi-monthly.

Over 25 English-language microcomputer periodicals as well as other publications that deal with microcomputers are indexed in this source. Hardware and software reviews at all educational levels are covered as well as book reviews and new products. Also accessed through this index are articles on developments in videotex and computer games. The index is also available online (with monthly updates) through DIALOG Information Retrieval Service.

Sources of Current Reviews

Classroom Computer Learning. Belmont, Calif.: Pitman Learning, 1981-. 9 issues/year.

Articles focus on the integration of computer-based learning with traditional classroom instruction. A regular column reviews software, hardware, and relevant literature.

Computer Equipment Review. Westport, Conn.: Meckler Publishing, 1979- . Semi-annual.

This source provides informative articles and reviews of computer hardware.

The Computing Teacher. Eugene, Ore.: International Council for Computers in Education, 1979- . Monthly.

Technical articles on the instructional use of computers at all educational levels are featured in this periodical. Each issue includes software and book reviews and news on conferences, projects, and resource centers.

Creative Computing. Morris Plains, N.J.: Pertec Computer Corp., 1974-. Monthly.

A portion of each issue features articles on educational uses of computers. Special issues include software reviews and listings of computer games.

Educational Computer Magazine. Cupertino, Calif.: Edcomp Inc., 1981-. 10 issues/year.

The pros and cons of instructional computing are addressed in this journal. Articles focus on conference reports and ongoing projects. Book and educational software reviews are included in each issue.

Educational Technology. Englewood Cliffs, N.J.: Educational Technology Publications, 1961- . Monthly

Developments in educational technology and educational computer applications are featured in this journal. Reviews of commercially available educational software are regularly included.

Instructional Innovator. Washington, D.C.: Association for Educational Communications and Technology, 1956- . 8 issues/year.

Contains feature articles on developments in educational technology. Includes a new products section on hardware as well as special issues on microcomputers in education. Also gives announcements of reports available from the Educational Resources Information Center (ERIC).

Software Review. Westport, Conn.: Meckler Publishing, 1982- . Quarterly.

Reviews are given on software programs for library and educational applications. Includes articles on software concepts and evaluation.

MICROFORMS

Guide

Saffady, William. *Micrographics*. Littleton, Colo.: Libraries Unlimited, 1978.

A comprehensive text which serves as an introduction to the basics of microforms for librarians. The author discusses types of microforms, micropublishing, the use of microforms, bibliographic control, storage and retrieval, and the future of micrographics.

Non-Evaluative Sources

Guide to Microforms in Print. Westport, Conn.: Meckler Publishing, 1976- . Annual.

Over 60,000 titles from some 200 publishers are included in this cumulative alphabetical listing. Books are entered under authors, journals by title, newspapers by city and state, and manuscripts and archives by publishing organization. Entries indicate the basic bibliographic information as well as the price and type of microform.

The Microform Market Place: An International Directory of Micropublishing. Westport, Conn.: Meckler Publishing, 1976- . Annual.

Similar to other "Market Place" type directories, this one provides a list of commercial and institutional micropublishers with address, phone number, types of micropublications available, and the name and title of a contact person. The information is rearranged in other sections by geographical area and broad subject specialty.

Micropublishers Trade List Annual. Westport, Conn.: Meckler Publishing, 1975- . Annual.

A collection of catalogs issued by micropublishers in the United States and abroad. It is available only in microfiche.

National Register of Microform Masters. Washington, D.C.: Library of Congress, 1965- . Annual.

This union catalog lists the microform holdings of over 300 American and foreign libraries as well as commercial publishers. Entries are arranged alphabetically by author.

Subject Guide to Microforms in Print. Westport, Conn.: Meckler Publishing, 1976- . Annual.

This companion volume to *Guide to Microforms in Print* is arranged alphabetically under broad subject classifications.

Evaluative Sources

Index to Reviews

Reviews of microforms may be accessed in *Media Review Digest*.

Cumulative Microform Reviews 1972-1976. Westport, Conn.: Microform Review, 1979.

This compilation of microform reviews represents the first in a continuing series of five-year cumulations of reviews that have appeared in *Microform Review.* Entries are arranged under thirty-six subject categories.

Sources of Current Reviews

Microdoc. Surrey, England: S.J. Teague. Microfilm Association of Great Britain, 1962- . Quarterly.

Each issue includes reviews of several microform publications as well as book reviews. The articles are technical and aimed at the professional.

Microform Review. Westport, Conn.: Meckler Publishing, 1972- . Quarterly.

The emphasis in this basic reviewing publication is on the more scholarly microform publications. Both the content and the technical qualities of each publication are evaluated resulting in reviews which are lengthy and detailed.

Micrographics Equipment Review. Westport, Conn.: Meckler Publishing, 1976- . Quarterly.

Providing the same type of detailed coverage for equipment that *Microform Review* does for microforms, this publication reports on twenty-four to thirty pieces of equipment that are tested each year.

Microlist. Westport, Conn.: Meckler Publishing, 1977- . 10 issues/year.

This supplement to *Microforms in Print* provides an author, title, and subject approach to micropublications.

Selective Mediagraphy

Dodson, Suzanne Cates. *Microform Research Collections: A Guide*. 2nd ed. Westport, Conn.: Meckler Publishing, 1984.

Large and timely microform collections that are reviewed are described in this selective guide. A subject and title index provides access to over 370 entries which are arranged alphabetically by title. Each entry gives publisher, format, price (with date), citations to reviews, and date of publication as well as references to indexes and bibliographies listing the microform set, notes on content and arrangement, size of collection, and publishing status.

MUSICAL SCORES

Guide

Fling, Robert Michael, ed. *A Basic Music Library: Essential Scores and Books*. 2nd ed. Chicago: American Library Association, 1983.

This guide contains a series of selective lists of music-related books and scores considered primary for a basic music collection. Complete ordering information is provided for each entry.

Non-Evaluative Sources

Library of Congress Catalog: Music, Books on Music, and Sound Recordings. Washington, D.C.: Library of Congress, 1973- . Semi-annual with annual & quinquennial cumulations.

As part of the National Union Catalog, this reference tool represents a comprehensive bibliography of all music-related books, records, tapes, scores, sheet music, and libretti cataloged by the Library of Congress or other libraries participating in the NUC. Sound recordings listed are both musical and non-musical. Entries are arranged alphabetically by composer/author and give title, full bibliographic data (including size and speed for recordings), subject headings, LC card number, and classification number. A subject index is included. Formerly entitled *Library of Congress: Music and Phonorecords*.

Evaluative Sources

Index to Reviews

Critical commentaries on music-related materials are accessed in *Music Index* (see section on Recordings).

Sources of Current Reviews

Periodicals containing reviews of musical scores include *The Instrumentalist, Music and Letters, The Musical Times,* and *Notes.*

ORAL HISTORY

Guide

Davis, Cullom, et al. *Oral History: From Tape to Type.* Chicago: American Library Association, 1977.

An overview of the field of oral history as well as considerations and procedures for developing a local oral history collection is presented in this useful guide. A listing of reference works is also included.

Non-Evaluative Sources

Mason, Elizabeth B., and Louis M. Starr. *Oral History Collection of Columbia University.* 4th ed. New York: Columbia University, Oral History Research Office, 1979.

More than 3,700 titles in the oral history collection of Columbia University, which is considered a landmark in the field, are listed in this guide. Entries are alphabetically arranged by names of principal memorists or title of special projects and contain cross-references. Analytical annotations give information on background, contents, availability, microform, and limitations on use.

Meckler, Alan M., and Ruth McMullin. *Oral History Collections.* New York: Bowker, 1975.

The oral history holdings of libraries, archives, and other institutions in the U.S., Canada, and abroad are listed in this directory. Entries are arranged by the name or subject of the collection and include: location, language, and date of the interview, availability for use, and references to other interviews in which the person was discussed. A listing of U.S. and foreign oral history centers is included.

Evaluative Sources

There are no indexes which access reviews of oral history. However, oral history reviews are contained in the following journals: *American Archivist, History News, International Journal of Oral History, Oral History* (Great Britain), and *Oral History Association Newsletter.*

PAMPHLETS AND EPHEMERA

Guide

Miller, Shirley. *The Vertical File and Its Satellites.* 2nd ed. Littleton, Colo.: Libraries Unlimited, 1979.

This manual deals with the selection and organization of vertical file materials including pamphlets, clippings, maps, photographs, and other related resources. Also included is a discussion of methods for labeling, filing, circulating, and weeding materials as well as a listing of key publications and sources.

There is no reviewing source for pamphlets. The selection of pamphlets should be guided by the materials selection policy of the library. Sources that assist in the identification of pamphlets and related vertical file materials include the following:

Selected U.S. Government Publications. Washington, D.C.: Government Printing Office, 1928- . Monthly.

A pamphlet itself, this source lists currently available pamphlets on various topics. It is useful for public and school libraries.

Vertical File Index. New York: H.W. Wilson, 1935- . Monthly.

Many free and inexpensive materials are listed under subject categories in this well-known Wilson index. Sources listed cover a large variety of interests and are suitable for all levels of instruction. Complete ordering information and price are given.

Pamphlets are often listed in the standard reviewing journals (see Part I) as well as in the *Educators Guide Series, Free and Inexpensive Learning Materials, Monthly Checklist of State Publications, Public Affairs Information Service Bulletin,* and the *Monthly Catalog of United States Government Publications.*

Editorial Research Reports. Washington, D.C.: Congressional Quarterly, 1923- .Weekly.

This is a well-known pamphlet series suitable for use in high school, academic, and public libraries. Subject areas covered focus on topics of current interest. Semi-annual bound volumes area available.

As pictures are often part of the vertical file collection, selection sources for pictures should be consulted as well. (See following section.)

PICTURES

Guide

Appel, Marsha C. *Illustration Index V:1977-1981*. Metuchen, N.J.: Scarecrow, 1984.

The fifth edition of this work indexes illustrations found in such highly pictorial magazines as *American Heritage, Ebony, National Geographic, Sports Illustrated,* and *Smithsonian.* Entries are arranged under broad subject areas and provide in-depth cross-references, as well as an indication of the type of illustration, if other than a photograph, color, and size.

Bradshaw, David N., and Catherine Hahn, eds. *World Photography Sources*. New York: Directories; dist. New York: Bowker, 1982.

This comprehensive guide describes more than 1,700 international sources of pictures including stock agencies, institutions, and photographers. Entries are grouped under such broad subject areas as agriculture, industry, military, performing arts, social sciences, personalities, sports, and visual arts. Information for each source includes address, telephone number, contact person, subject areas, type of access to the collection, and fees. Several detailed indexes provide access to entries.

Evans, Hilary. *Picture Librarianship*. Hamden, Conn.: Shoe String, 1980.

This textbook provides useful instruction on the selection, access, and maintenance of picture libraries, which are defined as all types of illustrations such as postcards, newspaper clippings, cinema stills, and posters. A discussion of various types of picture libraries is also presented.

Reviewing sources for pictures do not exist. However, there are several tools for locating pictures.

McDarrah, Fred W. *Photography Market Place: The Complete Sourcebook for Still Photography*. 2nd ed. New York: Bowker, 1977.

The directory covers the major markets for selling photos, technical services, and equipment sources, including photographic supplies and support services. Entries give complete addresses, telephone numbers, and names of key personnel. An index lists the names of all firms and individuals appearing in the directory.

Picturescope. New York: Special Libraries Association, 1953- . Quarterly.

Tips on how to locate photographs and pictures and notes about new bibliographic aids in the field are included in this newsletter.

Parry, Pamela J. *Photography Index: A Guide to Reproductions.* Westport, Conn.: Greenwood Press, 1979.
Photographs found in more than eighty books are indexed in this work. Access to entries is through three major sections: a chronological index to anonymous photographs; an index by photographer; and a subject/title index.

Robl, Ernest H., ed. *Picture Sources Four.* Special Libraries Association. Ann Arbor, Mich.: Books on Demand, 1983.
Listed in this source are collections of prints, slides, and photographs in U.S. and Canadian libraries as well as private collections. Several commercial firms providing pictures are also included. Indexes aid the user in finding specific types of pictures which are arranged under various categories.

"Free and inexpensive" listings as well as U.S. Government publications often include pictures. (See sources listed in section on Pamphlets & Ephemera.)
Other sources of pictures include special interest groups such as the National Audubon Society, Sierra Club, etc. In addition, quality pictures are readily available in such highly pictorial magazines as *Arizona Highways, Ebony, National Wildlife, Life, National Geographic, Smithsonian,* and *Sports Illustrated.*

RECORDINGS: DISKS AND TAPES

Guides

Duckles, Vincent. *Music Reference and Research Materials.* New York: Free Press, 1974.
This text is a basis for reference materials in the field of music. Over 2,000 titles are listed and annotated in this guide. Entries are categorized by format (e.g., dictionaries, handbooks, bibliographies) with related subdivisions.

Non-Evaluative Sources

Chicorel, Marietta, ed. *Chicorel Index to the Spoken Arts on Disks, Tapes, and Cassettes.* Vols. 7 & 7A. New York: American Library Publishing Co., 1973-74.

Both commercial and non-commercial audiorecordings are listed in this index under such broad subject headings as essays, commentaries, poetry, readings from novels, political speeches, and readings of historical documents. Complete ordering information is given for each entry. The alphabetical listing is accessed through indexes by author, speeches, novels by title and poems by title and first line. The Chicorel Index series also includes the following titles: *Chicorel Index to Poetry in Collections on Discs and Tapes* (1979), *Chicorel Theatre Index to Plays in Anthologies, Periodicals, Discs, and Tapes* (1973).

Hoffman, Herbert H., and Rita L. Hoffman, comps. *International Index to Recorded Poetry*. Bronx, N.Y.: H.W. Wilson, 1983.

Over 1,700 recordings of the world's poetry on disks, tapes, cassettes, filmstrips, and 16mm films are listed in this sourcebook. Entries are arranged alphabetically by author and give the author's birth date, language of composition, format of the recording, and the poem's title and first line. Also included are indexes by title, first line, and poets under language.

McKee, Gerald. *Directory of Spoken Word Audio Cassettes*. 3rd ed. New York: J. Norton, 1983.

This directory lists thousands of available spoken-word audiocassettes appropriate for the adult or college level user. The offerings of nearly 700 producers and distributors are grouped under such headings as business, personal development, public affairs, and recreation. Entries include the price of the cassettes and are accessed by a comprehensive index.

National Center for Audio Tapes Catalog. Boulder, Colo.: University of Colorado, 1966- . Triennial.

This catalog lists tape recordings available for purchase from academic, commercial, government, and radio station sources. Emphasis is on educational recordings appropriate for all grade levels from elementary through university. Entries are arranged under broad academic subject areas and include full technical descriptions and recommended grade level.

Schwann-1 Record and Tape Guide. Boston: ABC Schwann Publications, 1949- . Monthly.

This reference tool is considered the "books in print" of sound recordings. Each monthly listing covers all stereo LP's and eight-track tapes and cassettes available on domestic labels, *except* children's recordings. Entries are classified according to classical or popular music with subsections on jazz, folk music, musicals, ballet, and opera. A sister publication, *Schwann-2 Record and Tape Guide*, is published semiannually and lists in-print spoken-word recordings, religious recordings, classics on lesser-known labels, and monophonic recordings as well as a listing of international popular music. The *Schwann Artist Catalog* lists, by performer, the titles covered in *Schwann-1* and *Schwann-2*.

Schwann also periodically publishes buying guides such as *A Basic Record Library, A Basic Jazz Record Library,* and *Children's Record and Tape Guide.*

Library of Congress Catalog: Music, Books on Music and Sound Recordings should also be consulted. (See section on Musical Scores.)

Evaluative Sources

Index to Reviews

Maleady, Antoinette O. *Index to Record and Tape Reviews: A Classical Music Buying Guide.* San Anselmo, Calif.: Chulainn Press, 1972- . Annual.

This practical guide provides access to reviews of recent classical music recordings. Citations for reviews are arranged under four sections by composer and individual work, recordings in collections, anonymous works, and by individual artist or group. Qualitative evaluations of recordings are included. Formerly published as *Record and Tape Reviews Index* (1972-1974).

Music Index. Detroit: Information Coordinators, 1949- . Monthly with annual cumulation.

Almost every subject in the field of music can be located through the index, but for the librarian needing music reviews, *Music Index* offers valuable assistance. Its price, however, may make it prohibitive for many libraries.

Myers, Kurtz, et al. *Index to Record Reviews.* Canton, Mass.: Music Library Association, 1948- . Quarterly.

This listing of citations to reviews appears in each issue of *Notes.* Each entry includes an indication of the reviewer's opinion of the performance. These reviews are cumulated at irregular intervals. The latest supplement covers 1978-1983.

Sources of Current Reviews

American Record Guide. Washington, D.C.: Heldref Publications, 1935-. (not published 1972-75). 6 issues/year.

Focusing on classical recordings, this source includes reviews of records as well as music-related books and contains articles on recordings.

Down Beat. Chicago: Maher Publications, 1934- . Monthly.
This magazine is devoted to the contemporary music world. Articles focus on new music groups, music theory, and current events. Record reviews are included.

Gramophone. Middlesex, England: General Gramophone Publications, 1923- . Monthly.
This English record and tape magazine features about 2,500 detailed critical reviews annually. The articles on music and audio equipment are also helpful. "The labels represent international companies but with a little use one may easily discover American equivalents. *Gramophone* has the advantage of often reviewing titles weeks or even months before they are noticed in America." (Katz, William A., *Collection Development.* New York: Holt, Rinehart, Winston, 1980. p. 260).

High Fidelity. New York: ABC Leisure Magazines, 1951- . Monthly.
The space in the magazine is about equally divided between reviews and articles on music and equipment. About 1,000 reviews a year are included; however the reviews are not so critical as those given in *Gramophone.* Classical records receive the major attention although pop, jazz, and folk do get wide coverage. The reviews in *High Fidelity* are cumulated annually into a separate book, *Records in Review.*

New Records. Philadelphia: H. Royer Smith Co., 1933- . Monthly.
A reviewing source for new recordings in the areas of orchestral and chamber music as well as choral, opera, and organ music.

Notes. Canton, Mass.: Music Library Association, 1942- . Quarterly.
Known as the *Book Review Digest* for records, *Notes* is considered a basic guide for all libraries. Each issue contains some 200 reviews of popular and classical recordings. "Index to Record Reviews" is cumulated annually as a separate publication entitled *Record Ratings.*

Rolling Stone. New York: Straight Arrow Publishers, 1967- . Biweekly.
Considered by many to be the dominant voice in the pop music field, *Rolling Stone* offers librarians, particularly those serving children and young people, reviews of this genre of music.

Stereo Review. New York: CBS Consumer Publications, 1958- . Monthly.
General articles on music, test reports, reports on new products, and surveys dealing with equipment are among the features of this guide to

equipment and recordings. The most important aspect of the magazine for librarians, however, is the review section, which includes all types of recordings. Like *High Fidelity, Stereo Review* includes approximately 1,000 reviews a year.

Selective Discographies

Halsey, Richard S. *Classical Music Recordings for Home and Library.* Chicago: American Library Association, 1976.

In this guide 4,000 recordings are listed with ratings. The age or listening level of each recording is given. Chapters on selection, ordering, and organizing a record collection are helpful.

Notable Children's Recordings. Association for Library Service to Children. Chicago: American Library Association. Annual.

Those recordings for children released in the United States during the previous year considered most notable are included in this annual list. The list is published in a spring (usually March) issue of *School Library Journal.* Other discographies directed towards young people are *Discovering Music* (New York: Scholastic Magazine, 1974) and *Recordings for Children* (New York Library Association, 1972).

Recordings for Children: A Selected List of Records and Cassettes. New York: Children's and Young Adult Services, New York Library Association.

Recommendations for a basic collection of recordings for a preschooler to the thirteen-year-old. Updated about every two years in *Illinois Libraries.*

Records and Cassettes for Young Adults: A Selected List. New York: Children's and Young Adult Services, New York Library Association.

Suggests a basic recording collection for listeners at the secondary school level. Updated every five to six years.

Tudor, Dean, and Nancy Tudor. *Contemporary Popular Music.* Littleton, Colo.: Libraries Unlimited, 1979.

Both mainstream popular music and rock music are covered in this selective, annotated discography. The introduction includes suggested priorities for collection development, identifying first-purchase items. Also included are directories of labels and specialized record stores. Complete ordering information is given. Entries are arranged by artist and are accessible through an artists index. Companion volumes to this source, which follow a similar format, are *Black Music* (1979), *Grass Roots Music* (1979), and *Jazz* (1979).

SLIDES

Guide

Irvine, Betty Jo, and P. Eileen Fry. *Slide Libraries: A Guide for Academic Institutions, Museums, and Special Collections.* 2nd ed. Littleton, Colo.: Libraries Unlimited, 1979.

While the manual supplies information on establishing and organizing slide libraries, there are also lists such as a directory of sources, producers, etc.

Non-Evaluative Sources

DeLaurier, Nancy, ed. *Slide Buyer's Guide.* 4th ed. Eugene, Ore.: Visual Resources Association, 1980.

Commercial firms, museums, and institutions producing art slides that are available for purchase are listed in this useful guide. Standard directory information is given for each source. American sources are emphasized though there are many entries for foreign sources as well. Both a general and a subject index are included.

Patrini, Sharon, and Troy Bromberger. *A Handlist of Museum Sources for Slides and Photographs.* Santa Barbara, Calif.: Slide Library, Art Department, University of California at Santa Barbara.

Slides made at museums are usually of higher quality than those available from commercial sources. This list should be of value to the librarian needing to identify slides and photographs.

Sources of Slides: The History of Art. New York: Metropolitan Museum of Art. Periodically updated and distributed free of charge.

A comprehensive list of commercial and museum art slide sources.

Evaluative Sources

Index to Reviews

Reviews of slides and slide sets may be found in *Media Review Digest.*

Sources of Current Reviews

Professional journals that contain reviews of slides include *Arts and Activities, Visual Education, Booklist, Choice, Library Journal,* and *School Library Journal.*

TRANSPARENCIES

A listing by broad subject areas of currently available commercially produced educational transparencies is provided in the *NICEM Index to Educational Overhead Transparencies*. Reviews of transparencies are accessible through the *Media Review Digest*. (See Part I).

VIDEOTAPES, VIDEODISKS, VIDEOTEX

Guides

Bensinger, Charles. *The Video Guide*. 3rd ed. Indianapolis: Howard W. Sams, 1982.
This useful guide provides an overview of developments in video technology. Video equipment and software, and video production are discussed as well as procedures for maintenance and trouble shooting. A glossary, a list of video program sources and an index are included.

Sigel, Efrem. *Videotext: The Coming Revolution in Home/Office Information Retrieval*. New York: Harmony Books, 1981.
This guide examines the prominent international videotext systems and how they may be accessed.

Sigel, Efrem, et al. *Video Discs: The Technology, the Applications and the Future*. 2nd ed. White Plains, N.Y.: Knowledge Industry Publications, 1984.
Developments in videodisk technology and applications are discussed in this comprehensive guide. A mediagraphy of currently available videodisks is included.

Non-Evaluative Sources

Chicorel Index to Video Tapes and Cassettes. New York: American Library Publishing Co., 1978- . Irregular.
The 4,000 annotated videotapes and cassettes, arranged by title with limited subject access, offer some guidance to the librarian. It should be pointed out, however, that the annotations are not critical since they were taken from producer/distributors catalogs.

Home Video and Cable Yearbook 1983-84. 3rd ed. White Plains, N.Y.: Knowledge Industry Publications, 1984.
This yearbook presents an overview of developments and resources in the home video industry. Topics covered include cable, interactive video, disks and cassettes, subscription television, satellites, personal computers and video games, and videotext, among others.

The Video Register. 7th ed. White Plains, N.Y.: Knowledge Industry Publications, 1984 Annual.

The most comprehensive listing of organizations and services in the field of non-broadcast video systems is given in this directory. Complete information is provided for manufacturers (listed under type of product), publishers/distributors, dealers and production/post-production facilities (listed by state), cable access centers, and user groups, all of which are listed alphabetically under their respective categories. A general index is included.

The Video Sourcebook. 6th ed. Syosset, N.Y.: National Video Clearinghouse, 1984.

The most comprehensive of its kind, this guide lists and annotates prerecorded educational and entertainment video programs available on videotape and videodisk. Arrangement of entries is alphabetically by title. Each entry gives the date, distributor, format, running time, producer, director, cast, and audience rating and a descriptive annotation. Indexes provide access by subject and by distributor/wholesaler.

The Video Tape/Disk Guide to Home Entertainment. 5th ed. Syosset, N.Y.: National Video Clearinghouse, 1984.

Complete bibliographic and ordering information is given for more than 4,000 videotapes/disks that are available for home viewing. Also included are articles on developments in home video as well as selected videographies. Several indexes provide various access points.

Evaluative Sources

Index to Reviews

The *Media Review Digest* includes citations to reviews of video recordings.

Sources of Current Reviews

Periodicals that contain reviews of video recordings include *Video Review, Videography, Instructor, Science and Children, Video Play Magazine, Videodisc/Videotex,* and *The Videoplay Report.*

Selective Videographies

Beardsley, Richard, ed. *Videolog: General Interest and Education 1980-81.* Guilford, Conn.: J. Norton, 1981.

Videolog identifies videotapes/cassettes suitable for adult/professional users. Programs for juveniles are excluded. Entries are listed alphabetically by title with access provided through a subject index. Each entry gives the distributor, date, series, a full technical description, price, restrictions, length, and a brief synopsis. Companion titles with identical formats are *Videolog in Business* (1981) and *Videolog in the Health Sciences* (1981).

As many films are recorded on videotapes/cassettes, selection tools for films should also be consulted. (See section on Films and Filmstrips.)

References

1. William Katz, *Collection Development: The Selection of Materials for Libraries* (New York: Holt, Rinehart, and Winston, 1980), pp. 228-29.

Mass Media Information Sources

Nancy Allen

THE mass media represent a part of our culture which critics decry and media specialists praise. They are difficult if not impossible to ignore. Television (free or pay), captures the attention of three-year-olds and Ph.D's alike. Newspapers are perused daily by all classes of people, and their content, ownership patterns, and circulation statistics are studied in university journalism classes, high schools, and by worried editors and publishers. Films entertained children in nickelodeons, raised the spirits of millions during World War II, and are now the subject of so much analysis that words like "pan," "take," and "track" have taken on new meaning in the vocabulary of most ordinary citizens.

WHY MASS MEDIA LIBRARIANSHIP?

Because the mass media communicate so much to so many, a great deal of interest has been generated in information sources about the media. Although information about media operations and effects is complicated, any librarian can grasp the nature of the body of literature about mass media and, with a few basic resources, can satisfy most of the general public's information needs. School, academic, and public libraries can all contain some sources of information on media, and awareness of interlibrary loan networks and media organizations will add to any librarian's access to answers. So . . . why mass media librarianship? Because library users' lives are changed by media, and people ask questions about these modern phenomena. Here are a few examples of common requests:

I want statistics on . . .
  minority ownership of the media
  advertising expenditures and costs
  the type of people who read *Readers' Digest*
  circulation of big city newspapers

I want a list of . . .
   radio programs for women
   ad agencies in Chicago
   Pulitzer Prize winners for newspaper writing
   newspapers carrying *Family Weekly*

I want the address of . . .
   the editor of *The New Yorker*
   the CBS station in New Orleans
   the owner of my local paper
   ten journalism schools

I want the name of . . .
   the actor playing Rhoda's father
   the agent for James Caan
   the vice president for public relations for Sears
   the distributor for "National Velvet"

How do I . . .
   get a radio broadcast license?
   find a job in advertising?
   write a TV script?
   turn in a terrific ad idea?
   videotape a PBS series legally?

I need some biographical information on . . .
   William Randolph Hearst
   Dan Rather
   Diane Keaton
   Federico Fellini

How does that cable selector box on my TV work?
How do I get an ad placed in one of the cable channels?
What are the pros and cons of putting a satellite dish in my yard?
What films has the cameraman Bill Butler made?
What other films did the screenwriter of "Chinatown" write?

Where can I read reviews of . . .
   "Superman II"?
   the book on which "Reds" was based?

    To begin to look for answers, media librarians need to know something about the fields of literature included in the subject area of mass communication.

WHAT IS MASS COMMUNICATION LITERATURE?

One way of itemizing the areas of mass communication literature is by medium. Cable television, subscription television, commercial television, and public television are all areas of concern and study. Television programming, effects, operation, and ownership are of interest in all categories. Other areas of broadcasting and telecommunications are radio, telephone, telegraph, and satellites. A lot of this literature is either historical or technical. New telecommunications fields include teletext and videotex, teleconferencing, interactive cable systems (in which a member of the home audience responds directly to the transmission), and electronic data transfer. Advertising also uses the media to get messages to the masses. Advertising literature can be broken down into areas such as design, marketing, audience research, direct mail, print, television, radio, and cinema advertising. Areas closely related are public opinion and public relations—the manipulation or measurement of opinion of large numbers of people through use of media. Journalism traditionally means newspaper and magazine writing. Computer technology plays an increasingly large part in this area of mass communications. Books on journalism include layout and graphics, reporting, writing, writers, editorial policy, ethics, management, international flow of news, and other topics such as feature and magazine writing. Films are written about from practically every angle—artistic aspects, social effects, production design, narrative structure, symbolism and language, script development, economic impact, psychological aspects of character or of audience reaction, cultural trends, interplay of music and soundtrack, and on and on. The seeming magic of moving images pulling us into another reality draws on the imagination and inspires philosophy, criticism, and worship.

All the mass media are subject to theoretical, cultural, social, psychological, and empirical analyses. It is no wonder that scholars are fascinated by questions about why people watch TV, go to the movies, and read papers, and what effects these activities have. Technical literature accompanies writing about these social and philosophical topics, since the science of communication is rapidly developing with fast-changing applications of electronic messages.

All the media are covered by information listed in bibliographies, handbooks, glossaries, encyclopedias, biographies, yearbooks, statistical reports, and other reference sources. For each field, a selected list of references will be provided. Both bibliographies and sources of fact are included, although technical information sources are for the most part omitted. Both general and academic library users are considered for this chapter.

JOURNALISM

Among the most basic and most wide-ranging resources in the field is the annual publication *Editor and Publisher International Yearbook* (New York: Editor and Publisher, 1921-). It is divided into six sections. For each listing in the first section (U.S. Newspapers), one finds local population, circulation, price, ad line rate, staff, equipment, and mechanical specifications. Papers are presented geographically in the categories of dailies, weeklies, black papers, national papers, newspaper groups, college papers, foreign language papers, professional and business papers, and employee and carrier publications. In section two, similar data are shown for dailies, weeklies, foreign language papers, and newspaper groups in Canada. Section three is on foreign papers, and similar listings are found for all foreign papers. Section four is on syndicated services, section five is on mechanical equipment supplies and services, and section six lists organizations and industry services. This includes newspaper representatvies, associations, foreign correspondents, journalism schools, newsprint statistics, clipping bureaus, and American Newspaper Publishers Association members.

Another basic resource is *Ayer Directory of Publications* (Bala Cynwyd, Pa.: Ayer Press, 1869-). A complete set of these would be useful as a source of historical data on magazine and newspaper publishing, and the current volume is invaluable. The lengthy, descriptive subtitle explains that it is "the professional's directory of print media published in the United States, Puerto Rico, Virgin Islands, Canada, Bahamas, Bermuda, the Republics of Panama and the Philippines. Economic descriptions of the states, provinces, cities, and towns in which all listees are published. 15 separate classified lists. 66 custom-made maps on which all publication cities and towns are indicated." The classified lists include newspaper feature editors, newspaper groups, daily newspapers, weekly, semi-weekly, and tri-weekly newspapers, and an alphabetical listing. The directory also lists magazines, trade publications, and other special-interest publications, all in order geographically by place of publication. Each publication listed shows editor and publisher, general line rate for newspapers and one-time black and white and four-color rates for magazines, circulation, subscription price, mechanical specifications, and other miscellaneous information.

A similar but lesser-known annual reference publication is called, simply, *Circulation* (Malibu, Calif.: American Newspaper Markets, 1962-). The subtitle for this describes it as "a comprehensive print analysis showing circulation and penetration in every U.S. county, in every U.S. metro area, in television viewing areas, for every U.S. daily newspaper, every U.S. Sunday newspaper, all regional sales groups, 5 national supplements, 23 leading magazines." The number of households is shown, with retail sales, average household income, and circulation and supplement data for each listing. This combination of demographic and readership data is very useful. The main sections are followed by rankings of newspaper markets and circulation.

Other reference materials offer lists of newspapers with circulation or market information. *Encyclomedia* (New York: Decisions Publications), a multimedia set, has a volume on newspapers which provides market data. *Working Press of the Nation* (Chicago: National Research Bureau) has a volume on newspapers which lists circulation and staff. Both of these multipart sets are annual, so information is current. For more details on these and other multipart sets, see the section on public relations. A useful guide to college and university newspapers is *Directory of the College Student Press in America 1980-81* (5th ed., New York: Oxbridge Communications, 1980). Information on currently syndicated columnists and the major syndicates is found in Richard Weiner's *Syndicated Columnists* (3rd ed., New York: Richard Weiner, Inc., 1979). It includes a directory by subject and name. The same author also produces *News Bureaus in the U.S.* (New York: Richard Weiner, Inc., 1979) which lists and discusses columnists and includes a directory of phone numbers and names by states.

An international directory of the world's press is *Willing's Press Guide* (West Sussex: Thomas Skinner Directories, 1874-). Like Ayer's, this annual has historical research value. The newspapers and periodicals are listed by country. A regional list of United Kingdom publications, and a reporting agency list are also included. Information for each entry includes address, subscription price, circulation, and major staff. There are a few books on individual countries, although they are not all annuals. A couple of examples are *The Japanese Press* (Tokyo: Nihon Shinbun Kyokai; The Japan Newspaper Publishers and Editors Association, 1981) and *INFA Press and Advertiser's Yearbook* (New Delhi: India News and Feature Alliance, 1962-).

In addition to directories based on geography, there are directories of specialized newspaper publishing. Some examples might include Henry G. LaBrie III, *A Survey of Black Newspapers in America* (Kennebunkport, Maine: Mercer House Press, 1979), *The Catholic Press Directory* (Rockville Centre, N.Y.: Catholic Press Association, 1923-) or Lubomyr R. and Anna T. Wyner's *Encyclopedic Directory of Ethnic Newspapers and Periodicals in the United States* (2nd ed., Littleton, Colo.: Libraries Unlimited, 1976).

For those interested in the history of newspaper publishing, special historical listings are available. An example based on a special collection is Powell Stewart's *British Newspapers and Periodicals, 1632-1800: A*

Descriptive Catalogue of a Collection at the University of Texas (Austin: University of Texas, 1950). A broader scope is covered in the two-volume work by Clarence S. Brigham, *History and Bibliography of American Newspapers, 1690-1820* (Worcester, Mass.: American Antiquarian Society, 1947). This is a state-by-state listing with narrative histories of individual papers.

Magazine and journal publishing information is often included in general reference volumes on journalism, or in multivolume media sets. However, there are two main listings which include consumer, trade, and business magazines and scholarly journals which should be in any library collection. *Standard Periodicals Directory, 1985-86* (9th ed., New York: Oxbridge Communications, 1985) is a mammoth listing by subject of basic data for more than 65,000 U.S. and Canadian periodicals with an alphabetic index. Publisher, address, frequency, circulation, phone, editor and key staff, indexing information, subscription rate, advertising rate, and other information is found in each entry. *Ulrich's International Periodical Directory: A Classified Guide to Current Periodicals, Foreign and Domestic* (New York: R.R. Bowker, 1932-) lists similar information for 64,000 titles. Hard-to-find small magazines are listed and described in *The International Directory of Little Magazines and Small Presses,* edited by Len Fulton and Ellen Ferber (19th ed., Paradise, Calif.: Dustbooks, 1983).

Magazines are listed, along with reference works, associations, a calendar of events, awards, advertising agencies and representatives, subscription agents, consultants, syndicates, artists, mailing lists and services, printers, paper suppliers, back-issue dealers, and other support services in *Magazine Industry Marketplace: The Directory of American Periodical Publishing* (New York: R.R. Bowker, 1979-).

For guidance on a wider range of writings in the area of journalism, consult bibliographies. There are a number of lengthy bibliographies in this field, although there are not many recent titles. Warren C. Price's *The Literature of Journalism: An Annotated Bibliography* (Minneapolis: University of Minnesota Press, 1959) contains 3,147 entries, with emphasis on newspapers and magazines. It was updated in Warren C. Price and Calder Pickett's *An Annotated Journalism Bibliography, 1958-1968* (Minneapolis: University of Minnesota Press, 1970) which contains 2,172 entries. Originally published in 1940, Ralph O. Nafziger's *International News and the Press* (New York: Arno Press, 1972) is one of the few large topical bibliographies in journalism. An enormous work on First Amendment issues for the press is Ralph E. McCoy's *Freedom of the Press: An Annotated Bibliography* (Carbondale, Ill.: Southern Illinois University Press, 1968). It includes eight thousand citations and·is followed by the same author's *Freedom of the Press, A Bibliocyclopedia: Ten Year Supplement (1967-1977)* (Carbondale, Ill: Southern Illinois University Press, 1979), which is just as large.

Compiling current bibliographies in journalism is no easy task, as there is no single index to serial literature for the field. *Journalism Abstracts* (Minneapolis: Association for Education in Journalism, University of Minnesota, 1963-) indexes master's theses and Ph.D. dissertations. Access to serial literature is gained through the use of *Communication Abstracts* (Beverly Hills, Calif.: Sage Books, 1978-) and other general magazine indexes such as *Business Periodicals Index, Humanities Index,* etc. This is the case as well for most mass media, with the exception of film and possibly television. *Journalism Quarterly* lists articles by topic which were published in a number of other journals in journalism and the mass media.

For biographical information on journalists, and for personal name listings, one can use general biographical sources. The task of finding such information, however, is made much easier through the use of *Journalists Biographies Master Index* (Detroit: Gale Research Co., 1979), which, like others in the series of master indexes, indicates which biographical dictionaries and encyclopedias contain entries under any name. Currency is a problem when it comes to directories of journalists. Several listings were published in the 1970s, but not as annuals. They inlcude Alan E. Abram's *Media Personnel Directory: An Alphabetical Guide to Names, Addresses, and Telephone Numbers of Key Editorial and Business Personnel at Over 700 United States and International Periodicals* (Detroit: Gale Research Co., 1979); *The Alphabetized Directory of American Journalists, Associated Press, United Press International, America's Daily Newspapers* (Box 231, Kokomo, IN 46901; 1977); and *Membership Directory and American Correspondents Overseas* (New York: Overseas Press Club of America, 1975). The most recent of these directories is a specialized listing for freelance writers— *American Society of Journalists and Authors Directory: A Listing of Professional Free-Lance Writers* (New York: ASJA, 1981).

Two works that do not fall into the category of bibliography or biography and answer frequent questions are John Hohenberg's *The Pulitzer Prize Story* (New York: Columbia University Press, 1959) and *The Pulitzer Prize Story II* (New York: Columbia University Press, 1980). These volumes reprint selected winners in many categories and together list awards from 1917 to 1980. A general encyclopedic reference including short entries on people, terms, and issues is *The Encyclopedia of American Journalism* (New York: Facts on File, 1983) by Donald Paneth.

BROADCASTING

Of all the areas of broadcasting covered in a mass media collection, commercial television is certainly of the most interest to the public, and all types of libraries need some basic reference sources on network television programming. Up to the mid 1970s, there was very little available to answer common questions about television actors, credits, and productions. The situation has improved, and it is now possible to find at least a brief listing on most television shows. The following citations illustrate the expansion of publishing in the area of television reference sources.

Tim Brooks and Earle Marsh's *The Complete Directory to Prime Time Network TV Shows, 1946-Present* (New York: Ballantine, 1979) includes "All network programs aired after 6 P.M. and which ran at least four consecutive weeks in the same time slot (or were intended to)," i.e., newscasts, sports, film series, etc., with descriptions, first and last telecast dates, emcees, panels, hosts, cast and characters, and broadcast histories. There are also schedule charts, award winners, top-rated shows in each season, and a name index. Les Brown's *Encyclopedia of Television* (New York: New York Zoetrope, 1982) is an encyclopedia-format list of entries for shows, people, terms, issues, and organizations. Larry James Gianakos' *Television Drama Series Programming: A Comprehensive Chronicle, 1959-1975, 1947-1959* (Metuchen, N.J.: Scarecrow Press), is a two-volume set. The 1947-1959 volume was published in 1980 and the other volume in 1978. Days and times for CBS, NBC, and ABC programs are shown. For each season, each episode of each series is listed with primary players, title, and date. *International Television Almanac*, edited by Richard Gertner (New York: Quigley, 1955-) is an annual including information on companies and people in the industry. The contents include: poll and award winners, a 300-page biography section, major credits for feature films, TV stations, companies, producers, distributors, ad agencies, services, program lists, organizations, the press, world market, and TV Code. Dennis La Beau's *Theatre, Film and Television Biographies Master Index* (Detroit: Gale Research Co., 1979) has a subtitle reading: "A consolidated guide to over 100,000 biographic sketches of persons living and dead, as they appear in over 40 of the principal biographical dictionaries devoted to the theatre, film and television." James Robert Parish's *Actors' Television Credits, 1950-1972* (Metuchen, N.J.: Scarecrow Press, 1973) was supplemented in 1978 for the period 1973-1975. It is a list of show titles, episode dates, special dates, and network indication for all appearances of each person listed. "Non-network" appearances are included. The main source of data is *TV Guide.* Harold and Marjorie Sharp's *Index to Characters in the Performing Arts, Part IV: Radio and Television* (Metuchen, N.J.: Scarecrow Press, 1972) lists and indexes characters. Moderators, hosts, etc., are also listed as themselves, although actors and actresses are not listed. *TV Facts* by Cobbett S. Steinberg (New York: Facts on File, 1980) begins with charts showing prime-time schedules from 1950 to 1980. Lists like the hundred longest running series, with dates and number of seasons, are mixed with statistics like the production costs of half-hour episodes of various shows in many categories. *Television Index* (New York: Television Index, Inc., 1949-) was published under the title *Ross Reports* from 1949-1963. It is a multipart group of weekly serials which cover networks (Network Program Report), public affairs, and performance (Program Performance Record) data. It looks like a newsletter, but the section on network programming has a quarterly cumulative index, so it can be used for efficient reference service. Vincent Terrace's *The Complete Encyclopedia of Television Programs, 1947-1979* (2nd ed., Cranbury, N.J.: A.S. Barnes, 1979) lists 3,500 entertainment shows including those imported for U.S. television stations. The two-volume set contains entries giving story line, cast and characters, announcers, major technical credits, network or syndication information, running dates, length of broadcast, sponsors, trivia, program openings, and number of episodes for each series. News, religious shows, sports, and specials are excluded. The index is in volume two. A source of bio-blurbs of TV people is *Who's Who in Television and Cable,* edited by Steven H. Scheuer (N.Y.: Facts on File, 1983).

All of these books contain answers to reference questions often asked, but there are hundreds of other publications on specific types of programs, or even on individual programs, artists, or performers. For instance, *The American Vein,* by Christopher Wicking and Tise Vahimagi (New York: Dutton, 1979) covers television directors, and a history of game shows can be found in *TV Game Shows* by Maxene Fabe (Garden City, N.Y.: Doubleday, 1979) and *The Directory of Religious Broadcasting,* edited by Ben Armstrong (Morristown, N.J.: National Religious Broadcasters), which has a 1982-83 edition listing stations, support services, and other information. George Woolery has prepared the first part of a two-part set called *Children's Television: The First Twenty Five Years, 1946-1981* (Metuchen, N.J.: Scarecrow Press 1983). Volume one covers animation, and volume two is on live, film, and tape series. *Universal Television: The Studio and Its Programs, 1950-1980,* by Ted H. Perry (Metuchen, N.J.: Scarecrow Press, 1983) lists hard-to-find technical credits along with many other facts about the series, TV films, and other productions of this prolific studio. There are several reference volumes or histories on animation, studies of particular shows and other areas of network broadcasting, such as particular companies or organizations (the BBC, for example).

Television business and market information is another major area of concern. Television program rating done by the Nielsen Company are in demand, but few libraries can afford to subscribe to the ratings themselves. Fortunately, seasonal ratings are regularly released to the press, and are generally available through magazine and newspaper indexing. It is also possible that local (Nielsen Station Index) biweekly ratings reports are available at local television stations.

Broadcasting Cablecasting Yearbook (Washington, D.C.: Broadcasting Publications, Inc., 1972-) is a valuable resource which includes radio information as well as television. It is the result of a merger of *Broadcasting Yearbook* and *Broadcasting Cable Sourcebook.* The yearbook is divided into sections. "A" includes information on the FCC and on group ownership, with lists of individuals and groups. "B" gives station maps for major markets, market rankings, and a geographical directory of all TV stations. There is also a list of stations by call letters and channels. "C" is on radio, and has a list of all FM and AM stations in the U.S., the territories, Canada, Mexico, and the Caribbean. The cross-index by call letters and frequencies is helpful. "D" is in three parts: "Broadcast Advertising" lists agencies, station representatives, services, and codes; "Networks and Programming" contains network directories and affiliates, lists of program producers, regional radio and TV networks, and news services. Lists of all kinds of other services are found here, such as cable services. Especially useful is a list of radio stations listed according to format and special programming. "Broadcast Summaries" is the third part of section "D" and contains statistics on the growth of broadcasting. "E" lists equipment and engineering related suppliers, companies, etc. "F" shows professional services, associations, broadcast education programs, international radio and television, international producers, and equipment manufacturers. "G" is the cable section and has information on markets, channel usage, and cable regulation.

A ceased annual devoted specifically to broadcasting statistics is *Statistical Trends in Broadcasting* (New York: John Blair and Co., 1964-1979). It shows charts and tables for such figures as station revenues, market rankings, advertising expenditures, and sales rates. *TV Guide Almanac,* edited by Craig T. and Peter G. Norback and the editors of *TV Guide Magazine* (New York: Ballantine, 1980) contains a very wide range of factual and statistical information. The contents include top TV advertisers, awards, associations, audience research data, education programs, TV stations, government agencies and regulations, histories of the networks, libraries, public and educational TV, syndicated columnists, ratings, satellite communications, scripts, studios, talent agencies, and videorecorders.

The television volume of the set *Encyclomedia* indexes U.S. stations by market area and call letter. Network affiliation, address, and station representatives are listed. Market data such as population, total and TV households, and some cable market information are provided. Canadian TV data, spot and network costs, and a glossary are also featured. *Television Factbook: The Authoritative Reference for the Advertising, Television, and Electronics Industries* (Washington, D.C.: Television Digest, 1949-), an annual two-volume set, is a thorough guide to the television industries. A quick look at the summary index shows abbreviations and initialisms, ad agencies, channel applications, educational programs, major communications corporations, associations and organizations, ownership, manufacturers, distributors, unions, market research data and companies, networks, cable and station data, and some international directories. *World Radio-TV Handbook* (New York: Watson-Guptill, 1946-) lists stations, wave bands, and programming for each country. There is a separate list of long and medium wave station data.

Radio information is often included in television sources; however, specialized radio programming reference sources can help locate a variety of radio facts, including production credits for shows, cast lists, awards, or other programming information. *The Big Broadcast, 1920-1950* (New York: Viking, 1972) by Frank Buxton and Bill Owen is an alphabetical listing of nationally known programs, with a name index. The previous edition of this work was called *Radio's Golden Age*. John Dunning's *Tune in Yesterday: The Ultimate Encyclopedia of Old-Time Radio, 1925-1976* (Englewood Cliffs, N.J.: Prentice-Hall, 1976) is a historical reference, with essays on each program entry rather than a chart-like listing. There is a name and title index. *Radio Programming Profile* (Glen Head, N.Y.: BF/Communication Services, 1967-) is a two-volume quarterly guide which covers both major and minor markets— Chicago and also Champaign—with descriptions of each day's programming and disk jockeys. Vincent Terrace's *Radio's Golden Years: The Encyclopedia of Radio Programs, 1930-1960* (San Diego: A.S. Barnes, 1981) is "an alphabetical listing of 1,500 nationally broadcast network and syndicated entertainment programs" with a name index.

There are now two indexes covering serial literature in the areas of broadcasting. In addition, broadcasting, along with the other mass media, is covered in indexes general literature. The major specialized index is the *International Index to Television Periodicals*, published by the International Federation of Television Archives in microfiche form, with annual cumulations planned.

The Cable-Video Index (Box 3451, Oak Park, IL 60303) began in 1983 and covers publications not in *Business Periodicals Index* or *Predicasts*, emphasizing U.S. trade publications. The trade journal *Broadcasting* publishes its own nicely bound index, *Broadcasting Index* (Washington, D.C.: Broadcasting Publication, 1972-), but the most recent volume is several years out of date.

Television news indexes help the user find out what was said on the air. There are two major indexes. The First is *Television News Index and Abstracts* (Nashville: Vanderbilt Television News Archive, 1972-), a monthly index to national network news broadcasts with abstracts that include dates, broadcasters, and a description of the broadcast's content. Special news events are also included. The other index is *CBS News Index* (Glen Rock, N.J.: Microfilm Corporation of America, 1975-). This is a subject index to news and public affairs broadcasts on CBS. The transcripts of all these broadcasts are published on microfilm, making the index a valuable and highly usable resource. The index and microfilm covers "60 Minutes" and "Face the Nation." One may find transcripts of other public affairs programs such as "Washington Week in Review" by writing the network. The literature on TV news is covered by Myron J. Smith's *U.S. Television Network News: A Guide to Sources in English* (Jefferson, N.C.: McFarland, 1983). One can discover details about broadcast archives by consulting one of these directories: *Television News Resources: A Guide to Collections* (Washington, D.C.: George Washington University Television News Study Center, 1982) or Donald G. Godfrey's *Directory of Broadcast Archives* (Washington, D.C.: Broadcast Education Association, 1983).

Book-length bibliographies containing citations to trade and research literature about broadcasting are numerous, plus broadcasting is always included in more general bibliographies on media effects, or mass communication research (see the section on multimedia resources). *Television and Social Behavior: An Annotated Bibliography of Research Focusing on Television's Impact on Children* by Charles Atkin, John P. Murray, and Oguz B. Nayman (Rockville, Md.: U.S. Dept. of Health, Education and Welfare, 1971), and *Effects and Functions of Television: Children and Adolescents: A Bibliography of Selected Research Literature 1970-1978* compiled by Manfred Meyer and Ursula Nissen (Munchen: K.G. Saur, 1979) are two guides to the literature on children and television.

Other more general bibliographies are *Television and Human Behavior* by George Comstock, et al. (New York: Columbia University Press, 1978), *World and International Broadcasting: A Bibliography* compiled by Lawrence W. Lichty (Washington, D.C.: Association for Professional Broadcasting Education, 1971), and *Radio and Television: A Selected, Annotated Bibliography* by William McCavitt (Metuchen, N.J.: Scarecrow Press, 1978), which was supplemented for the period 1977-1981 in 1982. Bibliographies for specific geographical areas and countries are available; an example is *British Broadcasting: A Selected Bibliography, 1922-1972* (London: BBC, 1972) which annotates over seven hundred books and articles.

In the last several years, a number of dictionaries covering terms in broadcasting and telecommunications have been published in the U.S.

and the U.K. to update the few older titles already on library shelves. This flurry of publishing is representative of the whole area of telecommunications. These dictionaries range from the highly technical to the illustrated list of terms for the layperson, and include S.J. Aries' *Dictionary of Telecommunications* (London: Butterworth, 1981); Donn Delson and Edwin Michalove's *Delson's Dictionary of Cable, Video, and Satellite Terms* (Thousand Oaks, Calif.: Bradson Press, 1983), which is a slim and selective volume; R. Terry Ellmore's *Illustrated Dictionary of Broadcast—CATV—Telecommunications* (Blue Ridge Summit, Pa.: TAB, 1982), a work by John Graham which was published in the U.S. as *The Facts on File Dictionary of Telecommunications* (New York: Facts on File, 1983) and in England as *The Penguin Dictionary of Telecommunications* (London: Allen Lane, 1983); Graham Langley's *Telephony's Dictionary* (Chicago: Telephony, 1982) which obviously emphasizes telecommunications; and Martin H. Weik's *Communication Standard Dictionary* (New York: Van Nostrand Reinhold, 1983) which is a weighty and technical tome. In addition, there are two recent dictionaries of terms in the related area of information technology, including computer science, called *Dictionary of Information Technology* by Dennis Longley and Michael Shain (New York: Wiley, 1982) and *Dictionary of New Information Technology* (London: Nichols, 1982) by A.J. Meadows.

NEW MEDIA

Technological change has affected all areas of the mass media and has allowed new ways of transmitting information to be created. In the area generally termed "electronic publishing," one may need to find descriptions of videotex and teletext systems, addresses for suppliers in these new businesses, or information on the topic of the electronic journal. The annual *Videotex Directory* (Washington, D.C.: Arlen Communication, 1982-) lists companies and personnel in videotex systems and organizations working in this area of interactive television. An overview of present systems is offered by John Tydeman and others in *Teletext and Videotex in the U.S.* (New York: McGraw-Hill, 1982) and by Richard H. Veith in *Television's Teletext* (New York: North-Holland, 1983) as well as by several other works. A directory of interactive cable systems and services with lists and descriptions of multiple system operators, governmental agencies and committees, law firms and a glossary is Rhonda Presser's *The Interactive Cable TV Handbook* (2nd ed., Bethesda, Md.: Phillips, 1982).

Satellites are crucial to a number of communication systems, relaying data, picture, and voice transmissions for telephone, data, cable, and broadcast systems. There are many technical discussions of these systems, and a number of consumer guides to satellite TV, such as Anthony Easton's *Home Satellite TV Book* (New York: Playboy, 1983). There is also a reference annual providing industry names and addresses—*Satellite Directory* (Bethesda, Md.: Phillips, 1982-).

Teleconferencing is an application of the satellite, telephone, or cable technologies which has been used extensively by business. An overview of teleconferencing principles, management issues, and economic impact is presented in *The Teleconferencing Handbook* by Ellen Lazer, Martin Elton, and James Johnson (White Plains, N.Y.: Knowledge Industry Publications, 1983). *The Teleconferencing Resources Directory* (White Plains, N.Y.: Knowledge Industry Publications, 1983-) lists audio and video conferencing equipment, facilities, and services.

Cable television is widely available, with pay-TV alternatives, and many information sources are now available, including a large number of journals and references for the consumer. Information about cable TV systems (or, as the Library of Congress terms them, community antenna television) is incorporated into the major broadcasting reference works such as *Broadcasting Cablecasting Yearbook* and *Cable and Station Coverage Atlas* (Washington, D.C.: TV Digest, annual). There are also sources especially for cable, such as the *Cable TV Databook* (Carmel, Calif.: Paul Kegan, 1981-) which provides a ranking and directory of cable systems, statistics on penetration and advertising, revenues, company profiles, and other lists. There are several short bibliographies compiled for the topic of cable, but the major book-length work is getting out of date. This title, *Cable Television*, by Felix Chin (New York: IFI/Plenum, 1978), is still useful for its other information, such a chronology and glossary, and represents the history of cable television. An ongoing bibliography on cable called *BCTV* is published every six months by the Communications Library of the Communications Institute (1550 Bryant St., San Francisco, CA 94103), and back issues are available.

Low-power TV is a newly approved use of older technology. A list of low-power stations is found in *Cable and Station Coverage Atlas* and a specialized newsletter is *LPTV Reporter* (Washington, D.C.: The Television Center).

Dozens of home video handbooks and directories have appeared in the last two or three years, generally directed toward the consumer who wants information on equipment, videocassette recordings to purchase or rent, and taping techniques. A work which annually lists sources of equipment and services internationally is *International Video Yearbook* (Poole, Dorset, U.K.: Blandford, 1977-). For North America, *The Video Register* (6th ed., White Plains, N.Y.: Knowledge Industry Publications, 1983) is, as the subtitle says, "the directory of professional video users, manufacturers, publishers, dealers, facilities, services, resources and cable access, origination centers."

Information policy is an increasingly complex area of government, community, and political concern. Two directories of information sources on information policy exist. The first, *Issues in International Telecommunications Policy: A Sourcebook,* edited by Jane H. Yurow (Washington, D.C.: George Washington University Center for Telecommunications Studies, 1983) lists a great deal of information on U.S. law, court decisions, key international organizations and their actions, international treaties and agreements, and public advisory committees to the U.S. government. This range of information is provided for each chapter, covering policy-making bodies, the International Telecommunication Union, regulatory environment, transborder data flow, telecommunications and trade policy, and intellectual property. The second source is a four-volume set edited by Forest Woody Horton, Jr., *Understanding U.S. Information Policy: The Infostructure Handbook* (Washington, D.C.: Information Industry Association, 1982). Selected literature, U.S. and foreign journals, congressional committees, organizations, litigation, conferences, and statutes are shown for all major areas of information and telecommunications policy.

There are two wide-ranging and ongoing sources available on telecommunication systems and policy emphasizing systems rather than policy production. One of these is a loose-leaf directory called *Changes, Challenges & Opportunities in the New Electronic Media,* by William L. McGee, Lucy E. Garrick, and Joseph H. Caton (San Francisco: BMC Publications, 1982-), which comes in five parts, one each for pay television, low power TV, direct broadcast services, videotex, and home video. Each part contains statistics, directories, and current news on issues. The other is *Telecommunications Systems and Services,* edited by John Schmittroth, Jr., and Martin Connors (Detroit: Gale Research Co., 1983-). It has a lengthy explanatory subtitle: "An international descriptive guide to new and established telecommunications organizations, systems and services, covering voice and data communications, teleconferencing, electronic mail, local area networks, satellite services, videotex and teletext, interactive cable television, transactional services, telegram, telex, facsimile, and others, including related consultants, associations, research institutes, publishers and information services, and regulatory bodies, with a detailed glossary of terms, acronyms, standards, and issues in the field." The first edition has 466 entries and several indexes. A new source of statistics and other information is Christopher Sterling's *Electronic Media: A Guide to Trends in Broadcasting and Newer Technologies, 1920-1983* (New York: Praeger, 1984).

FILM

Guides to literature on feature-length theatrical films, such as bibliographies, indexes, descriptions of special collections, and glossaries have been published in profusion for the last ten years. This activity has settled down somewhat recently, and this section is a selective guide to the most useful and most recent bibliographic and reference volumes.

A few bibliographies were published before 1980, but not many. A useful and unique guide to early literature was first published in 1941 by H.W. Wilson: *The Film Index,* edited by Harold Leonard (New York: Arno Press, 1966). It was a Writers Program project and includes books and articles on film as art. The annotated and fairly comprehensive volumes by George Rehrauer are the classic guides to all types of film literature. *Cinema Booklist* (Metuchen, N.J.: Scarecrow Press, 1972) was followed by a supplement in 1974 and a second in 1977. A total of four thousand books are described in the three volumes. Selections from these entries plus many new items are described and indexed by Rehrauer in the two-volume *Macmillan Film Bibliography* (New York: Macmillan, 1982). Of the many selective general film booklists, *The Film Book Bibliography, 1940-1975* by Jack C. Ellis, Charles Derry, and Sharon Kern (Metuchen, N.J.: Scarecrow Press, 1979) is annotated, well-indexed, and sensibly organized. A newer listing by Robert Armour, *Film: A Reference Guide* (Westport, Conn.: Greenwood Press, 1980) is a slightly unpredictable selection of basic film books and periodicals.

There are dozens of bibliographies and filmographies listing films and books about films on particular topics. Some examples of topics covered are women's films, western films, spy films, French films, film noir, costume in films, and musicals. One of the most useful recent titles is *The Film Audience: An International Bibliography of Research* by Bruce A. Austin (Metuchen, N.J.: Scarecrow Press, 1983).

Indexes to film journals and film reviews were also published in some number in the mid 1970s. Four similar retrospective indexes are arranged by topic and cover slightly differing lists of film journals. They are: Linda Batty's *Retrospective Index to Film Periodicals, 1930-1971* (New York: R.R. Bowker, 1975), Stephen Bowles' *Index to Critical Film Reviews in British and American Film Periodicals,* together with: *Index to Critical Reviews of Books About Film* (New York: Burt Franklin, 1974, 2 vols.), John C. and Lana Gerlach's *The Critical Index: A Bibliography of Articles on Film in English, 1946-1973, Arranged by Name and Topic* (New York: Teacher's College Press, 1974), and Richard Dyer MacCann and Perry Edward's *The New Film Index: A Bibliography of Magazine Articles in English, 1930-1970* (New York: Dutton, 1975).

The two ongoing film indexes are *International Index to Film Periodicals* (New York: St. Martin's Press, 1972-) and *Film Literature Index* (Albany, N.Y.: Filmdex, Inc. 1973-). The former is prepared by members of the International Federation of Film Archives as bound cumulations of their card index service (now on microfiche). Articles are arranged in broad topical chapters, and coverage is international. The latter is somewhat easier to use as a library reference, since it is arranged in one author-title-subject alphabetical order, and indexes considerably more journals than *International Index*. Film journals and articles on film are also indexed in many general indexes, such as *Reader's Guide, Art Index,* and *Humanities Index.* A retrospective index of film reviews which covers general magazines is *A Guide to Critical Reviews, Part IV: The Screen Play* (Metuchen, N.J.: Scarecrow Press, 1971) by James M. Salem.

Reference books in film abound. Because there are so many, this section will concentrate on the most-used resources which provide information about credits for films and individuals. There is no single source listing credits for every film ever made, and no single source listing credit for every filmmaker or performer. The sources overlap on coverage, in chronology, and in selectivity, and it is not an easy task to sort out all these factors. In addition, many of the most useful sources of credit data are serials, some of which are no longer published.

Credits for films can be found in a dozen or more books and serials. *Screen Achievement Records Bulletin* (Beverly Hills, Calif.: Academy of Motion Picture Arts and Sciences, 1960-1977) and its successor *Annual Index to Motion Picture Credits* (Westport, Conn.: Greenwood Press, 1978-) provide full credits for films made after 1960. The unfinished master list by the American Film Institute, *Catalog of Motion Pictures Produced in the United States* (New York: R.R. Bowker, 1971-) is presently composed of two parts, one for feature films in the twenties, and one for those released in the sixties. *Film Daily Yearbook* (New York: Film Daily, 1919-1970), with its various title changes, has always listed credits for each year's films. *Screen World,* edited by John Willis (New York: Crown, 1949-) annually lists credits for domestic and foreign films released in the United States. *Filmfacts* (Los Angeles: University of Southern California Division of Cinema, 1958-1977) has complete credits and a synopsis for each film listed. And the film reviews in *The New York Times* list credits, cast, and characters. These were reprinted in a multivolume set called *New York Times Film Reviews* (New York: Arno Press, 1970-) with annual supplements through 1976. *Variety* reviews contain the same sort of credit information, and since many foreign films are reviewed, the set of *Variety* reviews covering its entire publishing history is extremely valuable. *Variety Film Reviews, 1907-1980* (New York: Garland Publishing, 1982) is published in fifteen volumes with a title index and a four-volume credit index. Brief credits for fourteen thousand British films are in Denis Gifford's *British Film Catalogue, 1895-1970. A Reference Guide* (New York: McGraw-Hill, 1973) and Leslie Halliwell lists more complete credits in *Halliwell's Film Guide: A Survey of 8,000 English Language Movies* (3rd ed., New York: Granada, 1981).

Biographies and credit listings for individuals involved in filmmaking are also numerous. Many of the volumes already listed have name indexes so the user can compile credit lists or answer specific questions. Richard B. Dimmitt prepared *An Actor Guide to the Talkies: A Comprehensive Listing of 8,000 Feature-length Films from January 1949 until December 1964* (Metuchen, N.J.: Scarecrow Press, 1967-68) and *A Title Guide to the Talkies: A Comprehensive Listing of 16,000 Feature-length Films from October 1926 until December 1963* (Metuchen, N.J.: Scarecrow Press, 1965). Both volumes were supplemented by Andrew A. Aros in 1977. Credits for European actors are listed by James Robert Parish in *Film Actors Guide: Western Europe* (Metuchen, N.J.: Scarecrow Press, 1977) and the same author did a list of credits for directors—*Film Directors: A Guide to Their American Films* (Metuchen, N.J.: Scarecrow Press, 1974). Biofilmographies for over twenty thousand people are listed in David Ragan's *Who's Who in Hollywood, 1900-1976* (New Rochelle, N.Y.: Arlington House, 1976). David Thomson's *A Biographical Dictionary of Film* (2nd ed., New York: William Morrow, 1981) discusses important individuals on an international basis. Brief biographies are found in Evelyn Mack Truitt's *Who Was Who on Screen* (3rd ed., New York: R.R. Bowker, 1983). A pair of credit listings by John T. Weaver include production and direction credits for the silent and sound eras—*Forty Years of Screen Credits, 1929-1969* (Metuchen, N.J.: Scarecrow Press, 1970) and *Twenty Years of Silents, 1908-1928* (Metuchen, N.J.: Scarecrow Press, 1971). Searching for biographical information is time-consuming, and *Film and Television Biographies Master Index* (cited earlier) is of assistance.

Frequently, individuals and organizations want information about film rentals and programming. Several books list the necessary distribution information. Two of these are James L. Limbacher's *Feature Films on 8mm, 16mm and Videotape: A Directory of Feature Films Available for Rental, Sale, and Lease in the United States and Canada* (7th ed., New York: R.R. Bowker, 1982) and Kathleen Weaver's *Film Programmer's Guide to 16mm Rentals* (3rd ed. Albany, Calif.: Reel Research, 1980).

A few other miscellaneous works which can answer a lot of questions cover awards and history. A four-volume work edited by Frank N. Magill, *Magill's Survey of Cinema: English Language Films, First Series* (Englewood Cliffs, N.J.: Salem, 1980), provides historical perspective.

There are, of course, a large number of historical texts, many of which are international in scope. One of these is David Robinson's *The History of World Cinema* (2nd ed., New York: Stein & Day, 1981).

The question of awards comes up often. The Academy Awards are taken care of very nicely by Richard Shale in *Academy Awards* (New York: Frederick Ungar, 1978) which includes award nominations in all categories from 1927 to 1977, and by Paul Michael's *The Academy Awards*, now in its sixth edition (New York: Crown, 1982). Two recent dictionaries of film language are Frank Beaver's *Dictionary of Film Terms* (New York: McGraw-Hill, 1983) and Virginia Oakey's *Dictionary of Film and Television Terms* (New York: Barnes and Noble, 1983). There are half a dozen glossaries published before 1980, but, as in any medium, the language of film has changed with new technology.

PERSUASIVE COMMUNICATION

Advertising

Advertising is sometimes considered closer to business, marketing, economics, and finance than to mass communication, but since advertising research and practice literature is undeniably linked to the media, I will touch briefly on some information sources.

Specialized bibliographies separately published are infrequent. A very helpful guide to advertising history is the work edited and compiled by Richard W. Pollay, *Information Sources in Advertising History* (Westport, Conn.: Greenwood Press, 1979). It contains annotated listings and three bibliographic essays along with directories of special collections of unpublished materials and of professional associations. A substantial bibliography of advertising research is *Evaluation Advertising: A Bibliography of the Communication Process* by Benjamin Lipstein and William J. McGuire (New York: Advertising Research Foundation, 1978).

Indexes to periodical literature are more readily accessible for advertising than for other aspects of the mass media. *The Business Periodicals Index* (New York: H.W. Wilson, 1958-) covers many advertising journals, and advertising articles in business literature are also indexed. *Topicator: A Classified Article Guide to the Advertising/Communications/Marketing Periodical Press* (Golden, Colo.: Topicator, 1965-) indexes twenty trade and other journals by topic categories.

The two-part directory for advertising agencies and advertisers is really composed of two quite separate resources, called the "red books." *Standard Directory of Advertisers* (Skokie, Ill.: National Register Publishing Co., 1917-) lists seventeen thousand corporations. The classified edition published in April lists the advertisers in fifty-one classifications. The geographical edition published in May indexes them by state and city. The main listing, the classified edition, provides alphabetic and trade-name indexes. Each entry includes address and phone, sales, number of employees, products, executives, divisions, subsidiaries, and advertising agency. Other data about the film's advertising expenditures and the media used are also shown for most entries. The other red book, *Standard Directory of Advertising Agencies* (Skokie, Ill.: National Register Publishing Co., 1917-) is published annually in February. It lists advertising agencies geographically and alphabetically. The entries in the alphabetical list contain addresses, names of management, a list of clients, and other information on the amount and type of advertising. Media service and sales promotion agencies are listed separately at the back of the volume.

Various specialized sources are intended for use by those planning advertising campaigns. These give demographic information on users of various product types, advertising expenditures, advertising rates, and other data required by practitioners. These resources are not generally found in libraries, and will therefore not be described here in detail. *Standard Rate and Data Service* (Skokie, Ill.: SRDS, 1919-) comes in many editions, including consumer magazines, newspapers, spot radio, spot television, mass transit, and mailing lists. It shows advertising rates and other information, and each list is updated regularly. *Study of Media and Markets* (New York: Simmons Market Research Bureau, 1979-) is an annual set of audience and product advertising studies. *LNA Multi-Media Report Service* (New York: Leading National Advertisers) reports advertising expenditures in six major media. The quarterly reports are published in three formats—by brand name alphabetically, by company showing brand expenditures, and by brand within product classification. *Encyclomedia* (New York: Decision Publications, 1978-) is a quarterly set containing volumes on newspapers, consumer magazines, radio, and television. Information varies for every volume, but it is all designed to aid the media campaign planner.

In case a reader needs help with vocabulary, there is the *Dictionary of Advertising Terms* edited by Lawrence Urdang (Chicago: Tatham-Laird and Kudner, 1977).

Public Relations

Another allied area, public relations literature, varies from how-to books to bibliographies of scholarly research to directories. Since public relations practitioners deal with persuasion and public opinion, the literature and research are closely related to advertising, political communication, and propaganda. The mass media are used to communicate ideas and to form or influence opinion in all of these areas. Corporations are no longer simply advertising their products, they are spending vast amounts of money to promote an image of themselves. Politicians must hire media consultants in order to win elections—these consultants are manipulators of public opinion. Although the word "propaganda" has negative connotations, it means a way of influencing collective responses or of transmitting attitudes. A typical corporate public relations official does just that in his or her role as the person responsible for liaison between the firm and the public.

There are several major bibliographies covering early literature on public relations and public opinion. One of these is *Propaganda, Communication, and Public Opinion: A Comprehensive Reference Guide* by Bruce Lannes Smith, Harold D. Lasswell, and Ralph D. Casey (Princeton, N.J.: Princeton University Press, 1946). Books, periodicals, and articles on persuasive communication are listed, some with annotations, and accompanied by several essays. Keith A. Larson compiled writings about and by the parents of modern public relations in *Public Relations: The Edward L. Bernayses and the American Scene: A Bibliography* (Westwood, Mass.: F.W. Faxon, 1978). A more general bibliography was compiled by Scott M. Cutlip (the author of several guides to public relations practice), *A Public Relations Bibliography* (Madison: University of Wisconsin Press, 1965). It includes citations and brief annotations for almost six thousand books and articles in all areas of theory and practice. Robert Bishop's *Public Relations, A Comprehensive Bibliography: Articles and Books on Public Relations, Communication Theory, Public Opinion, and Propaganda, 1964-1974* (Ann Arbor, Mich.: A.G. Leighton-James, 1974) contains over four thousand entries arranged by subject and indexed by author. An annual list of current publications is found in a yearly special issue of *Public Relations Review: A Journal of Research and Comment* called "Comprehensive Bibliography."

The O'Dwyer guides are maps for the business of public relations. *O'Dwyer's Directory of Public Relations Firms* (New York: J.R. O'Dwyer, 1968-) is an annual which in 1982 listed twelve hundred public relations firms and departments in advertising agencies. There is an index to firms with special areas of emphasis, a geographical index, and a cross-index to client companies. Each entry includes the address, management, specializations, and clients of the public relations company or department. *O'Dwyer's Directory of Public Relations Executives* (New York: J.R. O'Dwyer, 1981-) shows brief biographies and has a corporate index. *O'Dwyer's Directory of Corporate Communications* (New York: J.R. O'Dwyer, 1975-) is an annual listing of public relations offices and personnel in twenty-six hundred companies and five hundred of the largest trade associations. Each entry shows address and phone, public relations director, responsibilities of the office, budget, sales of the firm, and staff size and reporting line of the office.

A multimedia resource designed for publicists is *Bacon's Publicity Checker* (Chicago: Bacon's Publishing Company, 1933-) which comes annually in two volumes, one for magazines and one for newspapers. It includes very brief listings for daily and weekly papers in the U.S. and Canada, and business, industrial, trade, farm and consumer magazines. For those public relations people who need international contacts, *Bacon's International Publicity Checker* (Chicago: Bacon's Publishing Company, 1975-) annually lists business, trade, and industrial publications and national and regional papers in twenty-five Western European countries. A one-volume list of media contacts is *All-in-One Gebbie Press Directory* (New Paltz, N.Y.: Gebbie Press, 1972-) which annually covers daily and weekly papers, AM-FM radio stations, television stations, general magazines, business papers, trade press, black press, farm publications, and news syndicates. Each listing gives address, phone, and few names, circulation, and a brief description of the market of the publication. *Working Press of the Nation* (Chicago: National Research Bureau, 1947-) is a five-part guide to the media with volumes on newspapers, including press services; magazines, including consumer, farm, service, trade, and industrial magazines; radio and television, including local programming by subject; feature writers and photographers, indicating areas of interest; and internal publications for U.S. companies, government agencies, and other groups. A one-volume guide to contacts, addresses, speakers, messengers, phone services, and many more practicalities is found in Richard Weiner's *Professional's Guide to Public Relations Services* (4th ed., New York: Richard Weiner, 1980).

Public Opinion

Public opinion poll results are widely available through general magazine and newspaper indexes, but there are other sources, both current and retrospective. *The Gallup Report: Political, Social and Economic Trends* (Princeton, N.J.: The Gallup Poll, 1965-) is a monthly report containing poll results and background information. *Public Opinion* (Washington, D.C.: American Enterprise Institute for Public Policy Research, 1977-) includes in each issue a twenty-page section tabulated by the Roper Center called "opinion roundup" summarizing surveys done by many different polling organizations. *American Social Attitudes Data Sourcebook, 1947-1978* by Philip E. Converse, Jean D. Dotson, Wendy J. Hoag, and William H. McGee III (Cambridge, Mass.: Harvard University Press, 1980) measures attitudes on areas such as education, economy, family, and employment. Gallup polls from 1935 to the recent past are cumulated in a set of volumes titled *The Gallup Poll: Public Opinion*. The first two-volume set covers 1935-1971 (New York: Random House, 1972) and the second two-volume set covers 1972-1977 (Wilmington, Del.: Scholarly Resources, 1978). Following years are in separate supplements. *The Index to International Public Opinion*, edited by Elizabeth Hann Hastings and Philip K. Hastings (Westport, Conn.: Greenwood Press, 1978/79-) is an annual prepared by Survey Research Consultants, International. It shows opinion data on a wide variety of current topics gathered by fifty-one survey organizations in twenty-eight countries, as well as by Radio Free Europe and other international organizations.

MULTIMEDIA RESOURCES

This section deals with reference and bibliographic resources that cover more than one medium, and also with general selection sources. There are many general references on a wide range of subjects as they relate to media, so this is a selective introduction to the kinds of materials available.

The primary general bibliography is Eleanor Blum's *Basic Books in the Mass Media* (2nd ed., Urbana, Ill.: University of Illinois Press, 1980). It covers major works, including but not limited to reference and bibliographic works. All 1,179 entries are annotated and indexed. They cover general communications, book publishing, broadcasting, journalism, film, magazines, and advertising and public relations.

Two bibliographies covering wide areas of mass communication research are *A Computerized Bibliography of Mass Communication Research, 1933-1964* by Wayne A. Danielson and G.C. Wilhoit, Jr. (New York: Magazine Publishers Association, 1967), which indexes by keyword twenty-three hundred entries; and *Mass Communication Effects and Processes; A Comprehensive Bibliography, 1950-1975* by Thomas F. Gordon and Mary Ellen Verna (Beverly Hills, Calif.: Sage Books, 1978) which lists citations to 2,703 articles and books.

Communication Policy and Planning for Development, edited by Syed A. Rahim (Honolulu: East-West Center, 1976) is an annotated bibliography including materials on communication policy for developing nations. Another publication of the same center is *Modern Communication Technology in a Changing Society: A Bibliography* by Godwin C. Chu and Brent Cassan (Honolulu: East-West Center, 1977). It covers media and social effects literature in regard to the use of media technology for developing nations. *Communications and Society: A Bibliography on Communications Technologies and Their Social Impact,* compiled by Benjamin Shearer and Marilyn Huxford (Westport, Conn.: Greenwood Press, 1983), is limited to books, magazines, newspapers, telegraph and cable, telephone, photography, film, radio, and television, and shows 2,732 citations to books, articles, and dissertations. *Media and Government: An Annotated Bibliography* by Oscar H. Gandy, Jr., Susan Miller, William Rivers, and Gail Ann Rivers (Stanford, Calif.: Institute for Communications Research, Stanford

University, 1975) shows methodology and conclusions for each article or book included. *Communications and the United States Congress: A Selectively Annotated Bibliography of Committee Hearings, 1870-1976,* by George Brightbill (Washington, D.C.: Broadcast Education Association, 1978) is a useful guide to congressional hearings. Leslie J. Friedman's *Sex Role Stereotyping in the Mass Media: An Annotated Bibliography* (New York: Garland Publishing, 1977) covers advertising, broadcast media, film, print media, popular culture, minority women, and children, among other areas. A last example of bibliographic literature comes out every few years. It is *Marxism and the Mass Media: Towards a Basic Bibliography* (New York: International General, 1972).

Related to bibliographies are two guides to archives and archival collections on the media. Collections in eleven western states are described by Linda Mehr in *Motion Pictures, Television and Radio: A Union Catalogue of Manuscripts and Special Collections in the Western United States* (Boston: G.K. Hall, 1977). Ernest Rose describes schools and archives internationally in *World Film and Television Study Resources; A Reference Guide to Major Training Centers and Archives* (2nd ed., Bonn-Bad: Friedrich Ebert-Stiftung, 1978).

The major communications index is *Communication Abstracts* (Beverly Hills, Calif.: Sage Books, 1978-), which covers a large number of media journals internationally, emphasizing communication research rather than the industries.

The media industries are described in many studies, but the next two works can be used for analysis as well as statistics. Christopher H. Sterling and Timothy R. Haight gathered statistical data and lists for *The Mass Media: Aspen Institute Guide to Communication Industry Trends* (New York: Praeger, 1978). Growth, ownership, jobs, media content, audiences, and international media are all covered. Organizational and financial data are presented in *The Knowledge Industry 200: America's Two Hundred Largest Media and Information Companies* (White Plains, N.Y.: Knowledge Industry Publications, 1983) along with rankings. A great deal of information is presented and analyzed in *Who Owns the Media: Concentration of Ownership in the Mass Communications Industry* by Benjamin M. Compaine with Christopher H. Sterling, Thomas Guback, and J. Kendrick Noble, Jr. (2nd ed., White Plains, N.Y.: Knowledge Industry Publications, 1982). The two-volume set, *World Press Encyclopedia* (New York: Facts on File, 1982) by George Thomas Kurian gives background information and media statistics for all countries. Another survey is *Global Journalism: A Survey of the World's Mass Media* (New York: Longman, 1983) edited by John C. Merrill. It is written as a text rather than as a reference book, but systematically discusses media worldwide. A guide to communications and communications education, research activities, and organizations is found in the *Aspen Handbook on the Media: A Selective Guide to*

Research, Organizations and Publications in Communications. (3rd ed., New York: Praeger, 1977-).

Media vocabulary is discussed in the wide-ranging *Longman Dictionary of Mass Media and Communication* by Tracy Daniel Connors (New York: Longman, 1982). Media law, as any other area of law, is a complex and ever-changing subject. There are several texts and casebooks on media law which are updated regularly. *Media Law Reporter* (Washington, D.C.: Bureau of National Affairs, 1977-) is a looseleaf service with annual bound cumulations. It reprints texts of court decisions and rulings of federal agencies in regard to media issues.

Guides to current literature can be used as selection sources, and two such guides exist for the mass media. The bibliographies and book reviews in *Journalism Quarterly* cover all areas of mass media, including advertising and other topics not usually considered part of journalism. *Mass Media Booknotes,* edited by Christopher Sterling, was published for twelve years by Temple University's Department of Radio-TV-Film. As of February 1982, this monthly annotated bibliography is called *Communication Booknotes: Recent Titles in Telecommunications, Information and Media* and is published by the Center for Telecommunications Studies of George Washington University. Sterling and a number of contributing editors provide valuable and lengthy annotations for new books, pamphlets, documents, and journals. In addition to these two sources, new booklists are issued by several universities and organizations, including University of Illinois Communications Library, Indiana University Journalism Library, Ohio State Journalism Library, the Library of the Canadian Radio-Television and Telecommunications Commission in Ottawa, and the Library of the International Telecommunication Union in Geneva. A number of non-English language new books lists exist as well. Two current contents-type services are published for the area of mass media. One is *Sommaire Mensuel des Livres et Revues* (Bry sur Marne: Documentation sur L'Audiovisuel, Institut National de l'Audiovisuel, 1980-) which is, as one might expect, an international selection of copies of title pages of more than 150 serials on media. *Teleclippings* (Geneva: International Telecommunications Union) comes monthly. It is a selection of reprinted articles in many languages, all on telecommunications, including radio, television, telephone, information, and space communication.

PERIODICALS

In this section, sixty English language news magazines and scholarly journals are listed for the subjects discussed in this paper. More complete listings, including newsletters, reports, and foreign language journals, are available with descriptive notes in the *Aspen Handbook on the Media* and in *World Directory of Mass Communication Periodicals,* compiled by Sylwester Dziki (Cracow, Poland: Bibliographic Section of IAMCR and Press Research Center, 1980). The latter does not include film periodicals.

Advertising: A Quarterly Review of the Communications Business. Advertising business, effectiveness, and processes are covered. The Advertising Association, Abford House, 15 Wilton Rd, London, SWIV INJ, England.

Advertising Age. This is the major national news weekly on the advertising business. Crain Communications, 740 Rush St., Chicago, IL 60611.

Alternative Media. This quarterly contains radical critiques of media and coverage of the alternative press, film, television, and culture. Alternative Press Syndicate, Box 1347, Ansonia Station, New York, NY 10023.

American Cinematographer: International Journal of Motion Picture Photography and Production Techniques. Discussion and illustration of how films are made is published monthly by the American Society of Cinematographers, Box 2230, Hollywood, CA 90028.

American Film Magazine. General news and commentary on films comes monthly with membership in the American Film Institute. American Film Institute, JFK Center for the Performing Arts, Washington, DC 20566.

Broadcasting. This is a major business news weekly covering radio, television, cable, video, and telecommunications. Broadcasting Publications, Inc., 1735 DeSales St., N.W., Washington, DC 20036.

Canadian Journal of Communication. Formerly *Media Probe*, this theoretical and critical quarterly on mass communication is published by the Canadian Communication Association, Box 272, Station R, Toronto, Ontario, Canada M4G 3TO.

Channels of Communications; The Magazine of Television and Society. This is a new bimonthly publication on general interest television effects topics. Box 2001, Mahopac, NY 10541.

Cineaste. This quarterly publishes theory and discussion of films with emphasis on radical film. 419 Park Ave. S. New York, NY 10016.

Columbia Journalism Review. Assessment of journalistic performance is the purpose of this bimonthly journal. 700 Journalism Bldg., Columbia University, New York, NY 10027.

Comm/ent: A Journal of Communications and Entertainment Law. Business law is covered as it relates to mass communication and entertainment industries in this quarterly specialized journal. Hastings College of Law, 200 McAllister St., San Francisco, CA 94102.

Communication. Each issue of this international biannual is on a specific theme related to communication theory. Gordon and Breach, 1 Park Ave., New York, NY 10016.

Communication News. This covers news of voice, video, and data communication industries, with information on regulation, technical developments, and products. Harcourt Brace Jovanovich, 124 S. First St., Geneva, IL 60134.

Communication Research: An International Quarterly. Interdisciplinary writings on communication research are published here. Sage Publications, 275 S. Beverly Dr., Beverly Hills, CA 90212.

Communications and the Law. This quarterly contains analysis of legal, judicial and legislative issues on media use and technology. Meckler Publishing, 520 Riverside Ave., Westport, CT 06880

Editor and Publisher. This is the major newsweekly for the newspaper business. Editor and Publisher, 575 Lexington Ave., New York, NY 10022.

Educational Broadcasting International: A Journal of the British Council. Articles are published quarterly on the use of radio and television in education, including Europe as well as developing nations. British Council, Tavistock House South, Tavistock Square, London WClH 9LL, England.

Electronic Publishing Review. This quarterly publishes scholarly and state-of-the-art articles on videotex, teletext, the electronic journal, and other aspects of the "paperless society." Oxford, U.K.: Learned Information.

Film Comment. This is a bimonthly magazine with comment and criticism of motion pictures. Film Society of Lincoln Center, 140 W. 65 St. New York, NY 10023.

Film Culture. Avant-garde film is emphasized in this quarterly on film aesthetics and criticism. Film Culture, Box 1499, G.P.O., New York, NY 10001.

Film Quarterly. This is a scholarly journal of film criticism which publishes articles from a variety of perspectives. University of California Press, 2223 Fulton St., Berkeley, CA 94720.

Folio: The Magazine for Magazine Management. This monthly covers advertising, circulation, sales, publishing and other aspects of the magazine publishing business. 125 Elm St. Box 697, New Canaan, CT 06840.

Gazette: International Journal for Mass Communication Studies. Editing journalism, advertising, politics, public relations, economics, and other areas are covered in this quarterly. Martinus Nijhoff Publishing, Box 566, 2501 CN The Hague, The Netherlands.

Historical Journal of Film, Radio, and Television. Published twice a year, this interdisciplinary journal is concerned with evidence provided by mass media for historians, and with the impact of the media in the twentieth century. Carfax Publishing Company, Box 25, Abingdon, Oxfordshire, OX14 1RW, England.

Human Communication Research. This is the quarterly journal of the International Communication Association. It covers broad areas of behavior research related to communication. Transaction Periodicals Consortium, Rutgers University, New Brunswick, NJ 08903.

Journal of Advertising. This quarterly on the theory and philosophy of communication as it relates to advertising is published by the American Academy of Advertising. 395 JKB, Brigham Young University, Provo, UT 84602.

Journal of Advertising Research. Papers are included which report findings related to advertising and marketing research. It is published by the Advertising Research Foundation. 3 E. 54 St., New York, NY 10022.

Journal of Applied Communications Research. Articles on mass, interpersonal, and organizational communication research are published semiannually. Department of Communication, University of South Florida, Tampa, FL 33620.

Journal of Broadcasting. This quarterly is the research journal of the Broadcast Education Association, covering radio, television, and related fields. 1771 N St., N.W., Washington, DC 20036.

Journal of Communication. Published by the Annenberg School Press in cooperation with the International Communication Association, this quarterly publishes interdisciplinary articles on mass and interpersonal communication. 3620 Walnut St., Philadelphia, PA 19104.

Journal of Communication Inquiry. Theoretical pieces on cultural, historical, legal, ethical, and other approaches to communication are published twice per year. School of Journalism, Iowa Center for Communication Study, University of Iowa, Iowa City, IA 52242

Journal of Popular Film and Television. This quarterly examines popular culture issues. Center for the Study of Popular Culture, Bowling Green State University, Popular Culture Center, Bowling Green OH 43403.

Journalism Educator. This quarterly is published by the Association for Education in Journalism for teachers in professional schools of print and broadcast journalism, advertising and public relations. Association for Education in Journalism and Mass Communication, College of Journalism, University of South Carolina, Columbia, SC 29208.

Journalism Quarterly. As the subtitle says: Devoted to research in journalism and mass communication. Association for Education in Journalism and Mass Communication, College of Journalism, University of South Carolina, Columbia, SC 29208.

Jump Cut: A Review of Contemporary Cinema. This contains radical perspectives on social and artistic aspects of film analysis. Frequency varies. Box 865, Berkeley, CA 94701.

Mass Comm Review. From the Mass Communications and Society Division of the Association for Education in Journalism, this is for academics and professionals. It is published three times per year. Department of Journalism, Temple University, Philadelphia, PA 19122.

Media, Culture, and Society. This is a general academic quarterly with writing on an international basis. Academic Press, 24 Oval Rd., London NW1 7DX, England. (111 Fifth Ave., New York, NY 10003 in North and South America).

Media Industry Newsletter (MIN). Although other newsletters are not included in this list, the statistics and financial data found in this weekly publication are valuable for the fields of radio, television, press, magazines, book publishing, cable, advertising, etc. MIN Publishing, 18 E. 53 St., New York, NY 10022.

Newspaper Research Journal. Research reports on press, readership, and related issues are published by the Newspaper Division of the Association for Education in Journalism. Department of Journalism, Memphis State University, Memphis, TN 38152.

Political Communication and Persuasion: An International Journal. This biannual contains analysis of international issues related to political communication, propaganda, and the media. Crane, Russak, & Co., 3 E. 44 St., New York, NY 10017.

The Press: Reporting How the Media Work. This includes news and opinion on media, bimonthly. Tone Arm Publications, 112 E. 19 St., New York, NY 10003.

Presstime: The Journal of the American Newspaper Publishers Association. A newsmagazine from ANPA, this monthly covers newspaper publishing. ANPA, 11600 Sunrise Valley Dr, Reston, VA 22091.

Public Opinion. Articles are published bimonthly on opinion issues. It also includes Opinion Roundup from the Roper Center. American Enterprise Institute, 1150 17 St., N.W., Washington, DC 20036.

Public Opinion Quarterly. From the American Association for Public Opinion Research, this includes pieces on polls, polling, survey research, and the mass media. Elsevier North Holland, 52 Vanderbilt Ave., New York, NY 10017.

Public Relations Journal. This is a monthly "serving public relations practitioners and educators and their managements" from the Public Relations Society of America. 845 Third Ave., New York, NY 10022.

Public Relations Quarterly. Both theory and practice are covered in this journal emphasizing societal issues. 4 W. Market St., Rhinebeck, NY 12572.

Public Relations Review: A Journal of Research and Comment. This is a general public relations quarterly, with one issue each year devoted to publication of "Comprehensive Bibliography." Foundation for Public Relations and Education, Communication Research Associates, Inc., 7100 Baltimore Blvd., Suite 500, College Park, MD 20740.

Public Telecommunications Review. From the National Association of Educational Broadcasting, this bimonthly publication includes news, research reports, and opinion pieces on public broadcasting. NAEB, 1346 Connecticut Ave. N.W., Washington, DC 20036.

Quarterly Review of Film Studies. Includes a range of articles on film theory and criticism. Redgrave Publishing Co., Box 67, South Salem, NY 10590.

The Quill. This monthly is for reporters, writers, editors, photographers, and others working with news writing. Society of Professional Journalists, 840 N. Lake Shore Dr, Suite 801W, Chicago, IL 60611.

Screen. This is a left-oriented quarterly journal on topics related to film education, theory, history, and criticism. 29 Old Compton St., London W1V 5PN, England.

Sight and Sound. This is from the British Film Institute and includes reviews, news, and features. 127 Charing Cross Rd., London WC2H OEA, England.

Studies in Visual Communication. This quarterly continues *Studies in Anthropology of Visual Communication* and includes articles on television, graphics, cartoons, photography, perception, etc. Annenberg School Press, 3620 Walnut St., Philadelphia, PA 19104.

TV Guide. This familiar listing of program information is issued in 88 regional editions. Triangle Publications, No. 4 Radnor Corporate Center, Radnor, PA 19088.

Telecommunication Policy. This is a frequently cited source of information on satellites and other communication systems and is international in scope. Guildford, U.K.: Butterworth Scientific.

Television and Children. Information, research reports, news, and opinion are published quarterly by the National Council for Children and Television. 20 Nassau St., Suite 200, Princeton, NJ 08540.

Television Quarterly, The Journal of the National Academy of Television Arts and Sciences. This is a quarterly magazine of reviews and articles by television professionals and others. 110 W. 57 St., New York, NY 10019.

Television/Radio Age. Business aspects of broadcasting are stressed in this biweekly trade magazine. 1270 Ave. of the Americas, New York, NY 10020.

University Film Association Journal. Both news and scholarly studies are published on film education. Department of Cinema & Photography, Southern Illinois University, Carbondale, IL 62901.

Variety. This well-known show-business weekly contains news and reviews for theater, television, film, music, and other entertainment industries. Variety, Inc. 154 W. 46 St., New York, NY 10036.

Wide Angle. This is a quarterly film magazine containing pieces on film criticism and theory. Ohio University, Department of Film, Box 388, Athens, OH 45701.

A Strategy for Purchasing Media Equipment

John W. Ellison and Clara DiFelice

Budget cuts or none, it is instilled in us to acquire the best materials available for the money. Buttressed by reviews, use-statistics, and word of mouth, the process of selecting non-print material (software) for library collections is usually rigorous and demands time and effort. Too often, however, the process used to select equipment (hardware) is not as thorough. Because the initial cost outlay for equipment may seem large, it is easy to become overly cautious and unsure in selecting equipment. Yet the cost of equipment is normally a small fraction of the expense of materials used with a piece of equipment. Equipment that is not up to the quality standards demanded for software can in turn downgrade the software.

Time and effort must be spent selecting quality equipment that provides reliable service. Time is needed to investigate the various demands that will be made upon the equipment, and effort is required to determine the best equipment to match those needs for the least amount of money.

The starting point in the process of selecting equipment is most often an expressed need for a certain type of hardware. In some rare instances, dollars are actually set aside to purchase equipment above and beyond the normal operating budget. Once the need has been expressed, it is important to determine the objectives of use to which the equipment will respond. Will it be in a fixed location? Used with large or small groups or individuals? Portable enough to carry easily? Durable enough to be transported by a variety of means—in the trunk of a car, on a mobile cart, or skidded down an ice-covered path? The patterns of use at individual libraries or institutions should form the basis for these questions. The answers will determine the necessary considerations of the selection process.

SOURCES OF INFORMATION

Beginning usually involves browsing through the *Audio Visual Equipment Directory*, published by the National Audio Visual Association. This publication gives some idea of available institutional equipment, basic specifications, and prices and includes photographs of equipment. A cursory examination of this publication will give information on the models and the options currently available.

Not all manufacturers list their products with the *Directory*. The many trade journals, most of them advertiser-supported and free to qualified equipment buyers, will help as well. *Video Systems, Audio-Visual Communication, Educational and Industrial Television* (E&ITV), *Audio Visual Directions, School Products News,* and *Broadcast Management* have ads which become a veritable shopping place for the newest in each type of equipment. Coded cards are provided to send for further information from the manufacturer on products that pique your interest. These journals also tend to publish annual equipment issues, which provide a nearly complete scope of equipment and manufacturers available in a given field. *Broadcast Engineering's* "Buyers Guide" issue is an example. It should be noted that these issues offer equipment lists and services, not reviews of equipment.

Written information on equipment of an evaluative nature is limited, but some can be found in the *EPIE Equipment Reports* and *EPIEgram: Equipment Newsletters* published by the Educational Products Information Exchange. They provide test results and wide-ranging articles on varied models of equipment. *Library Technology Reports* is another source of evaluative reviews of equipment. Additional sources for the techniques and tips on shopping for hardware are found in the bibliography accompanying this chapter.

SIGNIFICANT QUESTIONS

With an idea of the variety of equipment available, determining which model best meets the library or user needs is the next challenge. Flexibility often becomes an operative term here; sometimes with unfortunate results. Too much flexibility can mean the purchase of a piece of equipment which fills a variety of needs and never quite satisfies the one need that started the quest.

In the long run, a firm understanding of what is necessary must prevail. The cry, " . . . but for only a few hundred more we can get a videorecorder," simply clouds the decision. Why purchase a recorder if only playback is needed? Selecting more elaborate equipment just in case you may use it is not matching the expressed need and may cause problems in the future. If equipment is being used for recording, what will be used for playback? Keep eventual use in mind, but respond to the current expressed need with the best available piece of equipment for the lowest price. Flexibility may be a major factor when selecting equipment, especially when for a small collection. But if flexibility is not necessary, do not let it become the most important consideration.

Several factors begin to intrude at this point: ease of use, maintenance, standardization with models on hand. Each raises crucial questions. What unusual operating tips are required to use the equipment? How will users react to them? Operating instructions can often be tricky and may sway a decision for particular equipment models. Which button to push is usually all the user wants to learn. Ease of operation may have been proven with certain models, and continued familiarity helps soothe users' qualms. However, be aware that even tried and true models can raise problems. Design changes can occur at manufacturer's whim. Judge the ease of operation by using the equipment yourself, tempering that experience with what is known of users' preferences. Thoroughly understanding the operation of every piece of equipment considered for purchase is an important step in the selection process.

MANUFACTURERS AND VENDORS

The reputations of various manufacturers and vendors are important considerations. Contacting a local Better Business Bureau and talking with others who have purchased equipment under consideration are effective informal routes to this information. Does the manufacturer stand behind a warranty or service contract? How soon after purchase will the equipment arrive? How close are the vendor's ties to the manufacturer? Do they automatically supply buyers with new product information? Do they provide equipment for a demonstration period? In the case of a complex or large installation of new equipment, do they provide a training session for the staff? These questions should come up when considering vendors.

Who will service the equipment? Must it be returned to a vendor? What lamps, batteries, or other parts are necessary? Are they already on hand? Has this particular item been in the field very long? Has it been field-tested? Is it designed for institutional or home use?

Servicing and standardization of equipment can tip the balance in support of particular models. If equipment is serviced in-house, parts already stocked can save downtime. If it is sent out for servicing, vendor reputation becomes important. Also, the availability of a manufacturer's service center may be a factor.

Identifying vendors can be as easy as looking in the telephone yellow pages, contacting the manufacturer for the names of vendors nearby, or contacting the National Audio-Visual Association for vendors in your area. Local exhibits or conferences and seasoned media librarians in your community can usually supply necessary information to identify vendors.

The National Audio Visual Association, the trade association of the audio-visual industry, helps sales representatives stay abreast of developments in the industry through an active continuing education program. For their successful participation, they are designated Certified Media Specialists by the Association. This certification, according to the Association's literature, "gives recognition to those in the audiovisual industry who have attained a professional level of competency, efficiency, and skill in the sales, management, production, or manufacturing of audiovisual equipment, materials and systems."

Once a vendor has been identified, request that the equipment under consideration be brought to the library for demonstration and left for a three-day staff inspection. If other vendors carry comparable models of equipment, try to arrange for all equipment to be available for the same three days. This will make it easy to compare the different models.

Sales representatives can be the best friends of the media librarian all year, and particularly during the equipment selection process. They generally know the equipment and in the process of demonstrating it they can teach observers what question to ask the next representative. Their presentation is usually filled with statements like, "No other product can . . . " or "Some machines have problems . . . ." These bits of information help to focus on the strengths and weaknesses of their competition. Sales representatives almost never mention another company or product by name. The media librarian must evaluate each piece of equipment for the potential strengths and weaknesses learned from previous sales representatives. With models changing on a regular basis, this is sometimes the only way to compare equipment. Going to a conference where several models of equipment are on display for demonstration makes the process even easier since going back over each piece of equipment several times is possible. Large conferences may offer the potential buyer an opportunity to speak with a manufacturer's engineer.

When initially contacting sales representatives, be honest with them and give them your time. They need to know how many items you are planning to purchase. It may not seem fair on the surface, but when all is taken into consideration, the volume buyer pays for the visit to the single item buyer.

Sales representatives are usually very well-educated and almost always have a wealth of practical knowledge and experience worth the media librarian's undivided attention. Smart media librarians nurture their relationship with the valuable educator, assistant, and reference source found in most sales representatives.

Once the sales representative arrives, give the person time to properly demonstrate the equipment before asking questions, but then be prepared to ask: Are you an authorized vendor? How long has the company and distributorship been in business? Are you an authorized factory service representative? May I visit your service shop? Who has reviewed this equipment? Do you have life-cycle-cost records for this item? What are the maintenance and repair cost records for this equipment? Do you pick up and deliver equipment for repair? How does your service contract read? May I have a copy of it? What is the lamp projection life and cost? Does the vendor back both the guarantee and warranty? What is the library's cost for multiple or volume orders? Is the item on a state contract for which the library is eligible? These are not all the questions, but this list includes some of the major questions which should be asked.

SELECTING A VENDOR

Several types of vendors are in the equipment business. Each has advantages and disadvantages to consider prior to buying equipment. Is the vendor local, an out-of-town dealer, a warehouse dealer, or a "hit and run artist?" Local vendors have the obvious advantage of being close. They also depend on local institutions to stay in business. This is an advantage since they usually service their products, want return business from their customers, and therefore usually will not jeopardize this by selling a product not in the client's best interests. One disadvantage of local vendors may be small order purchase prices. They often do not buy in large quantities and therefore cannot pass savings on to their customers. When the media librarian buys in large volume, however, local vendors are usually competitive with other vendors.

Out-of-town vendors may have the disadvantage of not being able to service equipment as fast as local vendors. However, some local vendors are willing to service equipment under warranty, billing the cost to the equipment seller. Added expense of shipping is a factor one must consider when purchasing and returning equipment for repairs, though out-of-town vendors may have local repair services available.

Warehouse dealers usually have the advantage of low prices, but rarely have a service department or purchase guarantee. They seldom provide more than the factory warranty which all vendors provide. Unless your library has an excellent equipment service department, the warehouse vendor price may not be the cheapest in the long run.

Of all the vendors, the "hit and run artist" is the most undesirable. They usually buy in large volume directly from the factory and pass through communities with attractive prices because of their low (or nonexistent) overhead. However, they provide no guarantee or service with their equipment. In addition, they may not know the equipment they are selling.

Care should be taken when selecting a vendor. More is at stake than saving a few dollars on the initial purchase. Local vendors provide free reference services, engineers, and experts who make recommendations prior to writing specifications. They also generally support local media organizations with time, personnel, and even donations. These services cost money. The question becomes, is the price of equipment all that important?

SPECIFICATIONS AND BIDS

Most large institutional orders are sent out in a normal bidding process from the purchasing department. When requesting equipment, an understanding of this process and the importance of equipment specifications will demonstrate that the time spent selecting the best possible piece of equipment is not wasted.

Writing specifications will ensure that you receive the piece of equipment you identified to fulfill your needs. Working closely with the purchasing department can help assure they send the bid request to all eligible vendors rather than to the first three listed in the yellow pages. Any request for equipment should automatically include a request that operating, parts, and service manuals be provided with the equipment. This will save tracking down individual manuals at some point in the future and paying extra for them.

Written specifications give the vendor in detail all the requirements and the services the buyer wants with a piece of equipment. The motor size, lamp wattage, amperage, and length of power cord are just a few of the items a buyer may request. In addition, it is possible to request a specified number of demonstrations by the vendor over a given length of time in your library. Specifications may also require that the equipment must be set up and operating at the buyer's designated location a certain number of days after arrival. An indication of who will pay the shipping charges may also be written into the specifications. Some libraries write service contracts as part of the specifications.

A service contract may specify that equipment will be repaired within twenty-four hours or a replacement piece of equipment must be left for the library to use until the repaired equipment has been returned. Caution should be taken when writing service contracts into bid specifications. All services increase the bid price. Depending on the location of the vendor, the increase may be significant. It is advisable to examine carefully the implications when writing bids so tight that vendors are limited, and services so extensive that the equipment cost may actually be less than the add-on services requested.

Bids generally are of three types: formal, informal, and alternative. Formal bids usually have certain legal implications if not handled properly. Informal bids, on the other hand, do not carry legal constraints, but, like formal bids, they are usually based on written specification. Alternative bids are presented by vendors that have equipment that may not meet the written specifications but is comparable. Most institutions, cities, counties, or states have specific guidelines and categories that constitute types of bids and when bids are required. Some institutions require an item costing more than one hundred dollars to be placed on formal bid, while another institution may set the figure at fifteen hundred dollars.

Any bidding process should be used by the media librarian for the benefit of the library. Informal bids help the media librarian by knowing how much an item will cost and selecting items that will stay within the allocated budget. Formal bids help assure the institution that the lowest price is being paid for a piece of equipment. The alternative (or "equal") bid assures that all vendors will have an opportunity to bid on specifications even if their equipment does not meet the written specifications.

A purchasing agent or the institution's business office usually processes bids. These people centralize all purchasing and record-keeping, and make sure all legal requirements are met by the vendor and institution. The purchasing agent, like the media librarian, should be above bid-rigging, favoritism, direct bribery, and gifts from vendors. Their primary purpose is to make sure the institution pays no more than necessary for the equipment and service needed, and that the correct piece of equipment is selected and received. It is not the purchasing agent's job to select equipment for purchase or write bids, though they may assist. Where media librarians have permitted or even encouraged this practice, purchasing agents may have taken on this responsibility.

FINAL PHASE

The last step in selecting quality hardware is to examine the equipment thoroughly when it arrives before discarding its shipping box. Run a film through a projector and rewind. Play a cassette tape. Any damage which occurred in shipping should be immediately reported to the library's purchasing department or business office with a carbon to the vendor.

Use new equipment continuously for several hours. Better to find problems with the equipment while the manufacturer's warranty is still good. Resist the temptation to place it on the shelf and to protect it as a "new" piece of equipment. It is better to use it and determine how it will hold up than to find problems later.

Bibliography

Audio Visual Communications. United Business Publications. 475 Park Ave. So., New York, NY 10016.
Audio Visual Directions. Montage Publishing, Inc. 5173 Overland Ave., Culver City, CA 90230.

Audio Visual Equipment Directory. National Audio-Visual Association. Fairfax, Va. (annual.)

Broadcast Engineering. Intertec Publishing Corp. P.O. Box 12902, Overland Park, KS 66212.

Broadcast Management. Broadband Information Services, Inc. P.O. Box 6056, Duluth, MN 55806.

Educational & Industrial Television. C. S. Tepfer Publishing Co. 51 Sugar Hollow Rd., Danbury, CT 06810.

EPIE Equipment Reports, EPIEGram: Equipment. Educational Products Information Exchange. New York.

Grady, William F. "AV Hardware" in *Media and Methods*, September 1980-January 1981.

Laird, Dugan. *AV Buyer's Guide: A User's Look at the Audio Visual World*. Fairfax, Va.: National Audio Visual Association, 1977.

Library Technology Reports. American Library Association. Chicago.

Rosenberg, Kenyon C. and John S. Doskey. *Media Equipment: A Guide & Dictionary*. Littleton, Colo.: Libraries Unlimited, 1976.

School Product News. Penton/IPC, Inc. P.O. Box 95759, Cleveland, OH 44101.

Schmid, William T. *Media Center Management*. New York: Hastings House, 1980.

Video Systems. Intertec Publishing Corp. P.O. Box 12912, Overland Park, KS 66212.

Wyman, Raymond. *Mediaware: Selection, Operation and Maintenance*. Dubuque, Iowa: William C. Brown Co., 1976.

A Reader's Guide to Audiovisual Equipment

Joseph W. Palmer

LIBRARIANS are often unnecessarily intimidated by audiovisual equipment. The basic principles one must master are actually quite simple and a number of publications exist to give aid and comfort to the novice and the experienced practitioner. This article describes some of the publications that can help the librarian become more proficient in selecting, operating, and maintaining audiovisual equipment.

SELECTING EQUIPMENT

When purchasing audiovisual equipment, three basic rules apply. 1) Select the model that is most suited to your particular needs. Consider who will use it, where it will be used, for what, and how often it will be used. 2) Select the model that is easiest to use and maintain. 3) Select the model that is most durable and for which service and parts are readily available.

In the literature you will find: guidelines on how to evaluate equipment, information on characteristics and "specs" (specifications) of available models, and, if you are lucky, published evaluations of specific models that describe their strengths and weaknesses.

A good place to start is Kenyon C. Rosenberg and John S. Doskey's *Media Equipment: A Guide and Dictionary* (Littleton, Colo.: Libraries Unlimited, 1976). Part one offers guidelines for selecting various types of equipment. Fourteen excellent checklists detail the factors to consider in judging a wide variety of projectors, tape recorders (audio and video), and other audio equipment. Part two is a "dictionary of technical media equipment terms." It offers clear explanations, often accompanied by easy-to-understand diagrams, of the terminology most likely to be encountered in reading about audiovisual equipment. This is one book the media librarian will want to keep nearby.

Originally published in *Catholic Library World* 53 (September 1981) pp. 85-86.

Also worth examining is William F. Grady's column "AV Hardware" in *Media and Methods* magazine. The column began in September 1980 with a discussion of "Selection Criteria for AV Equipment." Specific hints on selecting audiocassette recorders also appeared in that issue. Hints on selecting 16mm projectors followed in October 1980 and on sound projectors for filmstrips and slides in January 1981. The November 1980 column provided advice on how to write justifications for audiovisual equipment, and the January 1981 article listed points to remember in "Writing AV Specs." Subsequent columns continue to offer excellent advice on a variety of subjects.

Issues of *EPIE Reports* and *Library Technology Reports* that deal with audiovisual equipment will also tell you what to look for when selecting equipment. These two publications provide in-depth evaluations of specific brand name models. Unfortunately, the models evaluated may not always be those currently on the market.

To find out which models are currently available, one can use *Audiovisual Marketplace* and *Audiovisual Equipment Directory* to identify manufacturers and write to them for catalogs, one can visit local dealers to examine, try out, and obtain literature on the models they stock, and one can consult the listings in the latest issue of *Audiovisual Equipment Directory*.

Audiovisual Marketplace (New York: R.R. Bowker, annual) attempts to "compress between two covers all sources of AV information and products." Of particular interest to the equipment user are the sections "AV Equipment Manufacturers" and "AV Equipment Dealers." The manufacturers section provides directory information and is indexed by type of equipment. The dealers section is arranged in geographic order so a nearby firm can be located easily. This section identifies the types of equipment sold and/or rented and also tells if repairs service is available. Valuable as this listing is, it is incomplete and can be supplemented by consulting the appendix of *Audiovisual Equipment Directory* as well as the yellow pages of the telephone book.

Audiovisual Equipment Directory (Fairfax, Va.: National Audio Visual Association, annual) is published every May. It provides technical descriptions plus a photograph of over 1,450 different equipment models. This is probably the easiest and one of the best ways (since specs are provided) to compare available equipment. The Appendix contains a geographic directory of "audiovisual dealers, film libraries, and consulting companies" as well as such useful addenda as a brief glossary, a trade-name directory, and a lamp substitution chart.

The Educational Products Information Exchange, a non-profit organization devoted to the concerns of the educational consumer, issues a number of *EPIE Reports* each year. Some deal with materials and programs (e.g., "Learner Verification and Revision," "High-Demand In-

Service Training Materials," "Junior High School Training Programs").
Others deal with hardware. Audiovisual equipment reports give results of
tests on specific brand name models. They sometimes provide results of
user satisfaction surveys as well as the EPIE technician's overall rating of
construction and performance. *EPIE Reports* relevant to this article
include:

#89e   Videocassette Recorder/Players: The State of the Art (1979)
#88e   Sound Slide Projectors (with audiocassettes) (1979)
#87e   Sound Filmstrip Projectors (with audiocassettes) (1978)
#86e   Audiotape Recorders and Players with Built-in Synchronizers (1978)
#84e   Copiers and Duplicators for Audiotape Cassettes (1978)
#83e   16mm Sound Motion Picture Projectors (1977)
#82e   Overhead Projectors (1977)
#72   Writing Equipment Specifications: A How To Handbook (1975)

EPIE also publishes two monthly newsletters that are packed with
miscellaneous news and information: *EPIEgram: Equipment* and
EPIEgram: Materials.

Library Technology Reports are published by the American Library
Association and provide in-depth surveys and evaluations for a wide
range of library hardware. Issues have dealt with topics as diverse as
microform readers, furniture, security systems, computer printers, and
online circulation systems.

Issues dealing with audiovisual equipment have included:

"One Half Inch Videocassette Equipment for Library Use," September-
     October 1978 (Vol. 14)
"Sixteen Millimeter Motion Picture Projectors for Library and Educational
     Use," November 1977 (Vol. 13)
"Sound Filmstrip Projectors," May 1976 (Vol. 12)
"Cassette Tape Recorders for Libraries," March 1976 (Vol. 12)
"Video Industry: Equipment, Software, and Library Applications," March
     1976 (Vol. 12)
"Sixteen Millimeter Motion Picture Projectors; Reports on Seven Automatic
     Loading and Slot Loading Machines," March 1975 (Vol. 11)
"Record Players," January 1973 (Vol. 9)

Articles in magazines and journals which discuss or evaluate specific
types of equipment may be located by consulting *Consumers Index to
Product Evaluations and Information Sources* (Ann Arbor, Mich.:
Pierian Press, quarterly and annual), a splendid index to consumer
information articles of interest to general audiences, businesses, and the
educational/library community. Relevant citations will be found in
Section Nine: Sight and Sound and in Section Thirteen: Education and
the Library.

OPERATING AND MAINTAINING EQUIPMENT

The single most useful publication for information on operating and maintaining a piece of equipment is the manufacturer's manual that accompanies it. Study it thoroughly and keep it in a safe place.

Other publications explain the principles that underlie the workings of audiovisual equipment and give advice concerning operation and care. Obviously the person who understood *how* equipment operates is in the best position to evaluate models and to use equipment and cope with minor problems that may arise. Unfortunately, most of these publications derive from 1960s editions and tend to give scant attention to video and to the most current innovations in traditional equipment. But for essential information on the ordinary projection and audio equipment found in schools and libraries, they are just fine. A number of excellent publications *are* available that concern themselves strictly with video. One of the better ones is Richard Robinson's *Video Primer* (New York: Quick Fox, revised ed., 1978).

Two publications that are good reference books for those handling traditional equipment are: Raymond Wyman's *Mediaware: Selection, Operation and Maintenance* (Dubuque, Iowa: William C. Brown, 2nd ed., 1976) and Raymond Davidson's *Audiovisual Machines* (International Textbook Co., 1969). Wyman is particularly good for its excellent diagrams, simple, clear explanations of the technical basis for various kinds of equipment's operation, and for good hints on selection, operation, and care. Davidson is similar but differs in that particular models of equipment are shown and step-by-step operating instructions are provided.

Two publications that emphasize the simple mechanics of equipment operation are: Sidney C. Eboch's *Operating Audiovisual Equipment* (Chandler Publishing Co., 2nd ed., 1969) and John R. Bullard and Calvin E. Mether's *Audiovisual Fundamentals: Basic Equipment Operation and Simple Materials Production* (Dubuque, Iowa: William C. Brown, 2nd ed., 1979). Eboch is very brief, simple, and lavishly illustrated with diagrams. It devotes the largest part of its pages to 16mm and super 8mm motion picture projectors, giving step-by-step operating instructions for various models of projectors. (While some of these models are no longer available, they often operate in a manner similar to the more current models.) Eboch also discussed in very elementary terms the essentials of projection and of audiorecording. Novices will find Eboch particularly easy to understand.

Bullard and Mether is among the most up-to-date of the publications described here. It includes 3/4-inch U-Matic videocassette recorders, open reel videotape equipment, and cathode-ray terminals in the 1979 edition. It features large labeled diagrams of equipment and step-by-step operation instructions. Unfortunately, the diagrams are not always completely labeled (it is frustrating to see a part in a diagram and no indication of its function). Also, the diagrams are only line drawings of the equipment itself. They do not illustrate the mechanics of operation. The novice is likely to be confused by some of the written instructions too since three columns of information (general instructions, instructions for particular models, and supplementary information) appear on the page side by side. The book does feature a useful troubleshooting guide and easy-to-follow instructions on such production techniques as lettering, thermal copying, spirit master duplication, mounting, and laminating.

Another potentially useful publication is Stanton Oates' *Audiovisual Equipment Self Instruction Guide* (Dubuque, Iowa: William C. Brown, 4th ed., 1979). Unfortunately, this writer was unable to examine a copy so no comment on its merits can be made.

Two extremely simple but very informative publications by George T. Yeamans are *Projectionists Programmed Primer* (Muncie, Ind.: Ball State University Bookstores, 4th ed., 1979) and *Tape Recording Made Easy: A Programmed Primer* (Muncie, Ind.: Ball State University Bookstores, 1978). While these "audiovisual self-instructional pictorial workbooks" concentrate on operation, they provide good information on utilization, maintenance, and troubleshooting as well.

Most of the publications we have listed deal to some degree with simple maintenance. The one publication that really concentrates on troubleshooting and minor repairs, skimping on the more elementary procedures dealt with in other publications in favor of somewhat more technical advice on how to deal with mechanical problems, is Don Schroeder and Gary Lare's *Audiovisual Equipment: A Basic Repair and Maintenance Manual* (Metuchen, N.J.: Scarecrow, 1979). In addition it provides step-by-step, well illustrated instructions on such operations as film splicing, audiocassette splicing, soldering, and cable and connector repair. This publication is valuable and unique.

Finally, mention should be made of the *Annotated Directory of Parts and Services for Audiovisual Equipment* (Denver: Association of Audiovisual Technicians, 1980-81). It lists brand names of audiovisual equipment and cross indexes them to the main service and information centers in the United States that one should contact for parts, publications, and servicing information.

With the help of publications listed in this article and a little practice, librarians can gain skill and confidence and lose their fear of audiovisual equipment.

ORGANIZING
NON-PRINT

Cataloging Non-Print Material

Sara Clarkson

T HERE are two reasons a media librarian would want to catalog a non-print collection: one has to do with organization, the other with control. A media librarian with a small collection may be acquainted with each individual title in that collection and may be able to work from memory when helping users to find the items they need. As the collection grows to hundreds and thousands of titles, however, the media librarian will probably need some other method of finding titles, and so will the user. One such method is to place the non-print materials in some logical order within the collection, for example by assigning call numbers, so that users will find materials on similar topics shelved near one another. Another method is to provide some external device, such as a catalog, which would help a user to select relevant items out of that large and confusing collection of titles.

ORGANIZATION

The methods of organization a media librarian selects will depend on the size of the collection and on the kind of use expected for the collection. Is the collection open for users to browse? If so, then some sort of classification scheme (such as call numbers by subject) will bring titles on similar topics together on the shelves. This will enhance the collection's "browsability" for the user. If the collection is closed to user browsing, putting the items in order by accession number (the order in which they were acquired) may be all the organization that collection needs.

Giving the media users the best possible access to titles in the collection is a primary goal of the media librarian. A sensible, orderly catalog should enable a user to select the most suitable items in the collection. Information on catalog entries should meet the user's needs: the catalog records should be complete enough to adequately describe the media; entries should use language that the user understands; enough entries or "access points" should be provided so that the user will find the item whether searching the catalog by author, title, subject, director, performer, or whatever.

CONTROL

If a collection is organized so that users can access it easily, the system of organization should also help the media librarian to control the collection. Adequate control means that the media librarian can determine how weak or strong the collection is in any one area; it means that staff can tell when items are missing and need to be replaced, or when they are already part of the collection so that unwanted duplicates will not be added.

Cataloging, then, is not an end in itself. It is a means of organizing and controlling a media collection so that other library functions (reference, inventory, collection development) can be carried out more effectively.

Depending on the needs of its users, two media collections could require very different cataloging for the same item. The users of a media collection that serves a botany department, for example, might want a slide showing a dandelion gone to seed accessible by its Latin name, and might want it housed near slides of other plants in the same species. In a collection of non-print materials used by architects, however, the same slide might be of interest only because of its shape and resemblance to certain man-made structures. In either case, the cataloging of the slide should emphasize the aspect of the item that is important to that particular collection's users.

The needs of users of one particular media collection might change over time, too. New words might be added to the vocabulary, or new courses added to a curriculum. The cataloger must be in touch with these changes, and must be sure that the catalog responds to such changes. It is the only way that the catalog will remain an up-to-date, useful tool.

HOW TO CATALOG

A variety of cataloging manuals, classification schedules, and subject heading lists exists to help, and to confuse, the cataloger of non-print materials. Decisions about which manuals and lists to use should be based on the type of use expected for the non-print collection. If the collection is small, independent, and for the use of local clientele only, locally devised cataloging procedures may suffice. If the collection is part of a larger system with a union catalog, or if the media service participates in, or is planning to participate in, a shared cataloging venture such as OCLC (the Online Computer Library Center), the media service may be expected to conform to some larger cataloging standards. If the media department is located within a college library system, for example, it may want to use the same call number and subject heading practices as the rest of the libraries on campus.

There are two steps involved in cataloging any item in any format: describing the item at hand so that the catalog user knows exactly what the media services owns; and providing suitable access points to enable the prospective user to find that item if it might possibly answer his or her needs.

Description

Until recently, the descriptive cataloging on non-print materials has been a sore spot for catalogers. The *Anglo-American Cataloging Rules (AACR)*,[1] the major cataloging code for large libraries in England, Canada, and the United States, was a major offender. Its rules for non-print materials were complicated and inconsistent in their approach to different formats, and they ignored some non-print formats completely. Because of this situation, a proliferation of other codes dealing only with non-print formats emerged to supplement or compete with *AACR*. The most widely used in North America were the "Canadian code"[2] and the rules issued by the Association of Educational Communications and Technology (AECT).[3]

In the late 1970s, a second edition of the *Anglo-American Cataloguing Rules (AACR2)*[4] appeared. One reason for its creation was to give non-print as much coverage as print materials. It was hoped that the one code could serve all sizes and types of libraries and media services, no matter how simple or complex they wanted their cataloging to be and regardless of format.

Appearing in times when shrinking library budgets, the sharing of materials with other libraries, and the growth of online shared cataloging systems were becoming the rule of the day, the standardization of descriptive cataloging for all types of library materials seemed to make sense. Authors of the Canadian code immediately released a new edition of their work,[5] bringing it into line with *AACR2*. The authors of the AECT rules announced their intention of revising their work as well.[6]

This chapter is not intended to be a manual for cataloging. Only formal cataloging courses and the use of an accepted code can provide that. This chapter merely gives an overview of types of information most catalogers think essential in describing a non-print item. These essential bits of information are:

Title
Statement of responsibility (name of persons or corporate bodies responsible
 for the creation of the work)
Edition
Publisher, producer, etc.
Date
Physical description

Other information can always be added if a cataloger thinks it is important to users.

Most cataloging codes describe a certain format or order in which these elements of description should occur and advise how to separate those elements. *AACR2*, for example, gives prescribed punctuation marks intended to distinguish and identify the elements of description. The resulting description, with all elements explicitly identified, can easily be converted into machine-readable form via the MARC (machine-readable cataloging) formats for use in computer databases.

An example of a finished cataloging record whose cataloging was done according to *AACR2* might look like this:

```
        Dandelion [slide ].  --Denver :
          Slide-Master, 1981.
          1 slide : col.

          Summary:  Close up color photo-
        graph of dandelion flower after it
        has gone to seed.

          1. Dandelions.  I. Slide-Master (Firm)
```

"Dandelion"	Title	(*AACR2*, Rule 8.1)
"[slide]"	General medium designator (optional)	(Rule 1.1C)
"Denver"	Place of publication	(Rule 8.4C)
"Slide-Master"	Name of publisher	(Rule 8.4D)
"1981"	Date of publication	(Rule 8.4F)
"1 slide: col."	Physical description (size 2″ × 2″ not given in this case because it is standard)	(Rule 8.5)
"Summary . . ."	Optional note describing the content of the item	(Rule 8.7B17)
"Dandelions"	Subject heading (From *Library of Congress Subject Headings*)	
"Slide-Master"	Tracing for name of publisher	(Rule 21.30E)

The cataloging description, no matter how basic, should always adequately describe what it is the media services owns. A user could come into a non-print collection looking for a motion picture on dolphins to show a large group and find a catalog record that looks like this:

```
     Dolphins / by Marianne Hammer.  --
       Quincy, Mass.   : Flipper Sea
       School, 1970.

     Summary: Describes the physical
   characteristics and behavior of
   dolphins
```

In this example the cataloger has not achieved the goal of telling the user whether this particular title suits his or her needs. From this catalog record the user cannot tell whether the item described is a motion picture, an audiocassette, or a book.

The user would be much better served if the catalog record looked like this:

```
   Dolphins [motion picture] / directed by
     Marianne Hammer. -- Quincy, Mass. :
     Flipper Sea School, 1970.
     1 film reel (20 min.) : sd., col., ;
   16 mm.

     Summary: Describes the physical
   characteristics and behavior of
   dolphins.

     1. Dolphins -- Physiology. 2. Dolphins --
   Behavior. I. Hammer, Marianne.   II.
   Flipper Sea School.
```

Access

The cataloger of non-print materials must also realize that users of the materials will look for an item in a variety of ways. Some users may know a specific title, others may search by subject, still others may only look under a name they associate with a certain work. Catalogers of non-print materials must take care to provide an access point under each possible approach to an item. To do this successfully the cataloger must know the users—their age level, educational level, their library habits, and their vocabulary. A motion picture that is being cataloged for a public libray, for example, might be cataloged adequately by giving access points for the title, the name of a famous director, and the subject of the film. The same motion picture cataloged for a college with a cinema studies program is likely to need access under title, director, persons responsible for screenplay and cinematography, major stars, name of the studio releasing the film, subject headings, and more.

In a card catalog a separate card would be filed under each access point provided by the cataloger. A complete set of cards for the preceding cataloging example would be:

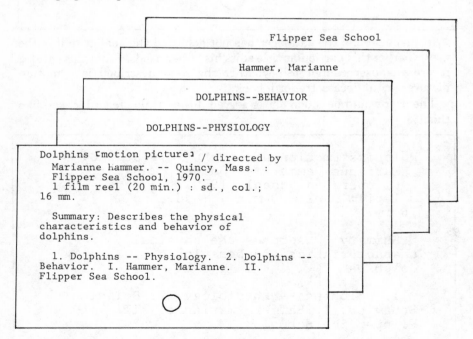

In an online catalog, each access point provided by the cataloger would be coded in such a way that someone searching under the access point would retrieve the relevant cataloging record.

Subject access deserves special attention here. Because media services users vary in their age, level of professional specialization, and interests, a particular media item might demand different subject treatment for different groups of users. Catalogers should strive to give subject headings that are as general or as specific as the item being cataloged. The catalog record for a work on suspension systems in cars would be more useful to students in an automobile repair program if the cataloger assigns the specific subject heading "Automobiles—Springs and suspension" rather than the general heading "Automobiles."

Subject headings should reflect the interests of the users of a particular non-print collection as well. A set of slides of dandelions might be accessible enough in one collection with the subject heading "Dandelions." In another non-print collection, perhaps a collection which has many users who are interested in nutrition, the same slide set might require the subject heading "Greens, Edible" as well.

Finally, when assigning subject headings a cataloger should know the terminology of that particular non-print collection's users. Many collections are committed to using standard lists of subject headings such as *Sears List of Subject Headings*[7] or *Library of Congress Subject Headings*.[8] Users benefit greatly when a cross-reference guides them from the term they search under to the term that is actually used as a subject heading. For example, a cataloger might prepare a cross-reference to tell catalog users:

NEW WAVE MUSIC

search under

MUSIC, ROCK

The advantage of cross-reference is that they can be made from any term currently in the vocabulary of the catalog users. As new words are added to users' vocabularies, or as old words take on new meanings, the cataloger must continually work to keep the subject catalog current by providing cross-references and by updating old subject headings. This is the only way that the subject catalog will remain a workable tool for the media services's users.

ISSUES IN NON-PRINT CATALOGING

Standardization

Is there a national standard for non-print cataloging? Do media services and non-print catalogers want such standardization? Do they need it?

As mentioned earlier, the *Anglo-American Cataloging Rules (AACR)* used by many of the larger libraries were difficult to use, inconsistent, and incomplete for the cataloging of non-print materials. Many smaller libraries bought catalog cards from the publishers of non-print materials and from the Library of Congress (LC) to save the expense of doing the original cataloging. Often it was unclear which cataloging code a publisher followed. Because the Library of Congress used *AACR*, this was the closest thing to a national standard for non-print cataloging. The Library of Congress, however, did not and still does not catalog all forms of non-print material.[9] Libraries had to resort to original cataloging for material in formats that LC did not catalog and for material for which publishers did not supply catalog cards. When they did do their own original cataloging, some libraries preferred the Canadian or the AECT rules, even though this resulted in a mixture of rules and different looking cards within individual catalogs.

This proliferation of cataloging codes made the sharing of information difficult. Non-print catalogers who had problems with a particular rule or a particular format would find it difficult, if not impossible, to work out a solution to the problem with a colleague who used a different cataloging code. Because of this, catalogers tended to develop local solutions to their problems. This made the likelihood of sharing cataloging expertise and the joint solving of problems even smaller.

This, then, is one major advantage of having standardized rules for non-print cataloging: with more catalogers using the same rules, problems and gaps in those rules would sooner surface, and joint solutions to those problems could be implemented more quickly. Such improvements should eventually make the cataloging rules easier to use.

National bibliographic databases such as the Online Computer Library Center (OCLC), the Research Libraries Information Network (RLIN), and the Washington Library Network (WLN) have revolutionized the work of cataloging. Because member libraries and media services can "copy" or "share" other libraries' cataloging, it saves them the time and expense of doing original cataloging for all items themselves. The databases of these bibliographic utilities, however, are made up mostly of records for printed material. OCLC is the largest of these utilities. As of July 1982, OCLC's database consisted of over 8.5 million cataloging records. Of these, just over 410,000 records (4.8% of the database) were records for non-print titles.[10] "Non-print" in this instance refers to those OCLC records which used the audiovisual format (motion pictures, filmstrips, slides, transparencies, videorecordings, filmloops, charts, dioramas, flash cards, games, microscope slides, models, realia, kits) or the sound recordings format (sound disk, sound tape, etc.) An additional 101,000 records (an additional 1.2% of the database) are for maps. It is likely that media services using OCLC will still have to resort to slow, expensive original cataloging for some of their non-print titles. Growing standardization, it is hoped, will make the cataloging of non-print titles easier and faster. More cataloging records for non-print titles would be added to the databases of the bibliographic utilities, and cataloging of non-print titles would become even cheaper and faster.

It remains to be seen whether *AACR2* (issued in 1978) will become the basis of standardization in non-print cataloging. The revision of the Canadian code and the proposed revision of the AECT code into conformity with *AACR2* are good signs that if anything does become a basis for such standarization at a national level, *AACR2* will. At this time, only if non-print catalogers from several types of institutions offer solutions to its problems can *AACR2* become a workable national standard for non-print cataloging.

Standardization Versus Local Needs

As original cataloging within each separate media service becomes more and more expensive, the prospect of sharing other institutions' cataloging becomes more attractive. Whether a media service is using cards supplied by a publisher, or using a record in online utility such as OCLC, the cataloging conforms to someone else's needs and standards. At what point does the cataloger make the compromise between the needs of local users and the demands of standardization? To some catalogers, the need to compromise at all is a disadvantage of standardization and sharing.

Standardization does not mean that a media service must give up its local integrity, however. "Shared" cataloging should always be adapted to the special needs of an individual media service's users, if necessary. Additional access points can always be added to a cataloging record, subject headings can be tailored to fit local needs and standards, and cross-references should always be provided to guide users to the chosen form of an access point used in a catalog. Thus, a media service can share in and contribute to a nationwide cataloging system and still meet its own user's special needs.

Communication in Non-print Cataloging

If standardization would be a boon to the cataloging of non-print materials, how do catalogers of these materials meet and share information on cataloging problems and solutions? National groups such as the American Library Association, the Canadian Library Association, and the Association of Educational Communications and Technology provide forums for such an exchange. Some have special subgroups which devote their energies to non-print cataloging issues (the American Library Association, Resources and Technical Services Division, Audiovisual Committee, for example). These groups hold open meetings at national conferences, and reports of their activities appear in the newsletters of their associations. A new national group emerged in 1980 to facilitate the sharing of information about non-print cataloging. It is called the On-Line Audiovisual Catalogers and issues a quarterly newsletter, the *On-Line Audiovisual Catalogers Newsletter*.

With input from individual catalogers of non-print materials in different sizes and types of institutions, groups such as these can become the focus for the concerns of non-print catalogers. Such concentrated attention should help to solve non-print cataloging problems more quickly than in the past. Solutions to problems in cataloging non-print material can be disseminated through publications such as the *RTSD Newsletter*,[11] the *On-Line Audiovisual Catalogers Newsletter*,[12] and *Cataloging Service Bulletin*[13] (a source of the Library of Congress' policy statements and of their interpretation of cataloging rules).

The cataloging of non-print materials, like the cataloging of materials in any other format, should not be done in a vacuum. Cataloging is the method by which the cataloger assists media users to find what they need in the collection of non-print materials. To do this successfully, the cataloger must know how to catalog and must know the users of the collection: be in tune with their changing vocabularies, their new interests, and how they look for material in the catalog. The cataloger must also be able to convey to those users, in language they can understand, what the media services owns that is relevant to their needs.

References

1. *Anglo-American Cataloging Rules*, North American Text (Chicago: American Library Association, 1967).
2. Jean Riddle Weihs, Shirley Lewis, and Janet Macdonald, *Nonbook Materials: the Organization of Integrated Collections* (Ottawa: Canadian Library Association, 1973).
3. Alma M. Tillin and William J. Quinly, *Standards for Cataloging Nonprint Materials: An Interpretation and Practical Applications*, 4th ed. (Washington, D.C.: Association of Educational Communications and Technology, 1976).
4. *Anglo-American Cataloguing Rules*, 2d ed., ed. by Michael Gorman and Paul W. Winkler (Chicago: American Library Association, 1978).
5. Jean Riddle Weihs, with Shirley Lewis and Janet Macdonald, *Nonbook Materials: The Organization of Integrated Collections*, 2d ed. (Ottawa: Canadian Library Association, 1979).

6. Although planned for release in 1980, to this author's knowledge the 5th edition has not been published yet.
7. Minnie Earl Sears, *Sears List of Subject Headings*, 11th ed., ed. Barbara M. Westby (New York: H. W. Wilson, 1977).
8. *Library of Congress Subject Headings*, 9th ed. (Washington, D.C.: Library of Congress, 1980).
9. The Library of Congress currently catalogs only filmstrips, kits, motion pictures, slides, sound recordings, transparencies, and videorecordings. Listed in "Display of General Material Designations Under *AACR2*," *Cataloging Service Bulletin* 6 (Fall 1979), 4-5.
10. *Cataloging File Statistics: Analysis of On-Line Catalog Records* (Dublin, Ohio: OCLC, Inc., July 17, 1982).
11. Available from: American Library Association, Resources and Technical Services Division, 50 E. Huron St., Chicago, IL 60611. Published six times per year.
12. Available to members. Membership applications available from: David Hedrick, Gettysburg College Library, Gettysburg, PA 17325. Published quarterly.
13. Available from: Library of Congress, Cataloging Distribution Service, Washington, D.C. 20541. Published quarterly.

Networking and Audiovisuals

Patricia Ann Coty

Bɪʙʟɪᴏɢʀᴀᴘʜɪᴄ control, while highly developed in the print realm, is painfully inadequate in the area of audiovisual media. A unified approach to bibliographic control is needed to present information to all library users about the wide variety of formats currently available. Because inadequate bibliographic control affects the availability of and the consequent demand for audiovisual materials, libraries can experience difficulty in servicing user needs for these items. How can library users request items unless they are aware of their existence and their location? How can librarians help their users, when often even the librarian does not know what is available?

Networking advances in the last dozen years have done much to correct this. Having bibliographic access to materials is the first step; making materials available through interlibrary loan networks is the second. These are areas where networking, especially computer-based networking, can have a great impact. Indeed, there are currently some exciting developments in this area.

Libraries have achieved good bibliographic control of print media. One of the contributing factors to this disparity between print and audiovisual bibliographic control is the development of many audiovisual collections outside of traditional library settings. In many cases, the standardization of bibliographic formats was not deemed a high priority by the audiovisual personnel, or by those who had possession of the audiovisual collections.

Another factor affecting the bibliographic status of audiovisuals is that many librarians view the cataloging of audiovisual materials as a more difficult enterprise than cataloging print items; audiovisual items commonly require more fields, or data elements, of bibliographic description than print media do. Examples of additional fields include producers, rental sources, media formats, and running time. Because of this real or perceived difficulty, audiovisuals have been given a low cataloging priority in many libraries. Additionally, rapid technological changes in the field of audiovisuals are continually creating new needs for describing an item, and it is a challenge to plan systems of control which will accommodate such rapid change.

An additional factor creating difficulty is the failure of audiovisual librarianship to develop a universal terminology for the field. Even basic terms such as "audiovisual," "non-print," and "multimedia" appear without apparent differentiation in the literature. What one librarian calls a "kit" will be designated a "sound-slide program" by another and a "sound recording" by a third. Some librarians refer to microforms as "print" media, while others relegate them to the realm of "audiovisual." The problem is compounded when an identical piece of information is encoded onto two or more different formats; one may be considered "print" while the others are not, for example, a monograph copied onto microfilm, videodisk, or computer software.

Information encoded into print, such as books and periodicals, tends to have some type of accompanying guide, such as a table of contents or an index. This allows the library user to rapidly scan the material in order to determine its suitability. It also can be used by the cataloger in creating descriptive cataloging. Audiovisual media, however, usually lack a mechanism for quickly browsing their contents. Even the purely descriptive information sometimes supplied by the producer or distributor on media packaging or in sales catalogs is often incomplete and sometimes inaccurate. For this reason, it is important that detailed abstracts of their contents be included in databases dealing with audiovisual media, so the user can quickly decide on an item's usefulness. Although there are presently many abstracting and indexing services that offer this type of analysis for print materials, there are only a few that do the same for audiovisuals. Of those that exist, only those that are available online offer searching with multiple subject access, so that topic, grade level, and medium can all be searched simultaneously. The fact that content abstracting is not readily available for most audiovisual materials complicates the task of establishing comprehensive databases.

A further hindrance to the creation of audiovisual databases stems from the peculiar copyright considerations of certain formats. Since duplication of certain media is easy and inexpensive, audiovisual materials are likely candidates for copyright infringement. Making audiovisuals freely accessible through large networks can increase the ease of illicit reproduction of titles, which is difficult to police. For these reasons, the producers and distributors of audiovisual material have hesitated to become involved in assisting networking activities. Additionally, some audiovisual items, unlike books, involve "residual rights" or royalty fees, applicable each time the item is used; the free flow of these items through networks can create confusion in the determination and collection of fees by the various parties involved.

Whereas most large collections of audiovisual materials are found in academic, public, and school libraries, audiovisual collections are also growing in special libraries, government agencies, museums, galleries, and historical societies. The current state of audiovisual collections in the majority of libraries discourages networking. Many libraries differ in their policies for interlibrary loan of print and audiovisual items; audiovisual collections are often partially or poorly cataloged, based on locally produced cataloging systems; interlibrary loan departments and audiovisual departments tend to be physically separate and speak different languages; and the special packaging and mailing requirements of audiovisual media is considered by many to be sufficient reason to simply refuse to include these items in the regular interlibrary loan program. These are just a few of the obstacles we face in trying to create more access to audiovisual materials through networking.

The reluctance of many libraries to become involved in audiovisual networking forces library users to make innumerable telephone calls and trips to many locations to find material to fill their needs. Even if they are lucky enough to find an item, they may yet be faced with restrictions on borrowing it. Some libraries do not circulate audiovisual material to their own users, let alone through interlibrary loan.

Somehow, in spite of all the obstacles, progress is being made. Various audiovisual databases are operational, and further development of these systems is anticipated. In general, existing audiovisual networks provide technical processing services and bibliographic information, but there are a few that offer resource-sharing, document delivery, booking and reservation systems, and information retrieval based on content. The good news for media librarians is that we can look forward to more comprehensive and useful systems in the future.

PROJECT MEDIA BASE

Jointly sponsored by the National Commission on Libraries and Information Science (NCLIS) and the Association for Educational Communications and Technology, Project Media Base was created in 1976 to examine the status of audiovisual materials as they related to the NCLIS objective, "to plan, develop, and implement a nationwide network of library and information services."[1] The hypothesis of Project Media Base was that "there is ample evidence that all the essential elements for a national bibliographic system for audiovisual informational resources currently exists, and that there is, therefore, no apparent reason why a national system cannot be developed, operated, and fully utilized to provide access to these resources."[2]

In examining existing machine-readable audiovisual databases, the Project identified over forty systems currently in operation, over half of which consisted of less than five thousand entries. Of these systems, nineteen were in colleges and universities, seven were in school systems, and the remainder were in government agencies and commercial or non-profit centers. Most existing systems were reported to be multi-disciplinary, with the exception of the National Library of Medicine's AVLINE (Audio Visuals On-Line). Almost half of the systems used locally developed bibliographic standards, designed to meet specific local needs. Over half of the systems used subject headings other than Sears (Dewey decimal system) or Library of Congress. Only a third of the systems reported compatibility of their records with the MARC (machine-readable cataloging) format.

Thus the audiovisual materials that are within some form of database structure are dispersed throughout the country, they are recorded using all types of bibliographic conventions, mostly non-standard, and the Project also found that citations were recorded in various degrees of completeness. The systems are serviced and controlled by a host of organizations and cooperative groups, at different levels of service—from local to national—and supported by the public, private, and non-profit sectors, or in some cases by multi-sector combinations. The audiovisual materials included in these databases are dispersed among different types of communities, generally categorized as library and non-library. These communities often do not share the same philosophies of free and unrestricted use of materials.

Project Media Base concluded that the principal uses of a nation-wide database for audiovisuals would be:

1. Reference: searching for material to fill stated needs and verification of data for publication of catalogs and/or mediagraphies.
2. Collection building: assessment and preliminary judgment about items considered for purchase.
3. Acquisition: for purchase, rental, or loan.
4. Cataloging: subjective and descriptive.
5. Processing: production of labels, booking and circulation cards.
6. Publication of checklists, catalogs, promotional literature.
7. Statistical support for collection management and for monitoring gaps, redundancies, replacements.
8. Production support including market analysis, determination of items already available, comparison of formats, subject coverage, currency.[3]

User needs identified by the Project were the need for holdings statements, statements of physical condition of media, circulation and use data, and analytical content treatment (for example, scene analysis in films).[4]

To create a nationwide database of audiovisual media, compatibility of records is requisite, with agreement on a system of bibliographic control. Without this agreement, and subsequent modification of existing databases, there is small chance of the possibility of unifying the bibliographic information now available. Without standards, it is impossible for separate databases to be merged. As long as databases continue to be created and maintained as separate, local units, their individualized systems of bibliographic control may be adequate; but if a broader, possibly even national database is to be created, bibliographic standardization is imperative.

It is expected that the relatively new MARC formats for audiovisuals and the ISBD(NBM) (International Standard Bibliographic Description for Non-Book Materials) rules will assist toward this goal. What the MARC and ISBD(NBM) communication formats have done is created conventions for recording bibliographic information. Bibliographic descriptions are composed of elements such as title, author, producer, and so on. Within the MARC and ISBD formats, the elements necessary for a complete bibliographical citation are specified, and an order for their arrangement is dictated. Additionally, certain symbols or punctuation marks are identified which are used between elements to denote their demarcation. For example, here is a citation using the ISBD(NBM) standards:[5]

Tacoma Narrows Bridge collapse [Motion picture].—Cambridge, Mass.: Ealing Film-loops, 1963.-1 filmloop (4 min., 40 sec.): col., si.: super 8mm
Notes Printed on container
£4.75

The intent of the ISBD standards, for non-book as well as other media (monographs, serials, cartographic materials, antiquarian materials, and printed music), is to aid the international exchange of bibliographic information; to promote the ease of interpretation of records between languages; and to facilitate the conversion of bibliographic records to machine-readable form.[6]

Because ISBD formats are meant to be universal, they do not provide guidelines for subject indication. Rather, the ISBD formats are meant to be used in conjunction with national or local cataloging rules. Library of Congress MARC records, which follow ISBD rules for ordering and punctuation, use the *Anglo-American Cataloguing Rules, Second Edition*[7] (*AACR2*), and assign LC subject headings, LC classification numbers, and Dewey decimal classification numbers. Library of Congress MARC records for audiovisuals are accessible online via the SDC

Information Services system,[8] DIALOG Information Services,[9] and the bibliographic utilities (OCLC, RLIN, UTLAS, and WLN).

NICEM

The National Information Center for Educational Media (NICEM),[10] headquartered at the University of Southern California, first published a computer-generated film catalog in 1959. This automated catalog aroused such interest that in 1964, a grant was awarded from the United States Office of Education, for the purpose of examining the cost-effectiveness of producing unique catalogs for selected schools through a central computer. Within two years, the project had established guidelines for automated cataloging of audiovisual material and had produced more than 350 computer-generated catalogs of holdings for schools and universities throughout the United States. Twelve thousand item records for films and filmstrips had been deposited by project participants, and these records formed a substantial database. The criteria for bibliographic formatting were the Association for Educational Communications and Technology's *Standards for Cataloging Nonprint Materials*[11] and the *Anglo-American Cataloging Rules*.

Over half a million items are presently accessible through the NICEM database, with about fifty thousand being added yearly. NICEM now gathers data from these three sources: institutional participants, media producers and distributors, and the Library of Congress. The database is accessed online through the DIALOG Information Services system, and is also available for purchase in book or microfiche format. Media represented in NICEM's files include films, filmstrips, audiotapes, overhead transparencies, videotapes, records, and slides. The DIALOG system has created a number of searchable fields for the database, such as a basic index of descriptors and all meaningful words from the title, descriptor, and abstract fields; a descriptor code index for subject searching; a media code index for searching by medium; color code, audience level, and length indexes; producer code and producer name indexes; index of sponsoring organizations; and indexes for publication date, LC catalog card number, and an update code index. The availability of this searching flexibility is an asset which cannot be matched in manual searching of the printed edition of the database.

Note that NICEM does not provide information on how the materials in the database may be borrowed or rented, or even basic holdings information. It is strictly a source of bibliographic data, with producer addresses furnished for those who may want to purchase an item.

THE CONSORTIUM OF UNIVERSITY FILM CENTERS

The Consortium of University Film Centers (CUFC) is an organization of fifty major film rental centers in the United States whose purpose is to share information related to collection development, distribution of resources, and an enhanced availability of audiovisual materials. The CUFC's main accomplishment toward these purposes has been the creation of a databank of the holdings of all its members, published by Bowker in 1977 (and revised in 1980) as the *Educational Film Locator*.[12] This was a monumental task which took years of planning to complete and was long awaited by media librarians throughout the country. About fifty thousand titles are included in the *Locator*, almost exclusively in 16mm format.

The *Locator* contains full technical and descriptive bibliographic citations, with additional rental and ordering information for each title. Also included are annotations, analyses, and evaluations. Entries are indexed under one thousand subject categories, with thousands of subject cross-references. Bowker and the CUFC began assigning ISBNs (international standard book numbers) to each title in 1976.

AVLINE

The National Library of Medicine, in cooperation with the Association to American Medical Colleges, has developed an online information and retrieval system for audiovisual materials in all aspects of medicine, nursing, dentistry, health, and related biomedical sciences. This system, AVLINE (Audio Visuals On-Line), is a subset of the MEDLINE[13] database, and is available internationally to qualified health professionals and related personnel. AVLINE is accessible online to those who have access to a terminal, either directly from the National Library of Medicine or through BRS[14] and DIALOG. AVLINE searches will also be done by staff at the National Library of Medicine in response to telephone or mail requests. AVLINE cataloging data is published quarterly in print as the *NLM AVLINE Catalog*,[15] available from the U.S. Government Printing Office.

AVLINE contains bibliographic data for over ten thousand items with one hundred to two hundred additional entries per month. All media formats are represented: films, videorecordings, audiotapes, slides, overhead transparencies, models, and others. Programs produced by the National Medical Audiovisual Center (NMAC),[16] currently numbering over one thousand, are included in the AVLINE database, as well as commercially produced college-level or continuing education materials. The NMAC programs can be purchased at rates much lower than comparable commercial items. A network of over fifteen hundred schools, hospitals, research institutions, and health-related businesses currently use the MEDLINE system, and thus have access to AVLINE records. Since MEDLINE charges are low, this system is very cost-effective for its users.

In addition to full bibliographic information, most records in AVLINE contain reviews and abstracts supplied by the Association of American Medical Colleges, which maintains a databank of about twenty-five hundred reviewers in major specialty areas. Reviews are assigned only to material which is designated as instructional; recorded events, seminars, and lectures, which make up about twenty percent of the database, are not reviewed but are entered with full cataloging data and subject analysis. All titles are entered into the AVLINE database when received at NLM, and updated by review data as received from the AAMC. Materials are given a review rating ("highly recommeded," "recommended," "not recommended," "no review," or "pending") in addition to having the full review text available as part of the online record.

The National Library of Medicine also contributes to the only existing index to audiovisual serials, the *Index to Audiovisual Serials in the Health Sciences*,[17] published and distributed by the Medical Library Association. The *Index* is available in print, as three quarterly issues with annual cumulations, or online through the MEDLINE sub-system CATLINE. Publications indexed include selected audiotape and video-tape serials that have undergone peer review procedures by the Association of American Medical Colleges. Citations are arranged under MeSH (Medical Subject Heading) terms which represent the central concepts in the programs. A separate author index is also included.

Publication of the *Index* is an important contribution to the problem of bibliographic access to audiovisual media. Having broader availability of computerized subject access to audiovisual serials, such as this index for the medical field, could greatly enhance their utility.

AGRICOLA

Begun in 1970 as the CAIN (cataloging and indexing) database, AGRICOLA (Agricultural On-Line Access)[18] consists of not only the cataloging and indexing files of the National Agricultural Library; it also contains substantial files on food and nutrition, from the Food and Nutrition Information and Educational Resources Center (FNIC); on agricultural economics, from the American Agricultural Economics Documentation Center; Environmental Impact Statements; and the Brucellosis subfile. The National Agricultural Library produces and maintains AGRICOLA to support research in the agricultural sciences, including such areas as farm management, forestry, animal breeding, entomology, veterinary medicine, and rural sociology.

FNIC maintains a collection of audiovisual materials (motion pictures, filmstrips, slides, games, charts, audiotapes and videocassettes). These items, which number over one thousand, are included in the AGRICOLA file. A controlled vocabulary is used for subject access to the AGRICOLA system, which is available online through BRS, DIALOG, or SDC. Citations are also available in print as the *Food and Nutrition Information and Educational Materials Center Catalog.*[19]

NICSEM/NIMIS

The National Instructional Materials Information System (NIMIS) of the National Information Center for Special Education Materials (NICSEM) is an online computer-based file of information about materials available for the education of exceptional children. Formats covered by the file include audiovisual, print, braille, and equipment and adaptive devices related to education of the handicapped, especially children. The file is a useful resource for educators, parents, and others who interact with the handicapped.

The file was created in the period between 1974-1977, by the National Information Center for Educational Media, under contract to the Bureau of Education for the Handicapped, of the Department of Health, Education and Welfare. File revisions have lapsed since 1977, due to insufficient funding. Hopefully, funding will be renewed to update this valuable database.

In addition to complete bibliographic data, records in NICSEM/NIMIS include abstracts and evaluative information. The evaluative information indicates who reviewed the materials and for which groups they have been judged suitable. Notes are also included for each citation to indicate any equipment required for use of the material, which is not readily apparent from the description of the material itself.

NICSEM/NIMIS is available through the DIALOG system and was just recently removed from the BRS system. Approximately forty thousand records are included in the NICSEM/NIMIS file. There is no printed equivalent for this service.

NATIONAL FILM BOARD OF CANADA

The National Film Board of Canada,[20] in cooperation with the University of Toronto Library Automation Systems (UTLAS), began work in 1978 toward a national information and distribution system for

Canadian audiovisuals. The goal of the project is the creation of a complete delivery service for Canadian audiovisual materials, to assist film producers and libraries in the selection, acquisition, and use of Canadian audiovisuals. The plan combines three related media projects and is designed to encourage the development of one or more audiovisual networks. These projects are: the Standard Catalog of Canadian-Produced Non-Print Materials and the PRÉCIS (Preserved Context Index System), both by the Univeristy of Toronto Centre for Research on Librarianship; and the Information/Distribution System for Canadian Audiovisual Products, sponsored by the National Film Board of Canada. The PRÉCIS project will produce a model computer-generated, multi-media catalog in which PRÉCIS designations will replace traditional subject headings, and thus provide a new method of indexing audiovisual materials.

Data gathering for the NFBC file was begun in 1978 with a drag of five UTLAS databases which contained significant audiovisual holdings. UTLAS dumped all records from these bases which contained any form of the NFBC name, in either the imprint or added entries, into a newly created file. Duplicate titles were eliminated, and remaining records were edited into consistent format, including MARC-compatible coding, ISBD, and AACR conventions. PRÉCIS indexing was added to each record as the form of subject access. Additional titles were obtained from the Canadian Film Institute, the LC MARC Films Source File, and other libraries in the UTLAS network. Also, producers and distributors of audiovisual materials have been invited to provide the NFBC with information on their new releases.

From its database of audiovisual materials, the NFBC has been able to create computer-generated subject lists. Reciprocal file-sharing agreements through UTLAS allow for the online availability of bibliographic data among libraries, reducing the need for original cataloging. The NFBC file is available for use by other libraries through the UTLAS system.

OTHER SPECIALIZED DATABASES

Many other databases exist which are wholly or partly composed of citations to audiovisual material. The Health Audiovisual Online Catalog,[21] available online through BRS, includes a union list of the audiovisual holdings of eight Ohio academic health sciences libraries. More than five thousand titles are included in the database, in medicine, nursing, psychology, and allied health. Each record includes title, author and/or producer, bibliographic data, physical description, and holdings information. This file is updated twice a year.

The Family Resources Data Base,[22] produced by the National Council on Family Relations, Family Resource and Referral Center, is an online database available through BRS and DIALOG. Included in this file are print and audiovisual resources in marriage and the family. Begun in 1970, this service lists more than 45,000 print and audiovisual citations, which include bibliographic and abstract information, as well as data on distribution, collation, and circulation. Updates are added monthly, at the rate of about a thousand per month. The printed *Information Guide to Family Literature, Programs, and Services* and the *Inventory of Marriage and Family Literature* correspond in part to the database.

The National Institute of Mental Health[23] database includes over four thousand audiovisuals of all types in its file of almost half a million citations. NIMH covers the biomedical and social aspects of mental health and mental illness. The print equivalent of the audiovisual file is *Selected Mental Health Audiovisuals*. NIMH is available online through BRS and DIALOG.

The National Rehabilitation Information Center (NARIC)[24] produces a database containing abstracted citations to both print and audiovisual materials relating to the rehabilitation of the physically or mentally disabled. About two hundred records a month were added to the file, which is available online through BRS. Citations include descriptors, sponsoring agency information, abstracts, and special notes on availability. Coverage dates from 1950.

IRIS, the Instructional Resources Information System, is produced by the U.S. Environmental Protection Agency, Instructional Resources Center.[25] Available online via BRS and DIALOG, this database contains citations, with abstracts, to print and audiovisual materials on water quality and water resources. Begun in 1979, about eight thousand records are included, with an additional 2,400 being added each year.

Other databases exist which consist partly or wholly of audiovisual materials, and these can be identified through perusal of the BRS, DIALOG, and SDC Database catalogs (available by writing to BRS, DIALOG and SDC), or by use of published guides to online bibliographic databases.[26]

THE BIBLIOGRAPHIC UTILITIES

The growth of the bibliographic utilities in the United States has certainly affected all libraries, whether or not they are direct users of one of these services. Development of the utilities has fostered concern among librarians for standards for machine-readable cataloging. Audiovisual materials have been included in the push to create large databases of bibliographic information.

OCLC (Online Computer Library Center)[27] began accepting materials covered by *AACR* chapter 12 (audiovisuals) in 1976. Loading of Library of Congress MARC tapes for maps and films occurred in 1979. As of February 1982, OCLC holdings included records for over 184,000 audiovisual titles, 94,000 maps, and 195,000 sound recordings.[28] An in-depth study produced in May 1981 revealed that about a third of the audiovisual records on OCLC were motion pictures; another third were filmstrips; and the remainder were divided among other formats, such as slides, overhead transparencies, videorecordings, and kits.[29]

OCLC records include cataloging data and library holdings symbols, so that it is possible to use the file for interlibrary loan purposes. Since the OCLC online interlibrary loan system allows for fairly quick response to a loan request, this is an efficient way to request audiovisual loans. However, the interlibrary loan policies of the various libraries on the system differ, and it is not possible to tell from the citation whether the libraries listed as holding the item will actually be willing to lend it. OCLC has a separate file (the Name-Address Directoy) in which interlibrary loan policies of individual libraries are often listed. It is best to consult this file before sending an interlibrary loan request.

OCLC is the only major bibliographic utility which does not at this time offer accessibility of records via subject. Records are accessible by title, author, series, ISSN and ISBD number, and various other routes. Since audiovisual records are stored in separate files, it is possible to narrow a search to include only audiovisuals; for instance, to search for the film *The Scarlet Letter* without retrieving print editions as well.

Online acquisition and cataloging of films, maps, music scores, and sound recordings are available through the Research Library Group's RLIN (Research Libraries Information Network).[30] Citations on the RLIN database are accessible by subject as well as title, author, and other modes. RLIN offers cataloging information and holdings data for each title. Online access to LC MARC records for maps and films is available in addition to access to members' cataloging records. As of February 1982, the RLIN database included 204,000 records (not individual titles) in the film, map, sound recording, and music formats (including musical scores).[31] RLIN has a message system whereby interlibrary loan requests can be exchanged by member libraries.

UTLAS (University of Toronto Library Automated Systems)[32] contains thousands of records for media of all formats, including films, filmstrips, kits, sound recordings, videotapes, and braille materials. Both

English and French progrms are included. Over fifty thousand LC film records are on the system. An electronic mailbox exists for the transmission of interlibrary loan requests, and responses are usually generated within days.

UTLAS allows subject searching of its files in addition to access by author, title, series title, and so forth. The audiovisual titles are not placed into a separate file, however, so searching by specified format is not possible.

WLN, the Washington Library Network,[33] includes approximately 210,000 records for projected media (films, slides, videotape) in its database. Since WLN discourages duplicate records for identical items, this number is probably a good indication of discrete titles available in WLN member libraries. These audiovisual titles compose about nine percent of WLN's database. Sound recordings, maps, and manuscripts are planned for inclusion in the future. Data records are input from LC MARC tapes, and locally cataloged materials are accepted from WLN member libraries. Although there is currently no message-switching system for interlibrary loan requests, many WLN members use the OnTyme electronic mail service to communicate interlibrary loan messages.

Subject searching is possible on the WLN system, in addition to other modes of access. Searching by format is possible to the extent that format types are included as Library of Congress subheadings.

Project Media Base identified five major conclusions in its final report to the NCLIS, and it seems appropriate to review them here:

- The library community and the audiovisual community differ in a number of ways, and have often developed separately.
- Much more progress has been achieved in bibliographic standardizations for print media than for audiovisuals, making the formation of networks an easier proposition for print materials than for audiovisuals.
- Efforts to date to establish such standards have been productive, but in the meantime separate efforts are growing in size and complexity, making the possibility of unification even dimmer.
- This lack of agreement on standard conventions is a major barrier to the development of a unified national network for audiovisual resources.
- In spite of these problems, the essential elements for a national network do exist.[34]

As progress is made in this regard, we media librarians must continue to serve our users as best we can with the resources that currently exist, while working to solve the problems that stand in the way of better alternatives. Many libraries have access to one of the bibliographic utilities (OCLC, RLIN, UTLAS, WLN) for acquisitions and cataloging information, or to one of the database vendors (BRS, DIALOG, SDC) which offer the various specialized networks such as NICEM, AVLINE, and AGRICOLA. The media librarian must be familiar with the use of these resources and take advantage of available databases. The *Educational Film Locator* and other print resources should be readily available to library users to assist them in identifying sources of information outside their local area. Media librarians cannot think solely in terms of their own collections, but should realize that there is a wealth of material available in other institutions which may be accessible to local users.

Through a realization that audiovisual materials are increasingly important sources of information for our users, it may someday be possible to grant these formats a status equal to that of the book. This is especially relevant in terms of the bibliographic control of audiovisuals, and its relationship to library activities such as reference, interlibrary loan, acquisitions, and technical services. Networking activities are an important step in realizing this goal. When the time comes that librarians see all formats as equally important to users, the dream of free and unrestricted access to information, regardless of its packaging, might be realized.

References

1. Gerald Brong et al., *Problems in Bibliographic Access to Non-Print Materials: Project Media Base: Final Report.* Association for Educational Communications and Technology, Washington, D.C., sponsored by the National Commission on Libraries and Information Science, Washington, D.C. October 1979. ERIC ED 185968. p. 4.
2. Ibid., p. 5.
3. Ibid., pp. 18+.
4. Ibid.
5. International Federation of Library Associations and Institutions. *ISBD (NBM): International Standard Bibliographic Description for Non-Book Materials.* (London: IFLA International Office for UBC, 1977), p. 59.
6. International Federation of Library Associations and Institutions. *ISBD(M): International Standard Bibliographic Description for Monographic Publications.* (London: IFLA International Office for UBC, 1977), p. 1.
7. *Anglo-American Cataloguing Rules, 2d ed., Revisions.* (Chicago: American Library Association), 1982.
8. SDC Information Services, 2500, Colorado Ave., Santa Monica, CA 90406.
9. DIALOG Information Services, Inc., 3460 Hillview Ave., Palo Alto, CA 94304.
10. National Information Center for Educational Media, University of Southern California, Research Annex, Suite 301, 3716 South Hope St., Los Angeles, CA 90007.
11. Association for Educational Communications and Technology. Information

Sciences Committee. *Standards for Cataloging Nonprint Materials, 3d ed.* (Washington, D.C.: Association for Educational Communications and Technology, 1972).

12. Consortium of University Film Centers. *Educational Film Locator of the Consortium of University Film Centers and R.R. Bowker Company, 2d ed.* (New York: R.R. Bowker), 1980.

13. National Library of Medicine, MEDLARS Management Section, 8600 Rockville Pike, Bethesda, MD 20209.

14. BRS, 1200 Route 7, Latham, NY 12110.

15. *National Library of Medicine AVLINE Catalog*, 1975/76-. (Bethesda, Md.: National Institutes of Health, National Library of Medicine).

16. National Medical Audiovisual Center, 8600 Rockville Pike, Bethesda, MD 20209.

17. *Index to Audiovisual Serials in the Health Sciences.* (Chicago: Medical Library Association, v. 1- 1977-). Quarterly.

18. U.S. Department of Agriculture, National Agricultural Library, Beltsville, MD 20705.

19. Food and Nutrition Information and Educational Materials Center. *Food and Nutrition Information and Educational Materials Center Catalog.* (Beltsville, Md.: U.S. Department of Agriculture, National Agricultural Library, 1976, with supplements).

20. National Film Board of Canada, Box 6100, Montreal, Quebec H3C 3H5 Canada.

21. Health Audiovisual Online Catalog, Northeastern Ohio Universities, College of Medicine, Basic Medical Sciences Library, Rootstown, OH 44272.

22. National Council on Family Relations, Family Resource and Referral Center, 1219 University Ave., SE, Minneapolis, MN 55414.

23. National Clearinghouse for Mental Health Information, 5600 Fishers Lane, Rockville, MD 20857

24. National Rehabilitation Information Center, 308 Mullen, Catholic University of America, Washington, DC 20064

25. Environmental Protection Agency Instructional Resources Center, Ohio State University, 1200 Chambers Rd., Room 310, Columbus, OH 43212

26. see Cuadra Associates, Inc. *Directory of Online Databases.* 1979-. Published quarterly by Cuadra Associates, Inc., Santa Monica, CA; and *Online Bibliographic Databases, a Directory and Sourcebook*, Third Edition, by James L. Hall and Marjorie J. Brown. (Detroit: Gale Research Company, 1983).

27. Online Computer Library Center, Inc., 6565 Frantz Rd., Dublin, OH 43017

28. *Online Union Catalog Statistics by Format (as of 1982 February 8).* (Dublin, Ohio: OCLC, Inc., 1982).

29. *Online Union Catalog, Audiovisual Format Statistics (as of 1981 May 22).* (Dublin, Ohio: OCLC, Inc., 1981).

30. RLIN, The Research Libraries Group, Inc., Jordan Quadrangle, Stanford, CA 94305

31. *The Research Libraries Group in Brief.* (Stanford, Calif.: The Research Libraries Group, Inc., March 1982).

32. UTLAS, Inc., 80 Bloor St. West, Toronto, Ontario M5S 2V1 Canada.

33. Washington Library Network, AJ-11, Olympia, WA 98504.
34. Brong, *Final Report*, pp. 43-44.

Bibliography

Avram, Henriette D. "International Standards for the Interchange of Biblio-graphic Records in Machine-Readable Form." *Library Resources and Technical Services*, vol. 20, no. 1 (Winter 1976) pp. 25-35.

Brong, Gerald R. et al. "Problems in Bibliographic Access to Non-Print Materials. Project Media Base: Final Report." Washington, D.C.: Association for Educational Communications and Technology, sponsored by the National Commission on Libraries and Information Science, Washington, D.C. October 1979. ERIC ED 185 968.

Ellison, John, and Sally A. Knight. "NIMIS: Serving Special Education Needs." *Audiovisual Instruction* (April 1979) p. 46.

Gardhouse, Judy. "NFB Develops Delivery Service for Canadian Non-Print Media." *Canadian Library Journal* vol. 37, no. 2 (April 1980) pp. 73-76.

Goodman, H. J. A. *The Development of National and International Information Systems and Networks Involving Combinations of Print and Non-Print Media.* August 1978. ERIC ED 168 533.

Jacob, Mary Ellen L. "Special Libraries and OCLC" in *The Special Library Role in Networks*. Ed. by Robert W. Gibson, Jr. (New York: Special Libraries Association, 1980).

Jonassen, David H. "National Audiovisual Data Base: A Deficient Knowledge Base." *Bulletin of the ASIS* vol. 5, no. 3 (February 1979) pp. 17-18.

Kudrick, Linda, comp. *Media Services at the National Library of Medicine.* Bethesda, Md.: National Library of Medicine, May 1981.

Rains, Ruth R. "Bibliographic Control of Media: One Step Closer." *Library Trends* vol. 27, no. 1 (Summer 1978) pp. 83-92.

Slusser, Margaret G. "NICEM, The Non-Print Data Base." *Database* vol. 3, no. 3 (September 1980) pp. 63-67.

Van Camp, Ann. "Health Science Audiovisuals in Online Data Bases." *Database* vol. 3, no. 3 (September 1980) pp. 17-27.

Non-Book Storage and Care Self-Evaluation Form

John W. Ellison

Libraries struggle to obtain funds for the acquisition of materials. Large investments are made in cataloging ... to make them usable. But it is too often the case that these same materials are put on the shelves in buildings without environmental control where they are subjected to extremes of heat and humidity and suffer abrasion from dust and particulate matter.[1]

—James W. Henderson

THE self-evaluation form presented here was designed to assist busy librarians who work with active non-book collections in evaluating the quality of their storage and care practices. An indication of significant variations from the information provided should warn you that additional study and possible alteration of conditions may be needed. You may choose to check: 1) the practices your library is *now* undertaking; 2) the practices you were not aware of (and would like more information on); 3) the practices you are *not* doing; or 4) to use the form to create an individualized priority list. In no situation should this form be considered the final authority on the storage and care of non-book material in active collections. It has attempted to be current and complete, but unique situations warrant individual considerations. Only after collection of data and careful study and observation should decisions be made by knowledgeable authorities regarding non-book collection storage and care.

HOW THE FORM WAS DEVELOPED

The form was initially developed from information gathered in an extensive literature search on the subject. An effort was made to concentrate on literature concerning *active* collections rather than

Originally published in *Catholic Library World* 53 (December 1982).

preservation, restoration, or long-term archival storage. Once the literature search was brought to a near end, a preliminary storage and care self-evaluation form for each of seven general formats was designed (Film, Tape, Maps, Microforms, Original Art, Phonorecords, and Photographs). Each form was then field-tested for its value and usability in twenty specifically selected participating institutions representing nearly every type of library situation. In addition, twenty-eight non-book authorities were sent copies of the preliminary form and asked to make recommendations. The form was then revised on the basis of all reasonable suggestions made by colleagues cooperating with the project, and copies were again mailed to the twenty institutions cooperating in the field-testing. All institutions were again encouraged to make final suggestions which would improve the form.

RATIONALE

The rationale for a storage and care program is: 1) to realize the full potential utilization a format has prior to unnecessary damage or deterioration; 2) to minimize the storage and care expense involved; 3) to provide the maximum care and service for the minimum amount of time and staff available; 4) to minimize any loss of content information; 5) to correct storage conditions in future construction or remodeling; 6) to more accurately report conditions, and finally; 7) to increase safe use of the collection. Within the environment, finances, and personnel available, a maximum effort can be made to properly store and care for all materials.

No attempt has been made to include the proper care or use of equipment which may destroy non-book materials. Persons responsible for archival or inactive collections will find this information helpful but should examine the literature thoroughly for specific recommendations for archival or long-term storage and care procedures.

Copies of all the individual storage and care of non-book self-evaluation forms are available from the Educational Resource Information Center (ERIC) under the following titles:

Films, Filmstrips, Filmloops, Transparencies and Slides: Storage and Care Self-Evaluation Form, ERIC, ED 178 091
Magnetic Tape (Audio, Video or Computer): Storage and Care Self-Evaluation Form, ERIC, ED 181 885
Maps: Storage and Care Self-Evaluation Form, ERIC, ED 181 882
Microforms: Storage and Care Self-Evaluation Form, ERIC, ED 181 883
Original Paintings/Prints and Non-Original Prints: Storage and Care Self-Evaluation Form, ERIC, ED 181 884
Phonorecords: Storage and Care Self-Evaluation Form, ERIC ED 178 084
Photographs and Negatives: Storage and Care Self-Evaluation Form, ERIC, ED 178 064

ADDITIONAL MATERIALS

A bibliography entitled *Storage and Care of Non-Book Materials in Libraries: An Annotated Bibliography*, compiled as part of the literature search for the self-evaluation form, is also available from ERIC (ED 179-246). Citations found in the literature search but not physically examined are also included in this bibliography.

Detailed information on the proper storage and care of non-book materials presented in this self-evaluation form is available for purchase in a series of six color slide/audiocassette programs for $160 from the National Audiovisual Center, GSA, Washington, DC 20409.

Storage and Care of Films, Filmstrips, Filmloops, Transparencies and Slides, 75 slides, 9 minutes, $30.

Storage and Care of Magnetic Tape (Audio, Video and Computer), 77 slides, 9 minutes, $30.50.

Storage and Care of Maps, 69 slides, 8 minutes, $27.75.

Storage and Care of Microforms (Films, Fiche and Ultra-fiche), 66 slides, 7 minutes, $29.

Storage and Care of Phonorecords, 68 slides, 7 minutes, $27.50.

Storage and Care of Photographs and Negatives, 65 slides, 7 minutes, $26.25.

The following sources will rent each slide/tape program for the cost of handling and postage:

Krasker Memorial Film Library
Boston University
765 Commonwealth Ave.
Boston, MA 02215
617-353-5272

Regional Film Library
Instructional Support Center
The Florida State University
Tallahassee, FL 32306
904-664-2820

Audio Visual Center
University of Iowa
C-215 East Hall
Iowa City, IA 52242
319-353-3724

Audio Visual Services
Merrill Library and Learning Resource Program
Utah State University
Logan, UT 84322
801-752-4100 ext. 7954

Film Library
The General Libraries
The University of Texas at Austin
Drawer W, University Station
Austin, TX 78712
512-471-3573

RECOMMENDATIONS

In the process of developing this self-evaluation form, numerous opportunities occurred to make general recommendations based on the literature and field-testing regarding information, attitudes, and practices related to storage and care of non-book material in active collections. Based on limited observations during this project, it was concluded:

- Little research has been done on the subject of storage and care of non-book material in *active* collections.
- Many published "authorities" make recommendations based on extensive experience, but with little or no scientific study to support their observations.
- Studies on almost every aspect of non-book storage and care need to be undertaken immediately.
- Based on the literature and personal observations, little accountability of those responsible for non-book collections was noted. This is particularly shocking when money, staff, or additional time may not be required to prevent significant amounts of destruction and deterioration of material.
- Finally, a comprehensive national study should be undertaken immediately to determine the quality of non-book collection care, knowledge of staff responsibility for non-book collections, preparation of personnel entering the profession who will manage non-book collections, and the general awareness for the need of quality collection care by leaders in the profession.

References

1. James W. Henderson, "Foreword," in *Library Conservation: Preservation in Perspective*, John P. Baker and Marguerite C. Soroka, eds. (Stroudsburg, Pa.: Dowden Hutchinson & Ross, 1978), p. v.

SELF-EVALUATION FORM

FILMS, FILMSTRIPS, FILMLOOPS, TRANSPARENCIES, AND SLIDES

Check the Following Items Practiced:

Temperature and Relative Humidity

__ Recorded temperature
__ Recorded relative humidity
__ The National Bureau of Standards recommends 70°F with relative humidity between 25%-40%; 40°F is ideal for color films. Kodak recommends below 75°F for black and white films at 15%-50% relative humidity and below 70°F at 40%-50% for color film. Temperature and relative humidity should be constant within the specified range.
When several formats of non-book materials are intershelved or stored in the same room, the temperature should be 69°F ± 1°F with a relative humidity of 40% ± 10%.

Containers

__ Containers are wiped free of dust.
__ The insides of containers are treated for mildew and fungus growth (or discarded if safe treatment products are not available).
__ Mildew and fungus preventives are applied in the containers so that they do not touch the film.
__ Films with magnetic sound tracks are stored in inert plastic, acid-free cardboard, or non-ferrous metal containers.
__ Filmstrips are stored in inert plastic containers.
__ Slide storage containers provide for the circulation of air.

Shelving

__ Motion picture films are stored vertically for short term storage.
__ Film racks with individual supports are used.
__ Motion picture films are stored at least six inches from the floor.
__ Inert baked enamel, steel cases are used for slides.
__ Inert plastic pages, mylar, or similar safe materials are used (vinyl slide storage sheets should not be used).
__ Storage area is uncarpeted.

Care (Motion Picture Films)

__ Motion picture films are inspected and cleaned after each use.

__ Motion picture films are cleaned once a year with antistatic, moisturizing, lubricating, and preservation chemicals.

__ Cement splices are used.

__ Measures are taken to prevent the twisting of the film.

__ Motion picture films are lifted by the lower flange or hub.

__ A five foot leader is at the head and tail.

__ A half-inch is allowed from the outside layer of a 16mm film to the edge of the reel.

__ To prevent shipping damage, motion picture films are tightly wound and the end secured with a special pressure-sensitive tape.

__ If in cold storage, film is allowed to warm up before using.

__ A quarter-inch is allowed from the outside layer of an 8mm film to the edge of the reel.

__ Cinching of filmstrips and films should be avoided.

Care (Slides)

__ A dry, soft brush should be used for dusting filmstrips and slides.

__ Blowing or breathing on a slide to remove dust should be avoided.

__ Silica gel may be used to treat moisture-impaired slides.

__ Slides are not projected for more than 30 seconds.

Care (General)

__ Lintless gloves are used when handling all film formats.

__ Check slide mounts for damage or frayed edges after each use.

__ Slides should be allowed to warm up gradually before projecting them if they are stored in or exposed to cold temperatures.

__ Glass-mounted slides are stored in carefully monitored environmental conditions to avoid moisture entrapment.

__ Cards or markers used for indexing should be made from an acid-free or inert product.

Measures Are Taken to Protect Film Formats from Coming into Direct Contact with

__ Acidic cardboard containers

__ Hydrogen sulfide

__ Sulfur dioxide

___ Ammonia
___ Illuminating gas
___ Motor exhaust
___ Solvent vapors
___ Mothballs
___ Turpentine
___ Mercury
___ Solvents and cleaners
___ Insecticides
___ Rubber bands containing sulfur
___ Paper clips

Heat and Light

___ Storage areas should be on intermediate floors of buildings in order to protect the collection from high humidity or temperature (particularly avoid basements and uninsulated attics).
___ Air conditioning systems should not bring in outside air, especially at night, that has excessive humidity.

MAGNETIC TAPE (AUDIO, VIDEO, AND COMPUTER)

Check the Following Items Practiced:

Temperature and Relative Humidity

___ Authorities generally agree that tapes should be stored at 67°F ± 3° with a relative humidity of 50% ± 10%. It is important that temperature and relative humidity remain constant within these ranges.

Containers

___ Non-conductive (inert plastic or cardboard) containers are used.
___ When non-ferrous aluminum containers are used they are stored on non-conductive shelves.
___ Containers are dust proof.
___ Containers are shielded from stray high intensity electrical and magnetic fields such as transformers, motors, generators, bulk erasers, speakers, etc. They are kept at a minimum of two or three feet from storage racks.
___ Containers support large reels at the hub.

__ Tapes are in plastic bags within the container when provided by manufacturer.
__ Tapes are always kept in a container when not in use.
__ Protective circulation containers are provided.

Shelving

__ Tapes are shelved vertically in boxes.
__ Wood or plastic shelving or electrically grounded metal shelving is used.
__ Stacking of tapes is avoided.

Care

__ Labels are on reels and containers.
__ Wrinkled and damaged ends are removed.
__ Tapes are entirely rewound loosely and evenly after each use.
__ Wind tension is six to eight ounces per half-inch if tape is in extended storage.
__ Tapes are stored "tails" out in extended storage.
__ Tapes are rewound every six months.
__ Tapes are played at least every two years.
__ Take-up reels are inspected weekly.
__ Recording tabs (on cassettes) are removed.
__ A Halon 1301 fire retardant system is available.
__ Water fire extinguishers are available for polystyrene fires.
__ Accumulations of dust, dirt, food particles, and tobacco ashes are avoided.
__ Room cleaning liquids are used that leave no residue.
__ Floors are not waxed.
__ Pressure-sensitive tape is used to "tab down" the end of tape prior to shipping or storage.

Heat and Light

__ Tapes are permitted to reach room temperature (usually twenty-four hours if they have been exposed to abnormally high or low temperatures).

Handling

__ Measures are taken to keep the touching of tape to a minimum.
__ Reels are lifted by the hub or lower flange.
__ Measures are taken to prevent dropping or bumping.

MAPS

Check the Following Items Practiced:

Temperature and Relative Humidity

__ Maps stored at a constant temperature of 68°F and a constant relative humidity of 30% theoretically could increase the life of the average U.S.G.S. map paper from 97.2 years to 361 years.

Container

__ Acid-free filters with a pH of 7.5 or higher are used.
__ Maps do not protrude from the map folders.
__ Folders do not contain more than fifty maps.
__ Folders are at least two inches shorter and narrower than the inside drawer dimensions.
__ Folders are at least one inch longer and wider than the largest maps they contain.
__ Folders are filed with folded edge towards front of drawer.
__ If acid-free folders are not used, then flat polyethylene envelopes open at one end and thermo welded at the other end are used.
__ If maps are circulated then flat, protective circulation containers are provided.

Shelving

__ Inert, baked enamel steel shelving is used.
__ Storage cabinets have six-inch bases.
__ Maps are stored in two-inch horizontal drawers.
__ Fabric dust covers are used.
__ Map drawers are no more than half- to three-quarters full.

Care

__ Maps are stored unfolded and flat.
__ Acid-free interleaf sheets are used.
__ Heavily used maps are laminated.
__ Reinforced maps are bonded with a water soluble medium.

Measures Are Taken to Protect Maps from the Following

__ Ink
__ Pressure adhesives

__ Unfinished wood
__ Sulfur dioxide
__ Rubber bands
__ Paper clips
__ Staples

MICROFORMS (FILMS, FICHE, AND ULTRA-FICHE)

Check the Following Items Practiced:

Temperature and Relative Humidity

__ The National Bureau of Standards recommends 70°F with a constant relative humidity between 25%-40%.

Container

__ Acid-free boxes or envelopes are used.
__ Microfiche are stored one per envelope.
__ Sealed (airtight) containers are used if the room temperature and humidity is not controlled.
__ Unsealed containers are used if the room temperature and humidity is controlled.
__ Plastic reels and clips free of chlorine, sulfur-free rubber bands, or acid-free paper/string ties are used.

Shelving

__ Inert, baked enamel steel, stainless steel, or aluminum cabinets and drawers are used.
__ Microforms are stored vertically.
__ Microforms are tightly packed.
__ Storage cabinets have a fire rating of at least one hour.

Care

__ Microforms are handled by their edges.
__ Microforms are inspected before returning them to storage.
__ Every microform is inspected on a five-year cycle.
__ Microforms are stored in areas without water sprinklers.
__ Microfilms have eighteen-inch leaders and tails.
__ Microfilms are wound loosely.
__ Users are educated to report tears and scratches.

Measures Are Taken to Protect Silver Halide Film from

— Paint fumes
— Hydrogen sulphide
— Sulfur dioxide
— Oxidizing agents
— Oil
— Fingerprints
— Chlorine
— Alum
— Peroxides
— Ammonia
— Turpentine
— Linseed oil
— Exhaust gases

Heat and Light

— Several hours of warm-up time are allowed when the storage area is cooler than the viewing room.
— Measures are taken to keep vesicular film from being exposed to high temperatures.
— Care is taken to prevent diazo film from long periods of exposure under ultraviolet rays.

PHONORECORDS

Check the Following Items Practiced:

Temperature and Relative Humidity

— A moisture content in equilibrium with a constant relative humidity of 50% and a constant temperature of 70°F is most ideal.

Containers

— The cellophane wrapping is removed from the jacket.
— Jackets are covered with a laminated plastic.
— Acid-free paper inner sleeves with polyethylene coated inner surfaces are used.
— Inner sleeves have no folds, wrinkles, or tears.
— The inner sleeve opening is toward the top of the jacket.

Shelving

___ Records are shelved vertically.
___ Shelves are thirteen inches high as well as thirteen inches deep.
___ Rigid separators are placed at three- to four-inch intervals.
___ There are only six records to every inch of shelving.
___ There is a slight even side pressure.
___ Jackets are shelved spine out.

Care

___ All records are parastated.
___ Records are cleaned after each use.
___ Records are inspected for damage after each use.
___ Records are handled only by the edge or label.
___ No part of a record is played more frequently than any other.
___ Records are played singly.
___ Records are not played repeatedly.
___ Records are covered if not in use.
___ Shelves and record jackets are vacuumed.
___ Records are shelved away from direct sunlight.

ORIGINAL PAINTINGS/PRINTS AND NON-ORIGINAL PRINTS

Check the Following Items Practiced:

Temperature and Relative Humidity

___ Art works stored at a constant temperature of 70°F and a constant relative humidity of 50% is considered ideal.

Storage

___ Framed prints are stored vertically.
___ Mounted prints are stored in jumbo files or placed flat in shallow drawers.
___ Inert, baked enamel steel cabinets and drawers are used.
___ Unmatted pictures are stored between acid-free paper.
___ Art is hung with a slight forward tilt.
___ Art is hung on inside walls.
___ UF1 or UF3 plexiglass or "picture" glass is used.
___ Art is not touching glass or plexiglass.
___ Cork tabs are on lower back corners of frames.

___ An all-rag mat board is used.
___ Art in backed with acid-free paper for dust protection.

Heat and Light

___ Art is away from radiators and air vents.

Care

___ Silica gel is used in drawers and cases, when humidity is not controlled.
___ Art is covered with acid-free paper, when not on display.
___ Art works on display are rotated at least once a month.
___ Art is dusted with a soft, silk cloth, absorbent cotton, or a soft brush.
___ Art is transported flat.

Measures Are Taken to Protect Art Works from the Following

___ Dirty hands.
___ Unnecessary movement.
___ Paper clips.
___ Pressure sensitive tape.
___ Gummed brown paper tape.
___ Rubber bands.
___ Rubber cement.
___ Heat sealing mounting tissue.
___ Wooden cabinets and drawers.

PHOTOGRAPHS AND NEGATIVES

Check the Following Items Practiced:

Temperature and Relative Humidity

___ The American National Standards Institute recommends a constant temperature within the range of 59°F-77°F preferably below 68°F with a constant relative humidity between 30%-50%. Temperature and relative humidity should be constant.

Containers

__ Photographs are stored in seamless acid-free envelopes or boxes.
__ Photographs are separated with acid-free interleaf sheets.
__ Photographs and negatives are stored in separate envelopes.
__ Negatives are stored in polyethylene transparent holders or acid-free envelopes.
__ Negatives are stored in seam-free envelopes or seams at edges.

Shelving

__ Steel cabinets with inert, baked enamel finishes are used.
__ Photographs are kept away from uncoated wood and fresh paint.
__ Photographs are filed firmly.

Care (Photographs)

__ Photographs are displayed under tungsten lights of 30-60 foot-candles.
__ Photographs are handled without touching surfaces.

Care (Negatives)

__ Negatives are stored in the dark.
__ Negatives are viewed away from ultraviolet light (direct sunlight and other heat and light sources).
__ Measures are taken to avoid the projection of negatives.
__ Negatives are cleaned with a camel-hair brush.

Care (General)

__ Lintless cotton gloves are used when handling.
__ Storage areas are located on intermediate floors.

*Measures Are Taken to Protect Photographs and Negatives
from Coming in Contact with*

__ Paint fumes.
__ Sulfur dioxide.
__ Rubber bands containing sulfur.
__ Bleached papers.
__ Printing ink.

__ Pastes, adhesives, and cements.
__ Uncoated wood.
__ Brown kraft paper.
__ Glassine envelopes.
__ Polyvinyl chloride folders.
__ Paper clips.

Mounting

__ Dry mount tissue and acid-free mounting board is used when permanently mounting.
__ Framed photographs are not in direct contact with glass or plexiglass, but an air space is provided by the matting.
__ Aluminum picture frames are used when photographs are displayed.
__ When framing, the use of plexiglass is avoided.

UNIVERSAL CONSIDERATIONS

The following storage and care practices are universally accepted for all non-book formats.

__ Protective circulation containers are used.
__ There is an established care and maintenance program.
__ Users are briefed on proper care (verbally or in writing).
__ Smoking, drinking, and eating are prohibited where materials are handled or stored.
__ Smoke, heat, and water detectors operate around the clock.
__ Air conditioning with a filtration system is used.
__ Materials are protected from ultraviolet sunlight and unshielded fluorescent lighting.
__ The temperature and relative humidity is recorded periodically.
__ Basements and uninsulated attics particularly are avoided as storage areas.
__ Storage cases are away from heat sources to avoid extremes in temperature and relative humidity.
__ Shelving is away from outer walls.
__ Each format is spot-checked once a year for deterioration and damage.
__ Temperature and relative humidity gauges are available.

PRODUCTIONS AND PRESENTATIONS

Rationale for Non-Print Production in Libraries

John W. Ellison and Ann Dausch

O VER the last twenty-five years, librarians have entered the media age somewhat reluctantly. The twenty-first century is almost upon us, and librarians are guilty of being too cautious and slow in adopting the new technologies and formats that will influence the functions of libraries in the near future.

Library users have embraced non-print and made it a necessary part of life. Media saturate our lives from the day we are born and exert tremendous power over nearly all of us. Joggers are equiped with headphones; teenagers are seldom without their portable radios and tape players. Automobiles, homes and stores contain thousands of dollars worth of equipment for media receiving and producing. One of the latest innovations is the microcomputer and its by-products which are capturing the minds of the young in schools, homes, and game rooms. Where has the library been during this entertainment and information revolution? Unfortunately, most libraries have been out of touch. It is ironic that while non-print materials are entertaining, informing, and educating library users and non-users, many librarians are dragging their feet when it comes to providing new information and entertainment formats and services to users.

The average American views twenty-nine hours and forty-six minutes of television per week, which amounts to roughly 17.70 percent of one's life. Women tend to watch the most television, with children, men, and teenagers following in that order. The number of radios per thousand Americans was 1,882 between 1970 and 1975. The average percent distribution of time adults eighteen years and older spend with four types of media daily is: magazines five percent; newspapers seven percent; radio forty-one percent; and television forty-seven percent. Librarians spend less than one percent of their time using these media to transmit information or entertainment programming. In 1977 the United States recreation dollar spent in millions of dollars was 4,388 for books and maps; 9,037 for magazines, newspapers, and sheet music; 18,055 for radios, television receivers, records, and musical instruments; and 3,200 for motion picture theaters.

Although these statistics, in and of themselves, do not justify the direction libraries should take, they do provide a strong indication of how people spend their time and money and how they can be reached. Public libraries, from 1978 to 1979, showed a total acquisition expenditure of: $165,957,968 for books; $18,869,482 for periodicals; and a penurious $14,012,949 for "audiovisuals." This would seem to indicate that public libraries are purchasing materials out of proportion with the information and entertainment use and interest of the general public. Clearly, this difference does not mean a direct proportion of the library acquisition budget should reflect the public's non-print use and spending patterns. However, libraries must recognize how and to what extent people use non-print information and entertainment formats, and make significant adjustments to reflect these patterns.

Some librarians become overly concerned about the current percentage of financial allocation and interest in non-print materials. Consider these recently published national figures: 6 percent of the total school media center budget; 6.4 percent of the total acquisition budget of public libraries; and 3.4 percent of the total library acquisition budget of college, junior college, and universities is allocated to non-print materials. Hardly overwhelming figures. Rather than continue to fight non-print information and entertainment materials, libraries should learn to use them and understand the value of their intellectual contribution and unique characteristics. Libraries can no longer view them as the enemy, the thing to do, or simply as a way to attract people to books. The idea that film, radio, television, and records are less valuable than books should be disposed of once and for all. We are in the communication business. People will use all formats of material whether librarians like it or not. Our best response would be to purchase and produce high quality materials, without regard for the format, based on the content, level, and format needs of our library community—be it a school, public, special, or academic library.

Simply put, if people are using all forms of non-print materials, libraries cannot afford to be anti-intellectual print snobs. Let us not forget that some "bad" books are published in rather large numbers every year. In view of recent studies that show that fewer than thirty percent of college students use library facilities during a week and about seventy percent of American adults do not use public libraries, many libraries would do well to examine their mission and priorities. Estelle Jussim put it best when she said that people often mistake "print and reading with thinking and acting." She went on to say, "Excessive emphasis on print-literacy, to the almost total exclusion of training and enlargement of other modes . . . may result in deep frustration and a sense of alienation from the 'real world.' "[1] Maybe this is why some librarians feel so alienated.

A RATIONALE FOR LIBRARY NON-PRINT PRODUCTION

Perhaps the greatest reason for non-print production from the point of view of the librarian is that it allows them to personally extend in many directions and through the variety of formats reach the widest possible audience. Librarians potentially reach large populations. In some states one professional librarian often has to serve ten or twenty schools and supervise a hundred or more volunteers or library assistants. The public library serves an even larger population. Without a way to reach all these people, communication may break down, financial support may wane, volunteers may be unsure of their duties or poorly trained, students may progress through school with little or no library service from a professional librarian, and the public may develop an erroneous view of the real functions and services of the library. The library has to find an effective way to reach all these people. Creation of materials can fulfill locally identified needs unique to a given library community.

With locally produced non-print, the librarian does not have to worry about breaking copyright laws, because the materials produced are library property. The librarian may design and produce non-print packages to teach library skills; the same sort of package might be used to teach the use of media equipment to library users, or it might be used to teach library procedures to library assistants and volunteers. Slides/tapes and videotapes can be produced by media librarians for student or volunteer library orientation programs to reach a wide audience. These are especially useful when a librarian has a large number of places to cover and not enough hours in a day. If video equipment and cable television are available, a librarian can reach the whole community with little expense using videotaped or live television presentations. In addition, through locally produced materials, librarians can share library-related materials with other libraries, thus widening professional knowledge.

Nancy Lane states that we are entering a totally new stage of library development that emphasizes non-print production, which will lead to opportunities for creativity and involvement.[2] Some media centers, community college libraries, and public libraries are already reaping the benefits of local production, and as information technology expands, other libraries will fulfill their function as producers and disseminators of all entertainment and information formats.

There are dozens of reasons for the production of non-print in all types of libraries. A few that come to mind are:

to enrich the education program
to allow for modification of materials
to make the library a total resource center

to allow users to become involved as active participants in learning and
  personal enrichment
to promote visual literacy
to promote ability to communicate in many modes
to disseminate public relations information
to assure timeliness of materials
to produce special materials for special groups
to match the channel users have selected for entertainment and information

Librarians must become non-print producers if they expect to keep
their credibility as professionals. A professional librarian must be an
expert in the design, operation, and management of systems and services
for the creation, organization, movement, and use of messages relevant
to the needs of any defined group of people.[3] In addition, a librarian must
also be able to produce in order to select and evaluate non-print.
Selecting non-print without production knowledge is analogous to
selecting print without the ability to read and write. Media librarians
usually have a wide variety of production skills that permit them to
supervise or become involved in the production of many non-print items.
The following is a very brief list of items most media librarians can
produce:

Black and white photographs
Colored slides
Wall charts, posters, and graphs
Super-graphics
Portable exhibits
Silkscreen posters
Radio programs
Television programs
Self-contained slide/tape programs
Transparencies for overhead pro-
  jectors
Black and white (8 × 10) transpar-
  encies for display or projection
Super 8mm films
Permanent mounting of ephemeral
  material for display
Window displays
Quality audiotapes (editing and
  dubbing)
Signs
Rear screens for displays
T-shirt designs

Non-print production will promote visual literacy, which is crucial if
we are to function in the world of knowledge-based societies. It is the
media librarian's job to educate the public in the literacies of the future
through production of the various forms of non-print. Media librarians
have a major responsibility to educate the "information deprived."[4]

Non-print production leads to the creation of new sources of non-print
research materials. This is especially true in connection with oral history.
Pfaff suggests that, "the public library is the most well equipped
institution to preserve the history of the community due to its access to

primary research sources and the traditional role of preserving perishable materials."[5] Cable and satellite television will create many new channels and thus lead to the creation of independent films and videotapes, special interest programs, and other creative non-print materials that will find their way into research library collections.

Library non-print production results in the user's learning the skills of production techniques and the use of production equipment. In addition, the librarian learns how to handle the software produced. The ability to master the equipment leads to a feeling of comfort, ease, self-confidence, and often great enthusiasm. At a library institute for para-professionals in New Mexico, people learned how to operate equipment and do simple non-print productions. They left the institute with a feeling of great enthusiasm, confidence, and commitment to establishing production projects in their own libraries.[6] Library nonprint production also allows the librarian to evaluate productions and to choose the most appropriate way of presenting an idea.

Libraries must become involved with producing "specialized materials for specialized groups."[7] If we do not, the public may totally abandon libraries and look for those services elsewhere. Libraries must provide these services to everyone at convenient places and times. In addition, they must serve the unemployed worker who needs courses to become more marketable, the blind person who wants taped book reviews of talking books,[8] the child who wants to illustrate a school report with slides, the person who wants to design and produce original computer games, the person who wants to record a family history on audiotape, the small-business person who needs continuing education, and the student who wants "on demand televised reference services."[9] In addition, library non-print production allows the library to reach people who normally would not use it because they are not readers.

BARRIERS TO LIBRARY NON-PRINT PRODUCTION

With few exceptions, the library profession has been resistant to integrating non-print production in libraries. There are several explanations for this situation.

In some libraries—such as special and academic, which are parts of larger institutions—non-print production may be a function of a separate non-print production center. For the library to have an additional production facility might seem to some a duplication of service and probably would not be approved by the parent organization. It is unfortunate that institutions develop in such a splintered way. In most cases, governing bodies simply have not realized that in order for our society to grow we need *convenient*, free access to all information and services,[10] and the best way to make it convenient is to have all materials and production services integrated.

The unwritten philosophy of a few "intellectuals" concerning libraries is that print is more important than non-print. This attitude usually results because of a fear of what is sometimes falsely perceived as the "high cost" of non-print. High fuel costs, taxes, inflation, and general economic conditions have caused some sectors of the public to question the need for libraries. Society is not ready to finance what they consider high-risk projects. Many people fail to realize that we are on the brink of an enormous information revolution and that the library will have the capacity to make all the new information technologies available. Again, education of the public about the library's expanding role as a dis-seminator of all formats of information and services, not just books, could lead to greater support of the library. Library-produced public relations efforts could bring accurate information to the public.[11]

Some library boards, school boards, and the public in general have a deep-seated stereotyped view of the library as a place to check out books. It is difficult to change narrow attitudes like this, even when there is an obvious need for changes in services to meet new information needs. People must be reeducated to see the library as a dynamic place where all kinds of services and all forms of information may be found.[12] It really comes down to the fact that the public and many librarians have a narrow concept of the basic purpose of the library. The National Commission of Libraries and Information Science has suggested the following common statement of function for all libraries:

> The function of libraries and information centers is to meet immediate and foreseeable information requirements of the greatest number of people ... to eventually provide every individual in the U.S. with equal opportunity of access to that part of the total information resource that will satisfy individual educational, working, cultural, and leisure time needs and interests, regardless of the individual's location, social and physical condition or level of intel-lectual achievement.[13]

Because of the dominant number of "print" faculty in library schools, librarians are often instilled with the idea that books are superior to other information and entertainment formats.[14] Potential librarians are some-times made to feel it is "unprofessional" to produce non-print, and they are taught that non-print materials are not very important. With so little attention being given to non-print and non-print production in library schools, it is not surprising that librarians have become so book-oriented and that the general public has such a narrow perception of the library's mission.

Most librarians are not adequately trained in non-print production. Courses in production are seldom required or advised. Library school faculty seldom produce non-print and have limited knowledge of production techniques; their students then usually perpetuate this ignorance of production skills. In fact, few library schools have even the most primitive production facilities or equipment. Many limit use to their faculty or have Gutenberg-style printing presses for "printing" courses. Production is simply not an aspect of librarianship that most library school faculty consider very important.[15] Librarians must be taught to produce non-print if they are to adequately serve the information needs of their users.

Many public, academic, and school libraries are facing serious budget and staff cuts that cannot be dismissed. It is not easy to convince the public that the library is one of their best buys when librarians have done a poor job of informing the public concerning the value of the library. States with laws like California's Proposition 13 and Massachusetts' 2½ are finding that libraries are fighting for their very existence. There often is no money for library materials. Maybe this situation would not exist on the present scale if libraries had made themselves an integral part of the community's information and entertainment resources.

Some media librarians have been so influenced that they manage the non-print services of their library much like the most traditional print services. That is to say, the media librarian arbitrarily selects the material, catalogs it, places it on the shelf, and waits for someone to discover "*their* wonderful world of non-print." Some have called it "media librarianship by personal convenience." It is little wonder that traditional librarians really question the need for media librarians.

These are all serious problems that cannot be overlooked or solved immediately. Perhaps if we start in the library school, and change attitudes there toward the importance of non-print production and then concentrate on changing the attitude of the public and some librarians concerning the real function of the library, the other problems may take care of themselves.

NON-PRINT PRODUCTION IN SCHOOL MEDIA CENTERS

One of the purposes of the library media center is to serve the needs of teachers and students by supplying them with all appropriate types of materials and services, including production service. With guidance from school media specialists, students in school media centers can produce a vast array of non-print materials to enhance learning and enrich their personal lives. Student productions may include sound/visual interpretations of author's works, non-print programs in place of reports, videotaped original skits and plays for English and drama classes, and the taping of sports, games, and other activities.

Teachers, to a lesser extent, produce non-print or have the school media center staff produce it for them. Teachers have been known to make photographs and slides of college campuses to show students, convert print lessons and activities into non-print format to add variety to teaching and meet individual needs, and create auto-tutorial modules for individualized learning.

School media specialists produce non-print and teach production fundamentals to students and teachers. They produce slide/tape programs for PTA and board meetings, they produce school media center orientation programs for students, library assistants, and volunteers, and they produce library skills packages geared to student needs.

NON-PRINT PRODUCTION IN THE PUBLIC LIBRARY

The public library certainly has an opportunity and a mandate to be a major producer of local-interest material, but librarians are cautious about their production endeavors and usually carry them out, if at all, on an elementary level. This may be a result of the self-stereotyping of the public library as a "book" place. Even large public libraries with non-print departments and media librarians seldom have production facilities. One exception is the Brooklyn Public Library. It supports an extremely popular production center where users and staff produce films, videotapes, and audiotapes at no cost to the users except for supplies.[16]

Some public libraries are beginning to experiment with the production of oral history tapes, the copying of old photographs for circulation, creation of slide/tape programs, and the audiotaping of books for the visually impaired. Often these projects are carried out by volunteers. At the San Mateo (California) Public Library, a volunteer produces many slide/tape and videocassette programs to be used in convalescent and retirement homes in the county. At other public libraries, volunteers provide talking books for the mentally impaired.

Video is a popular production service for some public libraries. With the help of grants, public libraries have initiated a number of innovative video projects. Through the "Sonoran Heritage Learning Library Programs and Resources" project, the Tucson Public Library has produced videotapes and also learning packets on subjects of local interest.[17] Maryland has initiated the first library video network to produce public announcements and staff learning tapes. Since a number of public library systems are involved, equipment and expertise were pooled for efficiency and cost-effectiveness.[18] The Mid-Hudson (New York) Library System has established nine video learning centers. These centers not only provide the public with production opportunities, but they provide new, never-before-broadcast tapes by independent producers, often on subjects of local interest.[19] The Cleveland Public Library has become involved with the production of videotapes for local television to stimulate public interest in their services. They also do video projects of an informational, educational, and promotional nature.[20]

In the San Francisco Bay area, public libraries are pioneering the use of microcomputers for library users. Two teenage computer entrepreneurs have installed coin-operated Apple II computers in several public libraries. These have proved extremely popular, and it is quite possible that within a year or two coin-operated computers will be widely available in libraries, and library users will be able to create their own software. The public schools are producing computer enthusiasts who will demand computer facilities and services in all their libraries. Projects like these, designed to actively involve users and attract and involve non-users or even non-readers, may give the library the support and integrity it has lacked in the past.[21] Indeed, the survival of the public library depends on its willingness to depart from old concepts of narrow service and embrace the expanded new information and enrichment services.

NON-PRINT PRODUCTION IN SPECIAL LIBRARIES

Special libraries in business and industry are frequently small operations run by one professional librarian. It is not difficult to demonstrate their need for production services, especially when some companies do not have their own non-print production centers staffed by non-print professionals, instructional designers, and specialists who develop sophisticated non-print materials for orientation and teaching of employees. In a situation like this, development and centralization of services is usually encouraged or expected.

Some special librarians are knowledgeable in production techniques and do produce their own materials. These special libraries produce slide tapes, video, and computer-assisted instructional programs. They tape speeches, produce training programs, create product and service announcements, and sometimes produce the company newsletter (a good vehicle for promoting library services).

NON-PRINT PRODUCTION IN ACADEMIC LIBRARIES

In universities and colleges, non-print production and instructional design and development have traditionally evolved as functions separate from the library. Some colleges have separate non-print services departments staffed by photographers, graphic artists, and technicians.

They produce slide/tape programs, slide reproduction, photocopying into slides, videotaping, and auto-tutorial packages. Students are not normally allowed to use the production center to produce their own materials. This places a real limit on accessibility of services to students and ignores the need for production services. The separation of the library from the production center causes an additional problem if you accept the rationale that the function of an academic library is to "make all media" and services available through a single facility.[22]

It is unfortunate that there are not more academic libraries like the one described in *Evergreen: Profile of a New College*. It is described as a "multi-media workshop library" where students learn how to use equipment and produce materials in a well-equipped production facility. There is a television studio, and the college buys superior student productions to encourage involvement. Here is a case where the philosophy of the institution and the philosophy of the library are in agreement.[23]

Academic librarians are not usually involved with production, although in conjunction with the non-print production center, some do produce general orientation programs, programs to introduce students to online computer catalogs, slide/tapes in English and foreign languages, and slide/tapes for use in introductory library courses. At DeAnza College in Cupertine, California, for instance, the library staff is working with the telecommunication staff in planning and developing a new television facility where, undoubtedly, the library will be able to present orientations and information programs in cooperation with public, school, and other libraries.

Although non-print production has been demonstrated to be an important, if not essential, part of the school library media center program and, to some extent, the public library program, this is not necessarily true in all other types of libraries. The importance of the need for non-print production depends on the type of library, knowledge of the staff, its philosophy, and upon the way that the institution with which the library is connected is functionally organized.

NON-PRINT PRODUCTION FOR THE FUTURE

No one can imagine what the library of 2001 will be like. There may be no library as we know it today, and information needs may be fulfilled by commercial vendors who sell information at a good profit. The library of the future depends on what we do today. If we begin to initiate innovative services such as non-print production, we may find our rightful place in the information society.

References

1. Estelle Jussim, "Confronting Our Media Biases: The Social Dimensions of Media," in *Expanding Media*, ed. Deirdre Boyle (Phoenix: Oryx Press, 1977), p. 33.
2. Nancy Lane, "The Library as a Media Producer, in *Reader in Media, Technology and Libraries*, ed. Margaret Chisholm (Englewood, Colo.: Microcard Editions Books, 1975), pp. 494-501.
3. Robert S. Taylor, "Reminiscing About the Future: Professional Education and the Information Environment," *Library Journal* (September 15, 1979), pp. 1871-75.
4. Ibid.
5. Eugene Pfaff, Jr., "Oral History: A New Challenge for Public Libraries," *Wilson Library Bulletin* (May 1980), p. 568.
6. Lucille Baird, *Library Media Institute for Paraprofessionals* (Portales, N.M.: Eastern New Mexico University, December 1978) ERIC ED 180 489.
7. Sylvia G. Faibisoff, *Functions and Services of Libraries* (March 1978, ERIC ED 158 761).
8. Harriet L. Eisman, "Public Library Programs for the Elderly," *Wilson Library Bulletin* (April 1979), p. 564.
.9 Susan K. Martin, *Technology in Libraries: 1960-2000* (March 1978, ERIC ED 158-764).
10. Elisabeth Israels Perry and Harold Hacker, *Access to the Past: The Librarian's Responsibility to the Future* (March 1978, ERIC ED 158 707).
11. Ibid.
12. Martin.
13. Charles Benton, "The National Commission: Visions of the Future," *Library Journal* (September 15, 1979), p. 1876.
14. John W. Ellison, "Media Accountability in Library Education," *Catholic Library World* (October 1980), pp. 129-31.
15. Ibid.
16. Louis Ebarb, "A Production House for the Public," *American Libraries* (December 1981), p. 692.
17. Helen N. Gothberg, "Videoworks at the Tucson Public Library," *Library Journal* (January 1, 1982), pp. 33-37.
18. Barbara Webb, "Maryland Creates First Video Production Network," *American Libraries* (May 1981), p. 186.
19. Michael Miller, "Video Learning Center Enrich Rural Libraries," *American Libraries* (February 1981), p. 103.
20. Frank R. Merrill, "Public Service Broadcasting and Libraries," *Wilson Library Bulletin* (February 1979), p. 448.
21. Paul V. Robinson, *The Public Library as a Multi-media Institution* (New York: Columbia University School of Library Service, 1974), ERIC ED 100 302.
22. Murray Phipps, "IMC—The Rationale" in *IMC: Selected Readings*, ed. Pearson and Butler (Minneapolis: Burgess Publishing Co., 1969), p. 19.

23. Don H. Coombs and James J. Prevel, *Evergreen: Profile of a New College* (Stanford, Calif.: Stanford University, 1973), ERIC ED 093 337.

Bibliography

A.V. Connection: Guide for Federal Funds for Audio Visual Programs, 3rd ed., NAVA, 1979.

Becker, Joseph. "Libraries, Society and Technological Change," *Library Trends* (Winter 1978): pp. 409-417.

Belland, John C. *1984 is Only Nine Years Away; Will School Media Programs Humanize or Dehumanize Schooling?* Maryland State Dept. of Education, Baltimore. April 9, 1975. ED 112 863

Bender, David R. and Rosa L. Presberry. *Services of a School Media Program.* Maryland State Dept. of Education, Baltimore. Div. of Library Development and Services. 1976. ED 126 908.

Brown, James and Kenneth Norberg, *Administering Educational Media*, McGraw-Hill, 1965.

Byrne, Richard B. "As Through a Glass Darkly: Planning for the Unknowable Media Future," *School Library Media Quarterly* (Fall 1981): pp. 22-28.

Carpenter, Ray L. "The Public Library Patron," *Library Journal* (Feb. 1, 1979): pp. 347-351.

Corbin, John. "Library Automation: A State of the Art," *Catholic Library World* (May/June 1979): pp. 427-429.

Delaney, Jack J. *The Media Program in the Elementary and Middel Schools*, Linnet Books, 1976.

Dennison, Lynn C. "The Organization of Library and Media Services in Community Colleges," *College and Research Libraries* (March 1978): pp. 123-129.

Ely, Donald P. *Future Training for Service, a Report to the Library and Information Science Profession.* Syracuse Univ., N.Y. Center for the Study of Information and Education. Oct. 1974. ED 098 940.

Evans, E. Edward. "Time for Decision: Yesterday, Today, and Tommorrow; Training for the New Breed Librarian," *Special Libraries* (May/June 1979): pp. 209-218.

Feingold, Karen E. *Library and Information Services for Improving Organizations and the Professions. A Discussion Guide.* National Commission on Libraries and Information Science, Washington, D.C. Oct. 1979. ED 179 243.

Galvin, Thomas J. "Libraries to Serve the Information Society," *Library Journal* (Sept. 15, 1979): pp. 1847-1851.

Giblin, Thomas R. "Don't Make a Four Letter Word," *Media and Methods* (January 1980): pp. 55+.

Gillespie, John T. and Diana L. Spirt. *Creating a School Media Program*, Bowker, 1973.

Guidelines for CA Library Media Programs: School, District, and State. CMLEA, 1977.

Gunter, Jonathan F. *Library and Information Services for Increasing International Understanding and Cooperation. A Discussion Guide.* National Commission on Libraries and Information Science, Washington, D.C. Oct. 1979. ED 179 244.

Lancaster, F. Wilfrid. "Whither Libraries? or, Wither Libraries," *College and Research Libraries* (Sept. 1978): pp. 345-357.

McGraw, Harold W. "Responding to Information Needs in the 1980s," *Wilson Library Bulletin* (November 1979): pp. 160-164.

Monroe, Margaret E. "Emerging Patterns of Community Service," *Library Trends* (Fall 1979): pp. 120-138.

Narrative Evaluation Report on the Institute for Training in Librarianship. Media: Production, Organization and Utilization, June 22, 1970-July 3, Marylhurst Coll., Oreg. 1970. ED 047 757.

Poston, Teresa G. "The Concept of the School Media Center and Its Services," *Peabody Journal of Education* (April 1978): pp. 198-204.

Prostano, Emanuel T. and Joyce S. Prostano. *The School Library Media* Center, 2nd ed. Libraries Unlimited, Inc., 1977.

Wilson, Pauline. "Librarianship and ALA in a Post-Industrial Society," *American Libraries* (March 1978): pp. 124-128.

Wyatt, Joe B. "Technology and the Library," *College and Research Libraries* (March 1979): pp. 120-124.

Zaslavsky, Gerald. *Media Services in an Academic Library. A Rationale With Special Implications for New York University's Bobst Library.* 1974. ED 110 033.

Considerations in Evaluating, Selecting, and Producing Visuals

John W. Ellison

MEDIA librarians have the major responsibility when it comes to evaluating, selecting, and producing visuals, whether they be still, film, video, three-dimensional, original, or art prints. They must know not only how the medium was created and what content it attempts to communicate, but why it is strong or weak in presentation. This knowledge does not generally come with age or work experience, even though both help. Visual knowledge is acquired with a great deal of concerted effort and study in the disciplines of visual composition and appreciation.

The media librarian may not have been exposed to visual composition as a formal academic subject even though seeing has always been a normal part of life's experiences. Like seeing, it is assumed those who hear also know how to listen. Exposure to formal visual composition may not have been presented in an academic curriculum until graduate school, if then. Media librarians must acquire the ability to understand visual composition and properly supervise image-makers within the library context.

A sound knowledge and appreciation of visual composition by media librarians is essential if they are to know the important questions one would ask to determine the visual information needs of their library community. Simply knowing what the library community likes will not provide the information necessary to develop a visual collection which is representative of the visual knowledge, means of accessing, and appreciation hierarchy of that community. The parallel with print librarianship would be the importance of knowing the special reading levels, formats, and interests of a library community. The media librarian must know the interests, format preferences, and visual knowledge level of the library community if visual appreciation and intellectual growth are to

Originally published in *Catholic Library World* 52 (April 1982) pp. 400–401 and (May/June 1982) pp. 443–445.

occur. The common denominator of visual communication is visual composition. This basic level provides the functional language which media librarians, image-makers, and the community use to communicate. The media librarian and image-maker must understand visual composition if effective communication and appreciation takes place. Unlike the written language, no universal acceptance of rules, principles, or guidelines has been adopted. However, most image-makers accept some notions of visual composition as a basis for expressing their work when it is discussed verbally or presented in written form.

Composition is a highly personalized set of factors determined and applied by individuals. They are simply the selection and arrangement of objects within a visual. Learning composition does not mean memorizing rules, principles, or guidelines; it means developing a style and sensitivity to what works or does not work for you and is communicated to others. Following rules, principles, and guidelines of visual composition will not make a good visual any more than they will make good prose. It is important to have a sensitivity to composition and develop the ability to recognize, compose, produce, select, or properly evaluate a visual with superior and emotional impact. Personal taste is a good guide since visual composition is highly personal.

There is a certain danger in the study of visual composition as rules, principles, and guidelines since the notions of composition are infinitely flexible. Describing visuals in terms of size, center of interest, color, balance, light, movement, and texture tends to exaggerate the importance of one quality and distort the delicate relationship of all the parts as a working harmony. The notions of visual composition described here make no pretense at being more than a set of basic considerations. Use of these considerations in combination with one's own creative imagination, organization, and awareness are the ingredients for effective visual communication, understanding, and appreciation.

Prior to evaluating, selecting, or producing visuals, the specific purpose should be identified. This means simply knowing what visual information is needed, what you want communicated, or what the image-maker intends to communicate. Often this first step is a major problem with most non-communicative visuals. Either the objective is unknown or the subject is inadequately analyzed. Therefore, the viewer is lost and effective communication does not take place. Failure to analyze the subject and the library community prior to evaluating, selecting, and producing visuals can be a troublesome burden later.

Let us begin learning about visual composition by assuming we are novice still photographers. We will start thinking about visual subjects from behind the camera. The content learned from this perspective can be easily transferred to evaluating, selecting, and supervising image-makers within the library context. It can also be applied to the other visual formats collected or created by the library.

THE SUBJECT

Good subjects are usually close at hand. Try to "see" things other people overlook—and capture them visually in a different and interesting way. Learn to use all the human senses to find interesting subjects, but once found, mute all senses but sight.

Develop a *viewfinder perception*. It might mean looking through a camera viewfinder or an empty slide mount for a period of time in order to experience a variety of visual composition possibilities by manipulating your view of the subject.

Select subjects with pleasing and *interesting forms*. It sometimes helps to study things common to your environment. This may require a great deal of tenacity on your part since familiarity may lead to boredom. However, the result may be heightened awareness of interesting forms we take for granted.

Learn about the subject so its visual and communicative properties are known. This may require extensive reading, talking with others, or observing the subject for an extended period of time.

Move close to the subject. Close-ups convey a feeling of intimacy while long shots suggest airiness and depth. Physically move closer or change the lens for a tighter shot. Look for a single idea, message, main subject, or center of interest.

Spontaneity is best captured by being inconspicuous while creating the visual and by not positioning the subject. It is usually difficult for most human subjects to remain natural once they are aware their picture is about to be taken. Expression, skin texture and muscle tone may all become unnatural when a camera is pointed at the subject.

Human interest can add a great deal to visuals. This is particularly true when the subject is associated with people. However, caution should be used when placing the person since the center of focus and all other elements of composition may be altered.

COMPOSITIONAL AESTHETICS

Simplicity is the key to effective visual communication. This can be accomplished by keeping the background unobtrusive. Try changing the angle higher or lower to a less cluttered background. Keep in mind that *low angles* (or shooting up at the subject) can create a feeling of height or grandeur while *high angles* can create a feeling of insignificance.

Taking a picture over the shoulder of someone working creates a *subjective* point of view while shooting in front of someone working creates an *objective* point of view. When demonstrating the proper manipulation of an object, the subjective position should be used. The objective position is used when a personal perspective is not important.

Provide a strong *center of interest* in each visual. Draw the viewer's eye into the visual. The center of interest is seldom in the exact center of the visual. The visual center is usually at the point where lines cross when a visual is divided vertically and horizontally into thirds. The most important part of the visual, or center of interest, is at one of the four places where the lines cross. This concept is better known as the "rule of thirds."

Use elements in the scene like trees, arches, leaves, and buildings to partially *frame the visual*. Also, nylon stockings, facial tissues, and textured glass can be used to frame subjects. Obvious overuse of such techniques can become very sterile and boring to the viewer. Simply moving closer to the subject reduces the visual content and makes framing easier. Overcast days when the sky is gray, white, and uninteresting are particularly important times to consider framing.

Some visuals need *balance* while others are weakened when balance is created. Size, weight, shape, color, and position are some of the factors that affect balance. Generally, the pleasing appearance of a visual tells the viewer balance is correct for that visual.

The eye tends to favor the *lower left area* of a visual field. Use this area accordingly when composing a visual. Sometimes having a line created by a fence, road, or river moving toward the center of interest from the lower left area adds strength to a visual.

Size (scale) in relationship to other subjects adds truth to a visual. This may be a major problem when unknown subjects are enlarged significantly or large unknown subjects are shown without a common item in the visual. Placing a common object in the scene usually helps the viewer gain proper perspective.

Visual ambiguity obscures compositional intent and meaning when ambiguity is not intended. Try to prevent trees from looking like they are growing out the subject's head or people in the background from standing on top of the subject.

Movement (motion) gives life to some otherwise dull visuals. This can be created by zooming, panning, and slow shutter speeds. Keep in mind, subjects in motion should not extend beyond the visual frame. This is accomplished by leaving the majority of open space in front of the subject in motion. The subject should appear to be moving toward the center of the frame rather than leaving the frame.

Color can enhance a dull scene. Proper contrast has the same effect when working with black and white film. Red and yellow are excellent choices when you want to add obvious color to a scene since they tend to direct the eye to the subject. Keep in mind the intensity of the color added since it may create a center of focus and detract from the intended subject in the visual.

Use of *light* can create excellent visuals where questionable subjects existed before. Avoid dominant front lighting unless it is particularly appropriate. Cross lighting created by early morning and late afternoon sun is better. It adds highlights, shadows, and the feeling of depth. Try taking color pictures when the sky is overcast and note the richness of color in particularly close-up visuals. Extreme brightness washes out colors. Front lighting, side lighting, back lighting, and flat light all have unique characteristics and should be used to create the appropriate feeling or contrast.

Texture is one compositional element that makes the viewer feel closer to the subject in the visual, almost eager to reach out and touch it. Usually a combination of closeness and proper lighting is required to create the feeling of texture.

Selective focusing techniques change the emphasis of a visual. For example, focus on a subject in the foreground and notice how the background, thrown out of focus, takes on a hazy, softened look. While this technique can be very effective in color photography, it can be very distracting in black and white photography if not used properly. The degree of background and foreground focus may also be critical since some subjects slightly out of focus create an unwanted focal point or area of interest in a visual.

Horizons should be level and at the upper or lower quarter of a visual. This is sometimes referred to as the Golden Section, Golden Mean, or Golden Ratio. Cutting the visual field in half with a horizon can be distracting to the viewer. Two equal areas in a visual usually eliminate singleness or unity and seem to create visual static.

Lines are an important consideration. Vertical lines impart feelings of dignity and strength, while horizontal depict quiet and tranquility. Diagonal lines are usually the most dynamic lines, symbolic of action and movement. Curved lines, depending on context and usage, can convey several meanings. The S curves and C curves are particularly pleasing to the eye. *Leading lines* are supposed to lead the eyes to the center of interest. A path, road, sidewalk, river, fence, hedge, stream, driveway, or shadow can be used. Proper use of lines can create a feeling of space in a visual which adds depth and shows relationship between subjects.

OTHER FACTORS

Vertical and *horizontal subjects* should usually be framed in like formats. However, mixing vertical and horizontal formats in a display or presentation can be disturbing to a viewer if they are not arranged properly. The *effective display* of the visual is sometimes just as important as the visual content itself. Sloppy presentation can nullify the intended appreciation or communication.

Remember that knowing a few considerations for visual composition are only as effective as the type of film selected, knowledge of equipment characteristics, and availability of optional equipment. Color filters, multi-image lenses, screens, black lights, and mirrors are but a few items which can be used to create special effects. Don't be afraid to experiment.

Take several shots of the same subject (select several angles, exposures, and shutter speeds) to improve the chances of having produced a superb visual. Consider recording each shot (shutter and f-stop) so there will be an accurate means of checking the results. When all is said and done, film is the cheapest element when creating visuals. Your time and the cost of processing and equipment are the expensive aspects of creating a visual.

The ability to evaluate, select, and produce good visuals is inherent in each of us. However, we must generate ideas and techniques by viewing many visuals, visiting art exhibits, going to the movies and to libraries, and practicing creative techniques.

Patience is the virtue of every creative image-maker. There may be only one time when the conditions are right for a perfect composition. Be patient and wait for that moment.

Please yourself. Success in composition is a matter of personal opinion and taste for the visual creator. On the other hand, knowing the community's visual information needs requires a formal assessment and may not reflect the image-maker's area of interest or personal taste.

VIEWING

The conditions under which one views visuals are sometimes just as important as the creation itself. Slides should be examined in a completely darkened room with a properly functioning projector and on a quality screen. Prints should be examined under natural daylight conditions. Fluorescence, tungsten, and tinted windows may emit light which is not true and consistent with natural daylight.

The distance from which one views visuals is also an important consideration. Some large visuals were designed to be viewed at a specific distance. Image-makers sometimes provide specific viewing instructions with their visuals. Other visuals encourage a variety of viewing angles to comprehend the image-maker's work.

One of the most difficult tasks for the novice image-maker is to reject or discard visuals. Learning that not everything is good or should be saved is acquired with experience and the ability to objectively judge one's own work.

It cannot be stressed enough that the above are "considerations," not golden rules or principles that can never be violated. Mixing and in some cases violating these considerations makes for creative visual composition. Only the rudiments of visual composition have been discussed. Shape, variety, order, unity, vitality, and repose are but a few advanced elements of composition which interact with several basic visual composition considerations to describe steps on the ladder of visual composition.

Bibliography

Asher, Harry R. *Photographic Principles and Practices*. Englewood Cliffs, N.J.: Prentice-Hall, 1975.

Bruce, Helen Finn. *Your Guide to Photography*. New York: Barnes and Noble, 1975.

Clements, Ben, and David Rosenfield. *Photographic Composition*. Englewood Cliffs, N.J.: Prentice Hall, 1974.

Feininger, Andreas. *Photographic Seeing*. Englewood Cliffs, N.J.: Prentice Hall, 1973.

Feininger, Andreas. *Principles of Composition in Photography*. New York: Amphoto, 1973.

Goldsmith, Arthur. *How to Take Better Pictures*. New York: Arco Publishing, 1960.

Henle, Fritz. *Photography for Everyone*. New York: Viking Press, 1959.

Highland, Harold Joseph. *Audel's Guide to Creative Photography*. Indianapolis: Audel and Co., 1960.

Jacobs, Lou. *How to Take Great Pictures with Your SLR*. Tucson, Ariz.: H.P. Books, 1974.

Jones, Paul. *Photographic Composition Simplified*. New York: Amphoto, 1975.

Litzel, Otto. *Litzel on Photographic Composition*. New York: Amphoto, 1974.

Robinson, Henry Peach. *Pictorial Effect in Photography*. Rochester, N.Y.: International Museum of Photography, 1971.

Wolchonok, Louis. *Art of Pictorial Composition*. New York: Dover Publishing, 1969.

Woolley, A.E. *Photography: A Practical and Creative Introduction*. New York: McGraw-Hill, 1974.

Zakia, Richard D. *Perception and Photography*. Englewood Cliffs, N.J.: Prentice Hall, 1974.

Factors That Determine Effective Library Displays

John W. Ellison

MEDIA librarians are called upon to provide many services, programs, and activities for the library. One responsibility is usually the preparation of library displays. A display may be in a fixed location and regularly changed or one for a special occasion in or outside the library. Displays include bulletin boards, booths in shopping ·centers, window displays, freestanding exhibits, or display cases.

Several basic factors should be taken into consideration by the media librarian during the creation of a display. Obviously, the purpose of a display should be determined before starting production. Next, sketch the display as envisioned upon completion. Label the colors, texture, small illustrations, and lettering on the sketch. Show the sketch to one or two members of the staff who have an artistic flair and willingly give objective criticism. Then, if you still feel the need, find four or five people in the library community and show them the sketch for reactions and suggestions which might improve the message you wish to communciate. Finally, if possible, have a graphic artist make suggestions.

At this point the novice might say, "Anyone can produce an effective display by simply following the suggestions in the above paragraph." However, other important factors must be taken into consideration. Displays that accomplish their objectives of attracting attention and communicating a message have producers who know that considerable thought, knowledge, and preparation go into the conceptualization, production, and exhibition of the library's image.

The conceptualization may be original or an idea from advertising, window displays, magazines, or other exhibits. Some of the best ideas are developed around a calendar of events with a group of brainstorming librarians over lunch.

Outstanding displays usually have three major ingredients: neatness, simplicity, and magnetism (or attention grabbing). Sloppy and crowded displays distract rather than attract attention. They are usually created because someone is in a hurry or wants to put too much information on

Originally published in *Catholic Library World* 53 (April 1982): 374-376 display. Displays that will make heads turn are made striking by colors, movement, or the message. Sometimes the combination of all three elements will be working in unison to direct attention to the display.

Talent to construct a display is available everywhere. Other staff members, trainees, aides, volunteers, and community library users are sometimes willing to help with display projects. Placing a notice on a public bulletin board will sometimes bring several dedicated helpers.

Construction is usually only twenty-five percent of the time dedicated to a display. Conceptualization of an idea and working out production problems such as determining what goes on the display, taking slides/ film, collecting materials, and making an audiotape may take seventy-five percent of the total time. When these percentages are disproportionally out of line, the end product may suffer.

Topics are numerous and should reflect a specific audience and the location of the display. Humor is always appreciated if appropriate and if it uses good taste and avoids the bizarre. Library book (and other material) displays should be avoided. People are stimulated by ideas—not formats! A well-illustrated display on space travel to whet the intellectual appetite with a simple notice that additional information is available at the library will suffice. Consumer displays in shopping centers and store windows with the library's logo have a way of being successful without being totally library oriented.

Locations other than in the library should be considered for display spaces. Store windows, shopping malls, doctors' offices, and theater lobbies are some locations to be considered. Portable circulating display units should be shifted to different locations where they will receive full utilization without overexposure and be cost-effective. Displays should not be left in one location for more than two weeks. Some feel displays should be changed or rotated every week. Since this may not always be feasible, sometimes background can remain, but the contents changed periodically.

Effective displays usually encourage viewer involvement. This is accomplished by having the viewer sniff, manipulate, move, or take something from the exhibit. Simple devices built into the display can encourage the viewer to press a button to light information, lift a window that provides additional insight, or open a door to receive a bibliography, bumper sticker, or bookmark. Nothing is impossible with a little imagination.

Captions should be brief, worthwhile, clear, and forceful. One idea is usually all a good display can convey. An exhibit has three seconds to convey a message. If a person must stoop and carefully examine the display to understand the message, the message is not simple. Avoid detailed explanations—they will not be read. If the message is good, people will stop and look more closely.

Displays should not totally depend on written words. Some unclear messages, when designed as such, will attract attention and encourage viewer participation. Take for example the caption, "These books should be burned!" This caption may attract immediate attention, but create confusion unless the viewer knows that the classical materials on display are part of an April Fool's Day prank. Examples of captions like *Come to the Library*, *Read These Books*, or *Libraries Are Fun* are not forceful even though the message is clear. They may also be disturbing when the person is standing in the library and reading, *Come to the Library* and *Libraries Are Fun* when there is no sign of fun in sight.

Seeing a display is essential if it is going to communicate a message. Nothing is more frustrating than watching children try to view a display designed for them, but well above their eye level. Always put yourself in the place of the viewer before construction starts on a display. Envision what they will see at their viewing level. Bulletin boards where children pass should be at their eye level just as all other displays should be lowered or raised to the level of the viewer. Viewers should be able to read the message from the back of a room or the end of a corridor. Store window displays are usually easy to read from the other side of the street. Effective displays have large enough messages to be seen from a reasonable distance. Test the lettering size by standing at a distance and viewing sample lettering sizes.

Two or three colors are usually adequate for a display. However, they must complement one another and be pleasing. Try to select attractive colors, but avoid the garish. Textured colors should also be considered such as those found in wallpaper and cloth. Remember that lettering need not always be black. Many times lettering can be the third color.

Lettering should be in good taste, simple, neat, well-spaced, and in harmony with the display. Expensive commercial plastic or vinyl letters can be purchased, but simple handmade construction paper, dry transfer, spray paint, or rubber stamp letters may be equally satisfactory for a few pennies. Another simple technique is to enlarge magazine or newspaper print with an opaque projector and trace the size letters needed. No more than two lettering styles should be used on one display. Again, remember the caption should be brief.

Some very effective displays create a total atmosphere by using the ceiling, floor, and wall to focus the viewer's attention. This notion should be considered for special occasions and where it is physically possible to create such an environment. The same feeling can be created by extending the display's colors in the immediate area. Signs, ribbons, string, crepe paper, and posters associated with the display can unify if they follow the same color scheme.

The use of motion such as rotating signs, fans, film, flashing lights, color wheels, clocks, or other mechnical devices have the advantage of attracting attention not usually found in static displays. Many of these devices are available gratis from old exhibits in local stores, bars, and restaurants. Minor alterations will make mechanical devices appropriate for a library display without advertising the original product for which it was designed. Easy-to-produce, fine-grain positive transparencies and color magazine picture lifts are especially effective when illuminated visuals are needed.

Items which extend from a display to make a three-dimensional appearance improve the overall visual quality. Raised letters, styrofoam, cardboard boxes, string-held shelves, and a table used as part of the display make for three-dimensional exhibits. They are items readily available and cost little or nothing, but improve a display significantly when properly used to add depth.

Continuous-play cassette tapes and rear screens made of frosted plastic add another dimension to library displays. Filmloops and carousel slide projectors can run continuously on rear screens without constant supervision. Placing the equipment inside the display can help prevent unauthorized removal. An extended power cord will start and stop the system. If the display is designed to function with or without equipment, to some extent, little is lost if mechanical problems occur until a staff member can make the proper repair.

Materials used to construct a display can be as simple as cloth, wallpaper, construction paper, newspaper, contact paper, aluminum foil, and burlap. Shipping crates use lightweight wood and make excellent framing material. Cardboard and styrofoam from the local appliance store is large enough for most display projects. It is usually important to keep the project cheap, simple to construct, and lightweight. Some people will add multi-purpose to the factors which should be considered.

When a bulletin board is the display, it is a good idea to leave it blank a few days between exhibits. The anticipation may bring suggestions for a future display and positive comments regarding the last exhibit. Some libraries place a large question mark on the original bulletin board. This technique has encouraged display discussions.

Background behind a portable display is extremely important when determining the location. Light color displays should be placed against darker backgrounds while dark displays look well against lighter backgrounds. Lively display colors go well against neutral backgrounds and neutral colors stand out from bright-colored backgrounds. When displays are moved to several locations and backgrounds vary, it is not necessary to select a neutral color. Special lighting which keys on the display will help make it stand out from any background. Notice how lighting is used in large department stores to highlight freestanding displays with cluttered backgrounds. This same technique will work on library displays.

The success of a display is determined by the degree it accomplishes a predetermined objective. Increased utilization, new users, and circulation of displayed topics are good measures of success. Library users, not staff, making reference to displays is also a factor in determining success. Periodic evaluation of displays should be recorded and formally published in annual reports to show that money and staff time are well-expended for display activities.

A photographic record should be made of each exhibit. These photographs can be used to stimulate future ideas, illustrate annual reports, supplement newspaper and journal articles on the library, and to enter the library's displays in public relations contests. A color negative film should be used to photograph displays. Negatives can reproduce black and white and color prints, slides, and enlargements of all sizes.

Outstanding library displays can be a vital and stimulating aspect of librarianship. The person responsible for this activity should be extremely energetic and creative. He or she should not only know the value of displays, but also understand every aspect of conceptualization, production, and exhibition of displays. This is not to say that the person will produce every aspect of the displays. However, the old adage, "You can't supervise what you don't know" is often at work when administrators assign staff to display projects without first determining their knowledge of the subject. All too often, media librarians see this at work.

Instructional Design: A Plan For Effective Learning

John W. Ellison

T HE first step in developing a plan for library instruction should be an assessment of learners' needs. This is accomplished by pretesting learners to determine answers to the following important questions: What do learners need to know? What do they already know? What are their problems in learning? Are they ready for the proposed content? After a thorough study of the answers to these questions via a formal needs assessment, development of the plan for instruction can start. (The terms "instruction" and "instructional" are used throughout to mean "managment of learning" rather than "librarian-centered teaching.") Should planning start prior to answering these questions, the librarian's needs may be fulfilled, but learners' needs may go unsatisfied.

CONCEPTUALIZATION

Conceptualization or determination of appropriate instructional strategies is the next step in the design process. Depending on the particular combination of learner needs, course/library content, librarian's teaching or management of learning style, and the learning environment, the librarian should choose the most appropriate instructional method for a given body of knowledge. Individualized learning, seminars, and lectures are but a few of the many options available. Verbal or printed word abstractions and vicarious experiences are the three broad categories of instructional methods. Usually a combination of the three methods are found in effective instruction.

GOALS AND OBJECTIVES

Once the instructional methods have been tentatively determined, the goals and objectives should be written. These terms are often treated synonymously. It is important to have a clear understanding of what each term means. Goals are *what* the librarian wants to accomplish and the objectives are *how* the goals will be accomplished. A presentation *goal* may read: "Students will learn the types of cards found in the card catalog." A learning *objective* that may accompany this goal might be: "Each freshman English student will be able to list all three types of catalog cards (presented in the film *Finding It!*) on the twenty-minute midterm examination." For each presentation goal, there should be at least one learning objective. Each objective should include the *target audience* (freshman English students), *terminal behavior* (three types of catalog cards), *level of proficiency* (know all three types), *conditions* (list, presented in the film, and on the examination), and *time* (midterm and twenty minutes). Objectives can be placed in three major categories: knowledge (cognitive), attitudes (affective), and skills (psychomotor). Using these categories helps the librarian establish some balance in instructional strategies.

Ultimately, the objectives will be used to give direction in an instructional experience and prepare any examinations or otherwise determine that learning occurred. It goes without saying that if the librarian does not clearly understand the objectives they will be of little value in planning and evaluating an instructional program. Learners will also have problems understanding and following unclear objectives in a syllabus or presentation.

FORMATS

Selecting the media formats to be used is the next step in the planning process. Choice of format should be consistent with projected goals and objectives and will also depend on available commercial material on the subject, production personnel, facilities, staff talent, production time, and, finally, available funds. Selection includes the consideration of specific formats such as slides, films, tapes (audio and video) phonorecords, overhead transparencies, filmloops, realia, models, readings, and theatrics. Each medium has a unique function in the learning process. The successful utilization of each format depends on a clear understanding of the strengths and limitations of each medium.

TIMING

Once all material formats have been selected, collected, or produced, it is important to work out the instructional timing. This may be no easy task for the novice presenter. Almost everything depends on the time available, importance placed on each objective, and length of time required to adequately cover the content. Many experienced librarians who use only the lecture method have problems effectively fitting content together in a given period of time. Imagine the problems when several instructional techniques and media formats are used. Often the problem is lack of clearly identified priorities for the selected objectives.

PRETESTING

It is important to try to pretest the material on a sample of the target audience for whom it is designed. However, time and opportunity will not always permit pretesting a new instructional approach. This makes it even more important to have several approaches available for the same content. Should one method fail, a quick shift to another technique may make the point or clarify the content. Some librarians will ask a group their learning preferences and proceed by lecturing or giving out modules, learning packages, or readings based on the styles identified.

FEEDBACK AND EVALUATION

During instructional sessions, it is essential for the librarian to keep track of successes and failures. The items noted should be dated so that specific improvements can be made for future instructional activities. Continuous self-evaluations and revisions are essential for effective presentations and learning experiences.

Once a given amount of material has been covered, it may be necessary to provide for learner satisfaction feedback (how well something has been taught), and a formal evaluation to determine the learners' level of proficiency (what has been learned). Both activities should occur since it is not possible to determine *successful presentations* or *degree of learning* without knowing both learner satisfaction and level of proficiency.

REFINE

After attitude and proficiency have been assessed, it may be important to refine the content. Usually it is necessary to start with the goals and objectives and review the complete instructional experience item-by-item. Other times it may require a time adjustment, a new approach for one topic, or different sequence of presentation. These adjustments are what eventually makes for continued successful instruction.

Media librarians are excellent instructional resource people. They usually have a sound understanding of instructional design and should be consulted during every step of the planning stage. Since they know both content and effective instructional techniques their knowledge should prove invaluable to successful library instruction.

Effective Library Instruction and the Learning Process

John W. Ellison

Effective library instruction, to a large extent, can only be determined when an extensive amount of learning has taken place. Experts feel learning tends to proceed most effectively and be most permanent when motivation, physical and intellectual ability, meaningful relationships, personality adjustment and social growth and knowledge of results are present. An examination of each will show they are critical in the learning process.

First, learners must be motivated. Two types of motivation are commonly exhibited: intrinsic and extrinsic. Intrinsic motivation occurs when learners have a stake in what is being taught and feel the subject is important. The feeling may be motivated by such things as a career, personal goals, or knowing the immediate benefit of the knowledge being acquired. Extrinsic motivation is usually provided by the librarian. It can be expressed by enthusiasm, a positive attitude toward the subject, or the importance of the content in relation to life in general.

Second, learners must have the proper physical and intellectual ability. Generally, an early activity or quiz will help the librarian identify potential physical and intellectual ability problems. A common misconception is that everyone, once they reach a given age, has nearly the same physical and intellectual ability. Nothing could be more false. Individuals differ significantly in their physical and intellectual ability even though they would seem, by their age, to be similar.

Learners differ in many ways and are seldom uniform even after the most careful homogenous screening. Learners may differ intellectually in mental abilities, verbal frequencies, spatial manipulation, and numerical reasoning.

Third, learners must perceive meaningful relationships. These relationships may relate to either what is being taught, life, or one specific concept in relation to other concepts in the same lesson.

Fourth, learners must have knowledge of results. This simply means the learner needs to know how well and how much progress is being

Originally published in *Catholic Library World* 53 (November 1981) pp. 182-184.

made. This can be expressed in reinforcement statements like, "you're doing fine," or in quizzes unless the content itself reinforces satisfactory progress.

Fifth, learners must experience satisfactory personality adjustment and social growth. Generally, this adjustment and growth will take place when learners see library instruction projects and content related to their reasons for selecting a specific profession, area of study or their future. It is sometimes wise to explain the content in relation to personal adjustment and social growth or assign projects with optional topics so learners can relate the content to career goals or areas of interest.

It is important to keep in mind that the objective of library instruction is learning—not teaching. So often decisions during preparation for library instruction, involving what should be taught, how it should be taught, when it should be taught, are made without much regard for learning. Every decision regarding content, method, and sequence should be made after giving the learning process thorough consideration.

The ultimate goal of effective library instruction is to stimulate life-long learning. The librarian should keep this notion in mind when considering the importance of the learner's attitude toward the subject. A positive library experience for learners goes a long way to reinforce lifelong learning.

The following considerations help improve the quality of learning and, ultimately, library instruction. Content, the librarian's style, the learner's attitude and ability, and the environment are the major factors that generally determine how much is learned. However, several other options need to be considered in relation to these factors.

Two major schools of thought exist regarding the librarian's role in library instruction. One notion follows the traditional model of the librarian standing in front of a group verbally dispensing information. The second school of thought has the librarian as an organizer or manager of learning. This librarian is less concerned with formal "librarian-centered" teaching and more interested in organizing the content and activities around the learner's needs. Learner-centered librarians are observed preparing specific materials for special needs, meeting with individuals and groups, selecting a variety of materials for individuals or special groups and developing activities unique to the individual learner's make-up. This librarian always keeps individual differences in mind when preparing for a presentation or learning activity. However, this librarian is usually in the minority of those specifically providing library instruction.

Learning theorists and researchers generally agree that using several techniques, thus providing a variety of learning experiences, based on the content, librarian's preferred presentation style, learner's preferred cognitive style, and the learning environment, produces the greatest amount of learning. Combinations of appropriate lectures, media activities, interactive sessions, practical experiences, individualized instruction, and so on for each topic seems to be most productive for learners. It also helps to have several approaches handy, depending on the response of a group or individual to an approach or topic. Learners must decide the process through which they best learn. The librarian should provide the instructional options. Here are forty instructional approaches from which to select:

Critical incident film	Study trip
Role-playing	Telelecture
Multimedia presentation	Television
Audio tape	Cartoon
Dramatized experience	Game
Vicarious experience	Audience reaction team
Self-instruction	Brainstorming
Simulation	Buzz session
Single-concept film	Case study
Sociodrama	Interview
Reading	Lecture
Discussion	Listening team
Conversation with librarian	Question period
Observation	Module
Demonstration	Skit
Guest lecture	Forum
Writing activity	Workshop
Library episode	Directed individual study
Self-evaluation	Practicum
Confrontation session	Media instruction

It is extremely important to discover your own presentation style. Seldom can we successfully model after other instructors or librarians. Content, personality, type of learners, and subject knowledge of the presenter are only four factors that make it difficult to copy another teaching style. It is usually not possible for every librarian to do equally well in seminar, lecture, or interactive teaching situations. The most important criterion, other than those discussed above, is to relax and be comfortable in the style you select.

If possible, it is a good idea to arrange the content in a flexible manner so that you can take advantage of "the teachable moment." This moment may come from a question, news item, or an experience everyone in the group can share. Some teachable moments can be contrived by the librarian.

Positive reinforcement is generally a very effective approach to bringing out the best in learners. Comments like, "You're on the right track," or "This has been a good group," provide the kind of continuous encouragement that stimulates quality work. The most positive benefits from this approach are derived when reinforcement is used early in the library instruction.

The librarian's knowledge of the subject does not guarantee learning will take place. A combination of subject knowledge, patience, and the ability to creatively present or organize learning alternatives to meet the learner's cognitive style goes a long way to increase learning.

The notion that mere exposure guarantees learning should be rejected. Some librarians feel their responsibility is to cover the material. This is often done without regard for the learner's cognitive style. This type of presentation is characterized by rigid schedules with little interaction between the librarian and the learners.

Improving the communication clarity of library instruction presentations is one way to increase learner achievement. Both the speaking voice and sequencing of content will help improve clarity. Subject matter and language are important functions of clarity.

Learners should be taught to share in the communication process. This may mean taking a few minutes at the beginning of the first library instruction to discuss a basic communication model, the role of learners in communication process and the importance of quality listening. The communication model selected should directly reflect the librarian's instructional methods.

Don't underestimate the learner's ability. Some test and observations reveal meaningless or at best questionable results. Usually combinations of several evaluation techniques and observations are required before a valid judgment can be made. Achievement in library instruction is more likely to be accurately measured when teaching and testing styles are related. That is to say, sessions that rely on a combination of lecture, note-taking, and reading will usually show high learner achievement on paper-pencil tests while laboratory (practical) sessions will usually show high achievement on practical tests. In summary, test like you present or organize the content.

A few institutions require formal evaluations. Some librarians are not happy with the tabulated results and find few helpful suggestions in the written comments. Should this be the case, develop your own short daily evaluation which rates clarity, content, presentation, and interest and leaves space for learners' comments. A 3 × 5 card format is usually sufficient. Guarantee anonymity by having one volunteer collect the evaluations, do the tabulations, and rewrite the comments each day for your perusal. Using this technique may provide valuable information not found in the traditional end of the term evaluations.

Self- and peer evaluations should also be considered as ways of improving and determining effective library instruction. Use of audio-tape or videotape recorders will help in the self-evaluation process while objective colleagues are essential in the peer evaluation process.

Never put off preparing for the next session or class until just before the starting date. It is wise to prepare for the next lesson immediately after the current session or no later than the end of the term. Presentation techniques and changes in content are usually fresh in your mind at these times.

Librarians should place themselves in the position of the learners at least once each semester. This is accomplished by attending courses, open lectures, seminars, conferences, and workshops. Study the presentation styles and note those you wish to try. Observing and critiquing others are excellent ways to learn effective presentation methods.

Finally, good library instruction is hard work. Those who make it look easy are usually not "naturals," but librarians who have worked at it.

Some may ask what library instruction has to do with media librarianship. It can be said that they go hand in hand, since the former usually cannot reach its full potential without the latter. Outstanding library instruction requires a support system and staff that understands what is required in the preparation of quality learning/presentations in addition to having the ability to apply the relevant suggestions noted above. Media librarians see learning and enrichment as major responsibilities in their daily activities as professionals.

Copyright Considerations in the Duplication, Performance, and Transmission of Television Programs in Educational Institutions

Jerome K. Miller

In the last twenty years, public schools and other educational institutions have purchased millions of dollars worth of television equipment for instructional use. Although this equipment is useful for teaching, the ease with which it can be used to duplicate copyrighted materials is a source of considerable controversy. The Copyright Revision Act of 1976 and its accompanying congressional reports offer some clarifications about the rights held by the copyright proprietor and the rights enjoyed by educators as they pertain to videorecordings.[1] Additional clarification appears in the recently issued guidelines for educational uses of television programs videotaped off the air.[2] Further clarifications (or contradictions) may be available through two recent court cases, the Betamax case and the BOCES case.[3] The information gleaned from these sources does not answer every question posed by educators, but they do provide reasonably clear answers for resolving the apparent conflict between the owner's rights and the educator's rights. These rights will be examined separately and then they will be applied to several examples.

THE OWNER'S RIGHTS

Live and prerecorded television programs are classified as performance materials and, as such, are given special protection by the copyright act.[4] Under these conditions proprietors enjoy a number of interrelated but divisible rights, called "the bundle of rights." These rights include: the right to duplicate the material in additional copies, the right to transmit the performance by means of the public airwaves or by cable, or a combination thereof. The owner also has the right to record the program in another medium or to develop derivative works from it. The proprietor also has the right to control public performances of the program. Finally, the proprietor has the right to control the distribution of copies of the work through rental, lease, lending, or sale. This "bundle of rights" may be transferred in its entirety, although the rights are usually sold, leased, or assigned separately or in pairs so that one right can be granted without affecting the other rights. Because of their complexity, each of these rights must be examined in greater detail.

Duplication Rights

Section 106 gives the owner of the work the exclusive right to "reproduce the copyrighted work . . . ."[5] The House Report comments on this point, that the owner has

> The right to produce a material object in which the work is duplicated, transcribed, imitated, or simulated in a fixed form from which it can be "perceived, reproduced, or otherwise communicated, either directly or with the aid of a machine or device." As under the present law, a copyrighted work would be infringed by reproducing it in whole or in any substantial part, and by duplicating it exactly or by simulation. Wide departures or variations from the copyrighted work would still be an infringement as long as the author's "expression" rather than merely the author's "ideas" are taken.[6]

The House Report goes on to comment that displaying an image on a screen is not a reproduction, as that term is understood in copyright law.[7]

Transmission Rights

Transmission rights include public transmissions by commercial and public television stations. Secondary transmissions include transmissions by cable television firms, hotel and apartment cable antenna systems which are independent of larger cable television systems, and a range of educational transmissions within and between educational institutions.[8] Many of these transmissions are regulated by the copyright owner and the Federal Communications Commission. The several transmission rights and retransmission rights provided for educational institutions are discussed separately.

Derivative Works

The copyright owner has an exclusive right to prepare derivative works from an earlier copyrighted work and this right is almost entirely immune from any educational exemption.[9] A derivative work is defined by the copyright law as

A work based upon one or more preexisting works, such as a translation, musical arrangement, dramatization, fictionalization, motion picture version, sound recording, art reproduction, abridgement, condensation, or any other form in which a work may be recast, transformed, or adapted. A work consisting of editorial revisions, annotations, elaborations, or other modifications which, as a whole, represent an original work of authorship, is a "derivative work."[10]

The House Reports adds that a derivative work is not an infringement unless it incorporates "a portion of the copyrighted work in some form; for example, a detailed commentary on a work or a programmatic musical composition inspired by a novel would not normally constitute infringements under this clause."[11] Under these conditions, we might assume that a television program that comments on and describes a literary or artistic work would not be a derivative work unless a portion of the original copyrighted work was included in the new television program.

Performances

The new copyright act makes changes in the definition of performances and in the control the copyright owner has over them. Under the 1909 act, proprietors could only regulate public performances for profit.[12] This enabled almost all performances by non-profit agencies to escape regulation or royalty payments. Under the new act, the copyright proprietor may regulate any public performance of a work.

To perform or display a work "publicly" means—
  (1) to perform or display it at a place open to the public or at any place where a substantial number of persons outside of a normal circle of a family and social acquaintances is gathered; or
  (2) to transmit or otherwise communicate a performance or display of the work to a place specified by clause (1) or to the public, by means of any device or process, whether the members of the public capable of receiving the performance or display receives in the same place or in a separate place at the same time or at different times.[13]

The House Report comments:

> To "perform" a work, under the definition in Section 101 [quoted above], includes reading a literary work aloud, singing or playing music, dancing a ballet or other choreographic work, and acting out a dramatic work or pantomime. A performance may be accomplished "either directly or by means of any device or process," including all kinds of equipment for reproducing or amplifying sounds or visual images, any sort of transmitting apparatus, any type of electronic retrieval system, and any other techniques and systems not yet in use or even invented.[14]

Some exemptions of this almost complete control over public performances are available through educational exemptions. The exemptions are narrowly circumscribed to avoid injuring the copyright owner's rights to regulate public performances.

Distribution Rights

This is sometimes known as "the right of first sale." Under this right, the owner may strictly control any distribution of a work until the product is sold or generally enters the market place. Having once sold a copy, the owner may no longer control the subsequent resale of the product.[15] To circumvent this loss of control, the owners of commercial film properties make it a policy never to sell a copy, but to distribute the product through rental, lease, or loan. Educational institutions that "buy" films and television programs frequently buy a "life of the print" or a "life of the tape" lease. Information about this practice is usually found in the fine print in the front of distributor's catalogs and in the fine print on invoices and packing slips.

EDUCATOR'S RIGHTS

Educators have seven clearly identified rights in the duplication of television programs which abridge the owner's rights, identified above. These rights include copying public domain programs, fair use copying, copying under a license, copying television news programs, copying by students as a learning exercise, copying programs to be captioned for the use of the deaf, and performing (showing) copies in classrooms and other places used in instruction. Some of these rights are conveyed by the copyright act and by the fair use of guidelines, while others are provided through agreements with the copyright holders. Each of these rights must be considered separately.

Copying Public Domain Programs

There are two types of public domain programs. Most programs that fall into this program are older works for which the copyright has expired. Under the 1909 act, the copyright in a work expired at the end of the twenty-eighth year, unless the registration was renewed during that twenty-eighth year.[16] Very little videotape existed twenty-eight years ago, but many educational and entertainment programs existed at that time on film. The copyright proprietors are vigilant about renewing the registration on their works, so most copyrighted films and television programs now enjoy seventy-five years of protection, beginning with the year of creation or publication.[17] If the copyright proprietor fails to renew the copyright during the twenty-eighth year, the copyright in the work expires at the end of the twenty-eighth year and the work enters the public domain. Although a given work has entered the public domain, the copyright proprietor may not have lost all of the means of protecting a work. Many films and television programs are based on older copyrighted works. If the copyright in the underlying work (e.g., a book or a song) is still in force, the copyright proprietor continues to exercise considerable control over the derivative work.[18] Some film and video companies distribute lists of films which have entered the public domain. These are films in which the copyright registration was not renewed in the twenty-eighth year. These lists must be used cautiously, since the compilers may not have checked to see if the underlying work was protected.

Works of the federal government also are in the public domain and they may be copied freely.[19] These programs include: televised addresses by the president, televised congressional hearings, and certain instructional or informational programs produced by government agencies. Few films or television programs exist in the later category, since most government agencies employ commercial producers to produce these materials. Contrary to popular belief, films and television programs produced under contract from the federal government can and do enjoy full copyright protection.[20] Several suggestions have been made for reducing or eliminating copyright protection for these programs, but this suggestion has not been incorporated in a congressional bill. Until Section 105 of the Copyright Act is amended, films and television programs produced under federal contracts should not be treated as public domain materials. When a public domain program has been identified, one may copy the program off the air or from another copy. The copy may be reproduced, sold, and edited, as long as the message is not distorted. Copies of public domain programs may be retained and used indefinitely.

Fair Use Copying

In practice, fair use copying falls into two categories: copying programs in their entirety off the air, and copying parts of copyrighted programs for the purpose of including the excerpt in a locally-produced program. Educators have been videotaping television programs off the air for the past twenty years as a form of fair use. Since the fair use criteria for videotaping off the air were not available until recently, nearly every media specialist had an interpretation of fair use copying of television programs. In a few instances, media specialists refused to videotape any programs off the air, while others videotaped every program that had any conceivable value, retained the tapes indefinitely, and duplicated when necessary. Now that the fair use guidelines are available, some may liberalize their policies, while many others should conduct wholesale erasing sessions to bring existing practices into conformity with the new guidelines. The guidelines may be summarized as follows:

1. The guidelines apply to educational uses of broadcast television programs in non-profit educational institutions. This would appear to apply to non-profit private, parochial, and tax-supported educational institutions from the preschool to the university level. It is unclear whether the guidelines apply to educational programs in public libraries, but many librarians will use the document for guidance in copying television programs for use in credit and non-credit instructional programs offered by public libraries. It seems reasonably clear that the guidelines do not apply to taping programs off the air for entertainment purposes (e.g., programs shown during the lunch hour or after school). The guidelines also do not apply to non-broadcast television programs carried by cable television networks (e.g., ESPN, C-Span, Home Box Office, and other programs available only from a cable television service or a satellite).
2. All copies made under this guideline must be made at the specific request of a teacher. The document does not authorize the common practice of copying a wide variety of programs with the expectation that they may be useful.
3. A teacher may not have a program copied more than once.
4. The copies may be retained for forty-five days for purposes of evaluation. This will allow schools time to purchase copies of the program or to obtain a license for its continued retention and use.
5. The copies may be used for instructional purposes for ten consecutive "school days." School days are defined as "school session days—not counting weekends, holidays, vacations, examination periods, or other scheduled interruptions—within the forty-five calendar day retention period." One may assume that the ten consecutive school days do not include days when schools are closed due to storms, teacher strikes, or other events which force the closing of the schools.
6. Tapes made under these guidelines may be duplicated for use by other teachers so long as the other criteria are met.

7. A teacher may show a program to several classes, if that is appropriate, and a program may be shown to a given class twice, the second time for reinforcement.
8. All copies made under these guidelines must include the copyright notice that appeared in the program.
9. A teacher may show all or part of a program to a class, but the program may not be edited or combined with other programs. This should not be interpreted so literally as to prevent a school from recording two programs on one tape, so long as they are not merged to create a single program.

Although these guidelines do not satisfy all of the users' requirements, they appear to be a reasonable compromise between the interests of users and proprietors. When a program needs to retained for a longer period of time (e.g., for the following semester), it may be possible to obtain a license for its retention from the Television Licensing Center or another source. If a television program is needed for a later semester, it frequently can be rented from a university film rental library or from other film or television rental or loan sources.

Copies Made or Retained Under a Distributor's License

Educators in Utah, Colorado, Washington, and elsewhere have attempted to establish television licensing agreements that would enable them to make video copies of films or to videotape off the air for educational purposes.[21] Few have been very successful. The first real success appeared with the opening of a commercial enterprise, the Television Licensing Center, in 1980.[22] The licensing center offers short-term and long-term licenses to duplicate and retain copies of network television programs. The licensing fees charged by the center appear to be reasonable and the licensing agreements are fairly simply to execute. In addition, some state agencies and educational broadcasters have executed state-wide or area-wide licenses to duplicate educational programs produced by Coast Community College, Great Plains Educational Network, and other educational agencies. Educators who wish to duplicate these programs should contact the educational program coordinator or the permissions officers at their local educational station to see which programs are cleared for long-term use by schools. Obviously these licensing agreements do not cover all the programs educators want to copy and retain, especially network television programs which are not cleared through the Television Licensing Center. Educators who wish to obtain licenses for the retention of these programs must negotiate individually with the copyright holder. The copyright holder is usually the producer, not the network. Unfortunately, the process of obtaining permission from producers is tedious, and the success rate is rather low.[23]

News Programs Authorized Under Section 108(f)(3)

Libraries and archives that are open to the public and meet the other requirements in Section 108(a) may videotape television news programs off the air.[24] Copies made under this provision are restricted to a "limited distribution to scholars and researchers for use in research purposes."[25] Copies made under these conditions and research purposes may be retained indefinitely, reproduced in a limited number of copies, and distributed by lending to individuals in institutions. It is clear from the congressional documents that this provision does not authorize copying for classroom use, but to provide scholarly access to these resources. It would be difficult for an elementary or secondary school library to justify copying under these provisions as they are more appropriate to university libraries with a major commitment to supporting research. Schools that wish to copy television news programs for formal instruction use may be able to justify that action under the fair use guidelines mentioned above. Schools that wish to duplicate the evening news programs for entertainment or out of class enrichment (e.g., for lunch hour showings) must obtain a license for that purpose from the television network. The McNeil-Lehrer Report, an evening news program shown on most public television stations, is licensed for school use through the Television Licensing Center.

Duplicating television programs for school use usually involves copying programs off the air for class use, but other forms of copying are occasionally employed, including incorporating parts of films and television programs in locally produced instructional programs. A small amount of this copying may be justified under the basic fair use criteria:

1. the purpose and character of the use, including whether such use is of a commercial nature or is for non-profit educational purposes;
2. the nature of the copyrighted work;
3. the amount and substantiality of the portion used in relation to the copyrighted work; and
4. the effect of the use upon the potential market for or value of the copyrighted work.[26]

The four criteria and their application to the publication of performance materials for educational purposes have been reviewed frequently, so the information need not be reviewed again here.[27] Two important points must be reaffirmed, though. Film and television materials are performance materials that are closely protected under the second criterion. Furthermore, the third criterion contains two points (amount and substantiality) which must be considered separately in applying the fair use criteria. A thirty-second segment of a film or television program which represents a substantial part of the work cannot be copied as a form of fair use, even though it represents a small part of the overall program.

Copying by Students as a Learning Exercise

The congressional reports suggest that it is a fair use for a student to copy a copyrighted work as a learning exercise, so long as the copy is erased or destroyed promptly.[28] This would seem to legitimate the duplication and editing of television programs by students in audiovisual or broadcasting classes. This provision may be applicable to copying and editing by students as part of an assigned exercise or as an examination. It should not be viewed as a loophole for copying materials for class showings which are not authorized by the copyright act or the fair use guidelines. Although the congressional reports suggest that copies should be destroyed or erased promptly, this probably should not be interpreted so rigidly as to prevent students from retaining a sample copy of edited videotapes for use in employment application files.[29]

Copies Made for Use as Captioned Programs for the Deaf

The House of Representatives Subcommittee on the Courts, Civil Liberties, and the Administration of Justice made a last-minute addition to the congressional comments on the fair use section and their application to educational institutions. This last-minute addendum appears in Representative Robert Kastenmeier's remarks from the floor of the House on the day the Copyright Revision Act was passed by the House of Representatives:

Also in consultation with Section 107, the committee's attention has been directed to the unique educational needs and problems of approximately 50,000 deaf and hearing-impaired students in the United States, and the inadequacy of both public and commercial television to serve their educational needs. It has been suggested that, as long as clear-cut constraints are imposed and enforced, the doctrine of fair use is broad enough to permit the making of an off-the-air fixation of a television program within a non-profit educational institution for the deaf and hearing-impaired, the reproduction of a master and a work copy of a captioned version of the original fixation, and the performance of the program from the work copy within the confines of the institution. In identifying the constraints that would have to be imposed within an institution in order for these activities to be considered as fair use, it has been suggested that the purpose of the use would have to be non-commercial in every respect, and educational in the sense that it serves as part of a deaf or hearing-impaired student's learning environment within the institution, and that the institution would have to insure that the master and work copy would remain in the hands of a limited number of authorized personnel within the institution, would be responsible for assuring against its unauthorized reproduction or distribution, or its performance or retention for other than educational purposes within the institution. Work copies of captioned programs could be shared among institutions for the deaf abiding by the constraints specified. Assuming that these constraints are both imposed and enforced, and that no other factors intervene to render the use unfair, the committee believes that the activities described could reasonably be considered fair use under section 107.[30]

These provisions give schools for the deaf considerable freedom in selecting and copying almost any television program for educational use so long as the copies are captioned for the deaf and restricted to use in schools for the deaf. Congressman Kastenmeier's statement was carefully crafted to deny this exemption to schools having a few deaf or hearing-impaired children who are mingled with children of average hearing ability under mainstreaming programs.

Educational Performances and Transmissions

Television programs duplicated under the above educational exemptions may be transmitted to classrooms and shown (performed) in classrooms under the following conditions:

1. "The performance ... is a regular part of ... systematic instructional activities of a ... non-profit educational institution."[31]
2. The program is shown by "instructors or pupils in the course of face-to-face teaching activities."[32]
3. The performance must take place "in a classroom or similar place devoted to instruction."[33]
4. Some programs may be transmitted to classrooms and laboratories in other buildings of a campus or cluster of buildings.[34]
5. Some programs may be transmitted to students who are ill or who are otherwise prevented from attending regular classroom instruction.[35]

These five exemptions for educational performances and transmissions meet most requests a teacher is likely to place on a delivery system. The first condition specifies that the program must be used for systematic instructional purposes in a non-profit educational institution. This would exclude showing television programs during the lunch hour or after school as a part of extracurricular or informal educational activities. The second condition indicates the programs can be shown by pupils or teachers in face-to-face teaching activities. The third point indicates that television programs may be shown in classrooms or other places "devoted to instruction." These other locations would include laboratories, auditoriums, gymnasiums, and the like.

The fourth point is controversial. Section 110 contains a clause that can be misinterpreted to authorize transmissions of films and television programs within a school building and from building to building. Because of the ease with which it is misunderstood, it must be examined carefully. The clause reads:

> Notwithstanding the provisions of section 106, the following are not infringements of copyright:
>
> . . .
>
> (2) performance of a nondramatic literary or musical work . . . by or in the course of transmission, if—
>
> . . .
>
> > (C) the transmission is made primarily for—
> >
> > > (i) reception in classrooms or similar places normally devoted to instruction . . . .[36]

It is obvious from this that dramatic works cannot be transmitted under this clause without a license (and many films and television programs are dramatic works), but one might assume non-dramatic works could be transmitted under this clause. The confusion arises over the word "literary." The term is defined in Section 101: " 'Literary works' are works, other than audiovisual works, expressed in words, numbers . . . ."[37] With the application of this definition, it appears that this clause only authorizes open- and closed-circuit transmissions of non-dramatic materials other than audiovisual works.

Two potential exemptions have been identified. The first appears in two vague comments in the House Report pertaining to face-to-face teaching:

> The concept does not require that the teacher and students be able to see each other, although it does require their simultaneous presence in the same general area.

and:

> However, as long as the instructor and the pupils are in the same building or general area, the face-to-face teaching exemption would extend to the use of devices for amplifying or reproducing sound and for projecting visual images.[38]

This has been interpreted to suggest that closed-circuit transmissions within a building or within a campus are acceptable applications of the face-to-face teaching exemption. This interpretation is supported by a statement in the "Guidelines for Off-Air Recording of Broadcast Programming for Educational Purposes": "off-air recordings may be used . . . within a single building, cluster, or campus . . . ."[39] Inasmuch as "used" is not defined, it can be defined in at least two ways—carrying the tape from place to place within a building, cluster, or campus, or transmitting the program from place to place within a building, cluster, or campus. Several informed observers indicate that this permits closed-circuit transmissions within a building, cluster, or campus. However, because of the vagueness of the word "used," closed-circuit transmissions could be protested by a copyright proprietor who wishes to recover lost income from the sale of transmission licenses.

The fifth condition pertains to transmitting programs to pupils who are unable to attend school due to illness, disability, or other reasons. Sections 110 (2) authorizes transmissions of non-dramatic works to home-bound pupils under the following terms: The transmission must be a regular part of systematic instructional activities; directly related and of material asssistance to the lesson; and accessible primarily to home-bound students.[40] The last point does not rule out transmissions which might be received by others. The House Report indicates these programs, including college courses for credit, may be transmitted by educational broadcasting stations.[41] It further comments that non-profit trans-missions on commercial cable television systems (e.g., on a school or public access channel) is acceptable under the right circumstances.[42]

The "Guidelines for Off-Air Recording of Broadcast Programming for Educational Purposes" authorizes the "use" of both dramatic and non-dramatic off-air recordings "in homes of students receiving formalized home instruction . . . ."[43] This is widely interpreted as authorizing trans-missions to home-bound students, but the vagueness of the language leaves ample room for dissent. In short, the guidelines can be interpreted to go beyond the provisions in Section 110 (2) authorizing transmissions of non-dramatic works to home-bound students. Inasmuch as this interpretation is tenuous, educators should exercise caution in trans-mitting dramatic works copied off the air to home-bound students. The degree of caution may be based on the number of people who could receive the program. A direct-wired transmission to a few home-bound students may be reasonably safe under the vague terms of the guidelines, but transmissions over an educational broadcasting station might not be prudent, since the copyright proprietor could readily substantiate a claim that this deprived the firm of income from the sale of a broadcast license.

EXAMPLES

At this point it may be useful to illustrate these points with several examples:

Example 1: The students in a university television production course copied a number of television programs off the air and edited them to produce a new program, with new music and sound effects inserted where appropriate. The finished programs were shown in class to be critiqued by the instructor and the students. Grades were assigned for the work. Some of the tapes were erased immediately, but others were retained for reuse by students. At the end of the semester each student was allowed to copy one or two finished programs he or she prepared, to include in his or her employment application file. All of the other first and second generation tapes were erased.

Comment: Brief passages in the House and Senate reports, especially the Senate report, suggest that copying by students as a learning exercise is a fair use.[44] In this instance, the students copied a substantial amount of material they needed to create new television programs. The point here is not the amount of copying but the purpose for the copying—to provide the raw material the students needed to complete assigned exercises. So long as the instructor determined that all of the materials were erased at the end of the semester and that none of the copies were diverted for other uses, this was probably a fair use. The practice of allowing students to copy one or two programs they created to show to prospective employers is reasonably safe, so long as those copies remain the students' personal property.

Example 2: An elementary school teacher asked the media coordinator to videotape a prime-time, dramatic television program for use in her class. The teacher used the program the day after it was broadcast and returned the tape to the media center. Another teacher heard about the program and asked to have it transmitted to her class—via the in-building closed-circuit television system. Other teachers asked to have the tape sent to their classes for class showing. Six teachers eventually showed the program or had it transmitted to their classes. One of the teachers assigned selected pupils to dramatize one of the scenes in the program. The students were sent to the media center the following day to see the scene again to refresh their memories. The students then wrote a script based on the scene they saw on television. The following week, the students presented the scene to their classmates. A discussion followed the presentation. All of the transmissions and showings were completed within ten school days of the original broadcast, but the student performance occurred after the ten-day period.

Comment: Most of these uses of the videotaped copy appear to fall within the "Guidelines for Off-Air Recording of Broadcast Programming for Educational Purposes." The program was videotaped off the air at the specific request of a teacher and that teacher used the program once within ten school days. The other teachers who used the program also completed the showings and transmissions within ten school days of the original broadcast. The closed-circuit transmission of the dramatic program within the building is the disputed point which may or may not fall within the terms of the guidelines. Reshowing one of the scenes to pupils in the media center for reinforcement also fell within the terms of the guidelines, since it was an assigned review showing and because it met the requirement that the programs be shown "in classrooms and similar places devoted to instruction . . . ."[45] If the teachers and the media specialist had difficulty scheduling the single videotape into six classrooms and the media center, additional copies could have been made to facilitate the use of the program within the ten-day period, so long as the classroom use was limited to the first ten school days and all of the copies were erased by the end of the forty-five day period.

The dramatization of one scene by students falls outside the scope of the "Guidelines for Off-Air Recording of Broadcast Programming for Eucational Purposes." However, this practice is authorized under Section 110 (1) of the act which authorizes the "performance or display of a work by instructors or pupils in the course of face-to-face teaching activities of a non-profit educational institution, in a classroom or similar place devoted to instruction . . . ."[46] Under the broad terms of this, teachers and students may perform any copyrighted work in class without restrictions.

Example 3: A school media specialist videotapes all of the presidents' television addresses and places the tapes in the media center's permanent collection. Each presidential address is cataloged, and a full entry appears in the card catalog. Some of the tapes are widely circulated.

Comment: The United States may not claim copyright protection on the works of its employees, including addresses by the president given as a part of his or her duties. Copying these addresses, cataloging them, and placing them in a permanent collection does not violate the law. The media director must be careful, though, about videotaping the network commentaries which follow presidential addresses. These commentaries by reporters and analysts are copyrighted by the networks.

There are three conditions under which these commentaries can be copied and used. First, a teacher may request that the post-address commentary be videotaped for classroom use within ten school days. In this instance, the presidential address could be retained and used indefinitely but the commentary would have to be erased within forty-five days and classroom use would be limited to the first ten school days. The post-address commentaries also can be copied for school use under licenses available from the television networks. The terms of the individual licenses will dictate the period of use and retention. In addition, these post-address commentaries are usually regarded as "on-the-spot coverage of news events . . . " which may be copied under the terms of section 108 (f) (3).[47] As noted earlier, copying under this provision is generally limited to research libraries and the copies are not available for classroom use.

Example 4: Because of financial exigencies, a high school's film rental budget is reduced by two-thirds. This is a handicap to many of the teachers but is particularly burdensome for the instructor of the film study courses. In order to keep his courses operating, the instructor begins videotaping films shown on the public and commercial television networks. In so doing, he is careful to observe the requirements of the "Guidelines for Off-Air Recording of Broadcast Programs for Educational Purposes." He frequently tapes three or four films per week on his home videorecorder for classroom use.

Comment: The fact that the copies are made in the instructor's home on his personal videorecorder does not, of itself, appear to violate the guidelines. So long as the instructor is scrupulous in observing the requirements in the guidelines, it would appear that his actions are a fair use. Unfortunately, this may not be the clear-cut example of fair use one might expect from reading the guidelines. An examination of the correspondence reprinted in the *Congressional Record* indicates that the guidelines were not adopted unanimously. The representatives of nineteen trade and professional associations and the actors' and writers' guilds were appointed to the negotiating team that wrote the guidelines. The representatives of two trade associations, the Motion Picture Association of America, Inc., and the Association of Media Producers, did not ratify the guidelines.[48] This does not suggest that the guidelines are invalid or that they do not apply to films and television programs produced or distributed by the members of those two associations. Firms which do not support the guidelines may attempt to sue or to gain out-of-court settlements with school districts for alleged copyright infringements in videotaping films shown on television.

Although the guidelines were issued as an official document of the House of Representatives Subcommittee on the Courts, Civil Liberties, and the Admininstration of Justice, they do not have the force of the law. If a film producer or distributor sues a school for videotaping films off the air, the complaint will probably center on the fourth fair use criterion: "the effect of the use upon the potential market for or value of the copyrighted work."[49] If the producer or distributor can clearly demonstrate that videotaping a film off the air for school use deprives the firm of income from rentals, leases, or sales, it may make a strong case against the school. The school district and the individual teacher could defend themselves on the grounds that they scrupulously observed the terms of the "Guidelines for Off-Air Taping of Copyrighted Works for Educational Use." This would present a very nice dilemma for the courts to resolve, and it is impossible to predict the outcome of such of case.

Two points can be made here. First, it is unclear whether the guidelines will protect a school district, an administrator, or a teacher from any and all types of copyright infringement suits or from pressure for out-of-court settlements for alleged copyright infringements. Second, teachers and media specialists are less likely to be sued for copyright infringement, or, if sued, they will be in a better position to defend themselves if they observe the guidelines to the letter.

Example 5: A science teacher requests that several installments of the PBS "Nova" series be recorded for classroom use. The teacher shows the programs in her class within ten school days and immediately erases the tape. An industrial arts teacher in the same school requests that each installment of the PBS "This Old House" series shown on PBS be recorded for use in one of his courses. All or part of each program is shown in his classes and erased within ten school days of the broadcast.

Comment: These two instances of copying from the Public Broadcasting Service appear to fall within the terms of the "Guidelines for Off-Air Taping of Copyrighted Works for Educational Use." Questions about the legitimacy of this action arise from the fact that those two series are listed in the "Not Authorized Series" list distributed by the local PBS station. The cover letter from the station's permissions officer indicates that programs on the "do not copy" list may not be copied for school use. This is an obvious contradiction of the more generous terms in the guidelines. Most PBS stations distribute monthly lists of instructional and cultural programming which may or may not be copied by schools for classroom use. These lists are not based on an interpretation of the guidelines, but on the contractual terms under which the station or the network acquired distribution rights.

The fact that PBS or the station could not obtain seven or ten-day convenience copying rights for teachers does not undercut the provisions of the "Guidelines for Off-Air Taping of Copyrighted Works for Educational Use." (The Public Broadcasting Service is a signatory to the guidelines.)[50] On the other hand, PBS stations sometimes distribute lists of programs which may be taped for classroom use and which may be retained and used for periods in excess of the ten- and forty-five-day terms in the guidelines. In such a case, the more generous terms acquired by the station or the network should be used by educators, if the programs have instructional value.

CURRENT LITIGATION

Although the Copyright Revision Act of 1976 and the "Guidelines for Off-Air Recording of Broadcast Programming for Educational Purposes" resolve many questions about the use of television programs in schools, the law is subject to revision by the courts. At the moment, two major cases are under consideration. The BOCES case, in New York, involves copying television programs off the air by an educational service agency. The tapes were retained indefinitely and duplicated in multiple copies for use by teachers.[51] The case was heard in the Federal District Court in 1980, but, at the time of writing, the judge has not announced his decision. The plaintiffs appear to have a strong case, and a victory for the plaintiffs probably won't change much for educators, so long as the educators' actions fall within the terms of copyright act and the guidelines for off-air recording. If the plaintiffs win their case, it will open the door to suits against educators for violations of the terms of the guidelines for off-air recording. If the educators win the case, it is safe to assume that the plaintiffs will file an appeal which will remain in the courts for some time.

There has been considerable publicity recently about the "Betamax case." The Federal District Court upheld the defendant's (Sony's) contention that selling home videorecorders and copying television programs off-the-air at home for personal use is a fair use.[52] The case was overturned by the Federal Appeals Court and Sony is appealing the case to the Supreme Court.[53] If the Supreme Court agrees to hear the case, it will probably be another year before it announces its decision.

The Appeals Court decision sparked numerous articles in the popular press, including editorials calling for legislative action to resolve the dilemma. A recent speech by David Ladd, the Register of Copyrights, delivered before the Appeals Court decision was delivered, called for a legislative resolution to the problem, with an eye toward the impact of future technological developments in home entertainment and information systems on the copyright laws.[54]The first step in the legislative process usually involves committee hearings by the House and Senate Judiciary Committees and the first round of hearings was held in December 1981.

Two questions necessarily arise from this problem. Will legislation regulating home videorecording activities affect the guidelines for off-air recording? Will the legislation affect copying programs on home videorecorders by educators for classroom use under the terms of the guidelines? It would be desirable to have the text of the guidelines incorporated in the amendment, or to at least have the guidelines identified by name and ratified in the amendment. Either of these steps would give the guidelines the force of law, which would be more desirable than their present status as part of the legislative history of the act. Inasmuch as Congress may want to skirt that question and concentrate on home videotaping, it will be important to see that the language of the amendment authorizes (or does not prevent) videotaping programs in the home for classroom use within the terms of the guidelines.

CONCLUSION

The duplication, performance, and transmission of television programs in educational institutions reflects a tradeoff between the interests of copyright proprietors and users. Educators enjoy unlimited rights to display legitimately-made television programs in classrooms. By contrast, most of the rights for duplication of copyrighted materials rest with copyright proprietors. Educators' rights to duplicate copyrighted programs are, with a few exceptions, limited to copying programs off the air for short-term use in the classroom or for evaluation. Transmission rights are divided between the users and the proprietors, with most the rights reserved for the proprietors. This balancing of interests embodied in the Copyright Revision Act and the related documents represents a compromise developed by Congress in an effort to satisfy the conflicting interests of the various parties. In its effort to arrive at a compromise, Congress delayed making decisions in several critical areas to permit further study and further efforts to arrive at a suitable compromise.[55] The "Guidelines for Off-Air Recording of Broadcast Programming for Educational Purposes," which was issued in October 1981, is a product of this extended deliberation. Although the document is unfortunately vague in one critical area, that vagueness is undoubtedly a product of a compromise between the competing interests of the participants.

Although the Copyright Revision Act and the "Guidelines for Off-Air Recording of Broadcast Programming for Educational Purposes" resolve many questions, some problems remain, most notably the problem of obtaining permission to use copies of television programs recorded off the air in classrooms beyond the ten-school-days period prescribed in the guidelines. The creation of the Television Licensing Center in 1980 by Films, Inc., was a major breakthrough by this progressive firm. Although the Television Licensing Center has a growing catalog of programs available for use by schools, some producers continue to withhold programs from the educational licensing market. One can hope that copyright clearinghouses will eventually provide convenient and inexpensive access to all films and television programs. Of course, the effort to expand licensing services will not work if educators fail to respect the proprietors' rights. It is unfortunate that, in spite of the work of the professional associations, many educators continue to "liberate" copyrighted materials "for the good of education," when it is obvious that the short-term benefits from those actions undermine the long-term benefits of obtaining convenient access to more and better programming. The copyright act and the guidelines for off-air copying were designed to provide a balancing of interests between the proprietors and the users. The full implementation of that compromise requires the cooperation of all parties.

APPENDIX

Guidelines for Off-Air Recording of Broadcasts for
Educational Purposes

In March of 1979, Congressman Robert Kastenmeier, Chairman of the House Subcommittee on Courts, Civil Liberties and Administration of

Justice, appointed a Negotiating Committee consisting of representatives of education organizations, copyright proprietors, and creative guilds and unions. The following guidelines reflect the Negotiating Committee's consensus as to the application of "fair use" to the recording, retention, and use of television broadcast programs for educational purposes. They specify periods of retention and use of such off-air recordings in classrooms and similar places devoted to instruction and for home-bound instruction. The purpose of establishing these guidelines is to provide standards for both owners and users of copyrighted television programs.

1. The guidelines were developed to apply only to off-air recording by nonprofit educational institutions.

2. A broadcast program may be recorded off-air simultaneously with broadcast transmission (including simultaneous cable re-transmission) and retained by a non-profit educational institution for a period not to exceed forty-five (45) calendar days after date of recording. Upon conclusion of such retention period, all off-air recordings must be erased or destroyed immediately. "Broadcast programs" are television programs transmitted by television stations for reception by the general public without charge.

3. Off-air recordings may be used once by individual teachers in the course of relevant teaching activities, and repeated once only when instructional reinforcement is necessary, in classrooms and similar places devoted to instruction within a single building, cluster, or campus, as well as in the homes of students receiving formalized home instruction, during the first ten (10) consecutive school days in the forty-five-day retention period. "School days" are school session days—not counting weekends, holidays, vacations, examination periods, or other scheduled interruptions—within the forty-five calendar day retention period.

4. Off-air recordings may be made only at the request of and used by individual teachers, and may not be regularly recorded in anticipation of requests. No broadcast program may be recorded off-air more than once at the request of the same teacher, regardless of the number of times the program may be broadcast.

5. A limited number of copies may be reproduced from each off-air recording to meet the legitimate needs of teachers under these guidelines. Each such additional copy shall be subject to all provisions governing the original recording.

6. After the first ten (10) consecutive school days, off-air recordings may be used up to the end of the forty-five (45) calendar day retention period only for teacher evaluation purposes, i.e., to determine whether or not to include the broadcast program in the teaching curriculum, and may not be used in the recording institution for student exhibition or any other non-evaluation purpose without authorization.

7. Off-air recordings need not be used in their entirety, but the recorded programs may not be altered from their original content. Off-air recordings

may not be physically or electronically combined or merged to constitute teaching anthologies or compilations.

8. All copies of off-air recordings must include the copyright notice on the broadcast program as recorded.
9. Educational institutions are expected to establish appropriate control procedures to maintain the integrity of these guidelines.

References

1. *United States Code*, Title 17 (Washington, D.C.: Government Printing Office, 1976); U.S. Senate, *Report No. 94-473* (Washington, D.C.: Government Printing Office, 1976); U.S. House of Representatives, *Report No. 94-1476* (Washington, D.C.: Government Printing Office, 1976); and U.S. House of Representatives, *Report No. 94-1733* (Washington, D.C.: Government Printing Office, 1976).
2. "Guidelines for Off-Air Taping of Copyrighted Works for Educational Use," *Congressional Record* 127 (October 14, 1981): E4750. (Hereafter cited as "Guidelines for Off-Air Recording.")
3. *Universal City Studios, Inc.* v. *Sony Corporation of America*, 480 F. Supp. 429, overturned by Ninth Circuit Court, *BNA's Patent, Trademark & Copyright Journal*, no. 551 (November 22, 1981), pp. D-1—D-7; and *Learning Corporation of America, Inc. et al.* v. *Crooks et al.*
4. U.S. Senate, *Report No. 94-473*, Sect. 107. (Hereafter cited as: Senate Report.)
5. *United States Code*, Title 17, Section 106 (1).
6. U.S. House of Representatives, *Report No. 94-1476*, Sect. 106. (Hereafter cited as: House Report.)
7. Ibid.
8. *United States Code*, Title 17, Sect. 111 (f).
9. Ibid., Sect. 106 (2).
10. Ibid., Sect. 101.
11. House Report, Sect. 106.
12. *United States Code*, Title 17 (1909 act), Sect. 101 (c-e).
13. *United States Code*, Title 17, Sect. 101.
14. House Report, Sect. 106.
15. *United States Code*, Title 17, Sect. 109 (a).
16. *United States Code*, Title 17 (1909 act), Sect. 24.
17. *United States Code*, Title 17, Sect. 304.
18. *G. Ricordi & Co.* v. *Paramount Pictures, Inc.* 187 F. 2d 469. Cert. denied. 342 U.S. 849.
19. Ibid., Sect. 105.
20. House Report, Sect. 105.
21. Jerome K. Miller, "Licenses to Videotape Film," *Library Trends* 27 (Summer 1978), pp.101-105.

22. The Television Licensing Center is a division of Films, Inc., 1144 Wilmette Ave., Wilmette, IL 60091.

23. Jeanne Mason Douglas, "Seeking Copyright Clearances for an Audiovisual Center," in *Fair Use and Free Inquiry: Copyright Law and the New Media,* ed. John Shelton Lawrence and Bernard Timberg (Norwood, N.J.: Ablex, 1980), pp. 122-126.

24. *United States Code,* Title 17, Sect. 108 (f) (3).

25. House Report, Sect. 108.

26. *United States Code,* Title 17, Sect 107.

27. Jerome K. Miller, *Applying the New Copyright Law: A Guide for Educators and Librarians* (Chicago: American Library Association, 1979), pp.11-61.

28. House Report, Sect. 107.

29. House Report, Sect. 107; and Senate Report, Sect. 107.

30. Robert Kastenmeier, [Remarks], *Congressional Record,* 122 (September 22, 1976): 10874-10875.

31. *United States Code,* Title 17, Sect. 110 (2) (A).

32. Ibid., Sect. 110 (1).

33. Ibid.

34. House Report, Sect. 110; and "Guidelines for Off-Air Recording," Sect 3.

35. *United States Code,* Title 17, Sect. 110 (2) (C) (ii); and "Guidelines for Off-Air Recording," Sect. 3.

36. *United States Code,* Title 17, Sect 110.

37. *United States Code,* Title 17, Sect. 101.

38. House Report, Sect. 110.

39. "Guidelines for Off-Air Recording," Sect. 3.

40. *United States Code,* Title 17, Sect. 110 (2) (A-C).

41. House Report, Sect. 110.

42. Ibid.

43. "Guidelines for Off-Air Recording," Sect. 3.

44. House Report, Sect. 107; and Senate Report, Sect. 107.

45. 'Guidelines for Off-Air Recording," Sect. 3.

46. *United States Code,* Title 17, Sect. 110 (1).

47. U.S. House of Representatives, Report No. 94-1733, Sect. 108.

48. *Congressional Record* 127 (October 14, 1981), p. E4752. Letters from officers of the two organizations indicate the boards of directors of the two organizations did not ratify the guidelines. The letters from Ivan R. Bender and James Bouras identify eight firms that assented to the guidelines.

49. *United States Code,* Title 17, Sect. 107 (4).

50. *Congressional Record* 127 (October 14, 1981), p. E4752.

51. *Learning Corp. of America, et al.* v. *Crooks, et al.*

52. *Universal City Studios, Inc.* v. *Sony Corporation of America,* 480 F. Supp. 429.

53. *BNA's Patent, Trademark, & Copyright Journal,* no. 551 (November 22, 1981), pp. D-1—D-7.

54. David Ladd, "Remarks ... to the Internationale Gesellschaft fur Urh-berrecht (INTERGU)" *BNA's Patent, Trademark, & Copyright Journal,* no. 548 (November 1, 1981), pp. E1-E5.
55. Other topics delayed for further study include performance rights for actors, actresses, and musicians; copyright protection for typefaces; industrial design protection; and copyright protection for computer programs. The first three items are still under study and there is no indication that those questions will be resolved soon. The fourth item, copyright protection for computer programs, was resolved by the 1980 amendment which rewrote Section 117 of the Copyright Act.

REACHING OUT

Media Programming

Don Roberts

MEDIA programming is crucial to the survival of library services in the late 20th century. The obvious reason is that programming gives libraries credibility in an age of mass communications. Our work in this area can be compared to the mass media in both a positive and negative sense, and inevitably we will be compared. We must professionalize our programming as much as possible, learning from the strengths and weaknesses of the "programs" which surround us in our immediate communities and in the "Global Village."

Audiovisual awareness began in the American Library Association around 1914, primarily in audio. It was not until 1924 that serious talk about film service began and programming was considered. The big problem in those days was the highly flammable nature of the 35mm nitrate film stock and the fact that portable projectors did not exist until the 1930s. World War II accelerated the use of 16mm safety stock, making it widely available for purposes of education, propaganda, and entertainment. Some future library directors came back from that war with a degree of audiovisual orientation. There was tendency to say yes to equipment, and a beginning in the design of audiovisual facilities in buildings (projection booths and the like). It was at this time that the first paid staff person for film began work at ALA headquarters. Non-print programming is only about thirty years old—just in its infancy, really—and the picture is still uneven.

Linear programming (carrot-and-stick programming) dominated library service throughout the middle and late 1960s. Projects funded under the Library Services and Construction Act (LSCA) and the needs of community information systems have provided a break through into what I call multilinear programming. The tradition of using film to draw people into the library in order to interest them in a library card, books, and reference services has been scrambled in part by the non-linear response of those who have been drawn in. Audiences have refused, for the most part, to be programmed in that way; they have instead insisted

Originally appeared in *Sightlines*, Winter 1979/80, published by the Educational Film Library Association.

that the initial program be something integral to their needs and their presence in the building. We have been challenged to respond to their needs.

The paradox is that I am often asked to speak about programming by conference or workshop organizers who, either explicitly or implicitly, still want linear programming to work. A children's librarian may want to know how to continue a storyhour with films which will lead the child to the book or to the "summer reading program," etc. Thus, the attitudes which must necessarily accompany the integration of materials into library service and the patron's information needs are sometimes lacking and program expectations are defeated for all concerned.

Multilinear programming takes into account the fact that things run in parallels, that all information modes and formats have integrity, and that today one must be able to work with parallel modes of communication in order to program successfully. For example, it may be important to have a community resource person in the building at the time of a program to give dimension to the information you are trying to share. Or you may want to assess the environment in which the information is presented, choosing perhaps to present the program outside the library building, on the "turf" of the group with whom you are working. Environment and its relationship to program effectiveness has been largely overlooked by library programmers.

Programming can begin in seemingly diverse areas: in building design (especially in interior environment, acoustical and optical space, and wiring of the building); in the preview and selection of software; in the work done by technical services (mediagraphic control, packaging, etc.); in relationships with fellow professionals both inside and outside the library, with other community institutions, organizations, and informal groups, and with other programmers in your area (TV affiliates and cable, film theaters, other educational and informational institutions, church groups).

Some of us will have the good fortune to plan new remodeled buildings, spaces which will really work for late twentieth-century "knowledge transfer." We may get a chance to develop areas both for group programming (meeting rooms, lounges) and for individual programming (carrels, media desks). We may even be able to participate in the design of media vehicles which will extend the possibilities previously realized in modified bookmobiles. If we lack these opportunities, we will have to try our best to improve the existing spaces and vehicles to insure the delivery of the information. Such factors as darkness in the room, good acoustics and sound systems, and a TV antenna or cable hookup to bring television signals into the building should be considered.

If the institutional situation is hopeless, then we must move beyond our buildings and vehicles—and our rationalizations—and into other community spaces, communication channels, whatever, to get the programming done. This is often necessary anyway and sometimes preferable if you have the staff time or volunteers to do it. You may not be able to "wire" to the cable station, so you may have to go there in order to fulfill your programming requirements with them. You may have shut-ins or institutionalized people to whom you must go. This is an important service. But my concern is that you not center an outreach program only around those who are "confined" with us as recipients of programming in which they have no voice, no preferences. The challenge is to offer meaningful programming to those groups and to go beyond them to other, less predictable groups.

Library programming is hampered by inadequate "mediagraphic" access to the materials available. Is selection done with programming in mind? Are the preview forms filled out with the idea that the content of the software will be readily available to both the professional and community person alike? I suggest that the preview form require the subject indexing of an item to reflect the needs of programming; the broad, often meaningless film headings will not do. Ideally, audiovisual entries should be integrated into the library's general catalog.

My feeling is that community programming will be much more successful if the selection of software and the programming are done with other community organizations and individuals. If you have vital interaction with the people you wish to reach all along the line, the chance of active rather than passive use and programming will be much enhanced. My experience is that this generalization holds true for all ages, from young children to senior citizens.

Media advisory work is intricate, many-levelled, and thoroughly multilinear. All of the developers of information and communications theory talk about choosing the most appropriate medium for the message to be communicated. It may be that our penchant for film causes us to set up a program which should not use a film at all. Or we may miss an obvious link with the information to be delivered because we were too close to our own preconceptions of how the particular program might proceed. "Objectivity" is a part of the problem, of course, but even more important is a thorough-going professionalism which can cut through to the bones of what a program can build upon.

New technology is constantly forcing us to reassess what programming will be, what we will need for it, and what our liaisons will have to be to perform successfully. Television/video will undoubtedly be the programming medium in the next two decades. Yet, our investment in earlier hardware and software may make contemporary programming impossible. It is paradoxical that just as we get set up with the technology of an earlier time, we are disrupted by the "future shock" of changing communication patterns. At worst, to borrow a McLuhanism, it is as if we are speeding into the future looking into a rear-view mirror.

Part of the justification for the purchase of expensive software, such as 16mm, must be programming. Thus, in order to prove the cost-effectiveness of film, it must spend a significant part of its life in programming. This is the mass communications aspect mentioned earlier. Undoubtedly, all library materials should be available to individuals and small groups; but for cost-effective use, some software will live or die with effective programming.

The vital literature on library programming is scarce. George Rehrauer's *The Film User's Handbook* (New York: R.R. Bowker, 1975) is very academic but includes many excellent suggestions. *New Media in Public Libraries* (Syracuse, N.Y.: Norton/Gaylord, 1976), by James W. Brown, and *Expanding Media* (Phoenix: Oryx Press, 1977), edited by Deirdre Boyle, are both very useful volumes. Of course, up-to-date examples are best found in the professional journals; *Sightlines, Wilson Library Bulletin, Previews, Library Journal,* and *American Libraries* sometimes provide useful articles and examples. I like *Media & Methods,* a magazine intended for high school educators and media center directors.

PRACTICAL SUGGESTIONS

Try to open a program with music to set a mood. If you cannot pick or choose music, you may just want to tune in to a suitable radio station which may approximate the tastes of the intended audience. Open with a personal welcome (music background?), and then go to a slide with the name of the library and perhaps other information which may be pertinent. Slides can be produced very cheaply at a local media center or camera shop and will professionalize your show. Make sure that you have an extension speaker or are plugged in to a PA system if, for example, the film projector is not adequate for the acoustical space. You can obtain extension speakers very cheaply.

Do not end a program abruptly by turning on the lights to an uneasy silence. Plan for some kind of closure which will provide for continuity and follow-up. Too often we have a graceless finish which makes people wonder what is going on. You can follow with a discussion, solicit suggestions for future programming, serve light refreshments and encourage informal conversation, or play more music. It might be well to do some role-playing to ascertain some options relating to the moods of the groups for which you will program.

Publicity is a vital part of programming and is one of the most difficult parts of it. Often we depend upon library bulletin boards or local newspapers. These are the least effective thing we can use, short of mimeographed announcements, which have the lowest success of all. Better that we work through the grapevine with the groups and individuals with whom we program. Next, we should try to reach the community through the channels where they actually exchange and receive information—radio and television, community bulletin boards, newspapers which feature a community events column, etc .

PROGRAMMING YOU MIGHT TRY

Library Welcome Wagon Single out groups and do a night of media with the community newcomers in mind (e.g., with the Lions Club, Scouts, Garden Club, etc.). This could be done with a "federated" group of community organizations every six months or so.

Family Programming Nuclear, extended, whatever; sometimes in homes is the best. The family can invite friends to extend the range of people involved. Program material of family interest, combining subject matter with entertainment—they may want to mix in some home movies or slides.

Crisis Intervention Watch newspapers, keep track of local television and radio and come right in on a subject of local concern (e.g., bicycle safety, fire prevention, drugs, etc.) Especially valuable is the use of local resource people to give the information immediacy and depth.

Community Information Event Create a multimedia information event which will be a celebration of the concerns of a local group (e.g., ecologists, co-ops). Such an event allows for a vital gathering of information which is often sequestered in the community.

School Assembly Prepared with the drama class, cheerleaders, and a school music group. You can combine your resources with theirs for a very powerful event which will reach the entire school body in a short time.

Seasonal Consideration Anticipate spring with a gardening program. Do less obvious holiday programs to get away from beating the event into the ground. Sports, leisure, and hobbies are a focus which will take the onus of the homework syndrome away from the library and put the library on the fun side of life. Combine with local people who have experience and feeling for recreation and leisure.

The library must be more active in helping individuals and groups in the community actually face and solve problems—it is not enough to send someone to the card catalog or give them a book on a subject. Through imagination, we must help move beyond the confines of their lives, to use their own personal resources and insights to achieve dignity and freedom. We must engage every format and avenue available to us to push the information through; flexibility is the name of the game.

In an age of shrinking budgets and increasing inflation, we are going to have to learn to do more with less. That means that we should learn to move quickly and imaginatively beyond the library's walls for program materials, resources, and allies. These can be employed inside or out, and the sky's the limit on the connections we make between those resources and the people we serve. Multidimensional programming is the product of an integrated system, one which is both people *and* information centered. This programming is based upon the premise that our patrons and resource persons are multidimensional beings, not fixed in a particular format or way of doing things. They are part of the Global Village, living in a particular locale, but a part of a complex universe. Thus, we can address a linear need or a multilinear one, and we can work with a group or an individual, in our place or theirs.

Programs and Activities for Media Librarians

John W. Ellison

Non-print collections should be more than stagnant rows of tapes, films, slides, realia, and holograms waiting to be discovered. Media librarians have a responsibility to develop inspiring programs and meaningful activities which will help inform users of the potential value of these untapped resources. Such efforts are particularly important in library situations where non-print collections are developing or where the non-print materials have been warehoused without adequate exposure.

Creative non-print programming starts with identifying library community needs. From there, the media librarian must develop a potential user-oriented collection based on this *need, material content* and *appropriate level*. Finally, the imagination must be fluid and free to explore the many ways non-print materials can be properly used to expose the potential library community to their availability and value.

The ideas expressed in this chapter come from a wide variety of sources and individuals. This collection of programs and activities provides media librarians with a source of ideas which they can develop, modify or reject according to their needs and philosophy. Detailed descriptions and citations were eliminated so more space could be used for ideas. No attempt was made to determine the merits or success of each program or activity. However, each idea has user appeal.

- Create an archival repository of our music heritage in 78 rpm and 33 rpm discs. Use local talents to stock a vast collection of music and fine arts. (Boston Public Library)
- In an academic or school library, develop a rock collection in cooperation with the geology department. Buy materials or use rocks collected on geology field trips.
- Sponsor art exhibits of local artists; advertise so they know the library is looking for local talent. (Toronto Public Libraries)
- Plan a travelling display of the art collection on an artmobile. Visits shopping plazas, senior citizen homes, and schools. (Eugene, Ore.)
- Plan an art workshop to introduce participants to art through original works, reproductions, and slides. A guest artist would be an excellent resources person. (South Brunswick Public Library, South Brunswick, N.Y.)

- Swap prints, sculpture, and other works with other libraries. In this way, new works are introduced at a minimum of expense. (Hudson Public Library, Hudson, Mass.)
- Specialize by concentrating in a certain subject area. Other libraries could concentrate in different areas.
- Plan workshops and courses in drawing and painting, macrame, kite-making, photography, and radio production. Charge a nominal fee to cover costs. (Toronto Public Libraries)
- Have children create a life map—drawing important events in their lives on a long piece of butcher paper rolled in a scroll. (Kean College, Union, N.J.)
- Get a button-making machine and make buttons. Using Polaroid photographs, make ID buttons, writing each person's name on the photo.
- Plan a photocopy-art program for young people. Great graphic effects can be achieved using black and white and color prints and three-dimensional objects as well.
- Provide a variety of music programs for children. Include a selection of classical music suitable for children. (John F. Kennedy Library, Solano County System, Calif.)
- Have young people tape oral history interviews with senior citizens in the community for the library collection. Plan an oral history fair and serve food prepared from recipes of the period. (Orange Public Library, Orange, N.J.)
- Have a contest for youngsters with a prize for the best original broadcast on tape. (Center for Understanding Media, New York)
- Using cassette tapes of children's stories, offer a Dial-a-Story programs for kids who call a special number. Change the story every week. (Fondulac District Library, East Peoria, Ill.)
- Install an induction coil loop system to allow listeners with headsets to move freely about the library without becoming entangled in wires.
- Make income tax information available on cassettes, and mail them free of charge to the visually handicapped. (Wayne County Library for the Blind and Visually Handicapped, Wayne County, Mich.)
- Wallpaper the restroom with photo prints or copies or with library/community snapshots. (Any room or wall space will do.)
- Have volunteers prepare audiotapes of stories, novels, newspaper stories, etc., and make them available to rest homes, hospitals, senior citizens' homes, and shut-ins. (Wolfboro Brewster Library, Wolfboro, N.H.)
- For people too busy or tired to read, loan popular books on ninety-minute cassette tapes. (Mayne Williams Library, Johnson City, Tenn.)
- Attach photographs to unused cards in the card catalog at random. This will make the catalog interesting, give an idea of what types of pictures are available in the books, and to encourage browsing of the card catalog.
- Collect pictures, posters, and large photographic prints from campaign headquarters during elections. Provide a display with these items. Provide the library as a forum. If a speaker cannot show up in person, provide a taped conversation with the candidate concerning questions of interest to the people. Provide an ongoing display, presenting *all* sides, with accurate visual feedback so that people at least know the faces of those running for office.

- Ask ad agencies, travel agencies, newspapers, and local stores for any photographs that might be usable for library display or use in the collection.
- Display maps (laminated, matted, or framed) as art prints to make users aware of the map collection.
- Plan a program for children. Have them collect magazine pictures depicting a special topic, make copy slides and an audiotape and have a special happening. (Kansas City, Missouri, School District)
- Have a giant "talking kangaroo" in the children's room. An audiotape starts when a child steps on a mat in front of the animal and the children can then enjoy listening to a story. (Mead Public Library, Sheboygan, Wisc.)
- If you are short of space and have very high ceilings, consider building a listening or viewing loft.
- Make a large plastic bubble which can hold up to sixteen students inside. Films can be projected on the outside of the bubble. (Knoxville/Knox Co., Knoxville, Tenn.)
- Tell young people "Rumor-Has-It" stories that have to be proved or disproved. For example, Abe Lincoln grew a beard from the suggestion of a little girl. (New Haven Public School, New Haven, Conn.)
- Have a holographic art display in your library.
- Take pictures of the library staff and display them prominently so staff members can be easily identified. (Milford Public Library, Milford, Conn.)
- Display a community calendar at the library.
- Offer licenses to kids and adults who have learned how to use library projectors and other hardware. Have workshops or programmed kits to teach them. (Fitchburg Public Library, Fitchburg, Mass.)
- Develop a course for freshmen on library orientation using a wide range of media resources. (Manchester High School Library, North Manchester, Ind.)
- Reach out to the community with TV and radio spots, in whatever languages are appropriate in your community. Publish "tell us what you want" coupons in local newspapers so the community can have input into materials selection. (Orange County Public Library, Orange County, Calif.)
- Sponsor a critic's club which meets to discuss and evaluate films, records, tapes, and books in the collection.
- Circulate materials and portable equipment from the media center by delivery van for home shut-in use.
- See if you can have library ads at your local drive-in or movie theater.
- Take tables, chairs, and a slide program onto street corners to show the public their library. (New York Public Library)
- Have a whistle-stop library van tour rural areas with films, folk singers, and any other mobile media. (South Central Kansas Library System)
- Use any kind of open board (poster board, bulletin board) to answer suggestions received in a suggestion box. It keeps the library honest and helps to stimulate constructive criticism. It also shows that someone cares about improving service.
- Use a bulletin board for buying, selling, or otherwise exchanging information and services for library users. (University of Toledo, Toledo, Ohio)
- Invite your local camera club to prepare a display of their photographs.

- In a storefront library, use a rear screen and a filmloop projector to create an interesting attraction for the passerby.
- Take pictures of library users. Display them in a collage or on a kiosk. (Richmond Public Library, Richmond, Calif.)
- Have old-time photography displayed and be sure to invite the old timers. Serve tea and cookies. (Memorial Library of Radnor Township, Wayne, Pa.)
- Ask people to bring in any old photographs they might have so that you can make copies for the library collection. Be sure to return the originals to them safely. (Willowbrook High School, Villa Park, Ill.)
- Get in touch with the public relations manager of business and trade organizations and companies. Most large companies and trade organizations are happy to provide, free or on loan, pictures of operations and products.
- Collect postcards for the picture file. Ask traveling staff members to drop a postcard in the mail or to bring a few back from their holidays.
- Have a cartoon caption contest. Post a captionless cartoon and ask for captions. Have a panel of judges choose the best caption and award a prize.
- Hang posters in employment offices advertising job hunting information that is available at the library—for free, too. Many people are unaware of the directories that provide information on businesses as well as advice on writing a resume and handling a job interview.
- Develop a circulating poster collection. If you can, get an old art print rack from a bookstore for display. Many posters can be obtained free of charge. (Dupage Public Library, Dupage, Ill.)
- Develop a library broadcast service broadcasting information of public interest and music from the library collection. (Nashville Public Library)
- Prepare tapes of interesting tidbits of information such as historical minutes to be broadcast on your local radio station. (Rockaway Meadow School, Parsippany, N.J.)
- On a public-library-operated FM radio station, sponsor a series of concerts featuring different views of local music with local musicians. (Nashville Public Library)
- Install news ticker-tape machine in the current affairs room so that users can see immediately the arrival of the latest news items. They also get the opportunity to view the operation of this machine. A bell rings if a bulletin comes through.
- Make a braille relief map of the library.
- Ask library staff going on holiday trips to bring back slides for the collection, or if they are planning to travel in particularly exotic lands, invite them to show their slides and talk about them in a special program. (Western Michigan University)
- Have students bring in old slides their families don't want. Obliterate bad shots by swabbing the dull (emulsion) side with bleach. Use transparency ink, crystal paint, or felt-tip pens to make new images. Build on washed-out images in over-exposed slides with the same inks and pens by adding lines. For black or near black exposures, swab off part of the emulsion with bleach and discover the blues and greens left.
- To show small, live organisms to a large group, place a sealer (Siligum) around the perimeter of the viewing area of a slide, place the organism inside with

water, place another piece of glass on top and insert into a slide mount. The small biological item then can be projected for large group viewing. (Ball State University, Muncie, Ind.)

- Using tennis ball containers or large tin cans and a frame, build a honeycomb-style poster rack. Use a photo album with small pictures of each poster indicating in which section the poster can be found.
- Use inexpensive wine rack to store posters.
- Equip the bookmobile with a solid state radio telephone for immediate reference queries, book orders, and emergency aid. (Washington County Library, Miss.)
- Provide service to the deaf over the phone with assistance of teletype machines and special phone adapters. (Martin Luther King, Jr., Library, Washington, D.C.)
- Inaugurate an after-hours information message center in which telephone reference requests are recorded and answered the next morning by librarians. (Monroe County, Mich.)
- Plan a closed-circuit system of telephone lines over which the audio collection can be played to city agencies as well as library branches. (Louisville Free Public Library, Louisville, Ky.)
- Produce stories on cassette tapes that are put on a twenty-four hour telephone player. Kids telephone the player to hear the story.
- Set up a telephone Dial-LIBRARY and have a couple of interesting questions on tape along with the answers or the names of the sources needed to find the answer. Questions might include: Where does Halley's Comet go? How can I train my dog? How can I beat Bobby Fisher? Change tape once a week.
- Provide twenty-four-hour-a-day, seven-days-a-week hotline telephone referral service for the elderly. (Tulsa City-County Library, Tulsa, Okla.)
- Use transparencies and slides projected as backdrops for special programs.
- Use an overhead projector with clear or colored sheets for story telling. (Flannel board figures can be easily used.) An advantage of the overhead is that you can read the script and manipulate figures while facing the children. (Hillside Public Library, New Hyde Park, N.Y.)
- Sponsor a videotape workshop to teach how to make tapes for showing on cable TV. (Nathan Straus Young Adult Library, New York)
- Tape a late-night TV program off the air for use in a discussion group the next day. Remember copyright laws and later wipe the tape.
- Provide video reference service wherein a camera focuses on the material in the library and is sent via cable TV to the user's home. The user can verbally communicate by phone. (Natrona County Public Library, Casper, Wyo.)
- To better understand what library users think about librarians, videotape people "on the street" to get opinions first-hand. (Baltimore County Public Library)
- Make a video camera and recorder available to groups or individuals for their use in exploring local community issues and cultural and social events for the benefit of public education. (Pocatello Public Library, Pocatello, Ida.)
- Make available a studio for producing audiotape and videotape programs. Have a library technician on hand to help out. (Kresge Library, Oakland University, Oakland, Mich.)

- Use videotapes to demonstrate athletic skills. Seeing them is a lot better than just reading about them.
- Tape public hearings and governmental functions, and make the tapes available.
- Install a "public access computer terminal" to be used by both adults and children. It can be connected to a university computer and can handle local input providing answers to questions. It can play games, do basic math, and can have self-taught instruction drills. (Venice Branch Library, Los Angeles, Calif.)
- In a school media center, use different types of programmed materials in special activity centers. (Reading Clinic of Northern Illinois University)
- Utilize computer-assisted instruction using a partial answer feedback technique which permits learners to direct the computer to print out sentences with spaces where errors occur or entirely correct sentences to compare with their own answers. (State University of New York)
- Have a "Home-Movie Night" where neighbors could get together and view everybody's home movies. A program like this could encourage interest in moviemaking and provide an enjoyable night out for those without families or funds.
- Have film talks like book talks.
- Super 8mm film is shot 18 frames per second (fps) and projected at the same speed thus, a whole day's library activity, filmed using a single frame technique, can be reduced to less than three minutes screen time. (Garrett County High School, Oxford, Ohio)
- Form an 8mm film circuit by moving blocks of films to different libraries at the end of every four to six months on a designated day. (Elyria Public Library, Elyria, Ohio)
- Sponsor a film seminar using independently made films and inviting the filmmakers. Interesting discussions will undoubtedly arise. (Newport Beach Public Library, Newport Beach, Calif.)
- Show films in the park or on the lawn on warm summer evenings. Invite your audience to bring their own blankets and chairs. (Oakville Public Library, Oakville, Ontario)
- Prepare a slide/tape presentation, a filmloop, or even a videotape to provide users with up-to-date library information about programs, new books and materials, or whatever is of current interest. Change it often. (Lawson McGhee Library, Knoxville, Tenn.)
- Make the vertical file more attractive: use multicolored cabinets with directional signs aplenty.
- Set up a pamphlet display in community areas—supermarkets, barber shops, churches, fire departments, butcher shops, etc. All materials should be free to anyone.
- Sponsor a booth at your local fair and hand out pamphlets giving information about the library.

- Collect and display video art.
- Operate community access television and provide free use of all facilities to community groups and all levels of government.
- Use a video bulletin board where audible announcements are not possible. (Gallaudet College, Washington, D.C.)
- Use video to assess and document community needs. (Livingston College, Rutgers University)
- In a school library, instead of the usual pen-pal letter exchange, have students prepare a videotape and exchange with another school located in another part of the country or world. (Harvest Park Middle School, Pleasanton, Calif.)
- To stimulate community interest display a model of your community as it is now or perhaps as it is planned to be in the future. You might have children prepare models of special buildings or their own homes for the display. (Webster Elementary School, Magna, Utah)
- Use models as well as other library materials to create effective displays. (James M. Milne Library, State University College, Oneonta, N.Y.)
- Instead of the usual pamphlet style, try distributing information to children in a comic book format. (John C. Calhoun State Community College, Decatur, Ala.)
- Sponsor a jazz festival in the library's park. Show jazz films, invite musicians, and plan a display on the musical history of jazz. (Pasadena Public Library, Pasadena, Calif.)
- Have IRS agents come to the library to answer questions and help prepare income tax forms for people with a gross adjustable income of $10,000 or less. Run a series of interviews and reports on a local radio station on topics of interest to the community. (Los Angeles Public Library)
- Offer English classes for non-English speaking community residents. (Dover Free Public Library, Dover, N.J.)
- Plan an open university concept with the use of audiotapes, videotapes, correspondence, special materials, set up in the library to allow degree courses to be given in public libraries—in conjunction with a university. (Scarborough Public Library, Scarborough, Ontario)
- Plan creative writing programs with local writers and people who are eager to learn the skills of creative writing. (San Francisco Public Library)
- Plan a hands-on workshop to instruct users in the operation of various types of library equipment and media. (St. Louis University)
- Sponsor a program to introduce four and five year olds to their cultural heritage through the use of their senses. Sessions alternate instruction with physical activity, entertainment, and crafts. Slides and prints are used along with music of a historical period—Picasso prints with modern music, African art with African music, etc. (South Brunswick Public Library, South Brunswick, N.J.)
- Let students experiment with optical items like the zoetrope and thaumatrope. (Crowlands Junior School Library, Romford, England)

- Use computer simulations on such things as repairing automobile engines and designing buildings.
- Collect recorded music which is of particular interest to people in your area.
- Play background music selected from the record collection in areas where people are browsing.
- Have people make photograms by placing small objects directly on photographic paper, exposing it to light, then removing the objects and developing the paper. Library users can then guess the identity of the photogram.
- Have young adults collect local history both in photographs and on tape. (Lebanon Hich School, Lebanon, Mo.)
- Sponsor a photography contest, with all submissions becoming part of the photo collection. Offer a prize to the winners.
- Collect historical photographs, making sure you have photos of important people, buildings, and landmarks in your community.
- Prepare fun and learning incentive packages (FLIP) according to the material available in the center on any particular subject. Various games and activities are designed to go along with each package at different age levels. (Akron Public Schools)
- Create a resource collection of preschool kits for story hour substitutes. Each kit should contain puppets, songs, finger plays, filmstrips, and felt boards. They could be available for use in the library system, or by teachers, students, nursery schools, day care centers, and adults working with children. (Quincy Public Library, Quincy, Mass.)
- Put together for children shoebox science kits with equipment and instructions for experiments. (Free Public Library of the Borough of Madison, Wisc.)
- Create a teaching package, including slidetape and simulation for instruction in library computer use. (Southampton University Library, Library School of the Polytechnic of London)
- Use a cassette tape and snapshot kit to introduce new users to material locations and library procedure and policies. You might also provide maps and pamphlets. (Garvis Area High School, Garvis City, Mich.)

Excuses by the hundreds have been used to avoid involving the library in developing programs and activities. Lack of money, time, talent, and responsibility are but a few. Once the decision has been made to meet the community's needs, resources and staff can be found to create stimulating programs and activities. When it is apparent that the community's information and enrichment needs are being met, increased financial support should be forthcoming.

Principles for Effective Group Media Presentations

Roberta Doctor Stevens and John W. Ellison

THE presenter of an effective media production must have a sound understanding of some basic principles of effective utilization. A lack of planning can result in an unsuccessful presentation not worth the audience's time or attention. The following is an attempt to identify some of the primary principles of effective utilization of media in group presentations.

PHYSICAL PREPARATION

1. Request a room which can be completely darkened and has acceptable acoustics. Rooms with blackout drape, carpeting, acoustical ceilings, etc., constitute a good environment for media presentations by eliminating noise from outside the room and distracting reverberations inside the room.
2. Provide adequate ventilation in the room.
3. Anticipate and assess the audience size so that there is adequate room and seating.
4. Arrange seating so that everyone can see the screen and hear.
5. Arrange a special section (ventilated if possible) for people who wish to smoke during the presentation.
6. Set up seating and equipment so that latecomers can enter the room without disrupting the presentation.
7. If possible, use ushers to guide audience traffic before and during the presentation.
8. When planning to speak during a media presentation and to act as the projectionist, leave an aisle between the speaker's platform and the projection equipment.
9. Label the door to the room and place directional signs throughout the building.

Originally published in *International Journal of Instructional Media* 2 (1974): 1-5.

SETTING UP EQUIPMENT

1. To make a smooth presentation, it is necessary to visit or acquire information regarding the facilities prior to the presentation time. Knowing the location of light switches, electrical outlets, circuit breakers, and temperature controls is the presenter's responsibility.
2. Working out arrangements with an unfamiliar projectionist takes time and should *not* be delayed until the last minute.
3. Be familiar with equipment used in the presentation.
4. Have spare equipment, parts (lamps, lenses, fuses, etc.) available during the presentation in case of mechnical or electrical problems.
5. Have extra extension cords and adapter available.[1]
6. Clean and check all equipment prior to the time the audience enters the room (If possible, this should be done prior to equipment delivery.) All media should be projected and/or played to insure proper operation and utilization without malfunction.
7. Wrap power cords around legs of carts and tape the cords to the floor to prevent movement or possible damage of equipment or people tripping.
8. If several reels of film must be used in the media presentation, have a projector for each reel so that there is minimal delay between reels.
9. Test all microphones for distracting feedback prior to the presentation.[2]
10. Projectors should be high enough to project over the heads of audience.
11. Rehearse the presentation and the handling of visuals.[3]
12. Use pen light during media presentations if no lectern light is available or if light is needed to operate equipment.
13. Make all last-minute adjustments prior to beginning the presentation.[4]
14. Use a pointer during a discussion-type media presentation.

SCREENS

1. Use the largest screen available for the room and audience. Seldom will a 70″ × 70″ screen satisfy the needs for groups over twenty. Most audience capacity tables disagree with this statement, but experience proves . . .
2. If more than one screen is required, use matched screens[5]
3. The front row of the audience should be no closer than two screen widths, the last row farther than six screen widths, and no row of seats wider than its distance from the screen.[6]
4. When stray light is unavoidable, place the back of the screen in front of the light source.
5. Place the screen in such a manner that opening the door after the presentation starts will not result in light hitting the screen.
6. Fill the screen with the visual image and be particularly careful not to extend the image onto the wall behind the screen.
7. Keep the white projection light off the screen unless it is part of the presentation.

8. Avoid keystoning the visual image.
9. Make sure the image is level.

AUDIO

1. Place audio speakers in front of the audience and near the projection screen. This might mean remote electrical extension cords will be needed to start and stop tape and/or record players when operating projectors simultaneously at the rear of the audience.
2. Place speakers at the ear level of your audience and on a cloth or soft surface to reduce reverberations.
3. Be sure sound is loud enough for the entire audience to be able to hear well.

INTRODUCTION

1. An explanation or introduction might precede the presentation. Avoid apologizing, indulging in false humility, or overdoing the introduction to the point that it takes away from aspects of the presentation that the audience should discover on its own.
2. Get in the proper frame of reference prior to the presentation—think showmanship, spirit, and humor.
3. Avoid continually interjecting comments and explanations during the media presentation. Let the presentation carry itself.

EFFECTIVE UTILIZATION OF MATERIAL AND ENVIRONMENT

1. If appropriate, provide a program and handouts for the media presentation.
2. Pace the presentation according to the age and sophistication of the audience and to the content of the presentation.
3. Use a variety of media and techniques to reach a large percentage of the audience. However, make sure the medium is appropriate to the content being presented.
4. Use only those portions of the film, tape, slide series, etc, which relate to the point.
5. Use slides and transparencies that are prepared in a horizontal format, as this is more easily seen by the audience when they are looming over the heads of persons in front of them.[7]
6. Total darkness and silence can be used effectively.
7. Direct attention of the audience by having the audio or visual on or off at various times during the presentation.

8. When appropriate, use audience participation during media presentations.
9. Show interest in the content during the presentation. The audience will see the presenter's reaction and be affected by it.
10. Repeat the media presentation if the audience expresses interest in seeing it again.
11. Keep the media presentation within time limits assigned as people may have other activities planned.

TYPES OF PRESENTATIONS

1. A "fine art" media presentation should be designed and programmed to please the presenter.
2. An "instructional" media presentation should be designed and programmed to educate and inform the audience.
3. Good media presentations in the affective domain are very difficult to produce. However, discussing the goals with the audience prior to the presentation will help make it meaningful and successful.

ENDING PRESENTATIONS

1. Bring lights up slowly at the end of a visual presentation.
2. Unless striving for a special effect, bring the sound up slowly at the beginning of a presentation and turn the sound down slowly at the end of the presentation.
3. If appropriate or desirable, allow time for questions or comments.

Although the above list is not all inclusive, we feel that the use of some of these principles could significantly improve the information gap in many group media presentations.

References

1. Daniel Levinson, "21 Ways to Ruin an Audiovisual Presentation," *Audiovisual Instruction*, (March 1969), p. 102.
2. Ibid.
3. Jerrold E. Kemp, "So You're On the Program," *Education Screen and Audiovisual Guide*, (March 1964), pp. 138-39.
4. Joel A. Benedict and Douglas A. Crane, *Producing Multi-Image Presentations* (Tempe, Ariz.: Arizona State University, 1973), p. 53.
5. Ibid., p. 51.
6. Mack R. Rowe et al., "Setting Up for the Presentation," *Audiovisual Instruction*, (March 1971), p. 105.
7. Ibid., p. 109

Planned Programhood, or Everything You Always Wanted to Remember but Forgot to Check

Maria Weinberger and Edie Hopkins

"He didn't ask for a pointer!"
"I had assumed the films were in proper order."
"The speaker thought she was coming next Thursday, not tonight!"

These comments or similar ones are familiar to everyone involved in library programming. Why? Because we tend to view the process as "old hat" and feel our experiences have taught us to cover all bases. But even the most experienced program directors have been embarrassed unnecessarily. A basic checklist can reduce consternation for them and for audiences. To help ensure a perfect program, here is a checklist of planning steps.

INITIAL CONTACT AND PROGRAM CONFIRMATION

In the initial contact with speaker or performer, establish the date, time, length, and location; suggested type and content of program; audience level; fee or honorarium; traveling expenses; and name, address, and telephone number of a contact person. Make the initial contact several months in advance, and indicate an acceptance deadline. Do not invite more than one person at a time.

After the initial arrangements for the program have been made, a letter should be sent confirming the above information and including a map. This letter should also contain such pertinent details as: size of expected audience, the date the speaker or performer should arrive (if different from the date of the program), where he or she will be staying, and means of transportation to and from accommodations. Mention should be made of any other plans you may have made, such as interviews or dinners.

Depending upon the type of program and the facilities of the individual library, a modified version of the following form (in duplicate) should accompany the letter of confirmation: Name the exact location you will meet (the airport, bus station, or railway depot or in the library) and if possible any strongly identifiable features by which speaker/performer can recognize you.

PROGRAMMING FORM

Program Title:

Date: Time:

Location:

PROGRAM REQUIREMENTS

Please fill in both copies. Retain one for your records and return the duplicate to:

Jane Smith, Program Co-ordinator
Foley Public Library
Foley, Minnesota 41250

Facilities Required (On your form, indicate the size of each room.)

SIZE

☐ Auditorium   ____
☐ Meeting room   ____
☐ Story room   ____
☐ Rehearsal room   ____

Audience Size

____ Preferred   ____ Maximum

Seating Arrangement Preferred

☐ Formal   ☐ Informal
☐ Special arrangements (e.g., circular seating)

_____
_____
_____

Introduction Preferred: _____

_____

Projectors Required

☐ 16mm
☐ Super 8 sound
☐ Dual 8 silent
☐ Slide
☐ Filmstrip
☐ Overhead
☐ Opaque
☐ Other, please specify _____

_____

☐ *Screens Required*

Tape Recorders/Players

☐ Reel-to-reel   (# of tracks _____)
☐ Cassette   ☐ sync
☐ 8-track   ☐ stereo
☐ mono

Record Players Required

☐ mono   ☐ stereo

☐ *Microphones Required*

☐ *Audio Speakers Required*
   Specific requirements: _____

_____

☐ *Lighting Required*
   Specific requirements: _____

_____

Video Equipment

Format: _____

☐ Playback/Record VTR
☐ Monitors   ☐ Color   ☐ B&W

[*NOTE:* Design this part of the form to list all video equipment available from *your* library and, for peace of mind, verify that the speaker/performer has indeed requested the equipment which will accommodate his or her videocassette or tape.]

Miscellaneous Requirements

☐ Lectern
☐ Chalkboard
☐ Easel
☐ Pointers   ☐ Wooden   ☐ Electric
☐ Other, please specify: _____
_____

Will you bring your own equipment?

☐ Yes   ☐ No
If yes, please specify: _____
_____

Do you provide:

☐ Posters
☐ Photographs
☐ Press releases
☐ Handouts
☐ Other, please specify: _____
_____

Do you wish to promote any materials?

☐ Yes   ☐ No
If yes, please specify: _____
_____

Do you allow any of the following interviews?

☐ Radio
☐ Press
☐ Television

Would you like someone from our library to accompany you on the interview?

☐ Yes   ☐ No
☐ Question and answer period after program

Do you allow any of the following during your program?

Photographing	☐ Yes	☐ No
Audiotaping	☐ Yes	☐ No
Videotaping	☐ Yes	☐ No

Are you willing to sign a release for photographs and tapes?

□ Yes   □ No
___ Number of people accompanying you
_____ Social Security Number (Provide only
if you are receiving an honorarium.)

Provide telephone numbers where you can be reached or messages can be left.
_____
_____

PREPARATION

Book all required facilities. Keep in mind that performers may require rehearsal time in the presentation room immediately preceding program or may need a room in which to relax before program.

Negotiate any necessary changes with speaker or performer.

Publicize well in advance: radio, television, newspaper, stores, and in-house.

Send copy of program to performer.

Make arrangements for introduction and thank-you of performers.

Reconfirm program by telephone two or three days prior to program date.

If necessary, arrange for delivery of equipment or other materials.

Double-check on hotel and restaurant reservations. Do not accommodate any performers or speakers in private homes.

Setting Up:

General Considerations

Have available:

□ Extension cords
□ Replacement parts for all relevant equipment, e.g., fuses, lamps, reels.
□ Adapter jacks
□ Multi-outlet plugs
□ Carts for equipment
□ Staff to carry equipment in and out of building

Facilities to Be Used

□ Confirm availability
□ Check conditions

Seating Arrangements

□ Number of seats
□ Arrangement of seats
□ Consider fire regulations

☐ Check specific requirements
☐ Technician Required (projection, control of lights, taping of session)

Projectors

☐ Spare bulbs and exciter lamps
☐ Take-up reels, slide trays, projection pens, blank transparencies, remote controls as required
☐ Special lenses
☐ Back-up projectors

Film

☐ Inspect for damagae
☐ Check for mislabelling
☐ Have on hand masking tape and quick splice for emergency repairs

Screens

☐ Choose appropriate type, e.g. daylight, rearview, cine (consider compatibility with lenses)
☐ Check placement

Tape Recorders/Players

☐ Determine placement depending on operation by staff or performer
☐ Check volume
☐ Have available, as required, take-up reels, blank cassettes or reels
☐ Have on hand, as required, any recordings

Microphones

☐ Number of microphones needed
☐ Placement of microphones
☐ Type of microphone (e.g. lavalier, gooseneck, omnidirectional, depending on needs of speakers)
☐ Check volume

External Speakers

☐ Placement and number depending on size of room or audience
☐ Check volume

Lighting

☐ Consider placement
☐ Check operation
☐ Have available staff to control lighting

Video Equipment

☐ Consider placement depending on audience size, type of program
☐ Check VTR
☐ Check monitors
☐ Check cables and connections

Miscellaneous Requirements

Lectern
☐ Consider position
☐ Provide ice water

Chalkboard, easel
☐ Provide, as required, chalk, eraser, paper, markers

Pointer
☐ Provide, as required, wooden or electric pointer

Piano
☐ Consider location

Promotional material
☐ Display

Admission

☐ Locate directional signs in halls and stairways for immediate reference.
   Tack posters on walls or use easels.
☐ Set up table and chair, cash box for ticket-taking

Refreshments and Hospitality:

For Audience

Consider:
☐ Number of people
☐ Type of refreshment and accessories (cups, spoons, etc.)
☐ Location

For Speaker/Performer

Consider:
☐ Number of people
☐ Type of refreshment and accessories (consider a bottle of wine)
☐ Location

Check with speaker/performer for any last-minute requirements.

WIND-UP

☐ Check all rooms. Leave everything in good order and remove all belongings, equipment, and material.
☐ Return all display material and equipment to their proper locations.
☐ Immediately forward thank-you letters to speakers. Include comments that you have heard from the audience.

COMPUTERS IN MEDIA SERVICES

Microcomputers

Clara DiFelice

Microcomputers have been around for only about ten years, with the home computer industry gearing up sometime in 1975. They have entered the media field in two ways—as education tools and as management tools. Media librarians must be prepared to deal with microcomputers from either standpoint; here, the intent is to concentrate on the microcomputer as management tool. Micros excel at providing rapid control of and access to information files. They provide a relatively inexpensive way to automate the variety of systems in media libraries to allow increased and more efficient service.

WHAT ARE MICROCOMPUTERS?

There are plenty of guidelines for defining a microcomputer. They are compared and contrasted with mainframe computers and minicomputer systems, most often in terms of cost, memory capacity, type of input and output, and type of program storage. Some are available in home assembly kits, most in a configuration known as the personal computer, with the newest ads mentioning the professional computer, between the micro and mini.

Essentially, the microcomputer is a microprocessor with added electronic components—memory and input/output circuitry which enable it to interact with keyboards, light pens, printers, and other equipment.

The microprocessor contains the central processing unit (CPU) of a computer reduced onto a logic chip using a technology known as large scale integration. The microprocessor also contains the central controller. It follows perfunctorily the steps laid out in a program to control a process.

Microcomputers handle five basic functions—the input, storage, processing, output, and control of data. In automation, the microprocessor's word length becomes the determining factor for an application. Word length is defined in numbers of bits or bytes. Bit stands for binary digit, the single element of a binary number with a value of zero or one. A byte is a group of eight bits that represent a piece of information, such as a letter of the alphabet, or a machine-language program step.[1]

The numbers used to describe word length are usually eight, sixteen, thirty-two, sixty-four, etc., bits. The microcomputer's memory is usually defined in kilobytes (K), 1,024 bytes, and the size of a program and its execution is limited by the amount of memory supplied with the microcomputer.

The memory in the microcomputer holds the information. It stores the programs which control the computer as well as all data entered. Memory is known by the acronyms ROM, PROM, EPROM, or RAM. *Read Only Memory* is designed for the storage of a specific program or set of instructions. It can be a single chip with specific circuits; it cannot be changed by the user. *Programmable Read Only Memory* provides a single chip which may be programmed by the user. Once programmed, it cannot be changed. *Electronically Programmable Read Only Memory* can be programmed and later re-programmed without replacing the chip. This memory type is the most expensive. *Random Access Memory* can be used to store varying data or programs. It requires the electrical power to hold its content. Once disconnected, all programs and instructions in RAM are lost unless first transferred onto a storage device.

Media library functions require external storage because of the extensive data utilized. The usual storage devices for microcomputers are either floppy disks or magnetic tape in the form of cassettes.

Microcomputers may execute only one program at a time. By interconnecting microcomputers, a distributed processing network may be formed. The micros would do their own processing and then send the results to a central computer for storage.

The microcomputer is itself a network of electrical components and circuits, packages of separate boards linked via the system bus. The system bus provides for data transfer from all the components of the microcomputer to its CPU for processing. For example, there could be a board which controlled graphics generation for display on a television screen, and a board which controlled interaction with a printer, allowing the graphics to be turned into hard copy.

WHAT ARE PERIPHERALS?

The devices connected to the microprocessor through the system bus are known as peripherals. They enter, display, or store data. Television screens are peripherals, attached as display units or constructed right onto the microcomputer as a monitor. They can be referred to as cathode-ray tubes (CRTs), video display tubes (VDTs), or television sets connected via radio frequency (RF) cables or direct video lines.

Keyboards are a usual peripheral, again part of the machine itself or connected by a cord. The keyboards are set by the manufacturer with each key having a separate signal. Some keys are programmed to perform a specific task, such as highlighting a line of print on the screen, moving the cursor, etc.

Storage devices are peripherals and commonly are either floppy disk drives or cassette recorders. The cassette recorders utilize magnetic tape for storage, recording data via an audio or digital signal. Disks are flexible plastic coated with magnesium oxide, 5¼ or 8 inches in diameter. A recording head reads and writes data onto the recording surface of the disk. A 5¼-inch disk can hold 130,000 to 180,000 characters of information. Access is quicker with a disk, since the read/write head can go directly to any preassigned portion of the disk. A cassette tape must usually rewind or fast forward to locate specific data, since it stores the data sequentially on the tape.

The printer is often the most costly device connected to the microcomputer. The range of sophistication is extensive. Type of print, speed, graphics capability, and dual-column printing are just a few aspects in which printers vary. Even the ways they accept paper can differ. Friction feed provides handling similar to a typewriter, while tractor feed uses holes on either side of the paper to pull it through the printer.

The printer interacts with the microcomputer via a serial or parallel interface. Serial interface sends information bit by bit. Parallel interface sends a sequence of bits at the same time. Printers often contain microprocessors, which allow for higher speeds or character variations such as underlining or bold printing of text.

Speed is measured by the number of characters printed each second. Different types of printers work at different speeds. Daisy-wheel printers position each letter over the paper, and the impact of the character on the inked ribbon creates the print. This provides a higher quality than a dot-matrix printer, which forms characters by using a combination of wires pressing against the ribbon. The greater the number of dots, the higher quality the print. Many dot-matrix printers are capable of producing graphics.

The number of columns refers to the number of characters that can be printed on a line. Eighty columns is the standard page width for typewriting. Bi-directional printing refers to a printer that prints to the end of a line, then begins printing the next line in the opposite direction. This increases the speed of the printer.

Light pens and touch-sensitive screens are additional peripheral devices for microcomputers. Each has its unique elements which are considered in conjunction with software when developing a system. The ease of input provided by a light pen which scans a bar-code or the ability of the touch screen to allow interactivity without a keyboard are just two examples.

The extent and quality of peripheral items in conjunction with memory size determines the cost of a microcomputer system. Microcomputers range from $150 to $15,000 for a system with high-quality peripherals. They are sold in types; turnkey systems designed for specific functions provided by commercial firms including both hardware and software, the basic electronics provided by chip or kit manufacturers, and the microcomputer itself—fully assembled but unprogrammed.

HOW MIGHT THE MICROCOMPUTER BE USED?

Any micro-based automated system, particularly as distributed processing and interfaced systems are developed, will bring about organizational change. Traditional areas will merge as computer files become accessible to everyone in the library. Media circulation records, for example, can be utilized by the collection development personnel. The management information available within the system challenges media librarians to provide even better services. In the long run, however, the data are just information which can be used or ignored. Many times, automating merely provides an expensive way to gather useless information or to perform an inefficient manual operation more rapidly.

Microcomputers are only beginning to be used in media centers and libraries. The applications are developed on-site in most cases, with many programs being written by students working with micros. Applications are most likely to be developed in school media centers, since student access to microcomputers is often first provided there. An eager student, a handy Apple, and a need for management information are the ingredients most often found. Some libraries may have different incentives. At IBM's Charlotte, North Carolina, technical library, the librarian was provided with an IBM Personal Computer, printer, and some available software. She uses the word processing program *Easywriter* and LC cataloging-in-publication data to produce catalog cards almost concurrently with the material's arrival. IBM's need to get materials onto the shelf and cards into the catalog quickly has instigated this application.

There does not appear to be much written in media or library literature on the applications of microcomputers in media centers and libraries. Some articles mention microcomputers but merely detail the use of micros and their software as a format in the media library, with computer-assisted instruction covered quite often. Some examples of microcomputers in actual usage can be found, such as the Ohio Scientific running circulation at the public library in Oakridge, Oregon. However, most writers agree that the potential uses for micros in libraries are limited only by the restrictions of the micro itself. The articles appearing in the monthly microcomputer journals *Creative Computing, Microcomputing* and *Popular Computing*[2] can lead to a better awareness of possible applications. The growth of consortia, networks, and other clearinghouses to share programs and information is encouraging.

The microcomputer works best on routine, repetitive tasks or manipulating files of words or numbers. Once desirable applications are determined, acquiring appropriate software becomes top priority. The cost of software is often underestimated. When computers first appeared, hardware consumed eighty percent of the costs of automating. Now, with relatively low-cost microcomputers, the software consumes that eighty percent. Some attribute that figure to the lack of programmers. The majority of microcomputer programmers these days are independents, with software development being known as a cottage industry.

At this time, unfortunately, not enough media librarians are utilizing microcomputers to stimulate commercial software development. Some are available, such as RTI's film rental and processing program; however, these are often tied exclusively to specific hardware packages. The cottage software industry for microcomputers has not yet discovered the media library or many other unique markets for which programs may be written.

Never underestimate the development costs involved in writing software. The hundreds of hours of time are only a fraction of the total costs involved. The need for expert knowledge in the computer area as well as the media area is essential for optimum flexibility in a program, its most desirable trait. It is unrealistic to expect programming of a complex nature, such as that involved in a circulation system, to be developed easily in-house. However, if an idea for an application occurs, thoroughly search the commercial software programs available for business and the home computer market. All kinds of payroll, accounting, inventory, cash and general ledger programs, and various database management programs are available.

For many possible applications, the commercial software which exists or can be modified provides adequate justification for getting involved with microcomputers. Once automated systems replace manual ones, they inevitably provide features which foster utilization, leading to increased output and better service.

SELECTING AND EVALUATING SOFTWARE

Selecting a software program for the microcomputer follows much the same steps involved in selecting media programs. Choose software before hardware if at all possible. The first thing to do is identify what is needed. List specific tasks and the inputs from which they are accomplished, for example, the forms used for circulating equipment. Outline all the capabilities necessary for an effective, flexible program. Consider the outputs needed from the system and ask advice from all staff involved in the service. Think in terms of expansion if possible, though this should be a secondary consideration. If the hardware is already present, keep in mind that all software must be compatible with system operating software and utility programs.

Read about computers, learn what they do best, and what their limitations are; then reduce the list of needs by eliminating those that are unrealistic for the microcomputer to handle. Watch particularly for routines that require human judgment—although it can make certain predetermined decisions, a microcomputer cannot guess.

Locate software by examining software catalogs and computing magazines' advertisements. Ask software manufacturers questions; many firms are small and often you'll talk to the program's author. Talk with other users of the program. Consider the impact if they mention the need to modify the program. Get a computer store salesperson to demonstrate programs for comparison. Once you've narrowed down the choices, invest if possible in the software manual. Consider how easy it is to understand and use as a training tool. If you've found the best possible program for your purposes but wish it to be modified for specific needs, hire a consultant to determine how easily it can be modified. How well-written the program and its documentation are indicates the effectiveness of the overall program design.

Word processing software is readily available for most microcomputers, and usually becomes the first software purchased in office-type environments. Word processing software and the microcomputer excel at media library applications. The production of printed materials: mediagraphies, guides, descriptive brochures, administrative reports, etc., are almost daily output. An obvious example is a printed catalog of media materials, easily edited and updated on a microcomputer using a word processing program.

With word processing programs, most microcomputer systems provide choices of software. The task of selecting the best possible program for your applications should be given the utmost attention. Word processing may be used for many things beyond ease of typing and updating catalogs. Any listing subject to change can be maintained by the microcomputer: an inventory of equipment with complete maintenance records, remote storage site holdings, stock/supplies lists, files of media catalogs, mailing lists, etc. Limitations need only be applied by the software and the microcomputer system. "Beyond the simple convenience and ease of a word processor, the bottom line in word processing is productivity ....[3] This comment is a succinct summation of the reason for the many word processing programs currently on the market.

The various elements of a word processing program should be examined thoroughly before selecting one for your applications. Use a published non-evaluative review of the elements to investigate the capabilities of any program considered. The review should cover the number of years the program has been available, price, which operating system is required, text display type, sorting and editing capabilities, and printing capabilities. The manual for the program is extremely useful and can outline many of the major functions such as method of file control, cursor movement, screen format, deletion and insertion methods, and search capabilities.

One of the first things to check is the file length provided by the program. A typed 8½″ x 11″ paper will require about two thousand bytes of storage. The amount of text a file can contain is measured in kilobytes, or 1,024 bytes. Word processing program file lengths can range anywhere from 2K to 250K, and the document length capability is of primary importance. Wordwrap refers to the ability of the program to automatically move a word to the next line once the line's end is reached. File insertion allows the merging or copying of contents between files. More complex is file merging, allowing the same letter to be addressed to numerous people and individualized as needed.

Block moves allow for the insertion or movement of whole paragraphs within a file. Search capabilities range from finding a specific word anywhere in the text to replacing it or a symbol for it wherever it appears. In typing this chapter, for example, "*" was assigned to stand for "microcomputer," and the search/replace function was used to correct the text once it was completely typed. Screen-oriented programs display exactly as the printed page will appear. Page display shows pages, and an element can be included to cause the printer to automatically print page numbers or header/footer lines (wording at the top or bottom of every page such as a magazine title, volume, and date notation).

Centering is useful for headings, and justified right margins can be an option. Proportional spacing refers to letters that occupy space proportional to their shape. An optional program often found coexisting with word processing is a dictionary program which provides a file of standard and user-specified words for comparison to the text. If incorrect spellings are present, the program flags them for correcting.

The elements referred to here give some idea of the complexity involved in evaluating program capabilities. They are by no means a complete listing of word processing program features. Overall, word processing programs and their application to media library services provide an excellent introduction to microcomputer technology. User-friendly and readily understood, word processing woos even the staunchest anti-computer types. After the introduction of word processing, invariably interest and output increases. More and more people utilize the technology and before long, the biggest headache becomes scheduling time on the microcomputer.

SOFTWARE FOR ADDITIONAL APPLICATIONS

Another area of commercial software to investigate for possible application is the computer-generated graphics programs which may be used for production purposes. The graphics editors allow you to manipulate colors and images to create charts, graphs, drawings, and even complex, 3-D, color moving pictures. Translating these computer graphics to slides, film, or video is possible. Investigate carefully the hardware support necessary for graphics if this application is of interest.

Additional software could include database management programs such as *Librarian* or *Visicalc* for budget management. *Librarian* is described as a storage and retrieval system for reference citations. Obviously such a program can be useful for access to media files by subject or other means.

Beyond word processing and general commercial software that can be applied or modified to apply to your situation, there is the development of single application software. Many procedures used in administering media library services are naturals for automation. Some examples would be the distribution of equipment on a daily basis, scheduling of facilities and personnel, monitoring the preview and evaluation of media, the process of renting materials from order to payment, and a control of production activities. Administrative use of the microcomputer could range from utilization data to budget tracking to needs assessments and cost-accounting.

These examples could involve the development of software in-house, for which the microcomputer is tailor-made. High level languages and simple operating systems provide an easier program development environment than has previously been available. Given an understanding of systems analysis and the principles of automation, a knowledge of a programming language and the microcomputer's capabilities, and plenty of time, the development of software is possible. Start with something that involves files of numbers or word strings (text) and has been working effectively as a manual system. Past the systems analysis and flow chart stages, programming may be relatively simple. Evaluation, debugging, and reprogramming can considerably lengthen the process of evolving an effective software package.

SELECTING AND EVALUATING HARDWARE

The microcomputer usually proves most effective when it serves a specific purpose. When appropriate, this should be the prime consideration in evaluating hardware for purchase. The applications programs form the parameters for specifying which microcomputer to buy. In many cases, where commercial software and systems are rejected for one reason or another, the media library may decide to invest in some general software and a microcomputer system with which any member of the staff may experiment. Programs developed by staff tend to be highly specific to the library and may prove the most effective. After thorough evaluation and debugging, another microcomputer may then be provided for the now automated function. Such programs may have limited usefulness in other media library environments.

While a micro-based automated system is dependent upon its software for ultimate success, the hardware utilized in the system must also match the needs of the user. There are guides available for selecting the best hardware for the applications you desire. A matrix of variables can be prepared to assist in the selection process.

Cost is often a major factor. Keep in mind the fact that actual cost is determined by what the equipment can do *and* the reliability and ease with which it performs. Often the fact that micros seem so cheap (compared with other automated systems) can cloud the fact that the equipment must match demonstrated needs in order to be cost-effective. Alternative purchasing possibilities, such as leasing arrangements, often work out more effectively in the long run.

The microcomputer industry is relatively young and the life of a micro under constant use, as in a media library system, is undetermined. Whatever maintenance history is available for the hardware can be an extremely useful indicator.

Actual usage of the microcomputer should be considered from the start. While most need only standard electrical power of 110AC volts, a grounded plug is essential. In addition, find out if a dedicated power line is required or if other electrical appliances can be on the line. Determine the effect a surge or brown-out will have if the equipment is operating at the time. In many cases, anything in RAM will be destroyed. Purchasing a surge protector with an adequate emergency power supply will ensure the safety of the equipment and any data or programs operating when a power failure occurs. These can provide battery power for three to five minutes, with some providing as many as twenty minutes of power. The fragility of electrical currents during even the mildest thunderstorm should not be overlooked.

If the micro will be in a public area security may be a factor to consider. Micros and their peripherals are fairly portable; investigate whether the equipment can be bolted to a desk. Noise level can be another consideration, depending upon where the micro will be used. Most microcomputers run silently, but printers and disk drives may be cause for complaint.

Adequate ventilation is another variable. Space must be provided around all the micro's vents to prevent internal overheating. A supplemental fan may be needed for some microcomputers if all expansion slots are filled with other boards. The temperature ranges tolerated by most micros are human levels. For optimum life of the equipment, controlled temperature and humidity for the micro and all its peripherals are recommended. At 85°F or higher, most micros exhibit fractious behavior. Avoid direct sunlight and closeness to a source of heat or cold such as a radiator or an air conditioning duct putting out 45°F air. Moisture and dirt should also be avoided. If the roof leaks in a spot or two, keep the micro well away. Care when using the micro cannot be stressed enough. Keep liquids and solids (even cigarette ash) far away. Damage can easily be caused to the micro or its peripherals if *anything* reaches the inside components.

In evaluating a microcomputer, both hardware and software capabilities should be closely examined. For hardware, evaluate the main board or CPU type with instruction set size; memory type, size, and expansion; software functions support (i.e., operating system and language in ROM chips); the interconnection for peripherals (bus type and number of ports); the video display; keyboard; printer; storage devices; audible output device; and finally, overall system configuration (integrated or detached).

Software evaluation should consider the operating system; support or utility functions (i.e., program monitoring, text editing, etc.); languages available and their level; applications programs available and their price; data communications software (to enable telephone connection to larger systems); and the database management system which supports software development.

Evaluate as well the manufacturer and individual vendors of the equipment. Are computers and their peripherals all the manufacturer makes? Are their sales international or local? Is their vendor a local service center, or is one available nearby? Where must the computer be shipped for repair? Does the manufacturer produce all needed peripherals for the system, and if so, what are they? How many peripherals does the vendor supply? What documents are provided to support the microcomputer? Service availability is a key issue. Do vendors supply service? Is there a maintenance contract available? Does the vendor stock spare boards (allows the return of just the board for repair)?

A systematic evaluation and examination of all variables involved in selecting a microcomputer will enable the user to match needs with the best available microcomputer system. Once selected, ordered, and received, unpack the micro carefully. Read the operating instructions and manuals thoroughly, first concentrating on the instructions for hooking up the system. If not followed properly, you'll be embroiled in the effects of your first case of human error!

References

1. Frank Herbert, *Without Me You're Nothing: The Essential Guide to Home Computers* (New York: Simon & Schuster, 1980) Glossary.
2. Other interesting journals include:
   Access: Microcomputers in Libraries. Quarterly. Provides product information and applications for hardware and software.
   Byte. Monthly. Hardware, software, applications and reviews. Highly technical articles provided.
   COMPUTE! Monthly. An example of system-related journal. For Apple Atari, and PET users, includes educational applications.
   Computer Graphics and Applications. Quarterly. Newsletter of the National Computer Graphic Association.
   Personal Computing. Monthly. Hardware, software, applications, reviews, developments in the fieled.
   Software Review. Biannual. Available software for computers.
   For additional titles, refer to the media-related periodicals listing in *Educational Media Yearbook.* Also useful for applications ideas are the four editions of the *Personal Computing Digest,* proceedings of the National Computer conferences of 1978, 1979, 1980, and 1981. They are published by the American Federation of Information Processing Societies, Arlington, Va.
3. Peter McWilliams, "An Introduction to Word Processing." *Popular Computing,* Vol. 1, No. 4 (February 1982).
4. *Librarian* available from Geosystems, Inc., 802 E. Grand River, Williamston, MI 48895. *Visicalc, Easywriter,* Apple, and any other hardware or software proper names mentioned in this chapter are registered trademarks of the individual manufacturers.

Bibliography

Christian, Deborah. "The Microcomputer at Oakridge, Oregon." *Library Journal,* Vol. 105 (July 1980), pp. 1470-71.
Consumer Guide. Editors. *Home Computers.* New York: Beekman House, 1978.

Ditlea, Steve. *A Simple Guide to Home Computers*. New York: A & W Visual Library, 1979.

Edwards, John. "Getting into Apple Graphics." *Popular Computing*, Vol. 1 No. 7 (May 1982), pp. 64-70.

Fosdick, Howard. "The Microcomputer Revolution." *Library Journal*, Vol. 105 (July 1980), pp. 1467-72.

Good, Philip. "Choosing the Right Business Software." *Popular Computing*, Vol 1, No. 6 (April 1982), pp. 32-38.

Herbert, Frank, and Max Barnard. *Without Me You're Nothing: The Essential Guide to Home Computers.* New York: Simon & Schuster, 1980.

Kelly, Mahlon G. "Buying Software." *Popular Computing*, Vol. 1, No. 6 (April 1982), pp. 27-30.

Krueger, Donald R. "Issues and Applications of Microcomputers for Libraries." *Canadian Library Journal.* Vol. 38 (October 1981), pp. 282-85.

Lundeen, Gerald. "The Role of Microcomputers in Libraries." *Wilson Library Bulletin,* Vol. 55 (November 1980), pp. 178-85.

McWilliams, Peter, "An Introduction to Word Processing." *Popular Computing*, Vol. 1, No. 4 (February 1982), pp.17-19.

Pratt, Allan D. "The Use of Microcomputers in Libraries." *Journal of Library Automation,* Vol.13, No. 1 (March 1980), pp.7-17.

Rorvig, Mark E. *Microcomputers and Libraries: A Guide To Technology, Products, and Applications*. White Plains, N.Y. : Knowledge Industry Publications, 1981.

Simpson, George A. *Microcomputers in Library Automation*. McLean, Va.: MITRE Corp., 1978. Report #7938. ERIC ED 174 217.

Computer Media Applications in Libraries: Issues and Problems (A Research Agenda)

James Rice

Decisions in media applications have often been made too hastily. Inspired by the availability of money and administrative support, media librarians have tended to implement and expand programs sometimes without sufficient evidence. Now that budget cuts are increasing so much, less effective programs are being closely scrutininzed. In some cases, unsuccessful media applications become an embarrassment when administrators evaluate them. We run the risk, then, of having an entire service or educational program lose credibility because one aspect isn't going well.

It is absolutely paramount that we consider all the elements of a problem before we make programmatic changes or additions. This means we must ask all of the necessary questions *during* the planning process—not afterwards. This chapter is a list of issues, problems, and concerns regarding media applications in our profession. Each is stated in the form of a question. Management decision-making should be very much like a research study. The steps in scientific investigation should be employed, research designs should be used, data should be collected or assembled, and various statistical methods should be applied to analyze and interpret the evidence.

All research begins with the recognition of a problem or concern. With this in mind, we may also look upon this list as a research agenda. It is assumed that readers must work with a given item on the list in order to develop a plan for research: refining the problem into a research question, formulating a hypothesis, reviewing the literature, developing the research methodology, etc. What the author provides here are some of the initial questions. These questions may also be useful to develop research for publication, grant proposals, or doctoral studies. Although the author obviously has opinions, an attempt has been made to eliminate any bias or implied position on any of the issues. Finally, it should be noted that this list is by no means exhaustive. The questions raised here are intended as a partial list only, and it is hoped that they will be helpful food for thought.

COMPUTER-ASSISTED INSTRUCTION (CAI)

This section includes issues and problems associated with all types of automated online instruction. Two primary examples of this are the PLATO and TICCIT projects, but the list also includes questions relevant to smaller projects. Generally, the questions relate to such CAI formats as automated programmed instruction, drill and practice, testing, simulations, instructional games, and other tutorial lessons via computers. Some questions on computer-managed instruction (CMI) are also included. This is the record-keeping function of computers in which testing and other diagnostic information is stored, compiled, and manipulated to make decisions. Students' progress in CAI projects is often monitored with CMI to form an integrated software package in a particular curricular design.

The section is split into two groups; instruction and learning with CAI and cost of CAI.

Instruction and Learning with CAI

A. Do users learn more from CAI compared to other instructional methods? How does CAI compare to audiovisual instruction, traditional lecture/demonstration instruction, or programmed instruction in print format?
B. What types of users learn best from CAI? How do slow learners compare with fast learners using CAI? Is CAI better for adult education, higher education, elementary or secondary education, or some other educational level? Do any special groups learn particularly well with CAI? How about handicapped people, deaf people, or emotionally disturbed people?
C. How long should CAI lessons be? Does this vary depending on the content of CAI lessons? Does the use of graphics enable the lesson to be longer and still maintain users' concentration? If lessons are mixed with non-computer display devices, does this affect the optimum length?
D. How long should testing or drill and practice programs be?
E. Does the level of learning in CAI vary with any particular techniques in developing lessons? Does the amount of graphics in a lesson affect

the level of learning? Does the degree of interaction in the lesson affect the level of learning? When the testing is mixed with instruction, does this affect learning level in CAI?

F. Is the learning level at all correlated with entertainment level in CAI? When lessons are specifically made to be more fun, do users learn more or less? Does this vary depending on the type of person who is using CAI?

G. What subjects are most effectively taught using CAI? Are there any subjects which are simply not effective at all using CAI?

H. In what cases, if any, is CAI most effective when supplemented with print materials? Are certain subjects most effectively taught when accompanied by supplementary materials? Are certain users more receptive to CAI when it is accompanied by other materials? Is CAI more effective when there are materials to take home between lessons or following a CAI course?

I. In what cases, if any, is CAI most effective when it is supplemented with the availability of a teacher (to answer questions, etc.)? Do certain users need personal assistance more than others? Are certain subjects more likely to demand that personal assistance be provided to people using CAI?

J. Does CAI impede the effectiveness of other instructional methods? Do people who have used CAI later have difficulty concentrating on lectures or print materials? If this phenomenon occurs, is it more likely to occur with certain types of users such as elementary students or special education students? Would this phenomenon be more prevalent with CAI in any particular subject areas?

K. Are there variations in retention levels when CAI is compared to other instructional methods? Do users remember more or less when CAI is compared to the lecture/demonstration method? When CAI is compared to programmed instruction in print format, is there any difference in retention level?

L. Does retention level vary with different types of CAI or different types of users? Would the use of graphics in a CAI lesson affect retention? Do elementary students retain better than adults when CAI is used?

M. Does CAI affect users' attitudes towards certain subjects? Are users' attitudes towards subjects such as math, chemistry, or statistics, improved or worsened by CAI?

N. Does CAI affect users' attitudes towards computers? Is CAI effective in desensitizing users to computers? Is CAI effective with users who are resistant to other forms of instruction?

O. Is CAI addictive? Is any form of CAI more likely to be addictive or habit-forming for users? Is any type of user more likely to become addicted to any type of CAI?

P. How many CAI computer languages are there and how do they compare? Are there any that are very effective or very ineffective? How long does it take teachers or other professionals to learn these non-programming languages? How do they compare in terms of ease of use or the amount of time it takes to learn them?

Q. To what degree is CAI copyrightable?

R. Does CAI have more credibility with users than other instructional methods? Do users believe the instruction more because the computer says so? Do computers have more credibility with users than teachers? How do parents, school administrators, rock and roll stars, or friends, compare with computers in credibility for various users?

S. Are any specific CAI techniques more effective with certain subject areas? For example, is simulation more effective with psychomotor instruction? Are graphics most effective with elementary subjects?

T. Are there any health hazards associated with extended use of a cathode-ray tube? Does long term use of the video display terminals cause cataracts, blurred vision, eye fatigue, headaches, or nervous tension? Are there any techniques such as supplementary materials or activity assignments which help to alleviate any of these problems if they occur?

U. To what extent is creative and original thinking possible when people use CAI as compared with other methods of instruction? How effective is CAI in promoting imagination or innovative thought when it is compared with other media or other methods? How effective is CAI in enabling the development of artistic creativity?

V. What types of computer terminals are most effective in CAI applications with different types of users?

W. What information should be considered in Computer Managed Instruction (CMI)? For example, should a user's successful completion of a lesson or test be supplemented by such information as length of time to complete, number of wrong responses, or other information?

X. What types of CMI profiles now exist? How do they compare with traditional educational record-keeping models? Are there benefits that would not be possible in manual systems?

Y. How are individual difference variables accounted for in CMI projects? Is it more or less possible to include individualization in CAI/CMI decision-making?

Z. Are there any legal problems with CMI? Is confidentiality or the right to privacy ever violated by CMI systems?

Cost of CAI

A. How does the cost of producing CAI compare with that of producing other instructional materials? Is CAI more or less expensive than videotapes, films, or lecture/demonstration instruction? Is the cost of CAI rising or falling?
B. What is the price tag on graphics versus text in CAI?
C. How do the production costs of page-turning CAI (simply the machine-readable form of a programmed text) compare with printed workbooks or programmed texts? If a CAI lesson is simply the automation of a printed programmed instruction text, what, if any, are the benefits of the CAI? Within any given collection of CAI lessons, how many are simply the machine-readable conversion of a programmed text?
D. How many CAI projects were (or are) funded by soft money? How many, if any, projects have had to be cancelled because grant money ran out?
E. How many CAI projects are self-sufficient (either part of an ongoing budget or cost supporting in some way)?
F. Does any type of CAI help to eliminate personnel? Has anyone ever been laid off because of the implementation of CAI?
G. How does programmed CAI compare in cost to CAI produced using a CAI computer language? When CAI is produced by a team of experts how does the cost compare with CAI produced only by teachers?
H. Does computer-managed instruction (CMI) save money? If not, are there benefits worth the expense? What are the cost considerations of CMI? Is the cost of CMI rising or falling?

MICROCOMPUTERS IN LIBRARIES

This section deals with all types of instructional applications that are delivered via microcomputers. Many microcomputer applications fall under the definition of computer-assisted instruction (CAI) and readers should refer to that section for those issues and problems. What appear here are questions that relate specifically to microcomputers.

Learning and Instruction with Microcomputers

A. What are microcomputers most often used for? In educational settings, are they usually supplements to the curriculum, or are a significant number of users self-sufficient with microcomputers? In schools, how much programming is being done by students beyond what is assigned in classes? How are micros primarily being used during free periods? Do users bring their own software packages from home to use on the institution's microcomputer?

B. In what proportions are various microcomputer applications being used? Are games, CAI, or programming dominating the use of microcomputers? Are librarians, teachers, or students making more use of microcomputers in schools? Are certain courses more likely to include microcomputers than others? How much of the micro-computer's time is devoted specifically to computer literacy?

C. Are any types of microcomputer applications addictive (chronically habit forming)? Are any specific applications more likely to be addictive than others? When users are supposed to be doing substantive work on a microcomputer, do they get side-tracked by the other capabilities of the microcomputer?

D. What are the instructional objectives of microcomputer games? Are there measurable benefits to games such as increased problem solving ability, increased reaction time or motor skill ability, or improved math/logic skills?

E. What types of users make the most effective use of microcomputers? Is there any correlation between math aptitude and microcomputer use or mechanical aptitude and microcomputer use? Do fast learners make more use of microcomputers than slow learners or vice versa? Do special education students like microcomputers? Do handi-capped, disabled, aged, or emotionally disturbed people use micro-computers more or less than other users?

F. For instructional applications, are there any types of users who consistently resist microcomputers?

G. In educational settings, do microcomputers detract from other instruction in any way? Do students lose interest in teachers as a result of microcomputers? Do students lose interest or concentration in their other courses because of microcomputers? Do students have any difficulty with grades as a result of microcomputers?

H. What are the implications of copyright and patent laws for micro-computers?

I. Do users (how many) copy software from the institution? How much trading of software is occurring between users? Is there any potential liability to the institution? Are people using the institution's microcomputer to trade software with each other? Is there any potential liability in this?

J. How much supervision of microcomputer facilities is needed? Should a microcomputer lab be staffed full-time? What type of personnel is most feasible? How much theft of microcomputers, facilities, equipment, or software has been reported?

K. How should a collection of microcomputer software be organized? Are there any particular storage facilities which are most effective? How should microcomputer software be cataloged or indexed?

L. How should microcomputer software be disseminated to users? Should media centers allow microcomputer software to circulate? If so, how long should it circulate and should it be renewable? What should the policy be for overdue software or lost software?

M. How should microcomputer software be protected or backed up in case of damage or loss?

N. What are the pros and cons of various programming languages available for microcomputers? What are the advantages or disadvantages of languages such as BASIC, PASCAL, ADA, and PL/1? Which microcomputers provide compilers or interpreters for various languages?

O. How long does it take users to learn various programming languages? Are certain programming languages simply beyond certain users' capabilities?

P. How do professionals select a microcomputer? What criteria should be applied in choosing?

Q. Are there any problems associated with prolonged or frequent use of microcomputers? Does extensive microcomputer use have any apparent relationship to reading, performance in math, socialization, or any other instructional or developmental characteristics?

R. How do microcomputers compare in reliability, ease of use, availability of parts and service, or other major characteristics?

S. Which microcomputers and microcomputer peripheral devices are intercompatible and to what degree?

T. How do user manuals and training materials compare for various microcomputers? Do certain microcomputers provide materials which are much more effective than others? Which microcomputers afford the greatest possibility for self-instruction?

U. Is software significantly more available for some microcomputers than for others? Can computer clubs, user groups, or microcomputer journals provide you with software which is compatible with any particular microcomputers?

V. Are given software packages or groups of packages intercompatible and to what degree?

W. Are there any health hazards associated with extended use of a microcomputer?

X. In educational settings, do students know more or less than teachers about microcomputers?

Y. What developmental characteristics are affected by the use of microcomputers? Do microcomputers improve or decrease problem-solving ability? Do they enhance or inhibit creativity? Do they lower or raise concentration level? What effect does the use of microcomputers have on verbal skills?

Z. How many microcomputers are needed in relation to the number of users in a given setting?

A1. How do administration policies of microcomputers vary? How many libraries provide open access? How many require a training session before use? How many libraries host a user's group?

Cost of Microcomputers

A. How do microcomputers affect personnel needs? Is additional personnel needed to supervise or instruct in the library or microcomputer lab? Have microcomputers ever eliminated the need for clerical, technical, or other personnel?

B. How many microcomputers are purchased with soft money and how many from regular budgetary sources?

C. What are the short-term and long-term implications of the purchase of microcomputers? Will owning microcomputers necessitate a software budget, equipment budget, or service budget? Will special facilities need to be purchased such as seating, lighting, wiring, or noise control facilities? Will volume of use exceed an institution's ability to supply access?

D. Where are microcomputers best located? Is it best to distribute them in different parts of an institution or should they all be together and centrally located? On what basis should this decision be made?

E. Are there hidden costs for microcomputers that should be considered in addition to the purchase price? What are the indispensable components of microcomputer facilities and services? Is video display for demonstration to large groups a necessity? What cables and hookups will be needed? How many printers, disk drives, or modems might be needed?

F. How do lease agreements, lease-purchase agreements and outright purchase compare in terms of total cost?

G. Which libraries are offering microcomputer use for a fee? Which microcomputer facilities are supported by fees either partially or totally?

AUTOMATED INFORMATION RETRIEVAL SERVICES

This section deals with issues and problems that relate to any type of automated information retrieval. The primary examples of these services are online databases such as Lockheed's DIALOG, SDC's ORBIT, BRS,

Medline (Elhill), Dow Jones News/Retrieval, The Source, Quotron, Compuserve, LEXIS, Westlaw, etc.

Information Retrieval/User Services

A. Which information retrieval services are used most often and by whom? Are certain online search services dominating the market significantly? Are certain search services growing faster than others? Are others declining in popularity? Are certain search services most popular in specific types of libraries or specific settings?

B. Which databases are used most often and by whom? Have any particular databases increased or declined in popularity?

C. How do various databases perform using various measures of effectiveness? How do certain databases compare in precision, recall, exhaustiveness, or depth of indexing?

D. How do search services compare in turnaround time or response time? Do certain search services provide equivalent searching with much less connect time than others? Do certain search services deliver printout much faster than other search services?

E. How do various online retrieval systems compare in user surveys or consumer evaluation studies?

F. Of the three major types of systems (weighted, menu-based, or boolean) which is easiest to use? Which of the three types of systems is most effective for searching? Which is most preferred by users? Which type of information seems most suited to each type of searching system? Which of the three types of systems is most commonly encountered in the information industry? Which type of system is currently being used most often?

G. What types of libraries offer what types of information retrieval systems? How do types of libraries compare in information retrieval services in general?

H. How are automated reference services promoted or publicized? How has publicity affected service or volume of use? Have any libraries avoided publicity to avoid drastic increases in volume of use?

I. How much training do searchers get in various libraries before they do online searches for users? How do libraries compare in terms of the training for online searchers?

J. How much training is needed for various levels of searching? Do certain databases require additional advanced training for effective searching: How do libraries compare in the amount of training they provide searchers, especially for advanced databases?

K. How many library education programs (schools or departments of library and information science) teach online searching and how much do they teach it? How many library schools require online searching competency? How many online searching systems are taught in different library schools?

L. How do search services compare on such features as frequency of update, searching aids provided, user training services, growth rate of databases, or user services such as help files or hotlines for troubleshooting? What other features should be used in comparing search services in a research study?

M. How do databases compare on such features as vocabulary control, accuracy of information, specificity of vocabulary, semantic or syntactic ambiguity, overlap with other databases, number and type of sources provided, frequency of update, help files, or searching aids provided? What other features should be used in comparing databases in research studies?

N. How do search service command languages vary in terms of such variables as ease of use, power of searching, or response time in retrieving given records. How do command languages compare in the amount of time it takes to become proficient? How do the databases offered by search services compare on these variables?

O. How do system translation languages affect these issues? If a software package is used to access several systems with a single language, is response time significantly affected?

P. How do searchers compare in effectiveness? Given equivalent reference questions, are there significant differences between search strategies which are used? If the same reference need is taken to various libraries, how can the various results be compared? Are there significant differences between online searchers in different libraries?

Q. What percentage of the public is aware of information retrieval services?

R. What types of users employ online searching? Are there any characteristics such as education level, income level, or occupation that are significantly associated with being a user of online services?

Cost of Information Retrieval

A. How are automated reference services paid for? Are they entirely budgeted or entirely self-supporting? Are they budgeted for some expenses and partially fee-based to support other expenses? How is the point determined where user fees begin and a library's support for online service end?

B. When online search services are budgeted, how does this affect the budget for other materials or services? Have any materials been cancelled in libraries that offer free online searching? Have any services been cancelled in these libraries?

C. When online search services are fee-based, how does this affect users' attitudes? Have users complained or taken legal action against fees for library service? Has there been measurable decline in a library's image or status in a community when it has charged fees to support online services?

D. Is effectiveness, exhaustiveness, searching time, user satisfaction, or anything else significantly affected by the cost of an online service to users? Does the fee-or-free question cause any variations in online searching services? When a search is free, is the connect time longer or shorter? When a search is fee-based, is there more or less output to the user? When users pay for online searching, is the reference interview longer or shorter than when online searching is free?

E. How do different databases compare in searching time needed? Apart from the per-hour cost, what are the real cost comparisons? Do logical operations take longer in some databases than others? How does CPU time compare to connect time in different databases? Are there significant differences in this proportion?

F. Is there any variation in searching time between expensive databases and more economical ones? Do searchers spend less time on a very expensive database or do they waste time when they are using an economical database? Do searchers hurry too much when they have to pay more?

G. How do different online searchers compare in cost? Do users pay significantly more depending on the searcher who helps them? Do searchers vary significantly in the length of time they allocate to the reference interview? Is there a relationship between the ultimate cost of a search and the amount of time previously spent on the reference interview before going online?

COMPUTER-BASED TELEVISION SERVICES

This section deals with questions relating to all types of television systems used for information retrieval/dissemination. Teletext, Videotex, and fully interactive two-way television are included.

Many applications of these systems are actually information retrieval and readers should refer to that section for those questions. Included here are some of the many questions regarding the large and rapidly growing technology of telereference services. An emphasis is placed on the capabilities of these systems most relevant to libraries and the effect these systems might have on library service.

A. What types of systems are currently in operation? What systems are being offered in libraries? How do systems in other countries compare with those in the United States? Of the systems which are in complete operation, which ones are commercially available to a significant number of subscribers? What capabilities do various systems offer? What information databases are available through various computer-based television services?

B. What television systems are being developed either in the United States or in other countries? What research and development is currently in progress? Are existing systems experimenting with new databases or new types of services? What kinds of television information systems do consumers want? What capabilities or services would users be most willing to pay for?

C. Of the various services that are technologically possible, which ones are most feasible? Which television information systems are currently popular enough to justify continuation?

D. What library services are most feasible via television systems? What library databases or library-related information services are now available in a telereference system and which of these are most popular? Are any libraries being paid by cable companies for such databases? Are there any problems with this?

E. How do telereference services affect other library services? Do they attract users who otherwise would not come to the library? Do they detract from other library services at all?

F. Does home delivery of library service cause a reduction in library personnel or in library use? Are there any benefits to the library when it offers home delivery of library service? Have users become interested in the library for the first time because of library services via television?

G. Which libraries are currently offering television information services in the library and to what extent?

H. How many librarians are resistant to library services via television information systems?

I. Do the subscribers to television information services have any common characteristics? Is education level, income level, or occupation associated with the use of television information systems? How does the user group of a given library compare with the user group of a given television information system in terms of education level, income level, or other characteristics?

J. If the library delivers programming in television information systems, will it be serving its regular clientele or a different clientele? If it offers access to a television information system in the library, will it be serving its customary user group or a different one?

For a list of issues and concerns relating to the cost of computer-based television services, refer to the list relating to the cost of information retrieval services. Although the cost of television systems is generally less than information retrieval systems, the issues and questions are very similar, since they both relate to some type of information retrieval or dissemination of information service.

Bibliography

Abshire, Gary M., ed. *The Impact of Computers on Society and Ethnics: A Bibliography*. Morristown, N.J.: Creative Computing Press, 1980.

ACM Committee on Computers and Public Policy. "A Problem-List of Issues Concerning Computers and Public Policy." *Communications of the ACM 17* (September 1974) 495-503.

Ball, A.J.S. "Videotext: Chimera or Dream Machine." *Canadian Library Journal* (February 1981) 11-15.

Callison, William. "Problems and Possibilities for Computer Assisted Instruction." *NASSP Bulletin* 65 (May 1981) 24-28.

Cambrell, James B., and Robert E. Sandfield. "Computers in the School: Too Much Too Soon?" *High School Journal* 62 (May 1979) 327-31.

Carter, J.B.R. "Editorial: A Library and Information Science Research Agenda for the 1980's." *Library Research* 4 (Spring 1982) 1-2.

Cawkell, A.E. "Will Information Flow to the Citizen be Improved with Videotex Systems?" *ASLIB Proceedings* 32 (June 1980) 264-69.

Cuadra Associates. "Library and Information Science Research Agenda for the 1980's: A Summary Report." *Library Research* 4 (Fall 1982) 235-77.

Curran, C.C. "Symposium on a Library and Information Science Research Agenda for the 1980's." *Library Research* 4 (Winter 1982): 385-400.

Ferguson, D. "Can We Shape the Future?" (agenda for library and information science research in the 1980's) *Online* 6 (January 1982) 8-9.

Ferguson, D. "Creating a Research Agenda: A Personal View." *Information Technology and Libraries* 1 (June 1982) 163-64.

Goldberg, Albert L. "After the Games-What?" *Media Spectrum* 7 (Third Quarter, 1980) 11.

Goldberg, Albert L. "Computers for Instruction: Many Questions, a Few Answers." *Media Spectrum* 5 (First Quarter, 1978) 3.

Hogrebe, Edmund F. "Digital Technology: The Potential for Alternative Education." *Journal of Communication* 31 (Winter 1981) 170-76.

Joiner, Lee Marvin, et al. "Potential and Limits of Computers in Schools." *Educational Leadership* 37 (March 1980) 498-501.

Kahn, Dean. "Use of VDT's Stirs Concerns for Health in the Workplace." *Columbia Missourian* (Columbia, Mo.) 14 March, 1982.

Laurie, Edward J. *Computers, Automation and Society*. Homewood, Ill.: Richard D. Irwin, Inc., 1979.

Lavin, Bebe L. "Can Computer-Assisted Instruction Make a Difference?" *Teaching Sociology* 17 (January 1980) 163-79.

Lawrence, Gail Herndon. "The Computer as an Instructional Device: New Directions for Library User Education." *Library Trends* 1 (Summer 1980) 139-52.

Lyon, B. J. "Mind Transplants; or, The Role of Computer-Assisted Instruction in the Future of the Library," *Clinic on Library Applications of Data Processing, 1975, University of Illinois. Proceedings.* University of Illinois, Graduate School of Library Science, 1976, pp. 127-36.

Mathews, Walter M., ed. *Monster or Messiah?* Jackson, Miss.: University Press of Mississippi, 1980.

"Microcomputer: Megachange." *EPIEgram Equipment* 9 (October 1980) 4-5.

Miller, Inabeth. "Micros Are Coming." *Media and Methods* 16 (April 1980) 32-34+.

"New Wave Is Not Quite With Us, Yet." *Canadian Library Journal* (February 1981) 5-9.

"Research Agenda for the Eighties." *ASIS Bulletin* 8 (December 1981) 369.

Sager, D.J. "Public Library Research Needs: An Agenda." *Public Libraries* 2 (Fall 1982) 111+.

Simonsen, Roger A., and Kent S. Renshaw. "CAI—Boon or Boondoggle?" *Datamation* 20 (March 1974) 90-102.

Wessel, Milton R. *Freedom's Edge: The Computer Threat to Society.* Reading, Mass.: Addison-Wesley, 1974.

White, H.S. "Research Agenda: No Panacea, But a First Step." *American Libraries* 13 (April 1982) 270+.

The Microcomputer and the Library Administrator

Inabeth Miller

ALL across the country, school libraries have sprouted microcomputers, used for a variety of functions from simple recreation to management of circulation, overdues, or indeed whole card catalogs. Public libraries are introducing "coin-op" word processors and cable interactive systems. Academic libraries have developed back-up microcomputer systems for their mainframes and minis, often used as intelligent terminals, tying in to national databases. Special libraries, too, are purchasing micro-computers for electronic communications systems and some data management. Where is the library administrator in this floodtide of activity? Along with the business executive prototype, the library director has remained largely in the background, an overall observer, even a catalyst, a purchaser, but seldom the planner, and rarely a user. The road from the library floor to the administrative offices is lengthy and poorly travelled. One administrator told me, "Frankly, that microcomputer has been sitting in my office for two years and nobody's really used it." Another remarked quite candidly, "Well, we've got the football pool on it, and a staff member came in to make a database out of his personal record collection, but that's about all." Why?

Without painting an idealized picture of the administrator and the micro locked in symbiotic embrace, this essay will examine some of the various uses of the microcomputer in the administrative office, along with the drawbacks, ending with a serious plea for preparation, careful planning, cost-effective decision-making, training, and evaluation.

Ted Hines (1982) has circulated a laundry list of microcomputer applications in libraries. It is an inspiration to the organized and to the frivolous to acquire, store, transmit, record, calculate with an efficiency that few humans can replicate. It promotes a piecemeal approach to technology which is unquestionably characteristic of experimentation and innovation throughout the country. It is valuable as a motivating force and was never meant to serve as an action plan or model. From Hines' thirty-one possibilities, from much of the literature over the past two years, and the tracking done by both Association of Research Libraries and Monroe C. Gutman Library of Harvard Graduate School of

Education, certain consistent patterns of administrative use appear. They can be categorized as financial, word-processing, record-keeping, facilities management, general, and staff development or training.

FINANCIAL

More libraries and business offices have purchased microcomputers for financial planning than for any other purpose. *Visicalc*, the first financial spreadsheet, and its many followers, particularly Lotus 1, 2, 3, brought to administrators the possibility of "what if" analysis. One library director asserts that this tool has reduced union negotiations from endless weeks to one short night. It is possible to look at a budget with a full accounting format that contains budgeting amounts, allocations of funds according to need projections, encumbrances, expenditures, balances, and percentage expended. Some libraries have used *Visicalc* for book fund allocations or for state accounting record-keeping. Hundreds of manual calculations would be necessary for these same operations without such a program. Libraries whose budgets are ultimately put on large computers still find the micro extremely useful for budget planning and decision-making. New integrated software (Symphony, Framework, Jazz) make it possible to move from budget to reporting with ease.

Although the rapid recalculations appear almost magical, the work involved in originally entering data into the system is arduous. New computers and inexperienced staff make the process even more difficult. Support and training for applications is the most cost-effective approach. Does the administrator need to know what's going on inside the financial package? Not really—but it is necessary to know how to manipulate the data. In most situations a staff member or systems department will do the entry work. Some administrators still ask for a review session before any budget presentation. It is most effective, however, when the director makes the actual presentation, works with any changes or impact questions, and knows what a spreadsheet can and cannot do. Financial forecasting and five-year plans will no longer be such labor-intensive tasks. They can be changed and updated to reflect the latest figures rather than filed and forgotten. Many other office functions that require considerable clerical or bookkeeping staff are prime candidates for computerization. Reliable programs exist for general accounting, receipts, expenditures, petty cash accounting, vendor reports, and purchase orders. Though the manager has little involvement with these tasks, results play an increasingly important part in day-to-day operations. Responsible financial management is a primary requirement for every administrator.

WORD PROCESSING

The latest discovery for library administration is the possibilities inherent in using a microcomputer with a word processing program. The word processing capabilities can be used for all manner of library publications. The library newsletter, often an underread and overwritten piece of publicity, is much simpler to produce. Bibliographies on current issues can be updated regularly, greatly increasing their usefulness, and making more efficient use of bibliographers. The microcomputer with word processing is grand for mailings, mailing lists, and labels. Letters to trustees, congresspeople, requests for free materials can be personalized and sent with a minimum of clerical time. Many hours used to be spent on repetitive mailings in my library. Even access to a magcard machine took a secretary away from other responsibilities for long hours. Now, form letters are stored on disk and sent instantly as the situation demands. The onus is upon my shoulders to continue generating letters and messages worthy of the delivery system.

Some questions to keep in mind before investing in a microcomputer for word processing are:

1. Are numerous drafts required for office typing?
2. Does the administrative office generate proposals and type manuscripts?
3. Does the office generate repetitive letters many times during the year?
4. Are there often mailings in batches of 100 or more?
5. Does the office keep lists or card records that must be manipulated for various purposes?
6. Is it necessary to have publications "camera ready" for the printer?

If the answer to all of these questions is positive, your demand exceeds the general capacity of microcomputers with floppy disks and you should probably be thinking about a dedicated word processor or a hard disk. For writing journal articles, small newsletters, library telephone directories, some list maintenance, and sending a great many letters, a microcomputer with a simple or sophisticated word processing program does the job. As you can readily discern, it is a matter of degree rather than function.

GENERAL

General office record-keeping and statistical analysis are two other functions ably handled by a small microcomputer if the tasks demanded

are narrow in scope. Staff records; patron, trustee, or faculty information; scheduling; project planning; and all of those statistical analyses
that give librarians a rush of adrenaline can be entered into a database
management system.

The inexperienced buyer is faced with an array of database management programs that perform either more or less complex tasks, and hold
more or less information. The librarian who is vague about a task and
unsure of its parameters is doomed to endure a frustrating experience.
Many of the comprehensive programs require a hard disk drive or more
capacity than a small microcomputer can hold. An attempt to place a
directory on a limited Apple microcomputer and retrieve information
according to nine separate fields (name, state, type of hardware, funding,
etc.) proved too complicated for the configuration of available hardware.
On the other hand, room reservations, equipment inventories and
reservations, calendars, community bulletin boards, and statistical
analyses are well within its abilities. It is always necessary to ask the
questions, "Will a limited memory computer perform this task? Must it
be done by a different equipment configuration?" This technology
encourages a compilation of ignorance which threatens to grow in
intensity as microcomputers become available in discount stores and
supermarkets. Trained salespeople are the exception rather than the
rule. As machines become "rigged" to complete tasks that they were not
designed to accomplish, the things that inevitably go wrong engulf an
administrative office.

A database management system combines many of the word processing and the financial functions addressed earlier. Special project and
grant management are neatly definable packages that can be appropriately controlled within the parameters of most systems. Public
libraries who employ numbers of JEPTA or CETA personnel find that
records can be kept discretely for the government reports. It is possible to
use programs in coordination with library forms for payroll, including
check calculations, and monthly bills. Reports on use statistics, patron
requests, and future projections can flow with far less effort than those
tasks previously consumed. A coordinated system of time management
and computer search billing is in the experimental stage at Gutman
Library. All of these wonderful-sounding applications took considerable
time to plan and even more time and people to implement. A staff
member inquired why we spent one hour generating a list that would
have taken five minutes to write by hand. Until staff is trained in the
operation of any system, time spent on tasks exceed that spent on
manual operations. Whatever information is to be generated from a
computer must be input. This is most often overlooked by administrators
in their haste to produce dramatic "results." The task of producing an
efficient, annotated software catalog on microcomputer has taken

months of frustrating false starts, and the seemingly simple matter of entering data onto an inadequate management program has been fraught with difficulties. Much is possible for those who know what they are doing or receive experienced assistance in the design of the overall function.

FACILITIES MANAGEMENT

Many aspects of building maintenance are now finding their way onto small microcomputer programs. Ground upkeep, snow removal, and energy management have been written about extensively. There are available programs through computer companies, and advertised in institutional journals for utilization and maintenance schedules. Claims of cost savings, particularly in the energy area, are most impressive. Small schools and libraries can take advantage of automatic heat adjustments and timed operations.

An immediate application, and one that is useful to most libraries, is the opportunity to inventory equipment. In this area, a microcomputer is uniquely suited to the task. It is possible to update, to analyze, to schedule, and to handle maintenance for office equipment, media equipment, and custodial supplies. Replacement budgets, ordering routines, become tied to actual statistics. The lengthy and arduous budgeting and procurement process becomes more a matter of being able to read and act upon the statistical data regularly generated. A by-product of all this record-keeping is general awareness that supplies and equipment are being carefully monitored. Somehow a reduction in both the loss rate and the level of consumption follows.

TRAINING

Libraries are beginning to use microcomputers in the training of staff and users, particularly in bibliographic instruction and the initiation of library assistant or aides to the mystical wonders of working at a circulation desk. A library slide tape, entitled "The Joys of Shelving," will soon be accompanied by an appropriate CAI (computer-assisted instruction) program. What are the implications in the administrative area? After a recent turnover of secretarial staff, it seems very obvious that the many routines of office management could have been programmed onto the computer, updated as they changed, and used with all of the accompanying forms, replacing the fifty file folders that are perpetually lost in the shuffle of new personnel.

A good training program for use of the microcomputer itself would be a welcome addition to the incomprehensible documentation that is available from dealers. Some of the self-instructional programs are so riddled with errors that they are unusuable. The Mid-Missouri Library Network has been experimenting with training quizzes and game formats for both staff and users. It is an interesting model to examine. Simmons College School of Library and Information Science is also developing training materials for users and for bibliographic instruction. Commercial programs in bibliographic or office procedures training are just beginning to appear. They are simplistic, lack graphics, and ordinarily take a question and answer format. Much of what is needed remains over the horizon.

THE FUTURE

All administrators would like to think that they have a crystal ball to peer into the future. Some would like to eradicate the images that they see of teletext terminals, of satellite communications, of homes accessing information through their personal microcomputers, using libraries in very different ways. Experiments by OCLC (channel 2000) look at reference services, public information service, community calendars, home banking, and a 32,000-article video encyclopedia. Time, Inc., and others have begun to publish electronic journals, accessible to home computers. Electronic transfer of information is just beginning in this country, and libraries will be an important part of much experimentation. Simple text transfer will be followed by document delivery, charts, graphs, maps, and photographs. Electronic mail systems, already often used in large institutions instead of simple memos or official notices, will be superseded by vast networks typing together new configurations of users and professionals. Each day I read my office mail, then open my electronic mailbox where requests are answered most promptly.

What are the advantages of microcomputers for today's library administrator? The capacity of small machines is growing daily without an accompanying elevation of price. They are not difficult to use though training and handholding are a necessity. A variety of applications are possible that will ultimately make certain administrative tasks more efficient. Software is now available that can be used in any library office. The general software does not require adaptation or lengthy training for implementation. All hardware and applications are controlled at the local level. It is possible to begin with a limited set of objectives in mind. Equipment can be installed in the office with minimal disruption of daily activities. Some flexibility is possible in using microcomputers as intelligent terminals when necessary, and expanding a system into a multi-user network. The small size and relative ease of operation reduces the threat of "computerization."

Looking at the down side, these are unpredictable machines with limited capacity and reliability. There are problems of maintenance and security. Initial training is necessary and hard to come by. Few people are qualified to give good advice, and the novice does not know whose words of wisdom to follow. Most software that is specifically designed for libraries is simplistic and of limited value outside the originating organization. It is still difficult to integrate data files, although more companies are recognizing the necessity for combinations, rather than duplicating data entry. Because of the limitations of the software, complex programs are too difficult for most libraries to develop. Many people are still fearful of a computer in the office, whatever its size. The introduction of any technology must take into consideration human factors and human impediments.

A microcomputer will never solve the many problems of a library. It is not the panacea that recent journals have led the world to believe. This tool can be useful, even valuable, to the administrator if it is neither oversold nor underutilized; if careful objectives are established in advance; if reliable advice is sought about hardware and software; if the staff is part of the decision-making process; and if appropriate steps are taken for training and support. Now is the time to become an informed consumer without compromising the library or its efficient operation in the process.

Bibliography

DeYoung, Barbara. "Impact of Microcomupters in Public Libraries," in *Microcomputers in Libraries*, ed. by Ching-chih Chen and Stacey Bressler. New York: Neal-Schuman, 1982.

Daly, Jay. "Confessions of a Computer Fraud," *Lincoln Review*, Vol. 6, No. 4 (September-October 1982), pp. 4-8.

Hines, Theodore C. "Library Applications of Microcomputers," *Classroom Computer News* (January/February 1982).

Johnson, Dale M. "The University's Role in Educational Computing," *NASSP Bulletin*, Vol. 66, No. 433 (September 1982), pp. 64-69.

Koven, Barbara. "Microcomputers in Academic Libraries," in *Microcomputers in Libraries*, ed. by Ching-chih Chen and Stacey Bressler. New York: Neal-Schuman, 1982.

McWilliams, Peter. "An Introduction to Word Processing," *Popular Computing* (February 1982), pp. 17-19.

Miller, Inabeth. *Microcomputers and the Media Specialist: An Annotated Bibliography*, Syracuse, N.Y.: ERIC Clearinghouse, 1981.

Miller, Inabeth. *Microcomputers in School Library Media Centers*. New York: Neal-Schuman, 1984.

Price, Douglas S. *Impact of Information Technology*. Issue paper prepared for the National Commission on Libraries and Information Technology, June 1982.

Rakov, Lucy S. *Administrative Uses of Microcomputers*. Cambridge, Mass.: Technical Education Research Centers, Inc., 1982.

Rosaschi, Jim. "Avoid Worthless Micro-related Purchases," *Access: Microcomputers in Libraries*, Vol. 2, No. 1 (January 1982).

Surprenant, Tom, "Future Libraries: The Electronic Environment," *Wilson Library Bulletin* (January 1982), pp. 336-41.

Tenne-Senne, Andrey. "Teledon Graphics and Library Applications," *Information Technology*, Vol. 1, No. 2 (June 1982), pp. 98-110.

"Use of Small Computers in ARL Libraries," *SPEC KIT, No. 77,* Washington, D.C.: Systems and Procedures Exchange Center, Association of Research Libraries (August-September 1981).

Wolman, Rebecca. "Training with Computers," *Training News*, Vol. IV, No. 3 (November 1982), pp. 6-8.

List of Contributors

Nancy Hill Allen is Assistant Director for Public Services at Wayne State University, Detroit. She is the author of *Unpublished Film and Television Scripts in the University of Illinois Library* and has published articles in *Collection Building, American Libraries,* and *Film Library Quarterly.*

Cheryll A. Bixby is Assistant Reference Librarian at Lockwood Memorial Library, State University of New York at Buffalo. She received her MLS in 1983 at the School of Information and Library Studies, State University of New York at Buffalo.

Marie Bruce is Director of Huntington Memorial Library, Oneonta, N.Y.

June B. Cawthon is Assistant Professor (Retired) in the Department of Educational Media and Librarianship at the University of Georgia, Athens, Ga. She is the author of *Tools of the Trade: Sources and Aids for Media Selection* and has also published in *Media Update.*

Sara Clarkson is former Head of Audiovisual and Microforms Cataloging at the University Libraries of the State University of New York at Buffalo.

Patricia Ann Coty is Associate Librarian at the Science and Engineering Library of the State University of New York at Buffalo.

Ann S. Dausch is Former District Elementary Librarian at the Morgan Hill Unified School District, Morgan Hill, Calif.

Clara DiFelice is Media Librarian at the Palm Springs Public Library, Palm Springs, Calif. She is the author of *Graduate Degree Programs in Instructional Technology 1978-1979* and has published articles in *Film Library Quarterly, The U*N*A*B*A*S*H*E*D Librarian, Media Spectrum, Ethnic Forum,* and *Public Library Quarterly.*

John W. Ellison is Associate Professor in the School of Information and Library Studies at the State University of New York at Buffalo. He is the author of the book *Graduate Degree Programs in Instructional Technology, 1978-1979.* His articles have appeared in *Journal of Library College, Omnibus, Educational Technology, Catholic Library World, International Journal of Instructional Media, Journal of Education for Librarianship, The U*N*A*B*A*S*H*E*D Librarian, Instructional Innovator, RQ, Views, Learning Today, Media Spectrum, New Library World, School Media Quarterly, Library-College Experimenter, Microfilm Review, Biomedical Communications, Ethnic Forum, Bulletin,* and *Information Systems Newsletter.* Several of his papers and reports are in ERIC Documents.

Kenneth R. Fielding is former Assistant Library Director of Steele Memorial Library, Elmira, N.Y. He has published articles in *Education and Industrial Television, Cable Libraries*, and *American Libraries*.

Edith Hopkins is Director of Adult Services at Oakville Public Library, Oakville, Ontario, Canada.

Amy R. Loucks-DiMatteo is Documentation Librarian/Loan Service Representative at Datek-InstaCard Corporation, Buffalo, N.Y.

Kathleen Lucisano is former Assistant Librarian at Phillips Lytle Hitchcock Baline & Huber, Buffalo, N.Y.

Nina Nix Martin is Associate Professor at the Graduate School of Library Service, University of Alabama, University, Ala. Her articles have appeared in *Audiovisual Instruction, Booklist, ALACS Open Circuit, The Southeastern Librarian,* and *The Alabama Librarian*.

Elizabeth Miller is part-time Reference Librarian at New City Library, New City, N.Y.

Inabeth Miller is former Librarian to the Faculty of Education, Graduate School of Education, Harvard University, Cambridge, Mass., and now an independent library consultant. She is the author of two books, *Kids and Parents: Learning Together with Micros* and *Microcomputers in School Library Media Centers*, and articles in *Electronic Learning* and *Media and Methods*.

Jerome K. Miller is President of Copyright Information Services, Friday Harbor, Wash. He is the author of *Using Copyrighted Videocassettes in Classrooms and Libraries, The Copyright Directory, Applying the New Copyright Law: A Guide for Educators and Librarians,* and *U.S. Copyright Documents: An Annotated Collection for Use by Educators and Librarians.* He has also published articles in *Audiovisual Instruction, Microform Review, Wilson Library Bulletin, Educational Media Yearbook, Social Education, Library Trends, Encyclopedia of Educational Media, Communications & Technology,* and *Journal of Education for Librarianship*.

Joseph W. Palmer is Associate Professor at the School of Information and Library Studies of the State University of New York at Buffalo. He has published articles in *American Libraries, Drexel Library Quarterly, Public Library Quarterly, Wilson Library Bulletin, Bookmark, Previews, NYLA Bulletin, RQ, Journal of Library Education, Journal of Library History, Catholic Library Bulletin, Illinois Libraries,* and *California Librarian*.

Naomi J. Rhodes is Librarian at Kenmore Public Library, Kenmore, N.Y., and has been published in *The U*N*A*B*A*S*H*E*D Librarian*.

James Rice is Assistant Professor in the School of Library Science at the University of Iowa, Iowa City. He is the author of *Teaching Library Use: A Guide for Library Instruction* and has published articles in *Library*

Journal, Wilson Library Bulletin, American Libraries, Journal of Library Administration, and *Journal of Education for Librarianship.*

Don Roberts is President of Independent Media, Minneapolis. He is the author of *Mediamobiles* and has published articles in *Catholic Library World, Technicalities, Drexel Library School Bulletin, School Library Journal, ERIC, IFLA Journal, New Mexico Library Bulletin, Film Library Quarterly, Wilson Library Bulletin, Focus, Choice, Library Journal, American Libraries,* and *Library Trends.*

Judith Schiek Robinson is Associate Professor in the School of Information and Library Studies at the State University of New York at Buffalo. Her books include *The Librarian and Reference Queries: A Systematic Approach* and *U.S. Government Scientific and Technical Information Sources.* She has published articles in *RQ, American Libraries,* and *Journal of Education for Librarianship.*

John S. Robotham is Principal Librarian (retired) of The New York Public Library. His books include *Freedom of Access to Library Materials* and *Library Programs: How to Select, Plan and Produce Them.* He has published articles in *Bulletin of The New York Public Library, Collection Building,* and *Sightlines.*

William T. Schmid is Manager of Quality Assurance at DELTAK, Inc., Naperville, Ill. He is the author of *Media Center Management: A Practical Guide* and his articles have appeared in *Media and Methods, Audio-Visual Instruction, Training, Video Systems, Technical Photography, Instructional Innovator,* and *Training and Development Journal.*

Roberta Doctor Stevens is Associate Director/Technical Operations at Fairfax County Public Library, Springfield Va. She is the author of *Multimedia Occupational Materials: An Annotated Bibliography.* Her articles have been published in *Library Journal, American Vocational Journal,* and *International Journal of Media.*

Paul B. Wiener is Audiovisual Librarian at the State University of New York at Stony Brook. His articles have appeared in *Library Acquisitions: Practise and Theory, Film Library Quarterly, Library Journal, Previews, School Library Journal, Choice, Science Books and Films, Collection Management,* and *The Reference Librarian.* He is also a columnist for *Catholic Library World.*

Maria L. Weinberger is Coordinator of Audiovisual Services at Hamilton Public Library, Hamilton, Ontario, Canada. She is the author of *Study of Audio-Visual Services in Ontario.*

Index

Compiled by Lisa A. Seivert

DATE DUE